DESIGNING AND MANAGING THE SUPPLY CHAIN

Concepts, Strategies, and Case Studies

SECOND EDITION

The McGraw-Hill/Irwin Series in Operations and Decision Sciences

DESIGNING AND MANAGING THE SUPPLY CHAIN

Concepts, Strategies, and Case Studies

SECOND EDITION

David Simchi-Levi

Massachusetts Institute of Technology (MIT), Cambridge, Massachusetts

Philip Kaminsky

University of California, Berkeley

Edith Simchi-Levi

LogicTools, Inc., Lexington, Massachusetts

Boston   Burr Ridge, IL   Dubuque, IA   Madison, WI   New York   San Francisco   St. Louis
Bangkok   Bogotá   Caracas   Kuala Lumpur   Lisbon   London   Madrid   Mexico City
Milan   Montreal   New Delhi   Santiago   Seoul   Singapore   Sydney   Taipei   Toronto

McGraw-Hill Higher Education ✎

A Division of The **McGraw-Hill**Companies

DESIGNING AND MANAGING THE SUPPLY CHAIN: CONCEPTS, STRATEGIES, AND CASE STUDIES

Published by McGraw-Hill/Irwin, a business unit of The McGraw-Hill Companies, Inc., 1221 Avenue of the Americas, New York, NY, 10020. Copyright © 2003, 2000 by The McGraw-Hill Companies, Inc. All rights reserved. No part of this publication may be reproduced or distributed in any form or by any means, or stored in a database or retrieval system, without the prior written consent of The McGraw-Hill Companies, Inc., including, but not limited to, in any network or other electronic storage or transmission, or broadcast for distance learning. Some ancillaries, including electronic and print components, may not be available to customers outside the United States.

This book is printed on acid-free paper.

domestic   1 2 3 4 5 6 7 8 9 0 DOW/DOW 0 9 8 7 6 5 4 3 2
international   1 2 3 4 5 6 7 8 9 0 DOW/DOW 0 9 8 7 6 5 4 3 2

ISBN 0-07-249256-2

Publisher: *Brent Gordon*
Executive editor: *Scott Isenberg*
Editorial Assistant: *Lee Stone*
Senior marketing manager: *Zina Craft*
Producer, Media technology: *Anthony Sherman*
Project manager: *Anna M. Chan*
Manager, new book production: *Melonie Salvati*
Coordinator freelance design: *Mary L. Christianson*
Senior supplement producer: *Susan Lombardi*
Senior digital content specialist: *Brian Nacik*
Freelance cover designer: *Maureen McCutcheon*
Cover illustration: © *Jeffrey Pelo/Folioplanet*
Typeface: *10.5/12 Times Roman*
Compositor: *UG / GGS Information Services, Inc.*
Printer: *R. R. Donnelley*

Library of Congress Cataloging-in-Publication Data

Simchi-Levi, David
    Designing and managing the supply chain: concepts, strategies, and case studies /
David Simchi-Levi, Philip Kaminsky, Edith Simchi-Levi.—2nd ed.
        p. cm.—(The McGraw-Hill/Irwin series in operations and decision sciences)
    Includes bibliographical references and index.
    ISBN 0-07-249256-2 (alk. paper)—ISBN 0-07-119896-2 (international : alk. paper)
    1. Pysical distribution of goods—Management.   2. Marketing channels—Management.
3. Business logistics.   4. Industrial procurement. I. Kaminsky, Philip.   II. Simchi-Levi,
Edith. III. Title. IV. Irwin/McGraw-Hill series in operations and decision sciences.
HF5415.7.S425   2003
658.5—dc21   2002026413

INTERNATIONAL EDITION ISBN 0-07-119896-2

Copyright © 2003. Exclusive rights by The McGraw-Hill Companies, Inc., for manufacture and export. This book cannot be re-exported from the country to which it is sold by McGraw-Hill. The International Edition is not available in North America.

www.mhhe.com

To our children, Sara and Yuval, who have the patience and humor to survive our work together

D.S.L., E.S.L.

To my family, for their support and encouragement

P.K.

ABOUT THE AUTHORS

DAVID SIMCHI-LEVI is a Professor of Engineering Systems at the Massachusetts Institute of Technogy (MIT). Prior to joining the faculty at MIT, he taught at Northwestern University and Columbia University. Professor Simchi-Levi received his Ph.D. in Operations Research from Tel-Aviv University and has won awards for his work in supply chain management, logistics, and transportation. At MIT he teaches logistics and supply chain management at the Leaders for Manufacturing program as well as Executive Programs at the MIT Sloan School of Management. In 2000, he was named the "Master of Design" by *Supply Chain Management Review*. He is co-author, together with Julien Bramel, of *The Logic of Logistic*, published by Springer, and a co-founder and president of LogicTools Inc., a company that provides decision support planning software for logistics and supply chain management.

PHIL KAMINSKY is Assistant Professor of Industrial Engineering at the University of California at Berkeley. He received his Ph.D. in Industrial Engineering from Northwestern University. Prior to his graduate studies, he worked for the production division of Merck & Co., Inc. He has consulted in the areas of supply chain and production management.

EDITH SIMCHI-LEVI is a co-founder and Vice President of Operations of LogicTools Inc., a leading supply chain planning software company. She has extensive experience in software development and has engaged in numerous consulting projects in logistics and supply chain management. She received her B.S. in Mathematics and Computer Science from Tel-Aviv University.

FOREWORD

In the last few years we have seen an explosion of publications on supply chain management; numerous books have been published and many articles have appeared in academic, trade, and popular magazines. These publications either are too technical—and therefore inaccessible to practitioners and students—or lack the breadth and depth that the topic deserves. Certainly, it is difficult to find a book appropriate for teaching supply chain management to business or engineering students. *Designing and Managing the Supply Chain* solves this problem!

The book is an important contribution and major milestone for the supply chain community. It is the first book that covers a comprehensive breadth of supply chain topics in depth, and addresses the major challenges in this area. It was written by experts from academia and industry who have been researching, consulting, and developing software for supply chain management for many years.

This book includes many classic and new case studies, numerous examples as well as in-depth analyses of some of the technical issues involved in inventory management, network design, and strategic partnering, to name a few. It is therefore an ideal textbook for classes on supply chain management at the undergraduate, Master's, and M.B.A. levels. Since each chapter is self-contained, instructors can pick the chapters they want to use, depending on the length of the class and its requirements. The book comes with two computerized games. The Computerized Beer Game provides an excellent instructional tool that engages students in managing a supply chain and provides a starting point for discussing the value of information in the supply chain, strategic partnering, centralized decision making, and so forth. The Risk Pool Game allows students to gain insight on an important concept in supply chain management, called risk pooling. The authors have been most creative in using games to motivate and expose students to challenging subjects.

Finally, since many companies view supply chain management as the core of their business strategy, this book will also be of interest to managers involved in any of the processes that make up the supply chain.

I want to compliment the authors for having written such an outstanding textbook for the supply chain community.

Hau L. Lee
Kleiner Perkins, Mayfield, Sequoia Capital Professor
Director, Stanford Global Supply Chain Forum
Stanford University

PREFACE

Two years ago, when we wrote the first edition of this text, our objective was to present, in an easily accessible manner, supply chain concepts, strategies, and models. We are pleased to note that the text was very successful; we received a tremendous response from adopters, students, executives, and consultants. The success of that edition, as well as new concepts and recent technological changes, have motivated us to revise the book. In this edition, we have attempted to build on the positive elements of the first edition and to include what we have learned in the last two years.

The first edition of this book grew out of a number of supply chain management courses and Executive Education programs we taught at Northwestern University over the past several years, as well as numerous consulting projects and supply chain decision-support systems we developed at LogicTools. Since then, we have continued teaching executive courses, both at Massachusettes Institute of Technology and at the University of California, Berkeley, and have continued to develop a variety of supply chain decision-support tools. These courses have spawned many innovative and effective supply chain education concepts. The focus in these programs has always been on presenting, in an easily accessible manner, recently developed state-of-the-art models and solution methods important in the design, control, and operation of supply chains. Similarly, the consulting projects and decision-support systems developed by LogicTools have focused on applying these advanced techniques to solve specific problems faced by our clients. In the last two years, we have added new models and techniques to these courses as they have been developed, and we have begun to put all of these techniques into perspective, and to develop frameworks to integrate all of these models and solution methods.

Interest in supply chain management, both in industry and in academia, has grown rapidly over the past several years, and continues to grow. A number of forces have contributed to this trend. First, in recent years it has become clear that many companies have reduced manufacturing costs as much as practically possible. Many of these companies are discovering the magnitude of savings that can be achieved by planning and managing their supply chain more effectively. Indeed, a striking example is Wal-Mart's success, which is partly attributed to implementing a new logistics strategy called cross-docking. At the same time, information and communication systems have been widely implemented, and provide access to comprehensive data from all components of the supply chain.

In particular, the influence of the Internet and e-commerce on the economy in general, and business practice in particular, has been tremendous. Changes are happening extremely fast, and the scope of these changes is breathtaking! For instance, the direct-business model employed by industry giants such as Dell Computers and Amazon.com enables customers to order products over the Internet and thus allows companies to sell their products without relying on third-party distributors or conventional stores. Similarly, business-to-business e-commerce, which is predicted by Forrester Research to skyrocket from $43 billion in 1998 to $1.3 trillion in 2003, has tremendous potential to increase the efficiency of a variety of businesses.

Finally, deregulation of the transportation industry has led to the development of a variety of transportation modes and reduced transportation costs, while significantly increasing the complexity of logistics systems.

It is therefore not surprising that many companies are involved in the analysis of their supply chains. In most cases, however, this analysis is performed based on experience and intuition; very few analytical models or planning tools have been used in this process. In contrast, in the last two decades the academic community has developed various models and tools for supply chain management. Unfortunately, the first generation of this technology was not robust or flexible enough to allow industry to use it effectively. This, however, has changed over the last few years, during which improved analysis and insight, and effective models and decision-support systems, have been developed; however, these are not necessarily familiar to industry. Indeed, to our knowledge there is no published work that discusses these problems, models, concepts, and tools at an appropriate level.

In this book, we intend to fill this gap by providing state-of-the-art models, concepts, and solution methods that are important for the design, control, operation, and management of supply chain systems. In particular, we have attempted both to convey the intuition behind many key supply chain concepts and to provide simple techniques that can be used to analyze various aspects of the supply chain.

The emphasis is on a format that will be accessible to executives and practitioners, as well as students interested in careers in related industries. In addition, it will introduce readers to information systems and decision-support tools that can aid in the design, analysis, and control of supply chains.

The book is written to serve as

- A textbook for M.B.A.-level logistics and supply chain management courses.
- A textbook for B.S. and M.S. industrial engineering courses on logistics and supply chain management.
- A reference for teachers, consultants, and practitioners involved in any one of the processes that make up the supply chain.

Of course, supply chain management is a very broad area, and it would be impossible for a single book to cover all of the relevant areas in depth. Indeed, there is considerable disagreement in academia and industry about exactly what these relevant areas are. Nevertheless, we have attempted to provide a broad introduction to many critical facets of supply chain management. Although many essential supply chain management issues are interrelated, we have strived wherever possible to make each chapter as self-contained as possible, so that the reader can refer directly to chapters covering topics of interest. The discussion ranges from basic topics of inventory management, logistics network design, distribution systems, and customer value to more advanced topics of strategic alliances, the value of information in the supply chain, information technology, decision-support systems, and international issues in supply chain management. Each chapter utilizes numerous case studies and examples, and mathematical and technical sections can be skipped without loss of continuity.

We have made substantial changes to the second edition of this text. As we continued to teach, consult, and research supply chain management issues, we have placed an increasing importance on finding or developing effective frameworks that illustrate many important supply chain issues. This is reflected in the second edition; many of the chapters have been reorganized around frameworks that will help the reader to understand the relationships between many critical supply chain issues. In addition, motivated by new developments in industry, for example, the impact of Internet technology on business practices, we have added a variety of new topics to the text and increased coverage of others. For example:

- We cover topics such as e-business and its impact on supply chain strategies (Chapter 5).
- We have added a chapter on procurement and outsourcing (Chapter 7).
- We discuss supply contracts and their impact on supply chain optimization (Chapter 3).
- We consider pricing and revenue management strategies and the implication of these strategies for supply chain management (Chapter 10).
- We cover additional inventory models (Chapter 3).
- We have increased coverage of forecasting (Chapter 3).
- We have increased our coverage of product and process modularity (Chapter 7 and Chapter 9).
- We have additional material concerning supply chain distribution strategies (Chapter 5).
- We introduce a new framework that illustrates the impact of various technologies on supply chain excellence (Chapter 11 and Chapter 12).
- We provide a detailed analysis of the latest information technology trends (Chapter 11).

We have also added supporting material:

- Several cases, including *Meditech Surgical, Sport Obermeyer, FreeMarkets OnLine,* and *Hewlett-Packard Company: Network Printer Design for Universality.*
- Numerous examples.
- Discussion questions and case exercises at the end of most of the chapters,

The book also includes two software packages, the **Computerized Beer Game** and the **Risk Pool Game**, that help to illustrate many of the concepts we discuss in the book. Indeed, in teaching executives and M.B.A. students, we have found that these games help students better understand issues and concepts such as the bullwhip effect, the value of information in the supply chain, and the impact of lead times, centralized decision making, and risk pooling on supply chain operations. For this edition, we have added a Microsoft Excel spreadsheet, which helps students understand many of the concepts introduced in Chapter 3, especially with regard to supply contracts.

Parts of this book are based on work we have done either together or with others. Chapters 1 and 2 borrow extensively from *The Logic of Logistics*, written by Julien Bramel and David Simchi-Levi and published by Springer in 1997. This, of course, is done by permission of the copyright owner. The Computerized Beer Game is discussed in an article by Philip Kaminsky and David Simchi-Levi that appeared in *Supply Chain and Technology Management*, edited by Hau Lee and Shu Ming Ng and published by The Production and Operations Management Society. Some of the material on the bullwhip effect appears in an article by Chen, Drezner, Ryan, and Simchi-Levi in *Quantitative Models for Supply Chain Management*, edited by Sridhar Tayur, Ram Ganeshan, and Michael Magazine, and published by Kluwer Academic Publishers. The material in Chapter 5 is taken from two papers, one written by the first and the third authors of this book and the second written by these two authors and M. Watson. This paper is going to appear in *The Practice of Supply Chain Management*, edited by C. Billington, T. Harrison, H. Lee, and J. Neale, to be published by Kluwer Academic Publishers.

ACKNOWLEDGMENTS

It is our pleasure to acknowledge all those who helped us with the first and the second editions of this manuscript. First, we would like to thank Dr. Myron Feinstein, former director of supply chain strategy development at Unilever, New York City, who read through and commented on various chapters. Similarly, we are indebted to the reviewers of the first edition, Professors Michael Ball (University of Maryland), Wendell Gilland (University of North Carolina, Chapel Hill), Eric Johnson (Dartmouth College), Douglas Morrice (The University of Texas, Austin), Michael Pangburn (Pennsylvania State University), Powell Robinson (Texas A&M University), William Tallon (Northern Illinois University), and Rachel Yang (University of Illinois, Urbana-Champaign). We are also grateful to Dr. Deniz Caglar of Booz Allen Hamilton for his comments on earlier drafts of the book.

The second edition benefited from comments and suggestions we received from many people. These include Professors Arjang Assad, Michael Ball, and their colleagues from the University of Maryland–College Park; Chia-Shin Chung (Cleveland State University); Brian Gibson (Auburn University); Boaz Golany (Technion, Israel); Isaac Gottlieb (Rutgers University); Shelly Jha (Wilfrid Laurier University, Ontario, Canada); Dana Johnson (Michigan Technical University); Mary Meixell (George Mason University); Dan Rinks (Louisiana State University); Tony Arreola-Risa (Texas A&M University); and Joel Wisner (University of Nevada–Las Vegas). These comments were invaluable in improving the organization and presentation of the book.

Professor Ravi Anupindi (University of Michigan, Ann Arbor), Professor Yehuda Bassok (University of Southern California), Dr. Jeff Tew (General Motors), and Professor Jayashankar Swaminathan (University of North Carolina, Chapel Hill) provided valuable insights that we have incorporated into the second edition of the text.

We are grateful to our colleagues at Massachusetts Institute of Technology; the University of California, Berkeley; and LogicTools who have provided us with opportunities to interact with some of the brightest minds in our field and to learn from their research and development. Three people stand out in this regard: Professors Charles H. Fine and Stephen C. Graves (MIT), with whom Professor Simchi-Levi has closely collaborated in the last two years, and Dr. Michael S. Watson from LogicTools.

We thank Dr. Kathleen A. Stair and Ms. Ann Stuart for carefully editing and proofreading many chapters. Ms. Ann Stuart has also provided invaluable assistance in preparing the second edition.

Finally, we wish to thank Ms. Colleen Tuscher, who assisted us in the initial stage of the project; our editor, Mr. Scott Isenberg; and his assistants, Ms. Nicolle Schieffer and Ms. Lee Stone of Irwin/McGraw-Hill, who encouraged us throughout and helped us complete the book. Also, thanks to Ms. Anna Chan, Mr. James Labeots, and the production staff at McGraw-Hill for their help.

David Simchi-Levi
Cambridge, Massachusetts

Philip Kaminsky
Berkeley, California

Edith Simchi-Levi
Lexington, Massachusetts

LIST OF CASES

BRIEF CONTENTS

CONTENTS

CHAPTER 1

Introduction to Supply Chain Management

1.1 WHAT IS SUPPLY CHAIN MANAGEMENT?

Fierce competition in today's global markets, the introduction of products with shorter and shorter life cycles, and the heightened expectations of customers have forced business enterprises to invest in, and focus attention on, their supply chains. This, together with continuing advances in communications and transportation technologies (e.g., mobile communication, Internet, and overnight delivery), has motivated the continuous evolution of the supply chain and of the techniques to manage it.

In a typical supply chain, raw materials are procured and items are produced at one or more factories, shipped to warehouses for intermediate storage, and then shipped to retailers or customers. Consequently, to reduce cost and improve service levels, effective supply chain strategies must take into account the interactions at the various levels in the supply chain. The supply chain, which is also referred to as the *logistics network*, consists of suppliers, manufacturing centers, warehouses, distribution centers, and retail outlets, as well as raw materials, work-in-process inventory, and finished products that flow between the facilities (see Figure 1-1).

In this book, we present and explain concepts, insights, practical tools, and decision support systems important for the effective management of the supply chain. But what exactly is *supply chain management*? We define it as follows:

> Supply chain management is a set of approaches utilized to efficiently integrate suppliers, manufacturers, warehouses, and stores, so that merchandise is produced and distributed at the right quantities, to the right locations, and at the right time, in order to minimize systemwide costs while satisfying service level requirements.

This definition leads to several observations. First, supply chain management takes into consideration every facility that has an impact on cost and plays a role in making the product conform to customer requirements: from supplier and manufacturing facilities through warehouses and distribution centers to retailers and stores. Indeed, in some supply chain analysis, it is necessary to account for the suppliers' suppliers and the customers' customers because they have an impact on supply chain performance.

Second, the objective of supply chain management is to be efficient and cost-effective across the entire system; total systemwide costs, from transportation and distribution

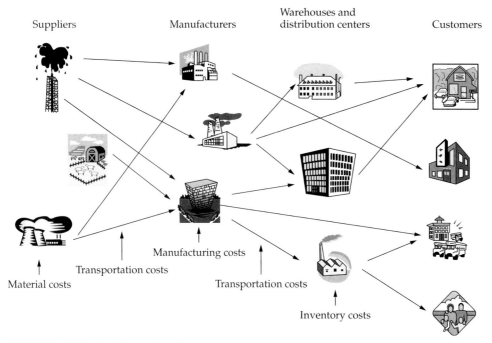

Suppliers   Manufacturers   Warehouses and distribution centers   Customers

Material costs

Transportation costs

Manufacturing costs

Transportation costs

Inventory costs

FIGURE 1-1 The logistics network.

to inventories of raw materials, work in process, and finished goods, are to be minimized. Thus, the emphasis is not on simply minimizing transportation cost or reducing inventories but, rather, on taking a *systems approach* to supply chain management.

Finally, because supply chain management revolves around efficient integration of suppliers, manufacturers, warehouses, and stores, it encompasses thc firm's activities at many levels, from the strategic level through the tactical to the operational level.

What about logistics management? What is the difference between supply chain management and logistics management? While the answer to this question depends on who is addressing this issue, we will not distinguish between logistics and supply chain management in this text. Indeed, our definition of supply chain management is similar to the definition of *logistics management* given by the Council of Logistics Management:

> The process of planning, implementing and controlling the efficient, cost effective flow and storage of raw materials, in-process inventory, finished goods, and related information from point-of-origin to point-of-consumption for the purpose of conforming to customer requirements.

What makes supply chain management difficult? Although we will discuss a variety of reasons throughout this text, they can all be related to one or both of the following observations:

1. It is challenging to design and operate a supply chain so that total systemwide costs are minimized, and systemwide service levels are maintained. Indeed, it is frequently difficult to operate *a single facility* so that costs are minimized and service level is maintained. The difficulty increases exponentially when an entire system is being considered. The process of finding the best *systemwide* strategy is known as *global optimization*.

2. Uncertainty is inherent in every supply chain; customer demand can never be forecast exactly, travel times will never be certain, and machines and vehicles will break down. Supply chains need to be designed to eliminate as much uncertainty as possible and to deal effectively with the uncertainty that remains.

In the next two sections we discuss each of these issues in detail.

1.2 GLOBAL OPTIMIZATION

What makes finding the best systemwide, or globally optimal integrated solution so difficult? A variety of factors make this a challenging problem:

1. **The supply chain is a complex network** of facilities dispersed over a large geography, and in many cases, all over the globe. The following example illustrates a network that is fairly typical of today's global companies.

EXAMPLE 1-1

National Semiconductor, whose list of competitors includes Motorola Inc. and the Intel Corporation, is one of the world's largest chipmakers whose products are used in fax machines, cellular phones, computers, and cars. Currently, the company has four wafer fabrication facilities, three in the United States and one in Great Britain, and has test and assembly sites in Malaysia and Singapore. After assembly, finished products are shipped to hundreds of manufacturing facilities all over the world, including those of Compaq, Ford, IBM, and Siemens. Since the semiconductor industry is highly competitive, specifying short lead times and being able to deliver within the committed due date are critical capabilities. In 1994, 95 percent of National Semiconductor's customers received their orders within 45 days from the time the order was placed, while the remaining 5 percent received their orders within 90 days. These tight lead times required the company to involve 12 different airline carriers using about 20,000 different routes. The difficulty, of course, was that no customer knew in advance if they were going to be part of the 5 percent of customers who received their order in 90 days or the 95 percent who received their order within 45 days [69].

---

2. **Different facilities in the supply chain frequently have *different, conflicting, objectives.*** For instance, suppliers typically want manufacturers to commit themselves to purchasing large quantities in stable volumes with flexible delivery dates. Unfortunately, although most manufacturers would like to implement long production runs, they need to be flexible to their customers' needs and changing demands. Thus, the suppliers' goals are in direct conflict with the manufacturers' desire for flexibility. Indeed, since production decisions are typically made without precise information about customer demand, the ability of manufacturers to match supply and demand depends largely on their ability to change supply volume as information about demand arrives. Similarly, the manufacturers' objective of making large production batches typically conflicts with the objective of both warehouses and distribution centers to reduce inventory. To make matters worse, this latter objective of reducing inventory levels typically implies an increase in transportation costs.

3. **The supply chain is a dynamic system** that evolves over time. Indeed, not only do customer demand and supplier capabilities change over time, but supply chain relationships also evolve over time. For example, as customers' power increases, there is increased pressure placed on manufacturers and suppliers to produce an enormous variety of high-quality products and, ultimately, to produce customized products.

4. **System variations over time** are also an important consideration. Even when demand is known precisely (e.g., because of contractual agreements), the planning

FIGURE 1-2 Order variations in the supply chain.

process needs to account for demand and cost parameters varying over time due to the impact of seasonal fluctuations, trends, advertising and promotions, competitors' pricing strategies, and so forth. These time-varying demand and cost parameters make it difficult to determine the most effective supply chain strategy, that is, the one that minimizes systemwide costs and conforms to customer requirements.

1.3 MANAGING UNCERTAINTY

Global optimization is made even more difficult because supply chains need to be designed for, and operated in, uncertain environments. A variety of factors contribute to this:

1. **Matching supply and demand** is a major challenge:
   (a) Boeing Aircraft announced a write-down of $2.6 billion in October 1997 due to "raw material shortages, internal and supplier parts shortages and productivity inefficiencies . . ." [161].
   (b) "Second quarter sales at U.S. Surgical Corporation declined 25 percent, resulting in a loss of $22 million. The sales and earnings shortfall is attributed to larger than anticipated inventories on the shelves of hospitals" [162].
   (c) "IBM sells out New Aptiva PC; Shortage may cost millions in potential revenue" [163].
   Obviously, this difficulty stems from the fact that months before demand is realized, manufacturers have to commit themselves to specific production levels. These advance commitments imply huge financial and supply risks.
2. Inventory and back-order levels fluctuate considerably across the supply chain, even when customer demand for specific products does not vary greatly. To illustrate this issue, consider Figure 1-2, which suggests that in a typical supply chain, distributor orders to the factory fluctuate far more than the underlying retailer demand.

3. **Forecasting doesn't solve the problem.** Indeed, we argue in the first principle of all forecasts, see Chapter 3, that "forecasts are always wrong. Thus, it is impossible to predict the precise demand for a specific item, even with the most advanced forecast techniques.

4. **Demand is not the only source of uncertainty.** Delivery lead times, manufacturing yields, transportation times, and component availability can also have significant supply chain impact. As supply chains become larger and more geographically diverse, natural and man-made disasters can have tremendous impact.

EXAMPLE 1-2

In September 1999, a massive earthquake devastated Taiwan. Initially, 80 percent of the island's power was lost. Companies such as Hewlett-Packard and Dell, who source a variety of components from Taiwanese manufacturers, were impacted by supply interruptions [7]. Similarly, fabric shipments from India were delayed in the wake of the Jan. 26 earthquake in the Indian state of Gujarat, impacting many U.S. apparel manufacturers [49].

Although uncertainty cannot be eliminated, we will explore various approaches that *minimize the effect* of uncertainty in the supply chain. When this is not possible, we will identify strategies that supply chain partners can apply so as to maintain, or increase, service level.

1.4 WHY SUPPLY CHAIN MANAGEMENT?

In the 1980s companies discovered new manufacturing technologies and strategies that allowed them to reduce costs and better compete in different markets. Strategies such as just-in-time manufacturing, *kanban*, lean manufacturing, total quality management, and others became very popular, and vast quantities of resources were invested in implementing these strategies. In the last few years, however, it has become clear that many companies have reduced manufacturing costs as much as is practically possible. Many of these companies are discovering that effective supply chain management is the next step they need to take in order to increase profit and market share.

Indeed, in 1998 American companies spent $898 billion, or about 10 percent of the U.S. gross national product (GNP), on supply-related activities. During 2000, this cost increased to $1 trillion, $6 billion ("State of Logistics Report," published by Roslyn Wilson and Robert V. Delaney). This figure includes the cost of movement, storage, and control of products across the supply chain, both within manufacturing plants and warehouses and between different components of the supply chain. Unfortunately, this huge investment typically includes many unnecessary cost components due to redundant stock, inefficient transportation strategies, and other wasteful practices in the supply chain. For instance, experts believe that the grocery industry can save about $30 billion, or 10 percent of its annual operating cost, by using more effective supply chain strategies [69].

To illustrate this issue, consider the following two examples:

1. It takes a typical box of cereal more than three months to get from the factory to a supermarket.

2. It takes a typical new car, on average, 15 days to travel from the factory to the dealership. This lead time should be compared with the actual travel time, which is no more than four to five days.

Thus, many opportunities exist to cut costs in the supply chain. Not surprisingly, a number of companies have been able to substantially increase revenue or decrease costs through effective supply chain management.

EXAMPLE 1-3

Procter & Gamble estimates that it saved retail customers $65 million in a recent 18-month supply chain initiative. "According to Procter & Gamble, the essence of its approach lies in manufacturers and suppliers working closely together ... jointly creating business plans to eliminate the source of wasteful practices across the entire supply chain" [160].

The example suggests that *strategic partnerships* between suppliers and manufacturers may have a significant impact on supply chain performance. What are the types of *business plans* and *partnerships* that can best reduce costs and improve service levels? Which one is appropriate for the particular situation at hand? What incentives and performance measures should be used to make the partnership successful? Finally, how should the benefits resulting from the strategic partnerships be shared? Should the cost savings be transferred to the customers, split between the different partners, or kept by the most powerful player?

EXAMPLE 1-4

In two years National Semiconductor reduced distribution costs by 2.5 percent, decreased delivery time by 47 percent, and increased sales by 34 percent by closing six warehouses around the globe and air-freighting microchips to customers from a new centralized distribution center in Singapore [69].

Of course, by switching to air carriers, National Semiconductor increased transportation costs significantly. This increase was offset by a reduction in inventory costs resulting from the shift from a decentralized distribution system with a number of warehouses to a centralized system with a single warehouse. This example motivates the following question: What are the correct trade-offs between inventory and transportation costs?

EXAMPLE 1-5

Nabisco, Inc., delivers 500 types of cookies and more than 10,000 candies to over 80,000 buyers and spends more than $200 million a year in transportation expenses. Unfortunately, too many trucks arrive at or depart from their destinations half empty. That is why Nabisco is pioneering a collaborative logistics effort, so that Nabisco can share trucks and warehouse space with other companies in order to lower logistics costs. In a recent pilot program, Nabisco shared warehouses and trucks with 25 other manufacturers, including Dole and Lea & Perrins. In one test involving 8,000 orders, grocer Lucky Stores reduced inventory costs by $4.8 million. Nabisco itself saved $78,000 in shipping costs, and combined, all of the manufacturers involved in the test saved nearly $900,000 [80].

Of course, this type of cooperation with other companies requires advanced information systems and entails a variety of risks. What systems are necessary for this approach to be a success? When should a company undertake this type of complicated partnership?

EXAMPLE 1-6

Dayton Hudson Corporation's Target stores rely on sophisticated relationships with suppliers. Target, for example, may agree that an earthenware manufacturer will supply a certain number of Italian bowls, without specifying details of style and color. As the delivery date draws nearer, Target forecasts styles that are likely to sell. Based on these forecasts, the manufacturer can produce trial lots, which can be sold in select Target stores to determine if the particular styles manufactured will indeed sell [147].

Clearly, this level of flexibility increases the complexity of the supplier's supply chain. Why would the supplier agree to this type of arrangement? How much does Target gain with this type of flexible ordering? Should Target be willing to pay more per bowl for this flexibility? If so, how much more? And finally, what type of information system needs to be employed by Target and its suppliers to support this level of flexibility?

EXAMPLE 1-7

In 1979 Kmart was one of the leading companies in the retail industry, with 1,891 stores and average revenues per store of $7.25 million. At that time Wal-Mart was a small niche retailer in the South with only 229 stores and average revenues about half those of Kmart stores. In 10 years Wal-Mart had transformed itself; in 1992 it had the highest sales per square foot and the highest inventory turnover and operating profit of any discount retailer. Today Wal-Mart is the largest and highest-profit retailer in the world. In fact, as of 1999, Wal-Mart accounted for nearly 5 percent of U.S. retail spending [78]. How did Wal-Mart do it? The starting point was a relentless focus on satisfying customer needs; Wal-Mart's goal was simply to provide customers with access to goods when and where they want them and to develop cost structures that enable competitive pricing. The key to achieving this goal was to make the way the company replenishes inventory the centerpiece of its strategy. This was done by using a logistics technique known as *cross-docking*. In this strategy, goods are continuously delivered to Wal-Mart's warehouses, from where they are dispatched to stores without ever sitting in inventory. This strategy reduced Wal-Mart's cost of sales significantly and made it possible to offer everyday low prices to their customers [145].

If the cross-docking strategy works so well for Wal-Mart, shouldn't all companies use the same strategy? Indeed, many successful retailers employ other distribution strategies: some keep inventory at their warehouses while others ship directly to stores.

EXAMPLE 1-8

The Home Depot Inc. moves over 85 percent of its merchandise directly from suppliers to stores, avoiding warehouses altogether. In addition, since such a high volume of goods moves through its stores ($44 million in annual sales on average), the products frequently are shipped in full truck loads, for additional savings [147].

The preceding examples describe a number of supply chain management success stories. They suggest that in some industries, supply chain management is perhaps the single most important factor determining the success of the firm. Indeed, in the computer and printer industries, where most manufacturers use the same suppliers and identical technologies, companies compete on cost and service levels, the two key elements in our definition of supply chain management.

The examples also raise an important question. If these firms have improved supply chain performance by focusing on strategic partnering, using centralized warehousing, or employing the cross-docking strategy, what inhibits other firms from adopting the same techniques to improve their supply chain performance?

The earlier discussion suggests that the answer involves two major issues:

- The ability to replace traditional supply chain strategies, in which each facility or party in the chain makes decisions with little regard to their impact on other supply chain partners, by those that yield a *globally optimized* supply chain.
- The ability to effectively manage uncertainty. Unfortunately, the level of demand uncertainty has increased in the last few years. Indeed, in high-tech industries, product life cycles are becoming shorter and shorter. In particular, many computer and printer models have life cycles of only a few months, so the manufacturer may have only one order or production opportunity. Unfortunately, since these are new products, no historical data are available that allow the manufacturer to accurately predict customer demand. At the same time, the proliferation of products in these industries makes it increasingly difficult to predict demand for a specific model. Finally, significant price declines in these industries are common, reducing the product value during its life cycle [112].

EXAMPLE 1-9

A Korean manufacturer of electrical products such as industrial relays is facing a service level of about 70 percent; that is, only about 70 percent of all orders are delivered on time. On the other hand, inventory keeps piling up, mostly of products that are not in demand. The manufacturer's inventory turnover ratio, defined as the ratio of the annual flow to average inventory at the manufacturer's main warehouse, is about four. However, in the electronics industry, leading companies turn inventory over about nine times a year. If the Korean manufacturer can increase its inventory turns to this level, it will be able to significantly reduce inventory levels. The manufacturer is thus searching for new strategies that will increase service levels over the next three years to about 99 percent and, at the same time, significantly decrease inventory levels and cost.

Just a few years ago, most analysts would have said that these two objectives, improved service and inventory levels, could not be achieved at the same time. Indeed, traditional inventory theory tells us that to increase service level, the firm must increase inventory and therefore cost. Surprisingly, recent developments in information and communications technologies, together with a better understanding of supply chain strategies, have led to innovative approaches that allow the firm to improve both objectives simultaneously.

Throughout the rest of this book, we endeavor to present these approaches and strategies in detail. We will focus on demonstrating why certain strategies are adopted, what the trade-offs are between different strategies, and how specific strategies are implemented in practice.

1.5 KEY ISSUES IN SUPPLY CHAIN MANAGEMENT

In this section, we introduce some of the supply chain management issues that we discuss in much more detail throughout the remaining chapters. These issues span a large spectrum of a firm's activities, from the strategic through the tactical to the operational level:

- The *strategic level* deals with decisions that have a long-lasting effect on the firm. This includes decisions regarding the number, location, and capacity of warehouses and manufacturing plants and the flow of material through the logistics network.

- The *tactical level* includes decisions that are typically updated anywhere between once every quarter and once every year. These include purchasing and production decisions, inventory policies, and transportation strategies, including the frequency with which customers are visited.
- The *operational level* refers to day-to-day decisions such as scheduling, lead time quotations, routing, and truck loading.

 Below we introduce and discuss some of the key issues, questions, and trade-offs associated with different decisions.

Distribution Network Configuration   Consider several plants producing products to serve a set of geographically dispersed retailers. The current set of warehouses is deemed inappropriate, and management wants to reorganize or redesign the distribution network. This may be due, for example, to changing demand patterns or the termination of a leasing contract for a number of existing warehouses. In addition, changing demand patterns may require a change in plant production levels, a selection of new suppliers, and a new flow pattern of goods throughout the distribution network. How should management select a set of warehouse locations and capacities, determine production levels for each product at each plant, and set transportation flows between facilities, either from plant to warehouse or warehouse to retailer, in such a way as to minimize total production, inventory, and transportation costs and satisfy service level requirements? This is a complex optimization problem, and advanced technology and approaches are required to find a solution.

Inventory Control   Consider a retailer that maintains an inventory of a particular product. Since customer demand changes over time, the retailer can use only historical data to predict demand. The retailer's objective is to decide at what point to reorder a new batch of the product, and how much to order so as to minimize inventory ordering and holding costs. More fundamentally, why should the retailer hold inventory in the first place? Is it due to uncertainty in customer demand, uncertainty in the supply process, or some other reasons? If it is due to uncertainty in customer demand, is there anything that can be done to reduce it? What is the impact of the forecasting tool used to predict customer demand? Should the retailer order more than, less than, or exactly the demand forecast? And, finally, what inventory turnover ratio should be used? Does it change from industry to industry?

Supply Contracts   In traditional supply chain strategies, each party in the chain focuses on its own profit and hence makes decisions with little regard to their impact on other supply chain partners. Relationships between suppliers and buyers are established by means of supply contracts that specify pricing and volume discounts, delivery lead times, quality, returns, and so forth. The question, of course, is whether supply contracts can also be used to replace the traditional supply chain strategy with one that optimizes the entire supply chain performance? In particular, what is the impact of volume discount and revenue sharing contracts on supply chain performance? Are there pricing strategies that can be applied by suppliers to incentivize buyers to order more products while at the same time increase the supplier profit?

Distribution Strategies   Wal-Mart's recent success story highlights the importance of a particular distribution strategy referred to as *cross-docking*. As observed earlier, this is a distribution strategy in which the stores are supplied by central warehouses that act as coordinators of the supply process and as transshipment points for incoming orders from outside vendors, but that do not keep stock themselves. We refer to such warehouses as *cross-dock points*. Consider the following questions: How many cross-dock points are necessary? What are the savings achieved using a cross-docking strategy? How should a cross-docking strategy be implemented in practice? Is the cross-docking strategy better than the classical strategy in which warehouses hold inventory? Which strategy should a particular firm employ: the cross-docking strategy, the classical distribution strategy in which inventory is kept at the warehouses, or direct shipping, a strategy in which items are shipped from suppliers directly to stores?

Supply Chain Integration and Strategic Partnering As observed earlier, designing and implementing a globally optimal supply chain is quite difficult because of its dynamics and the conflicting objectives employed by different facilities and partners. Nevertheless, the National Semiconductor, Wal-Mart, and Procter & Gamble success stories demonstrate not only that an integrated, globally optimal supply chain is possible, but that it can have a huge impact on the company's performance and market share. Of course, one can argue that these three examples are associated with companies that are among the biggest companies in their respective industries; these companies can implement technologies and strategies that very few others can afford. However, in today's competitive markets, most companies have no choice; they are forced to integrate their supply chain and engage in strategic partnering. This pressure stems from both their customers and their supply chain partners. How can integration be achieved successfully? Clearly, information sharing and operational planning are the keys to a successfully integrated supply chain. But what information should be shared? How should it be used? How does information affect the design and operation of the supply chain? What level of integration is needed within the organization and with external partners? Finally, what types of partnerships can be implemented, and which type should be implemented for a given situation?

Outsourcing and Procurement Strategies Rethinking your supply chain strategy not only involves coordinating the different activities in the supply chain, but also deciding what to make internally and what to buy from outside sources. How can a firm identify what manufacturing activities lie in its set of core competencies, and thus should be completed internally, and what product and components should be purchased from outside suppliers, because these manufacturing activities are not core competencies? Is there any relationship between the answer to that question and product architecture? What are the risks associated with outsourcing and how can these risks be minimized? When you do outsource, how can you ensure a timely supply of products? Finally, what is the impact of the Internet on procurement strategies? Should the firm use a private or public exchange when dealing with trading partners?

Product Design Effective design plays several critical roles in the supply chain. Most obviously, certain product designs may increase inventory holding or transportation costs relative to other designs, while other designs may facilitate a shorter manufacturing lead time. Unfortunately, product redesign is often expensive. When is it worthwhile to redesign products so as to reduce logistics costs or supply chain lead times? Is it possible to leverage product design to compensate for uncertainty in customer demand? Can one quantify the amount of savings resulting from such a strategy? What changes should be made in the supply chain to take advantage of the new product design? Finally, new concepts such as mass customization are increasingly popular. What role does supply chain management play in the successful implementation of these concepts?

Information Technology and Decision-Support Systems Information technology is a critical enabler of effective supply chain management. Indeed, much of the current interest in supply chain management is motivated by the opportunities that appeared due to the abundance of data and the savings that can be achieved by sophisticated analysis of these data. The primary issue in supply chain management is not whether data can be received, but what data should be transferred; that is, which data are significant for supply chain management and which data can safely be ignored? How should the data be analyzed and used? What is the impact of the Internet? What is the role of electronic commerce? What infrastructure is required both internally and between supply chain partners? Finally, since information technology and decision-support systems are both available, can these technologies be viewed as the main tools used to achieve competitive advantage in the market? If they can, then what is preventing others from using the same technology?

Customer Value Customer value is the measure of a company's contribution to its customer, based on the entire range of products, services, and intangibles that constitute the company's offerings. In recent years this measure has superseded measures such as quality and customer satisfaction. Obviously, effective supply chain management is critical if a firm wishes to fulfill customer needs and provide value. But what determines customer value in different industries? How is customer value measured? How is information technology used to enhance customer value in the supply chain? How does supply chain management contribute to customer value? How do emerging trends in customer value, such as development of relationships and experiences, affect supply chain management? What is the relationship between product price and brand name in the conventional world and in the on-line world? Can "smart" pricing strategies be used to improve supply chain performance?

Each of these issues and strategies is discussed in great detail in the remaining chapters. As you will see, the focus in each case is on either achieving a *globally optimized* supply chain or managing uncertainty in the supply chain, or both. A summary is provided in Table 1-1.

TABLE 1-1

KEY SUPPLY CHAIN MANAGEMENT ISSUES

	Global optimization	Managing uncertainty
Distribution network configuration	x	
Inventory control		x
Supply contracts	x	
Distribution strategies	x	x
Strategic partnerships	x	
Outsourcing and procurement		x
Product design		x
Information technology	x	x
Customer value	x	x

1.6 BOOK OBJECTIVES AND OVERVIEW

For many reasons, interest in logistics and supply chain management has grown explosively in the last few years. This interest has led many companies to analyze their supply chains. In most cases, however, this has been done based on experience and intuition; very few analytical models or design tools have been used in this process. Meanwhile, in the last two decades the academic community has developed various models and tools to assist with the management of the supply chain. Unfortunately, the first generation of this technology was not robust or flexible enough to be effectively utilized by industry. This, however, has changed in the last few years. Analysis and insight have improved, and effective models and decision-support systems have been developed—but these may not be familiar to industry.

This book aims to fill this gap by presenting state-of-the-art models and solution methods important in the design, control, operation, and management of supply chain systems. We intend this book to be useful both as a textbook for MBA-level logistics and supply chain courses and as a reference for teachers, consultants, and managers involved in any one of the processes that make up the supply chain.

Each chapter includes case studies, numerous examples, and discussion questions. In addition, each chapter is mostly self-contained, and mathematical and technical sections can be skipped without loss of continuity. Therefore, we believe the book is accessible to anyone with an interest in some of the many aspects of supply chain management. For example, transportation managers deciding which modes of transportation to use, inventory control managers wanting to ensure smooth production with as little inventory as possible, purchasing/supply managers designing contracts with their company's suppliers and clients, and logistics managers in charge of their company's supply chains can all benefit from the contents of this book.

The book includes chapters covering the following topics:

- Network configuration and site location.
- Inventory management and supply contracts.
- The value of information.
- Supply chain integration and the impact of the Internet.
- Strategic alliances.
- Outsourcing and procurement strategies.
- International supply chain management.
- Supply chain management and product design.
- Customer value.
- Information technology.
- Decision-support systems.

In addition, two software packages, the **Computerized Beer Game** and the **Risk Pool Game**, and a set of spreadsheets are included with the book. The Computerized Beer Game is an advanced version of a traditional supply chain management role-playing simulation, first developed at MIT. In addition to replicating the traditional board-based game, the Computerized Beer Game has many options and features that enable the reader to explore a variety of simple and advanced supply chain management concepts that cannot be easily taught using the traditional game. This includes the value of information sharing, the impact of long and short lead times, and the difference between centralized and decentralized decision making on supply chain performance.

This game complements much of what we discuss in the text; in particular, it helps to clarify many of the points raised in Chapter 4.

Similarly, the Risk Pool Game was developed to illustrate important issues in inventory management and, in particular, an important concept in supply chain management referred to as *risk pooling*, a concept that we discuss in Chapter 3. In the game, the player simultaneously manages both a supply chain with a single warehouse and a supply chain without any warehouse. In the latter case, the player delivers finished goods directly from the suppliers to the retail outlets. Throughout the game, the software records the profits of both supply chains, so that the player can compare the performance of the centralized and decentralized systems. Both software packages are described in detail in the appendix.

Finally, a series of spreadsheets is included with the book. These spreadsheets illustrate the various *supply contracts* described in Chapter 3.

DISCUSSION QUESTIONS

1. Consider the supply chain for a domestic automobile.
   a. What are the components of the supply chain for the automobile?
   b. What are the different firms involved in the supply chain?
   c. What are the objectives of these firms?
   d. Provide examples of conflicting objectives in this supply chain.
2. Consider a consumer mortgage offered by a bank.
   a. What are the components of the supply chain for the mortgage?
   b. Is there more than one firm involved in the supply chain? What are the objectives of the firm or firms?
   c. What are the similarities between product and service supply chains? What are the differences?
3. What is an example of a supply chain that has evolved over time?
4. A vertically integrated company is a company that owns, manages, and operates all its business functions. A horizontally integrated company is a corporation consisting of a number of companies, each of which is acting independently. The corporation provides branding, direction, and general strategy. Compare and contrast the supply chain strategies of the two types of companies.
5. If a firm is completely vertically integrated, is effective supply chain management still important?
6. Consider the supply chain for canned peaches sold by a major food processing company. What are the sources of uncertainty in this supply chain?
7. Consider a firm redesigning its logistics network. What are the advantages to having a small number of centrally located warehouses? What are the advantages to having a larger number of warehouses closer to the end customers?
8. Consider a firm selecting a supplier of transportation services? What are the advantages to using a truckload carrier? A package delivery firm such as UPS?
9. What are the advantages to a firm of high inventory levels? What are the disadvantages? What are the advantages of low inventory levels? The disadvantages?

Meditech Surgical

Three years after Meditech was spun off from its parent company, Meditech captured a majority of the endoscopic surgical instrument market. Its primary competitor, National Medical Corporation, had practically invented the $800 million market just over a decade ago. But Meditech competed aggressively, developing new, innovative instruments and selling them through a first-class sales force. The combination paid off, and Meditech had become a phenomenal success in a short period of time.

Despite the success, Dan Franklin, manager of Customer Service and Distribution, was concerned about growing customer dissatisfaction. Meditech had recently introduced several new products that were central to the entire Meditech product line. New product introductions, which were critical to Meditech's strategy of rapid product development, needed to be introduced flawlessly to protect Meditech's reputation and sales of other products. But Meditech consistently failed to keep up with demand during the flood of initial orders. Production capacity became strained as customers waited over six weeks to have their orders delivered. Poor delivery service, which is fatal in the health care industry, was jeopardizing Meditech's reputation.

COMPANY BACKGROUND

Endoscopic surgical techniques fall under a class of surgical procedures described as minimally invasive. Minimally invasive surgery, as opposed to traditional open surgery, requires only small incisions to perform an operation. As a result, procedures using endoscopic techniques often provide substantial benefits for the patient both physically and financially. The procedures often shorten patient recovery, which can translate into reduced surgical expenses overall. Despite the benefits and the multidecade history of endoscopic technology, the procedures have only become popular in the last 10 years.

Only three years ago, the market for endoscopic surgical instruments was expected to double its size in five years. Growth beyond five years also looked promising. Largo Healthcare Company, Meditech's parent company, decided to spin Meditech off as an independent company focused solely on producing and selling endoscopic surgical instruments. Largo management hoped that the new company would prosper without the distractions of other Largo businesses and capture market share of endoscopic instruments as quickly as possible.

Since its inception just over six years ago, Meditech has produced innovative, low-cost products. New products were brought to the market quickly and pushed by an aggressive sales force. Old products were updated with innovative features and presented to the market as new products. Consequently, the competition between Meditech and National Medical centered on the continuous development and introduction of new products by both companies. A dozen or more new products would typically be introduced by Meditech in any given year.

While the development strategies were similar, the sales strategies differed dramatically. National Medical concentrated on selling to surgeons. Meditech's sales force concentrated on selling to hospitals material managers as well as to surgeons. Material managers tended to be more concerned with cost and delivery performance. The surgeons, on the other hand, focused on product features. As the pressures increased on health care costs, the importance of the material manager's purchasing position also increased. Meditech was well positioned to take advantage of this important shift.

The success of Meditech's strategy quickly became evident. Within six years, Meditech had captured the leading share in the endoscopic surgical instrument market. This was no small feat by any market's standards, but with surgical instruments this was especially impressive. Market share changes in the professional health care industry tended to take place gradually. Surgeons and doctors often held onto preferred manufacturers. Hospitals frequently used group purchasing organizations (GPOs) that took advantage of extended contracts with suppliers. The process of

Source: Copyright © 1995 by Massachusetts Institute of Technology. This case was prepared by LFM Fellow Bryan Gilpin under the direction of Professor Stephen C. Graves as the basis for class discussion.

"converting" a hospital to a new supplier often took months of negotiation and convincing.

Most endoscopic surgical instruments are small enough to fit into the palm of a surgeon's hand. They are mechanical in nature, typically having several intricate mechanisms to provide the required functionality. Materials used to produce the instruments include plastic injection–molded parts, metal blades, springs, and so forth. In all cases of use, surgeons use the instrument for one operation and then immediately dispose of it. Instruments are never resterilized and reused for another patient. All in all, the Meditech product line consists of over 200 separate end-products.

DISTRIBUTION

Meditech distributes all its goods from a central warehouse, using two primary channels—domestic dealers and international affiliates—to distribute its products from the central warehouse to end-customers (i.e., hospitals). The first channel, for domestic sales only, uses domestic distributors, or dealers, to ship to hospitals. The dealers order and receive products from multiple manufacturers, including Meditech, typically stocking hundreds of different products. Stocked products range from commodity items, such as surgical gloves and aspirin, to endoscopic surgical instruments. By using dealers to supply products, hospitals do not need to order directly from manufacturers for their diverse needs. Additionally, since dealers maintain regional warehouses all over the United States, the distance between dealer warehouses and most hospitals tends to be quite small. The short distance permits frequent replenishments of hospital inventories; in some cases, trucks from dealers drop off supplies once or twice per day. Hospitals enjoy the frequent replenishments, which reduce hospital inventory and, consequently, reduce material costs.

The regional dealer warehouses act as independent entities, autonomously determining when to order new supplies and how much to order. Therefore, while Meditech only uses four or five major distribution companies, it still receives orders from, and ships to, hundreds of regional, individually run warehouses. Each warehouse in turn ships to about a dozen or more hospitals, resulting in thousands of hospitals that receive Meditech products.

The distribution channel for international sales uses Largo Healthcare's international affiliates. International affiliates are wholly owned subsidiaries of Largo Healthcare residing outside of the United States. As with domestic dealers, affiliates distribute to hospitals in their regional area. However, in contrast with domestic dealers, which may locate within just a few miles of customer hospitals, an affiliate ships product throughout an entire country. From Meditech's point of view, affiliates' orders essentially look no different than dealers'—international affiliates submit orders to Meditech and Meditech fills them with available product.

INTERNAL OPERATIONS

The production processes to manufacture endoscopic instruments are composed of three major steps: assembling of component parts into individual or "bulk" instruments, packaging one or more bulk instruments into a packaged good, and sterilizing the packaged goods. Each of these steps is described below.

Assembly

The assembly process is manually intensive. Component parts arrive into the assembly area from suppliers following a brief inspection by Quality Assurance (QA). The parts are placed into inventory until ready for use by one of several assembly lines. Each assembly line is run by a team of cross-trained production workers who can produce any of several instruments within a product family. Line changeovers within a family are quick and inexpensive, merely requiring a warning from the production team leader and a supply of the appropriate component parts. The typical cycle time for assembly of a batch of instruments— the time required to schedule assembly of a batch of instruments and then actually assemble them, assuming that component parts are available in component parts inventory—is on the order of two weeks. Lead time for component parts is on the order of 2–16 weeks. Assembled instruments are moved from the assembly area into bulk instrument inventory, where they wait to be packaged.

Packaging

The packaging process makes use of several large packaging machines. The machines direct bulk instruments into plastic containers and then adhere a flexible sheet of material over the top of the container. The entire plastic container is then placed into a finished cardboard container and shipped immediately to the sterilizer. Capacity at the packaging area has not restricted output.

Sterilization

The sterilization process uses a large Cobalt radiation sterilizer. After batches of packaged instruments (cardboard container, plastic container, and instruments) are placed into the sterilizer, the sterilizer is turned on for about an hour. The radiation penetrates cardboard and plastic to destroy any potentially harmful contaminants. The sterilizer can sterilize as much product as will fit inside its four walls. Capacity limitations have not been a problem thus far. Sterilized instruments are immediately moved into finished goods inventory.

The Operations Organization

The entire operations organization reports up through the vice president of Operations, Kenneth Strangler (see Figure 1-3 for an organization chart for Operations). Functions immediately reporting to Strangler include several plant managers (one for each of Meditech's four manufacturing facilities), a director of supplier management, and a director of planning, distribution, and customer service. Other vice presidents (not shown) exist for marketing and sales,

product development, and finance. All vice presidents report to the highest officer in the company, the president of Meditech. The plant managers in the organization have responsibility for production personnel, engineering technicians, quality assurance, support services, and material supply for their respective facilities. Reporting directly to the plant managers are several business units. Each business unit has full responsibility either for the assembly of a particular product family or, in the case of packaging and sterilization, for an entire production process. The most important job of each assembly business unit is to meet the production schedule every week. Meeting the schedule ensures a constant supply of bulk instruments to the packaging/sterilization process. The process of determining assembly and packaging/sterilization schedules will be discussed below.

Also reporting to the vice president of Operations are Supplier Management and Planning, Distribution, and Customer Service. Supplier Management works on relationships with suppliers, including establishing purchasing contracts and finding new suppliers if necessary. The Planning, Distribution, and Customer Service department does everything it can to ensure that customers receive product when needed. The positions within the Customer Service department include the manager of Customer Service and

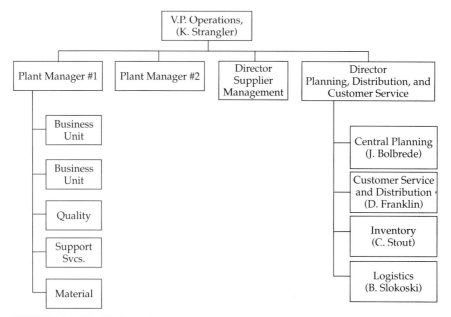

FIGURE 1-3 The Meditech Organization Chart for operations.

Distribution, Dan Franklin; the manager of Central Planning; the manager of Inventory; and a manager of Logistics. Customer Service deals with everything from occasional customer complaints to establishing strategies to improve delivery service to customers. Customer Service representatives work with dealers and affiliates to keep them updated on product delivery schedules and problems. Often this responsibility places the Customer Service representative in direct contact with hospital personnel.

While Customer Service handles issues concerning the movement of product out of finished goods inventory, Central Planning ensures that adequate finished goods are available to meet incoming orders. They develop monthly production plans that are used by the business units to determine weekly and daily schedules.

Charles Stout, the Inventory manager, determines the finished goods inventory policy and establishes parts and bulk inventory guidelines for the business units. When a mandate to reduce inventory is passed down from higher levels of management, the Inventory manager must determine where inventory can be reduced and then begin enforcing those reductions. Through recent efforts, Stout had successfully eliminated several million dollars of obsolete and slow-moving inventory.

PRODUCTION PLANNING AND SCHEDULING

The production planning and scheduling process is broken down into two parts: planning, based on monthly forecasts, of assembly and component parts orders and daily scheduling of packaging and sterilization based on finished goods inventory levels.

During the fourth quarter of each fiscal year, the marketing and finance organizations determine an annual forecast. The annual forecast is then broken down proportionately, based on the number of weeks in the month, into monthly forecasts. As the year progresses, the Central Planners work with the Marketing organization to make forecast adjustments according to market trends and events. At the beginning of each month, the month's forecasts are adjusted and agreed upon by the Marketing organization and the Central Planners.

The planning of assembly for a particular instrument begins with the monthly demand forecasts. Based on the month's forecast, the Central Planners determine the amount of product that needs to be transferred from bulk inventory into finished goods inventory to "meet" the expected demand. This amount, termed the finished goods "transfer requirement," is determined by subtracting the current finished goods inventory level from (1) the demand forecast for the month plus (2) the required safety stock. (The current safety stock policy is to maintain three weeks' worth of demand).

The transfer requirements, once completed for all 200-plus product codes, are passed throughout the organization for approval. This process typically takes place one to two weeks into the current month. While not actually used to schedule assembly or to alter the packaging and sterilization processes, the transfer requirements provide an estimate of the required overall production for the month. Any problems in being able to deliver to the plan can then be identified and resolved.

Assembly schedules and replenishment orders for parts are based on the monthly demand forecasts and current inventory levels. By mid-month, the completed monthly plans, which contain the monthly forecasts, are sent to the assembly business units. A planner in the business unit plugs the forecasts into a Materials Requirement Planning (MRP) system, which determines weekly production schedules and component parts orders for each finished product. The MRP system determines assembly schedules and parts orders based on (1) the monthly forecasts; (2) the lead times for assembly, packaging, and sterilization, and (3) current parts, bulk, and finished goods inventory levels. Although the MRP calculation may be run several times each week, the planner is careful not to change weekly production schedules with less than a week's notice. (A schedule change often requires rescheduling workers and procuring more component parts. One week's notice for responding to scheduling changes, therefore, has been deemed adequate by the business unit managers.)

In contrast to the forecast-based scheduling of the assembly operation, the packaging and sterilization operations are scheduled based on as-needed replenishment of finished goods inventory. For purposes of scheduling, the packaging and sterilization operations are considered one operation because bulk instruments flow through packaging, into the sterilizer, and into finished goods without being inventoried. (See Figure 1-4 for a diagram of the entire production process.) The entire packaging/sterilization process can be completed for a batch of instruments in about

FIGURE 1-4 The Meditech production process.

one week. The scheduling of packaging/sterilization is done on an order point/order quantity (OP/OQ) basis [i.e., when finished goods inventory drops below the predetermined order point (OP), a replenishment order for more packaged/sterilized product is initiated. The size of the order in terms of number of instruments is always equal to the predetermined order quantity (OQ).]

Another way to view the scheduling process is to think of material as being "pushed" through assembly into bulk instrument inventory and as being "pulled" through packaging/sterilization into finished goods inventory. The push through assembly is based on the monthly forecast determined before the month's demand actually arrives. The pull through packaging/sterilization simply replenishes what was sold from finished goods the day before.

NEW PRODUCT INTRODUCTIONS, HIGH LEVELS OF INVENTORY, AND POOR SERVICE LEVEL

Over the past several years, Meditech has introduced dozens of new products into the market, mostly by updating existing products. Meditech plans to continue this strategy of continuously obsoleting its own products by constantly introducing innovations. While the innovative products have been well accepted by the marketplace, each new product introduction has resulted in a nightmare of supply problems. Dan Franklin felt that customers were beginning to tire of the poor service resulting from each introduction. Through many meetings with

hospital material managers, Dan began to realize the full scope of his customers' frustrations.

Franklin could not figure out why Meditech consistently had shortages with each introduction. Forecasting had definitely been a problem, but determining its extent was difficult. Data to measure forecast accuracy had not previously been tracked, nor had forecasts and demand information been kept. Data gathering requires a lengthy process of going back through hard copies of prior monthly plans and entering the information by hand into a computer. Even if a better methodology could be determined, forecasts can only be improved by so much.

In addition to new product introduction problems, finished goods inventory levels appeared to be remarkably high. A consultant had recently been hired to study Meditech's inventory. Her findings indicated that overall inventory could be reduced by at least 40 percent without an impact on the delivery service level (see Figure 1-5).[1] Despite the high levels of inventory, the actual service level over the past year was disappointing and below corporate objectives. Management feared that reducing inventory would further damage the already subpar level performance.

Another possible cause of the problem is "panic ordering" from dealers and affiliates. Panic ordering occurs when a dealer or affiliate is unsure of whether or not product will be received in time and therefore increases the size of its orders hoping that Meditech will deliver at least part of the order. The increased orders would cause demand to temporarily rise, helping to explain Meditech's problems with demand consistently exceeding supply. Familiar with past delivery problems, dealers and affiliates had every

---

[1]Note on replenishment assumption: For simplicity, this chart assumes that finished goods (FG) inventory is replenished once per week with a lead time of one week. At the beginning of each week, enough product is "ordered" so that the "pipeline" plus FG inventory equals $2\frac{2}{3}$ demand-weeks of product. The pipeline in this case refers to in-process product that has not yet reached FG inventory. On average, one week's worth of demand will reside in the pipeline. This leaves, again on average, $2\frac{2}{3} - 1 = 1\frac{2}{3}$ demand-weeks in FG inventory at the beginning of each week.

FIGURE 1-5 Weekly demand pattern for a representative stable product demonstrating current levels of inventory versus consultant's recommended inventory policy.

FIGURE 1-6 Typical demand pattern for a new product introduction. The product was officially introduced near the end of week #4.

reason to want to panic order. In one conversation with a representative from Meditech's largest dealer, the representative had indicated that panic ordering was a possibility. Given the decentralized nature of the regional warehouses, the dealer has little control over what an individual warehouse actually orders.

Warehouses could therefore panic order without the knowledge of the central dealer. On the other hand, the possibility of panic ordering does not mean that it actually occurs. To make matters worse, data proving or disproving its existence had been hard to find.

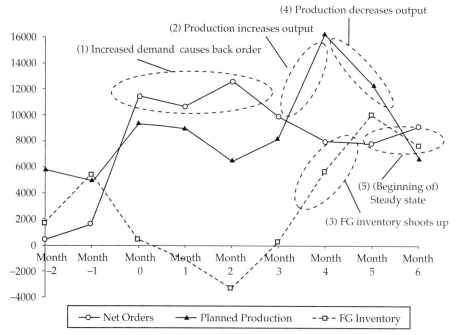

FIGURE 1-7 Production reaction to a new product introduction. The product was introduced in the last 2 weeks of Month 0.

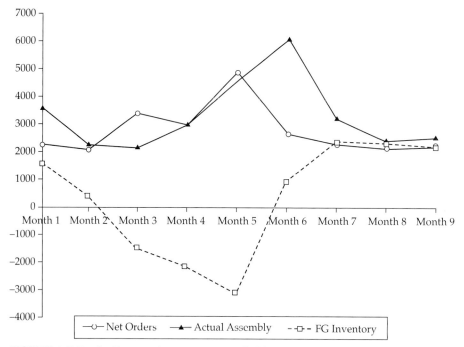

FIGURE 1-8 Production reaction to unexpectedly high demand (not a new product introduction). The unexpected demand occurred during Month 3, Month 4, and Month 5. Note that only monthly assembly output is shown; packaging/sterilization output was not obtained.

Dan asked one of his staff members to investigate the new product introduction problem and inventory/service level paradox. The staff member spent several months compiling information on demand patterns, production rates, and forecasts. Consistent with Meditech's decentralized nature, the information existed on many different systems in several different areas of the organization. There was no routine way to see incoming demand, inventory, or production rates for a particular instrument. Developing a common format for the data had also been difficult. Some data were expressed in terms of calendar months, other data in terms of weeks, and still other data in terms of the corporate financial calendar (alternating 4-week, 4-week, and 5-week months). Once put together, the information conveyed the following:

- New product demand after an introduction followed a consistent pattern of reaching a high peak during the first few weeks, but becoming relatively stable immediately afterward (see Figure 1-6).

- Variation in production schedules often exceeded variation in demand (see Figures 1-7 and 1-8).
- Monthly forecasting could be improved substantially using a simple statistical method: generating a linear regression through past data.

With this information in mind, Dan Franklin began thinking about how to fix Meditech's delivery problems.

CASE DISCUSSION QUESTIONS

1. What are Meditech's problems in introducing new products? In manufacturing ALL products?
2. What is driving these problems, both systemically and organizationally?
3. Why is the customer service manager the first person to recognize the major issues?
4. How would you fix these problems?

CHAPTER 2

Logistics Network Configuration

CASE
The Bis Corporation

The Bis Corporation is a company that produces and distributes soft drinks. Currently, two manufacturing plants located in Atlanta and Denver serve about 120,000 accounts—that is, retailers or stores—all over the United States. The current distribution system requires that all products be shipped to the three existing warehouses in Chicago, Dallas, and Sacramento prior to delivery to the retail accounts. The company was established in 1964 as a family venture and grew in the 1970s and 1980s at a fairly steady rate. Bis is now owned by 12 shareholders and run by a newly appointed CEO.

The gross margin in the soft drink industry is about 20 percent, and the value of each SKU (stockkeeping unit) is $1,000 for all products. Despite high profitability, the new CEO is concerned that the distribution network is not the most efficient one. In a recent shareholder meeting, he pointed out that the current distribution strategy used by Bis was designed about 15 years ago and was never modified. It consists of the following steps:

- Produce and store at the manufacturing plants.
- Pick, load, and ship to a warehouse/distribution center.
- Unload and store at the warehouse.
- Pick, load, and deliver to stores.

Thus, the shareholders decided to look for outside help in modifying their logistics network. Your company was able to secure the engagement, after six months of continuous work by the sales division. The commitment you made when you received the engagement was to improve the effectiveness and to align the cost of service with account profitability. In your original proposal you mentioned that "this will be accomplished by reengineering the sales and distribution functions." It seems that the concept of reengineering the entire distribution network, together with your commitment not only to the design but also to the implementation of the new distribution strategy, is what made your proposal attractive to Bis shareholders.

Since this is a huge project, you recognize that you can do a number of things rather quickly. In particular, in the first phase, which you have just completed, you identified about 10,000 accounts that should receive deliveries directly from the manufacturing plants. This was based on

- Dock receiving capabilities.
- Storage capabilities.
- Receiving methodologies.
- Merchandising requirements.
- Order-generation capabilities.

Source: Bis is a fictional company. The material in this case is loosely based on our experience with several companies.

- Delivery time window constraints.
- Current pricing.
- Promotional activity patterns.

It is now time to redesign the distribution network. For this purpose, you have grouped the accounts into 250 zones and the different products into five product families.

The data collected include the following:

1. Demand in 1997 by SKU per product family for each customer zone.
2. Annual production capacity (in SKUs) at each manufacturing plant.
3. Maximum capacity (SKUs) for each warehouse, new and existing (35,000).
4. Transportation costs per product family per mile for distributing products from the manufacturing plants and from the warehouses.
5. Setup cost for establishing a warehouse.

Customer service is of particular concern to Bis because there are a number of competing products in the markets. No specific dollar figure can be attached to a specific level of service; however, the CEO insists that to remain competitive, delivery time should be no more than 48 hours. This implies that the distance between a warehouse and a customer zone should be no more than 900 miles.

TABLE 2-1					
ESTIMATED YEARLY GROWTH					
Family	1	2	3	4	5
Multiplier	1.07	1.03	1.06	1.05	1.06

The Bis Corporation has just finished a comprehensive market study that shows significant volume growth in its markets. This growth is estimated to be uniform across the different zones, but it varies from product to product. The estimated yearly growth for 1998 and 1999 is given in Table 2-1.

The variable production cost at the two manufacturing facilities varies by product and by manufacturing plant. The CEO and company shareholders oppose building a new manufacturing plant because of the costs and risks involved. They are willing, however, to expand production capacities at the existing plants as needed. They estimate that increasing production capacity for a family would cost about $2,000 for every 100 SKUs.

The Bis Corporation would like to address the following issues:

1. Does the model developed truly represent Bis's logistics network? How can the Bis Corporation validate the model? What is the impact of aggregating customers and products on the model accuracy?
2. How many distribution centers should be established?
3. Where should they be located?
4. How should the plant's output of each product be allocated between warehouses?
5. Should production capacity be expanded? When and where?

At the end of the chapter, we suggest one way to analyze the case.

By the end of this chapter, you should be able to understand the following issues:

- How a company can develop a model representing its logistics network.
- How a company can validate this model.
- How aggregating customers and products affects the accuracy of the model.
- How a company knows how many distribution centers to establish.
- How a company knows where to locate these distribution centers.
- How a company allocates the output of each product in its plants among its distribution centers.
- How a company knows whether, when, and where to expand its production capacity.

2.1 INTRODUCTION

The logistics network (see Chapter 1) consists of suppliers, warehouses, distribution centers, and retail outlets as well as raw materials, work-in-process inventory, and finished products that flow between the facilities. In this chapter, we present some of the issues involved in the design and configuration of the logistics network.

Network configuration may involve issues relating to plant, warehouse, and retailer location. As explained in Chapter 1, these are strategic decisions because they have a long-lasting effect on the firm. In the discussion below, we concentrate on the following key strategic decisions:

1. Determining the appropriate number of warehouses.
2. Determining the location of each warehouse.
3. Determining the size of each warehouse.
4. Allocating space for products in each warehouse.
5. Determining which products customers will receive from each warehouse.

We therefore assume that plant and retailer locations will not be changed. The objective is to design or reconfigure the logistics network so as to minimize annual systemwide costs, including production and purchasing costs, inventory holding costs, facility costs (storage, handling, and fixed costs), and transportation costs, subject to a variety of *service level* requirements. Note that one other key decision, the selection of transportation *mode* (e.g., truck, rail), is a tactical decision discussed in Chapter 3.

In this setting, the trade-offs are clear. Increasing the number of warehouses typically yields

- An improvement in service level due to the reduction in average travel time to the customers.
- An increase in inventory costs due to increased safety stocks required to protect each warehouse against uncertainties in customer demands.
- An increase in overhead and setup costs.
- A reduction in outbound transportation costs: transportation costs from the warehouses to the customers.
- An increase in inbound transportation costs: transportation costs from the suppliers and/or manufacturers to the warehouses.

In essence, the firm must balance the costs of opening new warehouses with the advantages of being *close* to the customer. Thus, warehouse location decisions are crucial determinants of whether the supply chain is an efficient channel for the distribution of products.

We describe below some of the issues related to data collection and the calculation of costs required for the optimization models. Some of the information provided is based on logistics textbooks such as [11], [75], and [132].

Figure 2-1 and Figure 2-2 present two typical screens of a decision-support system (DSS) that the user would see at different stages of optimization. One represents the network prior to optimization and the second represents the optimized network.

2.2 DATA COLLECTION

A typical network configuration problem involves large amounts of data, including information on

1. Location of customers, retailers, existing warehouses and distribution centers, manufacturing facilities, and suppliers.
2. All products, including volumes, and special transport modes (e.g., refrigerated).
3. Annual demand for each product by customer location.

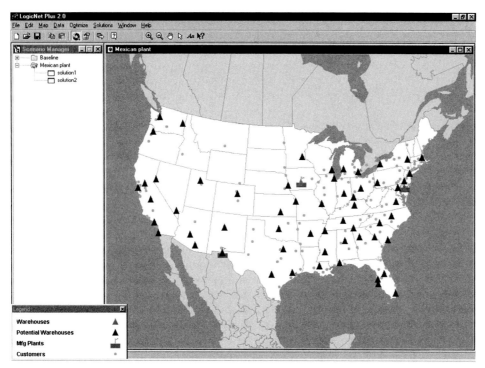

FIGURE 2-1 The DSS screen representing data prior to optimization.

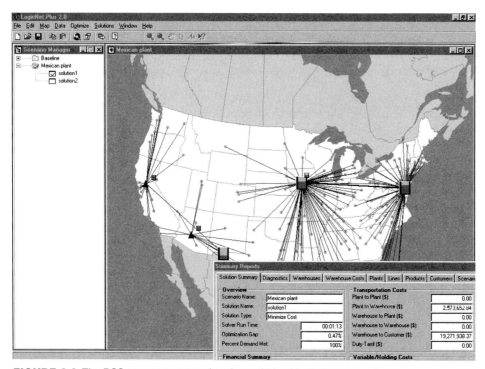

FIGURE 2-2 The DSS screen representing the optimized logistics network.

4. Transportation rates by mode.
5. Warehousing costs, including labor, inventory carrying charges, and fixed operating costs.
6. Shipment sizes and frequencies for customer delivery.
7. Order processing costs.
8. Customer service requirements and goals.

2.2.1 Data Aggregation

A quick look at the above list suggests that the amount of data involved in any optimization model for this problem is overwhelming. For instance, a typical soft drink distribution system has between 10,000 and 120,000 accounts (customers). Similarly, in a retail logistics network, such as Wal-Mart or JC Penney, the number of different products that flow through the network is in the thousands or even hundreds of thousands.

For that reason, an essential first step is data aggregation. This is carried out using the following criteria:

1. Customers located in close proximity to each other are aggregated using a grid network or other clustering technique. All customers within a single cell or a single cluster are replaced by a single customer located at the center of the cell or cluster. This cell or cluster is referred to as a customer zone. A very effective technique that is commonly used is to aggregate customers according to the five-digit or three-digit zip code. Observe that if customers are classified according to their service levels or frequency of delivery, they will be aggregated together by classes. That is, all customers within the same class are aggregated independently of the other classes.
2. Items are aggregated into a reasonable number of product groups, based on
    a. *Distribution pattern*. All products picked up at the same source and destined to the same customers are aggregated together. Sometime there is a need to aggregate not only by distribution pattern but also by logistics characteristics, such as weight and volume. That is, consider all products having the same distribution pattern. Within these products, we aggregate those SKUs with similar volume and weight into one product group.
    b. *Product type*. In many cases, different products might simply be variations in product models or style or might differ only in the type of packaging. These products are typically aggregated together.

An important consideration, of course, is the impact on the model's effectiveness caused by replacing the original detailed data with the aggregated data. We address this issue in two ways.

1. Even if the technology exists to solve the logistics network design problem with the original data, it may still be useful to aggregate data because our ability to forecast customer demand at the account and product levels is usually poor. Because of the reduction in variability achieved through aggregation, forecast demand is significantly more accurate at the aggregated level.

EXAMPLE 2-1

To illustrate the impact of aggregation on variability, consider an example in which two customers (e.g., retail outlets) are aggregated. Table 2-2 provides data on demand generated by these customers over the last seven years.

TABLE 2-2

HISTORICAL DATA FOR THE TWO CUSTOMERS

Year	1992	1993	1994	1995	1996	1997	1998
Customer 1	22,346	28,549	19,567	25,457	31,986	21,897	19,854
Customer 2	17,835	21,765	19,875	24,346	22,876	14,653	24,987
Total	40,181	50,314	39,442	49,803	54,862	36,550	44,841

Assuming that these data correctly represent the distribution of next year's demand for each customer, Table 2-3 provides a summary of average annual demand, the standard deviation of annual demand, and the coefficient of variation for each customer and for the aggregated one. For a discussion on the difference between the standard deviation and the coefficient of variation, see Chapter 3.

TABLE 2-3

SUMMARY OF HISTORICAL DATA

Statistics	Average annual demand	Standard deviation annual demand	Coefficient of variation
Customer 1	24,237	4,658	0.192
Customer 2	20,905	3,427	0.173
Total	45,142	6,757	0.150

Note that the average annual demand for the aggregated customer is the sum of the average demand generated by each customer. However, the variability faced by the aggregated customer, measured using either the standard deviation or the coefficient of variation, is smaller than the combined variabilities faced by the two existing customers.

2. Various researchers report that aggregating data into about 150 to 200 points usually results in no more than a 1 percent error in the estimation of total transportation costs; see [11] and [72].

In practice, the following guidelines are typically used when aggregating the data:

- Aggregate demand points for 150 to 200 zones. If customers are classified into classes according to their service levels or frequency of delivery, each class will have 150–200 aggregated points.
- Make sure each zone has approximately an equal amount of total demand. This implies that the zones may be of different geographic sizes.
- Place the aggregated points at the center of the zone.
- Aggregate the products into 20 to 50 product groups.

Figure 2-3 presents information about 3,220 customers all located in North America while Figure 2-4 shows the same data after aggregation using a three-digit zip code resulting in 217 aggregated points.

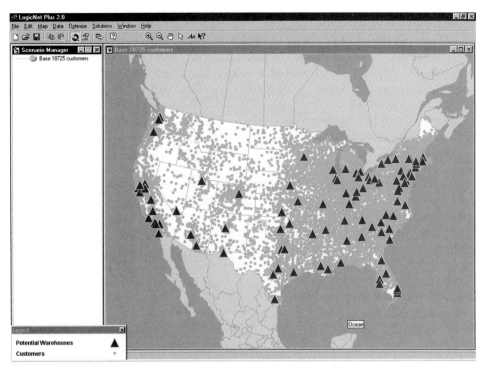

FIGURE 2-3 The DSS screen representing data prior to aggregation.

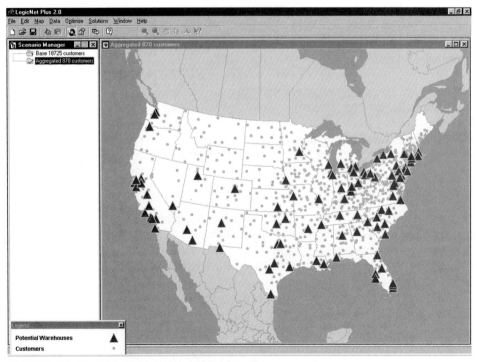

FIGURE 2-4 The DSS screen representing data after aggregation.

2.2.2 Transportation Rates

The next step in constructing an effective distribution network design model is to estimate transportation costs. An important characteristic of most transportation rates, including truck, rail, and others, is that the rates are almost linear with distance but not with volume. We distinguish here between transportation costs associated with an *internal* and an *external* fleet.

Estimating transportation costs for company-owned trucks is typically quite simple. It involves annual costs per truck, annual mileage per truck, annual amount delivered, and the truck's effective capacity. All this information can be used to easily calculate cost per mile per SKU.

Incorporating transportation rates for an external fleet into the model is more complex. We distinguish here between two modes of transportation: truckload, referred to as TL, and less than truckload, referred to as LTL.

In the United States, TL carriers subdivide the country into zones. Almost every state is a single zone, except for certain big states, such as Florida or New York, which are partitioned into two zones. The carriers then provide their clients with zone-to-zone table costs. This database provides the cost per mile per truckload between any two zones. For example, to calculate TL cost from Chicago, Illinois, to Boston, Massachusetts, one needs to get the cost per mile for this pair and multiply it by the distance from Chicago to Boston. An important property of the TL cost structure is that it is not symmetric; that is, it is typically more expensive to ship a fully loaded truck from Illinois to New York than from New York to Illinois (why?).

In the LTL industry, the rates typically belong to one of three basic types of freight rates: *class*, *exception*, and *commodity*. The class rates are standard rates that can be found for almost all products or commodities shipped. They are found with the help of a *classification tariff* that gives each shipment a *rating* or a *class*. For instance, the railroad classification includes 31 classes ranging from 400 to 13 that are obtained from the widely used *Uniform Freight Classification*. The National Motor Freight Classification, on the other hand, includes only 23 classes ranging from 500 to 35. In all cases, the higher the rating or class, the greater the relative charge for transporting the commodity. There are many factors involved in determining a product's specific class. These include product density, ease or difficulty of handling and transporting, and liability for damage.

Once the rating is established, it is necessary to identify the *rate basis number*. This number is the approximate distance between the load's origin and destination. With the commodity rating or class and the rate basis number, the specific rate per hundred pounds (hundred weight, or cwt) can be obtained from a carrier tariff table (i.e., a freight rate table).

The two other freight rates, namely *exception* and *commodity*, are specialized rates used to provide either less expensive rates (exception), or commodity-specific rates (commodity). For an excellent discussion, see [75] and [118]. Most carriers provide a database file with all of their transportation rates; these databases are typically incorporated into decision-support systems.

The proliferation of LTL carrier rates and the highly fragmented nature of the trucking industry has created the need for sophisticated rating engines. An example of such a rating engine that is widely used is SMC[3]'s RateWare (see www.smc3.com). This engine can work with various carrier tariff tables as well as SMC[3]'s CzarLite, one of the most widely used and accepted forms of nationwide LTL zip code–based rates. Unlike an individual carrier's tariff, CZAR-Lite offers a market-based price list derived from

FIGURE 2-5 Transportation rates for shipping 4,000 lb.

studies of LTL pricing on a regional, interregional, and national basis. This provides shippers with a fair pricing system and prevents any individual carrier's operational and marketing bias from overtly influencing the shipper choice. Consequently, CZAR-Lite rates are often used as a base for negotiating LTL contracts between shippers, carriers, and third-party logistics providers.

In Figure 2-5 we provide LTL cost charged by one carrier for shipping 4,000 pounds as a function of the distance from Chicago. The cost is given for two classes, class 100 and class 150. As you can see, in this case, the transportation cost function is not linear with distance.

2.2.3 Mileage Estimation

As explained in the previous subsection, the cost of transporting products from a specific source to a specific destination is a function of the distance between these two points. Thus, we need a tool that allows us to estimate distances. We can estimate distances using either street network or straight-line distances. Specifically, suppose we want to estimate the distance between two points, a and b. For this purpose, we need to obtain lon_a and lat_a, the longitude and latitude of point a (similarly for point b). Then, the straight-line distance in miles from a to b, D_{ab} is calculated as follows:

$$D_{ab} = 69\sqrt{(lon_a - lon_b)^2 + (lat_a - lat_b)^2}$$

The value 69 is approximately the number of miles per *degree* of latitude in the continental United States because longitude and latitude are given in degrees. This equation is accurate for short distances only; it does not take into account the curvature of the earth. To measure fairly long distances and correct for the earth's curvature, we use the approximation suggested by the U.S. Geological Survey, see [97]:

$$D_{ab} = 2(69) \sin^{-1}$$

$$\times \sqrt{\left(\sin\left(\frac{lat_a - lat_b}{2}\right)\right)^2 + \cos(lat_a) \times \cos(lat_b) \times \left(\sin\left(\frac{lon_a - lon_b}{2}\right)\right)^2}$$

These equations result in very accurate distance calculations; in both cases, however, the equations underestimate the actual road distance. To correct for this, we multiply

D_{ab} by a *circuity* factor, ρ. Typically, in a metropolitan area $\rho = 1.3$, while $\rho = 1.14$ for the continental United States.

EXAMPLE 2-2

Consider a manufacturer shipping a single fully loaded truck from Chicago, Illinois, to Boston, Massachusetts. The manufacturer is using a TL carrier whose rate is 105 cents per mile per truckload. To calculate transportation cost for this shipment, we need geographic data. Table 2-4 provides information about the longitude and latitude of each city.

TABLE 2-4

GEOGRAPHIC INFORMATION

City	Longitude	Latitude
Chicago	−87.65	41.85
Boston	−71.06	42.36

Note: The degrees in the table are in decimal representation so that 87.65 is 87° 39′ in a degrees/minutes representation, typical of paper maps. Longitude represents east-west position; any position west of the meridian has a negative value. Latitude represents north-south position; any location south of the equator has a negative value.

Application of the above equation leads to a straight-line distance from Chicago to Boston equal to 855 miles. Multiplying this number by the circuity factor, 1.14 in this case, leads to an estimate of the actual road distance equal to 974 miles. This number should be compared with the actual road distance, which is 965 miles. Thus, based on our estimate of the road distance, the transportation cost in this case is $1,023.

Applications in which exact distances are more appropriate can typically be obtained from advanced geographic information systems (GIS), as discussed in Chapter 12. However, this approach typically slows down the operation of decision-support systems dramatically, and the approximation technique described above usually provides enough accuracy for many applications.

2.2.4 Warehouse Costs

Warehousing and distribution center costs include three main components:

1. *Handling costs.* These include labor and utility costs that are proportional to annual flow through the warehouse.
2. *Fixed costs.* These capture all cost components that are not proportional to the amount of material that flows through the warehouse. The fixed cost is typically proportional to warehouse size (capacity) but in a nonlinear way (see Figure 2-6). As the figure shows, this cost is fixed in certain ranges of the warehouse size.
3. *Storage costs.* These represent inventory holding costs, which are proportional to *average* positive inventory levels (see Chapter 3).

Thus, estimating the warehouse handling costs is fairly easy while estimating the other two cost values is quite difficult. To see this difference, suppose that during the entire year 1,000 units of product are required by a particular customer. These 1,000 units are not required to flow through the warehouse *at the same time*, so the average inventory level will likely be significantly lower than 1,000 units. Thus, when constructing the data for the DSS, we need to convert these annual flows into actual

FIGURE 2-6 Warehouse fixed costs as a function of the warehouse capacity.

inventory amounts over time. Similarly, annual flow and average inventory associated with this product tell us nothing about how much space is needed for the product in the warehouse. This is true because the amount of space that the warehouse needs is proportional to peak inventory, not annual flow or average inventory.

An effective way to overcome this difficulty is to utilize the *inventory turnover ratio*. This is defined as follows:

$$\text{Inventory turnover ratio} = \frac{\text{Annual sales}}{\text{Average inventory level}}$$

Specifically, in our case the inventory turnover ratio is the ratio of the total annual outflow from the warehouse to the average inventory level. Thus, if the ratio is λ, then the average inventory level is total annual flow divided by λ. Multiplying the average inventory level by the inventory holding cost gives the annual storage costs.

Finally, to calculate the fixed cost, we need to estimate the warehouse capacity. This is done in the next subsection.

2.2.5 Warehouse Capacities

Another important input to the distribution network design model is the actual warehouse capacity. The question is how to estimate the actual space required, given the specific annual flow of material through the warehouse. Again, the inventory turnover ratio suggests an appropriate approach. As before, annual flow through a warehouse divided by the inventory turnover ratio allows us to calculate the average inventory level. Assuming a regular shipment and delivery schedule, such as that given in Figure 2-7, it follows that the required storage space is approximately *twice* that amount. In practice, of course, every pallet stored in the warehouse requires an empty space to allow for access and handling; thus, considering this space as well as space for aisles, picking, sorting, and processing facilities, and AGVs (automatic guided vehicles), we typically multiply the required storage space by a factor (>1). This factor depends on the specific application and allows us to assess the amount of space available in the warehouse more accurately. A typical factor used in practice is three. This factor would be used in the following way. Consider a situation where the annual flow through the warehouse

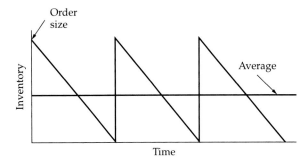

FIGURE 2-7 Inventory level as a function of time.

is 1,000 units and the inventory turnover ratio is 10.0. This implies that the average inventory level is about 100 units and, hence, if each unit takes 10 square feet of floor space, the required space for the products is 2,000 square feet. Therefore, the total space required for the warehouse is about 6,000 square feet.

2.2.6 Potential Warehouse Locations

It is also important to effectively identify potential locations for new warehouses. Typically, these locations must satisfy a variety of conditions:

- Geographical and infrastructure conditions.
- Natural resources and labor availability.
- Local industry and tax regulations.
- Public interest.

As a result, only a limited number of locations would meet all the requirements. These are the potential location sites for the new facilities.

2.2.7 Service Level Requirements

There are various ways to define service levels in this context. For example, we might specify a maximum distance between each customer and the warehouse serving it. This ensures that a warehouse will be able to serve its customers within a reasonable time. Sometimes we must recognize that for some customers, such as those in rural or isolated areas, it is harder to satisfy the same level of service that most other customers receive. In this case, it is often helpful to define the service level as the proportion of customers whose distance to their assigned warehouse is no more than a given distance. For instance, we might require that 95 percent of the customers be situated within 200 miles of the warehouses serving them.

2.2.8 Future Demand

As observed in Chapter 1, decisions at the strategic level, which include distribution network design, have a long-lasting effect on the firm. In particular, decisions regarding the number, location, and size of warehouses have an impact on the firm for at least the next three to five years. This implies that changes in customer demand over the next few years should be taken into account when designing the network. This is most commonly addressed using a scenario-based approach incorporating net present value calculations. For example, various possible scenarios representing a variety of possible future demand patterns over the planning horizon can be generated. These scenarios can then be directly incorporated into the model to determine the best distribution strategy.

2.3 MODEL AND DATA VALIDATION

The previous section documents the difficulties in collecting, tabulating, and cleaning the data for a network configuration model. Once this is done, how do we ensure that the data and model accurately reflect the network design problem?

The process used to address this issue is known as model and data validation. This is typically done by reconstructing the existing network configuration using the model and collected data, and comparing the output of the model to existing data.

The importance of validation cannot be overstated. Valuable output of the model configured to duplicate current operating conditions includes all costs—warehousing, inventory, production, and transportation—generated under the current network configuration. These data can be compared to the company's accounting information. This is often the best way to identify errors in the data, problematic assumptions, modeling flaws, and so forth. In one project, for example, the transportation costs calculated during the validation process were consistently underestimating the costs suggested by the accounting data. After a careful review of the distribution practices, the consultants concluded that the effective truck capacity was only about 30 percent of the truck's physical capacity; that is, trucks were being sent out with very little load. Thus, the validation process not only helped calibrate some of the parameters used in the model but also suggested potential improvements in the utilization of the existing network.

It is often also helpful to make local or small changes in the network configuration to see how the system estimates their impact on costs and service levels. Specifically, this step involves positing a variety of what-if questions. This includes estimating the impact of closing an existing warehouse on system performance. Or, to give another example, it allows the user to change the flow of material through the existing network and see the changes in the costs. Often, managers have good intuition about what the effect of these small-scale changes on the system should be, so they can more easily identify errors in the model. Intuition about the effect of radical redesign of the entire system is often much less reliable. To summarize, the model validation process typically involves answering the following questions:

- Does the model make sense?
- Are the data consistent?
- Can the model results be fully explained?
- Did you perform sensitivity analysis?

Validation is critical for determining the validity of the model and data, but the process has other benefits. In particular, it helps the user make the connection between the current operations, which were modeled during the validation process, and possible improvements after optimization.

2.4 SOLUTION TECHNIQUES

Once the data are collected, tabulated, and verified, the next step is to optimize the configuration of the logistics network. In practice, two techniques are employed:

1. Mathematical optimization techniques that include:

- Exact algorithms that are guaranteed to find optimal solutions, that is, least-cost solutions,
- Heuristic algorithms that find *good* solutions, not necessarily optimal solutions.

2. Simulation models that provide a mechanism to evaluate specified design alternatives created by the designer.

2.4.1 Heuristics and the Need for Exact Algorithms

We will start our discussion by considering mathematical optimization techniques. In order to understand the effectiveness of heuristic algorithms and the need for exact algorithms, consider the following example developed by Geoffrion and Van Roy in [60].

EXAMPLE 2-3

Consider the following distribution system:

- Single product.
- Two plants, referred to as plant $p1$ and plant $p2$.
- Plant $p2$ has an annual capacity of 60,000 units.
- The two plants have the same production costs.
- Two existing warehouses, referred to as warehouse $w1$ and warehouse $w2$, have identical warehouse handling costs.
- Three markets areas, $c1$, $c2$, and $c3$, with demands of 50,000, 100,000 and 50,000, respectively,
- Table 2-5 provides distribution cost per unit. For instance, distributing one unit from plant $p1$ to warehouse $w2$ costs $5.

TABLE 2-5

DISTRIBUTION COSTS PER UNIT

Facility warehouse	$p1$	$p2$	$c1$	$c2$	$c3$
$w1$	0	4	3	4	5
$w2$	5	2	2	1	2

Our objective is to find a distribution strategy that specifies the flow of products from the suppliers through the warehouses to the market areas without violating the plant $p2$ production capacity constraint, that satisfies market area demands, and that minimizes total distribution costs. Observe that this problem is significantly easier to solve than the logistics network configuration problem discussed earlier. Here we assume that facility location is not an issue, and we merely attempt to find an effective distribution strategy.

For this purpose, consider the following two intuitive heuristics:

Heuristic 1

For each market we choose the cheapest warehouse to source demand. Thus, $c1$, $c2$, and $c3$ would be supplied by $w2$. Then, for this warehouse choose the cheapest plant; that is, distribute 60,000 units from $p2$ and the remaining 140,000 from $p1$. The total cost is:

$$2 \times 50{,}000 + 1 \times 100{,}000 + 2 \times 50{,}000 + 2 \times 60{,}000 + 5 \times 140{,}000 = 1{,}120{,}000$$

Heuristic 2

For each market area, choose the warehouse where the total delivery costs to and from the warehouse are the lowest; that is, consider inbound and outbound distribution costs. Thus, for market area $c1$, consider the paths $p1 \rightarrow w1 \rightarrow c1$, $p1 \rightarrow w2 \rightarrow c1$, $p2 \rightarrow w1 \rightarrow c1$, $p2 \rightarrow w2 \rightarrow c1$.

Example 2-3 *Continued*

Among all these alternatives, the cheapest is $p1 \rightarrow w1 \rightarrow c1$, so choose $w1$ for $c1$. Using a similar analysis, we choose $w2$ for $c2$ and $w2$ for $c3$.

This implies that warehouse $w1$ delivers a total of 50,000 units while warehouse $w2$ delivers a total of 150,000 units. The best inbound flow pattern is to supply 50,000 from plant $p1$ to warehouse $w1$, supply 60,000 units from plant $p2$ to warehouse $w2$, and supply 90,000 from plant $p1$ to warehouse $w2$. The total cost for this strategy is $920,000.

Unfortunately, the two heuristics described earlier do not produce the best, or least-cost, strategy. To find the best distribution strategy, consider the following *optimization model*. Indeed, the distribution problem described earlier can be framed as the following linear programming problem.[1]

For this purpose, let

- $x(p1, w1)$, $x(p1, w2)$, $x(p2, w1)$, and $x(p2, w2)$ be the flows from the plants to the warehouses.
- $x(w1, c1)$, $x(w1, c2)$, and $x(w1, c3)$ be the flows from warehouse $w1$ to customer zones $c1, c2$, and $c3$.
- $x(w2, c1)$, $x(w2, c2)$, and $x(w2, c3)$ be the flows from warehouse $w2$ to customer zones $c1, c2$, and $c3$.

The linear programming problem we need to solve is

$$\text{Minimize}\{0x(p1, w1) + 5x(p1, w2) + 4x(p2, w1)$$
$$+ 2x(p2, w2) + 3x(w1, c1) + 4x(w1, c2)$$
$$+ 5x(w1, c3) + 2x(w2, c1) + 1x(w2, c2) + 2x(w2, c3)\}$$

subject to the following constraints:

$$x(p2, w1) + x(p2, w2) \leq 60,000$$
$$x(p1, w1) + x(p2, w1) = x(w1, c1) + x(w1, c2) + x(w1, c3)$$
$$x(p1, w2) + x(p2, w2) = x(w2, c1) + x(w2, c2) + x(w2, c3)$$
$$x(w1, c1) + x(w2, c1) = 50,000$$
$$x(w1, c2) + x(w2, c2) = 100,000$$
$$x(w1, c3) + x(w2, c3) = 50,000$$

All flows are greater than or equal to zero.

One can easily construct an Excel model for this problem and use the Excel linear programming solver to find the optimal strategy. For more information on how to construct the Excel model, see [87]. This strategy is described in Table 2-6.

TABLE 2-6

OPTIMAL DISTRIBUTION STRATEGY

Facility warehouse	p1	p2	c1	c2	c3
w1	140,000	0	50,000	40,000	50,000
w2	0	60,000	0	60,000	0

The total cost for the optimal strategy is $740,000.

---

[1]This part of the section requires a basic knowledge of linear programming. It can be skipped without loss of continuity.

This example clearly illustrates the value of optimization-based techniques. *These tools can determine strategies that will significantly reduce the total system cost.*

Of course, the logistics network configuration model that we would like to analyze and solve is typically more complex than the simple example described above. One key difference is the need to establish optimal locations for warehouses, distribution centers, and cross-dock facilities. Unfortunately, these decisions render linear programming inappropriate and require the use of a technique called *integer programming*. This is true because linear programming deals with continuous variables while a decision on whether or not to open a warehouse at a specific city is a binary variable—0 if we do not open a warehouse in that location and 1 otherwise.

Thus, the logistics network configuration model is an integer programming model. Unfortunately, integer programming models are significantly more difficult to solve. The interested reader is referred to [18] for a discussion on exact algorithms for the logistics network configuration problem.

2.4.2 Simulation Models and Optimization Techniques

The mathematical optimization techniques described earlier have some important limitations. They deal with static models—typically by considering annual, or average, demand—and they do not take into account changes over time. Simulation-based tools take into account the dynamics of the system and are capable of characterizing system performance for a *given design*. Thus, it is up to the user to provide the simulation model with a number of design alternatives.

This implies that simulation models allow the user to perform a microlevel analysis. Indeed, the simulation model may include (see [67])

1. Individual ordering pattern.
2. Specific inventory policies.
3. Inventory movements inside the warehouse.

Unfortunately, simulation models only model a prespecified logistics network design. In other words, given a particular configuration of warehouses, retailers, and so forth, a simulation model can be used to help estimate the costs associated with operating that configuration. If a different configuration is considered (e.g., a few of the customers are to be served by a different warehouse), the model has to be rerun. As you will see in more detail in Chapter 12, simulation is not an optimization tool. It is useful in characterizing the performance of a particular configuration, but not in determining an effective configuration from a large set of potential configurations.

In addition, a detailed simulation model that incorporates information about individual customer ordering patterns, specific inventory and production policies, daily distribution strategies, and so on may require enormous computational time to achieve a desired level of accuracy in system performance. This implies that typically one can consider *very few* alternatives using a simulation tool.

Thus, if system dynamics is not a key issue, a static model is appropriate and mathematical optimization techniques can be applied. In our experience, this type of model accounts for almost all the network configuration models used in practice. When detailed system dynamics is an important issue, it makes sense to utilize the following two-stage approach, suggested by Hax and Candea [67], which takes advantage of the strengths of both simulation- and optimization-based approaches:

1. Use an optimization model to generate a number of least-cost solutions at the macrolevel, taking into account the most important cost components.
2. Use a simulation model to evaluate the solutions generated in the first phase.

2.5 KEY FEATURES OF A NETWORK CONFIGURATION DSS

One of the key requirements of any decision-support system for network design is flexibility. In this context, we define *flexibility* as the ability of the system to incorporate a large set of preexisting network characteristics. Indeed, depending on the particular application, a whole spectrum of design options may be appropriate. At one end of this spectrum is the complete reoptimization of the existing network. This means that each warehouse can be either opened or closed and all transportation flows can be redirected. At the other end of the spectrum, it may be necessary to incorporate the following features in the optimization model:

1. *Customer-specific service level requirements.*
2. *Existing warehouses.* In most cases, warehouses already exist and their leases have not yet expired. Therefore, the model should not permit the closing of the warehouse.
3. *Expansion of existing warehouses.* Existing warehouses may be expandable.
4. *Specific flow patterns.* In a variety of situations, specific flow patterns (e.g., from a particular warehouse to a set of customers) should not be changed, or perhaps more likely, a certain manufacturing location does not or cannot produce certain SKUs.
5. *Warehouse-to-warehouse flow.* In some cases, material may flow from one warehouse to another warehouse.
6. *Bill of materials.* In some cases, final assembly is done at the warehouse and this needs to be captured by the model. For this purpose, the user needs to provide information on the components used to assemble finished goods.

It is not enough for the decision-support system to incorporate all of the features described above. It also must have the capability to deal with all these issues with little or no reduction in its *effectiveness*. The latter requirement is directly related to the so-called *robustness* of the system. This stipulates that the relative quality of the solution generated by the system (i.e., cost and service level) should be independent of the specific environment, the variability of the data, or the particular setting. If a particular decision-support system is not robust, it is difficult to determine how effective it will be for a particular problem.

It is also essential that the system running time be reasonable. Of course, the term *reasonable* depends on the particular problem at hand. The running time in seconds of one popular DSS, running on a Pentium-200 personal computer, is listed in Table 2-7. The table provides running times for variety of problems. For each instance, the table provides the number of aggregated customers (Num Customers), the number of products (Num Products), the number of suppliers (Num Suppliers), the number of potential

TABLE 2-7

RUNNING TIMES (SECONDS)

Num Customers*	Num Products	Num Suppliers	Num Potential	Num Exist	Min-Max	Distance	Running Time 1.0%	Running Time 0.5%
333	1	2	307	2	3–3	1,300	12	12
333	1	2	307	2	3–7	1,300	140	223
333	1	2	307	2	3–10	1,300	184	209
2,448	12	4	73	0	3–32	**	126	300
2,066	23	23	52	0	3–25	700	393	500

*After aggregation.
**No service level requirement.

locations for warehouses (Num Potential), and the number of existing warehouses (Num Exist). In addition, the table provides the range of values (Min-Max) of the number of new warehouses considered by the DSS. This implies that the number of warehouses considered by the DSS was no less than the Min value and no more than the Max value. In each case, the model includes a service level requirement, defined as a limit on the distance between a customer and a warehouse serving it. This value is provided in the Distance column. The decision-support system found solutions guaranteed to be within 1.0 percent and 0.5 percent of the optimal solution, and the running times to get each of the solutions is listed. All of the problems listed were based on real-world data for a number of companies in the United States.

2.6 SOLVING THE BIS CORPORATION DISTRIBUTION PROBLEM

We now go back to the Bis Corporation case described at the beginning of the chapter. An important issue in the analysis is an effective way to predict the impact of the estimated increase in demand on the network design. One way of doing that is to design the network based on the current demand and then evaluate the impact of future demand on the total cost; that is, fix the number and location of warehouses based on current (1997) demands and calculate total cost for 1997, 1998, and 1999. Compare this, for instance, to designing the logistics network based on, say, 1998 demands.

Specifically, consider the following three options.

Option I: Find optimal network design based on 1997 demands.

Option II: Find optimal network design based on 1998 demands.

Option III: Find optimal network design based on 1999 demands.

Consider Option I. In this case, we need to calculate total cost for 1998 and 1999, assuming that the network configuration does not change. We fix the network configuration according to this design option and evaluate the impact of the increase in demand on total cost. By calculating net present value of total logistics costs for 1997, 1998, and 1999, we get the total cost associated with this design option. Note that during this process, we are able to address capacity issues. For instance, the analysis of 1998 demand data will allow us to evaluate whether there is enough production capacity or whether production capacity needs to be increased to satisfy customer demands.

The same analysis is also applied to the other two design options, and the three net present values are used in making the final decision.

SUMMARY

In this chapter, we examined issues important in the design of the logistics network. One question often raised is the efficiency of demand aggregation. Since information is available on individual retailer demands, it is not clear why the analysis combines groups of customers and treats them as a single aggregate customer. As we have seen, there are two main reasons for aggregating demand data. The first is the size of the model that results from the input data. Indeed, the time it takes to solve a network design problem grows exponentially as the number of facilities and products increases. Even if optimization time is not an issue, aggregating demand is important because it improves the accuracy of forecast demand. This is true because our ability to forecast customer demand at the account and product levels is usually poor. By contrast, because of the reduction in variability achieved through aggregation, forecast demand is significantly more accurate at the aggregated level.

A second issue often raised in practice is the need for a decision-support system to optimize the logistics network. The question is whether a sophisticated tool is required or spreadsheets alone are sufficient. The chapter argues that a thorough logistics network analysis should consider complex transportation cost structures, warehouse sizes, manufacturing limitations, inventory turnover ratios, inventory cost, and service levels. These issues require the use of optimization-based decision-support systems that can solve large-scale problems efficiently. For a detailed discussion, see Chapter 12.

DISCUSSION QUESTIONS

1. Why is it important for a firm to periodically review its logistics network design? How do a firm's requirements for its logistics network change over time?
2. Within the organization, who is involved in a network design project (Operations, Sales, marketing executives, etc.)? How?
3. KLF Electronics is an American manufacturer of electronic equipments. The company has a single manufacturing facility in San Jose California.

   KLF Electronics distributes its products through five regional warehouses located in Atlanta, Boston, Chicago, Dallas, and Los Angeles. In the current distribution system, the United States is partitioned into five major markets, each of which is served by a single regional warehouse. Customers, typically retail outlets, receive items directly from the regional warehouse in their market area. That is, in the current distribution system, each customer is assigned to a single market and receives deliveries from one regional warehouse.

   The warehouses receive items from the manufacturing facility. Typically, it takes about two weeks to satisfy an order placed by any of the regional warehouses. In recent years, KLF has seen a significant increase in competition and huge pressure from their customers to improve service level and reduce costs. To improve service level and reduce costs, KLF would like to consider an alternative distribution strategy in which the five regional warehouses are replaced with a single, central warehouse that will be in charge of all customer orders.

   Describe how you would design a new logistics network consisting of only a single warehouse. Provide an outline of such an analysis; what are the main steps? Specifically, what data would you need? What are the advantages and disadvantages of the newly suggested distribution strategy relative to the existing distribution strategy?
4. In selecting potential warehouse sites, it is important to consider issues such as geographical and infrastructure conditions, natural resources and labor availability, local industry and tax regulations, and public interest. For each of the following industries, give specific examples of how the issues listed above could affect the choice of potential warehouse sites:
   a. Automobile manufacturing
   b. Pharmaceuticals
   c. Books
   d. Aircraft manufacturing
   e. Book distribution
   f. Furniture manufacturing and distribution
   g. PC manufacturing
5. Consider the pharmaceutical and the chemical industries. In the pharmaceutical industry, products have high margins and overnight delivery typically is used. On the other hand, in the chemical industry, products have low margins and outbound

transportation cost is more expensive than inbound transportation. What is the effect of these characteristics on the number of warehouses for firms in these industries? Where do you expect to see more warehouses: in the chemical industry or the pharmaceutical industry?

6. In Section 2.2.2 we observe that TL transportation rate structure is asymmetric. Why?

7. Discuss some specific items that make up the handling costs, fixed costs, and storage costs associated with a warehouse.

8. What is the difference between using an exact optimization technique and a heuristic to solve a problem?

9. What is simulation, and how does it help solve difficult logistics problems?

Inventory Management and Risk Pooling

JAM Electronics: Service Level Crisis

JAM Electronics is a Korean manufacturer of products such as industrial relays. The company has five Far Eastern manufacturing facilities, each in a different country, with headquarters in Seoul, South Korea.

JAM USA is a subsidiary of JAM Electronics and was established in the United States in 1978. The U.S. subsidiary provides distribution and service functions in this country. It has a central warehouse in Chicago that serves two types of customers: distributors and original equipment manufacturers (OEMs). Distributors typically keep inventory of JAM's products and supply them to their clients as needed. OEMs use JAM's products to produce different types of items such as automatic garage door openers.

JAM Electronics produces about 2,500 different products, all of them manufactured in the Far East. Finished products are stored in a central warehouse in Korea and are shipped from there to different countries. In particular, items sold in the United States are transported by ship to the warehouse in Chicago.

In recent years, JAM USA has seen both a significant increase in competition and huge pressure from its clients and distributors to improve service levels and reduce costs. Unfortunately, as Al Jones, the inventory manager, points out, "the service level right now is at an all-time low. Only about 70 percent of all orders are delivered on time. On the other hand, inventory, primarily that of low-demand products, keeps piling up."

In a recent meeting with Chan Moon, the president of JAM USA; Ken Hall, vice president and general manager; and Li Chan, a representative of the Korean headquarters, Al pointed out several reasons for the low service level:

1. *Difficulty forecasting customer demand.* Indeed, many factors, including changes in the economy and changes in customer behavior, have had a major impact on demand, and these are quite difficult to predict.
2. *Long lead time in the supply chain.* A typical order placed by the warehouse in Illinois arrives in about six to seven weeks. There are two primary reasons for the long lead time. First, there is a week of processing time in the central distribution center in Korea; second, the ocean transit time is very long.
3. *The large number of SKUs handled by JAM USA.* Recall that JAM USA distributes about 2,500 different products, ranging from small relays to large programmable controllers, to its customers.
4. *The low priority given the U.S. subsidiary by headquarters in Seoul.* An order that arrives at the Korean headquarters from Japanese or Korean clients typically receives a higher priority over an

---

Source: JAM Electronics is a fictional company. The material in this case is loosely based on our experience with several companies.

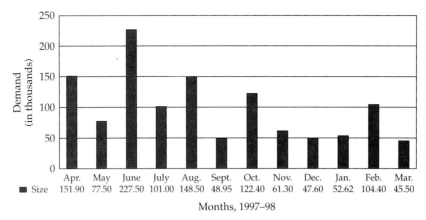

	Apr.	May	June	July	Aug.	Sept.	Oct.	Nov.	Dec.	Jan.	Feb.	Mar.
■ Size	151.90	77.50	227.50	101.00	148.50	48.95	122.40	61.30	47.60	52.62	104.40	45.50

Months, 1997–98

FIGURE 3-1 Monthly demand for item xxx-1534.

order received from the United States. Thus, the lead time to the United States is occasionally much longer than seven weeks.

To illustrate the difficulty in forecasting customer demand, Al provided a graph that showed monthly demand information for item xxx-1534, a relay product used in the manufacture of refrigerators (see Figure 3-1). As the graph demonstrates, variability in customer demand is very high; demand changes from month to month and it is difficult to predict what customer demand is going to be even with sophisticated forecasting techniques.

Ken, the general manager, was very critical of Al's analysis. He pointed out that if long lead time is an issue, then JAM USA needs to reduce it, perhaps by using air carriers, which would probably reduce lead time to about two weeks. Ken, however, was unsure of the impact of this change on the overall supply chain. He pointed out that "transportation costs are certainly going to increase, but where are the savings?"

The meeting ended with a decision to establish a task force, headed by Ken, to address the service level crisis.

As Al left the meeting, he could not help but think that many companies must be facing similar problems: high demand variability, long lead times, unreliable supply processes, and a large number of SKUs. "What is the competition doing to cope with these problems?" he wondered.

By the end of this chapter, you will understand the following issues:

- How firms cope with huge variability in customer demand.
- What the relationship is between service and inventory levels.
- What impact lead time and lead time variability have on inventory levels.
- What an effective inventory management policy is.
- How buyers and suppliers use *supply contracts* to improve supply chain performance.
- What approaches can be used to forecast future demand.

3.1 INTRODUCTION

The importance of inventory management, and the need for the coordination of inventory decisions and transportation policies, has long been evident. Unfortunately, managing inventory in complex supply chains is typically difficult, and may have a significant impact on the customer service level and supply chain systemwide cost.

As we discussed in Chapter 1, a typical supply chain consists of suppliers and manufacturers, who convert raw materials into finished products, and distribution centers and warehouses, from which finished products are distributed to customers. This implies that inventory appears in the supply chain in several forms:

- Raw material inventory.
- Work-in-process (WIP) inventory.
- Finished product inventory.

Each of these needs its own inventory control mechanism. Unfortunately, determining these mechanisms is difficult because efficient production, distribution, and inventory control strategies that reduce systemwide costs and improve service levels must take into account the interactions of the various levels in the supply chain. Nevertheless, the benefits of determining these inventory control mechanisms can be enormous.

EXAMPLE 3-1

General Motors (GM) has one of the largest production and distribution networks in the world. In 1984 GM's distribution network consisted of 20,000 supplier plants, 133 parts plants, 31 assembly plants, and 11,000 dealers. Freight transportation costs were about $4.1 billion with 60 percent for material shipments. In addition, GM inventory was valued at $7.4 billion, of which 70 percent was WIP and the rest was finished vehicles. GM has implemented a decision tool capable of reducing the combined corporate cost of inventory and transportation. Indeed, by adjusting shipment sizes (i.e., inventory policy) and routes (i.e., transportation strategy), costs could be reduced by about 26 percent annually [14].

Of course, the key question is: Why hold inventory at all? Some of the reasons include

1. Unexpected changes in customer demand. Customer demand has always been hard to predict, and uncertainty in customer demand has increased in the last few years due to
   a. The short life cycle of an increasing number of products. This implies that historical data about customer demand may not be available or may be quite limited (see Chapter 1).
   b. The presence of many competing products in the marketplace. This proliferation of products makes it increasingly difficult to predict demand for a specific model. Indeed, while it is relatively easy to forecast demand across product groups—that is, to forecast demand for all products competing in the same market—it is much more difficult to estimate demand for individual products. We discuss this in more detail in Section 3.3 and in Chapters 5 and 9.
2. The presence in many situations of a significant uncertainty in the quantity and quality of the supply, supplier costs, and delivery times.
3. Even if there is no uncertainty in demand or supply, there is a need to hold inventory due to delivery lead times.
4. Economies of scale offered by transportation companies that encourage firms to transport large quantities of items, and therefore hold large inventories. Indeed, many of the transportation providers try to encourage large-size shipments by offering all sorts of discounts to shippers (see Chapter 2).

Unfortunately, managing inventory effectively in this environment is often difficult, as the following examples illustrate:

- In 1993, Dell Computer's stock plunged after the company predicted a loss. Dell acknowledged that the company was sharply off in its forecast of demand, resulting in inventory write-downs [164].
- In 1993, Liz Claiborne experienced an unexpected earnings decline, as a consequence of higher-than-anticipated excess inventories [165].
- In 1994, IBM struggled with shortages in the ThinkPad line due to ineffective inventory management [166].
- In 2001, Cisco took a $ 2.25B excess inventory charge due to declining sales.

These examples raise two important issues in inventory management:

1. Demand forecasting.
2. Order quantity calculation.

Since demand is uncertain in most situations, forecast demand is a critical element in determining order quantity. But what is the relationship between forecast demand and the optimal order quantity? Should the order quantity be equal to, greater than, or smaller than forecast demand? And, if order quantity is different than forecast demand, by how much? These issues are discussed below.

3.2 A SINGLE WAREHOUSE INVENTORY EXAMPLE

What are the key factors affecting inventory policy?

1. First and foremost is customer demand, which may be known in advance or may be random. In the latter case, forecasting tools may be used in situations in which historical data are available to estimate the average customer demand, as well as the amount of variability in customer demand (often measured as the standard deviation).
2. Replenishment lead time, which may be known at the time we place the order, or may be uncertain.
3. The number of different products.
4. The length of the planning horizon.
5. Costs, including order cost and inventory holding cost.
   a. Typically, order cost consists of two components: the cost of the product and the transportation cost.
   b. Inventory holding cost, or inventory carrying cost, consists of
      i. State taxes, property taxes, and insurance on inventories.
      ii. Maintenance costs.
      iii. Obsolescence cost, which derives from the risk that an item will lose some of its value because of changes in the market.
      iv. Opportunity costs, which represent the return on investment that one would receive had money been invested in something else (e.g., the stock market) instead of inventory.
6. Service level requirements. In situations where customer demand is uncertain, it is often impossible to meet customer orders 100 percent of the time, so management needs to specify an acceptable level of service.

3.2.1 The Economic Lot Size Model

The classic *economic lot size model*, introduced by Ford W. Harris in 1915, is a simple model that illustrates the trade-offs between ordering and storage costs. Consider a warehouse facing constant demand for a *single* item. The warehouse orders from the supplier, who is assumed to have an unlimited quantity of the product. The model assumes the following:

- Demand is constant at a rate of D items per day.
- Order quantities are fixed at Q items per order; that is, each time the warehouse places an order, it is for Q items.
- A fixed cost (setup cost), K, is incurred every time the warehouse places an order.
- An inventory carrying cost, h, also referred to as a *holding cost*, is accrued per unit held in inventory per day that the unit is held.
- The lead time, the time that elapses between the placement of an order and its receipt, is zero.
- Initial inventory is zero.
- The planning horizon is long (infinite).

Our goal is to find the optimal order policy that minimizes annual purchasing and carrying costs while meeting all demand (that is, without shortage).

This is an extremely simplified version of a real inventory system. The assumption of a known fixed demand over a long horizon is clearly unrealistic. Replenishment of products very likely takes several days, and the requirement of a fixed order quantity is restrictive. Surprisingly, the insight derived from this model will help us to develop inventory policies that are effective for more complex realistic systems.

It is easy to see that in an optimal policy for the model described above, orders should be received at the warehouse precisely when the inventory level drops to zero. This is called the *zero inventory ordering property*, which can be observed by considering a policy in which orders are placed and received when the inventory level is not zero. Clearly, a cheaper policy would involve waiting until the inventory is zero before ordering, thus saving on holding costs.

To find the optimal ordering policy in the economic lot size model, we consider the inventory level as a function of time (see Figure 2-7 in Chapter 2). This is the so-called saw-toothed inventory pattern. We refer to the time between two successive replenishments as a *cycle* time. Thus, total inventory cost in a cycle of length T is

$$K + \frac{hTQ}{2}$$

since the fixed cost is charged once per order and holding cost can be viewed as the product of the per unit per time period holding cost, h; the average inventory level, $Q/2$; and the length of the cycle, T.

Since the inventory level changes from Q to 0 during a cycle of length T, and demand is constant at a rate of D units per unit time, it must be that $Q = TD$. Thus, we can divide the cost above by T, or, equivalently, Q/D, to get the average total cost per unit of time:

$$\frac{KD}{Q} + \frac{hQ}{2}$$

Using simple calculus, it is easy to show that the order quantity Q^* that minimizes the cost function above is

$$Q^* = \sqrt{\frac{2KD}{h}}$$

This quantity is referred to as the *economic order quantity* (EOQ).

FIGURE 3-2 Economic lot size model: Total cost per unit time.

This simple model provides two important insights:

1. An optimal policy balances inventory holding cost per unit time with setup cost per unit time. Indeed, setup cost per unit time $= KD/Q$, while holding cost per unit time $= hQ/2$ (see Figure 3-2). Thus, as one increases the order quantity Q, inventory holding costs per unit of time increase while setup costs per unit of time decrease. The optimal order quantity is achieved at the point at which inventory setup cost per unit of time (KD/Q) equals inventory holding cost per unit of time $(hQ/2)$. That is:

$$\frac{KD}{Q} = \frac{hQ}{2}$$

or

$$Q^* = \sqrt{\frac{2KD}{h}}$$

2. Total inventory cost is insensitive to order quantities; that is, changes in order quantities have a relatively small impact on annual setup costs and inventory holding costs. To illustrate this issue, consider a decision maker that places an order quantity Q that is a multiple b of the optimal order quantity Q^*. In other words, for a given b, the quantity ordered is $Q = bQ^*$. Thus, $b = 1$ implies that the decision maker orders the economic order quantity. If $b = 1.2$ ($b = 0.8$), the decision maker orders 20 percent more (less) than the optimal order quantity. Table 3-1 presents the impact of changes in b on total system cost. For example, if the decision maker orders 20 percent more than the optimal order quantity ($b = 1.2$) then the increase in total inventory cost relative to the optimal total cost is no more than 1.6 percent.

TABLE 3-1

SENSITIVITY ANALYSIS

b	0.5	0.8	0.9	1	1.1	1.2	1.5	2
Increase in cost	25.0%	2.5%	0.5%	0	0.4%	1.6%	8.0%	25.0%

3.2.2 The Effect of Demand Uncertainty

The previous model illustrates the trade-offs between setup costs and inventory holding costs. It ignores, however, issues such as demand uncertainty and forecasting. Indeed, many companies treat the world as if it were predictable, making production and inventory decisions based on forecasts of the demand made far in advance of the selling season. Although these companies are aware of demand uncertainty when they create a forecast, they design their planning processes as if the initial forecast was an accurate representation of reality. In this case, one needs to remember the following principles of all forecasts (see [113]):

1. The forecast is always wrong.
2. The longer the forecast horizon, the worse the forecast.
3. Aggregate forecasts are more accurate.

Thus, the first principle implies that it is difficult to match supply and demand, and the second one implies that it is even more difficult if one needs to predict customer demand for a long period of time, for example, the next 12 to 18 months. The third principle suggests, for instance, that while it is difficult to predict customer demand for individual SKUs, it is much easier to predict demand across all SKUs within one product family. This principle is an example of the **risk pooling** concept (see Section 3.3).

To illustrate the importance of incorporating demand uncertainty and forecast demand into the analysis, and to characterize the impact of demand uncertainty on the inventory policy, consider the following example.

C A S E

Swimsuit Production

Consider a company that designs, produces, and sells summer fashion items such as swimsuits. About six months before summer, the company must commit itself to specific production quantities for all its products. Since there is no clear indication of how the market will respond to the new designs, the company needs to use various tools to predict demand for each design, and plan production and supply accordingly. In this setting the trade-offs are clear: overestimating customer demand will result in unsold inventory while underestimating customer demand will lead to inventory stockouts and loss of potential customers.

To assist management in these decisions, the marketing department uses historical data from the last five years, current economic conditions, and other factors to construct a *probabilistic forecast* of the demand for swimsuits. They have identified several possible scenarios for sales in the coming season, based on such factors as possible weather patterns and competitors' behavior, and assigned each a probability, or chance of occurring. For example, the marketing department believes that a scenario that leads to 8,000 unit sales has an 11 percent chance of happening; other scenarios leading to different sales levels have different probabilities of occurring. These scenarios are illustrated in Figure 3-3. This probabilistic forecast suggests that average demand is about 13,000 units, but there is a probability that demand will be either larger than average or smaller than average.

Additional information available to the manufacturer includes:

- To start production, the manufacturer has to invest $100,000 independent of the amount produced. We refer to this cost as the *fixed production cost*.
- The *variable production cost* per unit equals $80.
- During the summer season, the selling price of a swimsuit is $125 per unit.

Source: This case is based loosely on [53] and course material prepared at the Columbia University Graduate School of Business.

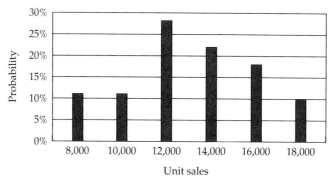

FIGURE 3-3 Probabilistic forecast.

- Any swimsuit not sold during the summer season is sold to a discount store for $20. We refer to this value as the *salvage value*.

To identify the best production quantity, the firm needs to understand the relationship between the production quantity, customer demand, and profit.

Suppose the manufacturer produces 10,000 units while demand ends at 12,000 swimsuits. It is easily verified that profit equals revenue from summer sales minus the variable production cost minus the fixed production cost. That is:

$$\text{Profit} = 125(10{,}000) - 80(10{,}000)$$
$$- 100{,}000$$
$$= 350{,}000$$

On the other hand, if the company produces 10,000 swimsuits and demand is only 8,000 units, profit equals revenue from summer sales plus salvage value minus the variable production cost minus the fixed production cost. That is:

$$\text{Profit} = 125(8{,}000) + 20(2{,}000) - 80(10{,}000)$$
$$- 100{,}000$$
$$= 140{,}000$$

Notice that the probability that demand is 8,000 units is 11 percent while the probability that demand is 12,000 units is 27 percent. Thus, producing 10,000 swimsuits leads to a profit of $350,000 with probability of 27 percent and a profit of $140,000 with probability of 11 percent. In similar fashion, one can calculate the profit associated with each scenario given that the manufacturer produces 10,000 swimsuits. This allows us to determine the *expected* (or average) profit associated with producing 10,000

units. This expected profit is the total profit of all the scenarios weighted by the probability that each scenario will occur.

We would, of course, like to find the order quantity that maximizes average profit. What is the relationship between the optimal production quantity and average demand, which, in this example, is 13,000 units? Should the optimal order quantity be equal to, more than, or less than the average demand?

To answer these questions, we evaluate the *marginal profit* and *marginal cost* of producing an additional swimsuit. If this swimsuit is sold during the summer season, then the marginal profit is the difference between the selling price per unit and the variable production cost per unit, which is equal to $45. If the additional swimsuit is not sold during the summer season, the marginal cost is the difference between the variable production cost and the salvage value per unit, which is equal to $60. Thus, the cost of not selling this additional swimsuit during the summer season is larger than the profit obtained from selling it during the season. Hence, the best production quantity will in general be less than the average demand.

Figure 3-4 plots the average profit as a function of the production quantity. It shows that the optimal production quantity, or the quantity that maximizes average profit, is about 12,000. It also indicates that producing 9,000 units or producing 16,000 units will lead to about the same average profit of $294,000. If, for some reason, we had to choose between producing 9,000 units and 16,000 units, which one should we choose?

To answer this question, we need to better understand the *risk* associated with certain decisions. For this purpose, we construct a frequency histogram (see Figure 3-5) that provides information about potential

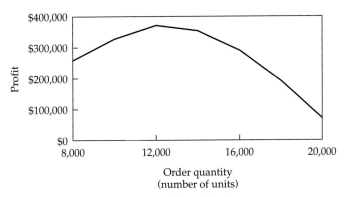

FIGURE 3-4 Average profit as a function of production quantity.

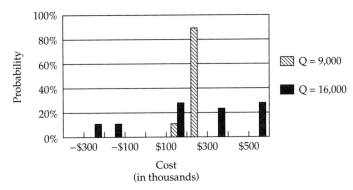

FIGURE 3-5 A frequency histogram of profit.

profit for the two given production quantities, 9,000 units and 16,000 units. For instance, consider profit when the production quantity is 16,000 units. The graph shows that the distribution of profit is not symmetrical. Losses of $220,000 happen about 11 percent of the time while profits of at least $410,000 happen 50 percent of the time. On the other hand, a frequency histogram of the profit when the production quantity is 9,000 units shows that the distribution has only two possible outcomes. Profit is either $200,000 with probability of about 11 percent, or $305,000 with probability of about 89 percent. Thus, while producing 16,000 units has the same average profit as producing 9,000 units, the possible *risk* on the one hand, and possible *reward* on the other hand, increases as we increase the production size.

To summarize:

- The optimal order quantity is not necessarily equal to forecast, or average, demand. Indeed, the optimal quantity depends on the relationship between marginal profit achieved from selling an additional unit and marginal cost. More importantly, the fixed cost has no impact on the production quantity, only on the decision whether to produce or not. Thus, given a decision to produce, the production quantity is the same independently of the fixed production cost.
- As the order quantity increases, average profit typically increases until the production quantity reaches a certain value, after which the average profit starts decreasing.
- As we increase the production quantity, the risk—that is, the probability of large losses—always increases. At the same time, the probability of large gains also increases. This is the risk/reward trade-off.

THE EFFECT OF INITIAL INVENTORY

Suppose now that the swimsuit under consideration is a model produced last year, and that the manufacturer

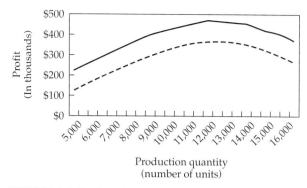

FIGURE 3-6 Profit and the impact of initial inventory.

has an initial inventory of 5,000 units. Assuming that demand for this model follows the same pattern of scenarios as before, should the manufacturer start production, and if so, how many swimsuits should be produced?

If the manufacturer does not produce any additional swimsuits, no more than 5,000 units can be sold and no additional fixed cost will be incurred. However, if the manufacturer decides to produce, a fixed production cost is charged independent of the amount produced.

To address this issue, consider Figure 3-6, in which the solid line represents average profit excluding fixed production cost while the dotted curve represents average profit including the fixed production cost. Notice that the dotted curve is identical to the curve in Figure 3-4 while the solid line is above the dotted line for every production quantity; the difference between the two lines is the fixed production cost.

Notice also that if nothing is produced, average profit can be obtained from the solid line in Figure 3-6 and is equal to

$$225,000 \text{ (from the figure)} + 5,000 \times 80 = 625,000$$

where the last component is the variable production cost already included in the $225,000.

On the other hand, if the manufacturer decides to produce, it is clear that production should increase inventory from 5,000 units to 12,000 units. Thus, average profit in this case is obtained from the dotted line and is equal to

$$371,000 \text{ (from the figure)} + 5,000 \times 80 = 771,000$$

Since the average profit associated with increasing inventory to 12,000 units is larger than the average profit associated with not producing anything, the optimal policy is to produce $7,000 = 12,000 - 5,000$ units.

Consider now the case in which initial inventory is 10,000 units. Following the same analysis used before, it is easy to see that there is no need to produce anything because the average profit associated with an initial inventory of 10,000 is larger than what we would achieve if we produce to increase inventory to 12,000 units. This is true because if we do not produce, we do not pay any fixed cost; if we produce, we need to pay a fixed cost independent of the amount produced.

Thus, if we produce, the most we can make on average is a profit of $375,000. This is the same average profit that we will have if our initial inventory is about 8,500 units and we decide not to produce anything. Hence, if our initial inventory is below 8,500 units, we produce to raise the inventory level to 12,000 units. On the other hand, if initial inventory is at least 8,500 units, we should not produce anything.

The swimsuit analysis motivates a powerful inventory policy used in practice to manage inventory: Whenever the inventory level is below a certain value, say s, we order (or produce) to increase the inventory to level S. Such a policy is referred as an (s, S) policy or a *min max* policy. We typically refer to s as the *reorder point* and to S as the *order-up-to-level*; in the swimsuit production example, the reorder point is 8,500 units and the order-up-to level is 12,000 units. The difference between these two levels is driven by fixed costs associated with ordering, manufacturing, or transportation.

3.2.3 Supply Contracts

The analysis of the swimsuit case so far was under the assumption that the swimsuit manufacturer had an adequate supply of raw materials, which would always be delivered on time and in the exact quantity the manufacturer ordered. For this purpose, buyers and suppliers typically agree on supply contracts. These contracts address issues that arise between a buyer and a supplier, whether the buyer is a manufacturer purchasing raw materials from a supplier or a retailer purchasing manufactured goods from a manufacturer. In a supply contract, the buyer and supplier may agree on

- Pricing and volume discounts.
- Minimum and maximum purchase quantities.
- Delivery lead times.
- Product or material quality.
- Product return policies.

As we will see, supply contracts are very powerful tools that can be used for far more than to ensure adequate supply of, and demand for, goods.

To illustrate the importance and impact of different types of supply contracts on supply chain performance, consider the following set of examples, based on the swimsuit case analyzed in the previous section.

EXAMPLE 3-2

Consider once again the swimsuit example discussed in Section 3.2.2. In this case, we assume that there are two companies involved in the supply chain: a retailer who faces customer demand and a manufacturer who produces and sells swimsuits to the retailer. Demand for swimsuits follows the same pattern of scenarios as before, and the retailer pricing and costing information are the same:

- During the summer season, a swimsuit is sold to customers at $125 per unit.
- The wholesale price paid by the retailer to the manufacturer is $80 per unit.
- Any swimsuit not sold during the summer season is sold to a discount store for $20.

For the manufacturer, we have the following information:

- Fixed production cost is $100,000.
- The variable production cost per unit equals $35.

Observe from these data that the marginal profit of the retailer is the same as the marginal profit of the manufacturer, $45. Also, notice that, excluding the fixed production cost, the retailer selling price, salvage value, and variable cost are the same as the selling price, salvage value, and production cost in the original example. This implies that the retailer's marginal profit for selling a unit during the season, $45, is smaller than the marginal loss, $60, associated with each unit sold at the end of the season to discount stores.

How much should the retailer order from the manufacturer? Recall our conclusion at the end of the swimsuit case study: the optimal order quantity depends on marginal profit and marginal loss but not on the fixed cost. Indeed, the solid line in Figure 3-6 represents average profit for the retailer since it does not account for the fixed cost. Thus, the optimal policy for the retailer is to order 12,000 units for an average profit of $470,700.

If the retailer places this order, the manufacturer's profit is

$$12,000(80 - 35) - 100,000 = 440,000$$

Notice that the sequence of events described in the previous example is sequential in nature. The retailer makes a purchasing decision to optimize his own profit, and the manufacturer reacts to decisions made by the retailer. This is referred to as a **sequential supply chain**, that is, a supply chain in which each party determines its own course of action independent of the other parties. As we observed in Chapter 1, this cannot be an effective strategy for supply chain partners.

It is natural to look for mechanisms that enable supply chain entities to move beyond this sequential optimization and toward **global optimization**. More specifically, are there mechanisms that the supply chain parties can use to improve all profits? To answer that question, observe that in the supply chain in the previous example, the retailer assumes all of the risk, of having more inventory than sales, while the manufacturer takes no risk. Indeed, since the manufacturer takes no risk, the manufacturer would like the retailer to order as much as possible, while the retailer is willing to order only 12,000 units because of the huge financial risk. If the manufacturer is willing and able to share some of the risk with the retailer, it may be profitable for the retailer to order more than 12,000 units, thereby increasing profit for both the manufacturer and the retailer.

It turns out that a variety of supply contracts will allow this risk sharing, and therefore increase profits for both supply chain entities.

Buy-Back Contracts   In a buy-back contract, the seller agrees to buy back unsold goods from the buyer for some agreed-upon price. Let's return to the swimsuit example.

EXAMPLE 3-3

Suppose the manufacturer offers to buy unsold swimsuits from the retailer for $55. Under this contract, the solid line in Figure 3-7 illustrates the retailer's average profit while the dotted line represents the manufacturer's average profit. The figure shows that in this case the retailer has an incentive to increase its order quantity to 14,000 units, for a profit of $513,800, while the manufacturer's average profit increases to $471,900. Thus, the total average profit for the two parties increases from $910,700 (= $470,700 + $440,000) in the sequential supply chain to $985,700 (= $513,800 + $471,900) when a buy-back contract is used.

The buy-back contract is effective because it allows the manufacturer to share some of the risk with the retailer, and thus motivates the retailer to increase the order quantity, in this case by about 17 percent. The manufacturer compensates for its increase in risk

FIGURE 3-7 Buy-back contract.

by being able to sell more products at full price if demand turns out to be larger than 12,000 units.

Revenue-Sharing Contracts Observe that in the sequential supply chain, one important reason for the retailer to order only 12,000 units is the high wholesale price. If somehow the retailer can convince the manufacturer to reduce the wholesale price, then clearly the retailer will have an incentive to order more. Of course, a reduction in wholesale price will decrease the manufacturer's profit if it is unable to sell more units. This is addressed by revenue-sharing contracts. In a revenue-sharing contract, the buyer shares some of its revenue with the seller, in return for a discount on the wholesale price. Consider the swimsuit example.

EXAMPLE 3-4

Suppose the swimsuit manufacturer and retailer have a revenue-sharing contract, in which the manufacturer agrees to decrease the wholesale price from $80 to $60, and, in return, the retailer provides 15 percent of the product revenue to the manufacturer. Under this contract, the solid line in Figure 3-8 illustrates the retailer's average profit while the dotted line represents the manufacturer's average profit. The figure shows that, in this case, the retailer has an incentive to increase his order quantity to 14,000 (as in the buy-back contract) for a profit of $504,325, and this order increase leads to increased manufacturer's profit of $481,375, in spite of lower wholesale prices. Thus, the supply chain total profit is $985,700 (= $504,325 + $481,375). That is, the reduction in the wholesale price coupled with revenue sharing leads to increased profits for both parties.

Other types of supply contracts can be equally effective [22].

Quantity-Flexibility Contracts Quantity-flexibility contracts are contracts in which the supplier provides full refund for returned (unsold) items as long as the number of returns is no larger than a certain quantity. Thus, this contract gives full refund for a portion of the returned items, whereas a buy-back contract provides partial refund for all returned items [22].

Sales Rebate Contracts Sales rebate contracts provide a direct incentive to the retailer to increase sales by means of a rebate paid by the supplier for any item sold above a certain quantity.

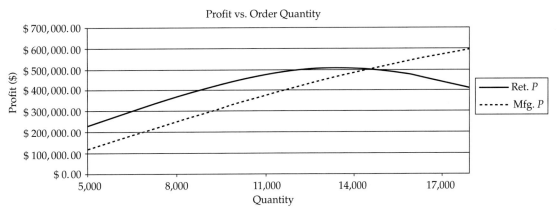

FIGURE 3-8 Revenue-sharing contract.

Global Optimization The various contracts described earlier raise an important question: what is the most profit both the supplier and the buyer can hope to achieve?

To answer this question, we take a completely different approach. What if an unbiased decision maker is allowed to identify the best strategy for the entire supply chain? This unbiased decision maker would consider the two supply chain partners, the manufacturer and the retailer, as two members of the same organization. That is, the transfer of money between the parties is ignored.

EXAMPLE 3-5

In the swimsuit example, the only relevant data in this case are the selling price, $125; the salvage value, $20; the variable production costs, $35; and the fixed production cost. In this case, the cost that the retailer charges the manufacturer is meaningless, since we are only interested in external costs and revenues. Evidently, in this case the supply chain marginal profit, $90 = 125 - 35$, is significantly higher than the marginal loss, $15 = 35 - 20$, and hence the supply chain will produce more than average demand. Indeed, Figure 3-9 suggests that in this global optimization strategy, the optimal production quantity is 16,000 units, which implies an expected supply chain profit of $1,014,500.

The examples above illustrate some of the power of supply contracts. Effective supply contracts provide incentives for supply chain partners to replace traditional strategies, in which each partner optimizes its own profit, with global optimization, where supply chain profit is maximized. The difficulty with global optimization is that it requires the firm to surrender decision-making power to an unbiased decision maker.

This is precisely why supply contracts are so important. They help firms achieve global optimization, without the need for an unbiased decision maker, by *allowing buyers and suppliers to share the risk* and the potential benefit. Indeed, in the examples above, the contracts we discussed came close to, but did not reach, the profit obtained by the global optimization strategy. In fact, it is not difficult to show that a more careful design of these contracts can achieve the exact same profit as the profit in global optimization. For example, in revenue sharing this is achieved by carefully selecting the wholesale price and the level of revenue sharing, while in the buy-back contract,

FIGURE 3-9 Profit using global optimization strategy.

FIGURE 3-10 Globally optimal buy-back contract.

it is achieved by choosing the buy-back price and, sometimes, the wholesale price. Figure 3-10 shows the retailer's, manufacturer's, and system profit with the same buy-back contract discussed earlier, except that the wholesale price has been decreased to $75 and the buy-back price has been increased to $65. In this case, the retailer will elect to buy 16,000 units, and system profit will be $1,014,500.

In addition, from an implementation point of view, the main drawback of global optimization is that it does not provide a mechanism to allocate supply chain profit between the partners. It only provides information on the best, or optimal, set of actions that need to be taken by the supply chain to improve profit. Supply contracts allocate this profit among supply chain members.

More importantly, effective supply contracts allocate profit to each partner in a way that no partner can improve his profit by deciding to deviate from the optimal set of decisions. That is, there is no incentive for either the buyer or the seller to deviate from the set of actions that will achieve the global optimal solution. For example, observe that in the improved buy-back contract illustrated in Figure 3-10, the retailer's optimal order quantity is 16,000 units, which is equal to the manufacturer's optimal supply quantity.

The following example illustrates the impact of supply contracts in practice.

EXAMPLE 3-6

Until 1998, video rental stores used to purchase copies of newly released movies from the movie studios for about $65 and rent them to customers for $3. Because of the high purchase price, rental stores did not buy enough copies to cover peak demand, which typically occurs during the first 10 weeks after a movie is released on video. The result was low customer service level; in a 1998 survey, about 20 percent of customers could not get their first choice of movie. Then, in 1998, Blockbuster Video entered into a revenue-sharing contract with the movie studios in which the wholesale price was reduced from $65 to $8 per copy, and, in return, studios were paid about 30–45 percent of the rental price of every rental. This revenue-sharing contract had a huge impact on Blockbuster revenue and market share. Today, revenue sharing is used by most large video rental stores [23].

3.2.4 Multiple Order Opportunities

We now return to the single-decision-maker models we considered in Section 3.2.2. The models described and analyzed in Section 3.2.2 assume that the decision maker can make only a single ordering decision for the entire horizon. This may be the case for fashion items such as swimsuits or ski jackets, where the selling season is short and there is no second opportunity to reorder products based on realized customer demand. In many practical situations, however, the decision maker may order products repeatedly at any time during the year.

Consider, for instance, a distributor of TV sets. The distributor faces random demand for the product and receives supply from the manufacturer. Of course, the manufacturer cannot instantaneously satisfy orders placed by the distributor: there is a fixed lead time for delivery whenever the distributor places an order. Since demand is random and the manufacturer has a fixed delivery lead time, the distributor needs to hold inventory, even if no fixed setup cost is charged for ordering the products. At least three reasons explain why the distributor holds inventory:

1. To satisfy demand occurring during lead time. Since orders aren't met immediately, inventory must be on hand to meet customer demand during the period between the time the distributor orders and when the order arrives.
2. To protect against uncertainty in demand.
3. To balance annual inventory holding costs and annual fixed order costs. We have seen that more frequent orders lead to lower inventory levels and thus lower inventory holding costs, but they also lead to higher annual fixed order costs.

While these issues are intuitively clear, the specific inventory policy that the distributor should apply is not simple. To manage inventory effectively, the distributor needs to decide when and how many TV sets to order. We distinguish between two types of policies:

- **Continuous review policy**, in which inventory is reviewed every day and a decision is made about whether and how much to order.
- **Periodic review policy**, in which the inventory level is reviewed at regular intervals and an appropriate quantity is ordered after each review.

3.2.5 Continuous Review Policy

We make the following additional assumptions.

- Daily demand is random and follows a normal distribution. In other words, we assume that the probabilistic forecast of daily demand follows the famous bell-shaped curve. Note that we can completely describe normal demand by its average and standard deviation.
- Every time the distributor orders TV sets from the manufacturer, the distributor pays a fixed cost, K, plus an amount proportional to the quantity ordered.
- Inventory holding cost is charged per item per unit time.
- Inventory level is reviewed at the end of every day and if an order is placed, the order arrives after the appropriate lead time.
- If a customer order arrives when there is no inventory on hand to fill the order (i.e., when the distributor is stocked out), the order is lost.
- The distributor specifies a required *service level*. The service level is the probability of not stocking out during lead time. For example, the distributor might want to

ensure that the proportion of lead times in which demand is met out of stock is 95 percent. Thus, the required service level is 95 percent in this case.

To characterize the inventory policy that the distributor should use, we need the following information:

AVG = Average daily demand faced by the distributor
STD = Standard deviation of daily demand faced by the distributor
L = Replenishment lead time from the supplier to the distributor in days
h = Cost of holding one unit of the product for one day at the distributor
α = service level. This implies that the probability of stocking out is $1 - \alpha$

In addition, we need to define the concept of *inventory position*. The inventory position at any point in time is the actual inventory at the warehouse plus items ordered by the distributor that have not yet arrived minus items that are backordered.

To describe the policy that the distributor should use, recall our previous definitions of s and S, the reorder point and order-up-to level. An effective inventory policy in this case is an (s, S) policy where the difference between S and s is due to the fixed cost. Hence, in this case, whenever the inventory position level drops below level s, the distributor should order to raise its inventory position to level S.

The reorder level, s, consists of two components. The first is the average inventory during lead time, which is the product of average daily demand and the lead time. This ensures that when the distributor places an order, the system has enough inventory to cover expected demand during lead time. The average demand during lead time is exactly

$$L \times AVG$$

The second component represents the *safety stock*, which is the amount of inventory that the distributor needs to keep at the warehouse and in the pipeline to protect against deviations from average demand during lead time. This quantity is calculated as follows:

$$z \times STD \times \sqrt{L}$$

where z is a constant, referred to as the **safety factor**. This constant is associated with the service level. Thus, the reorder level is equal to

$$L \times AVG + z \times STD \times \sqrt{L}$$

The safety factor z is chosen from statistical tables to ensure that the probability of stockouts during lead time is exactly $1 - \alpha$. This implies that the reorder level must satisfy:

Probability {Demand during lead time $\geq L \times AVG + z \times STD \times \sqrt{L}$} $= 1 - \alpha$

Table 3-2 provides a list of z values for different values of the service level α.

What about the order-up-to level, S? This value is calculated following the intuition developed in the economic lot size model. Recall from this model that the order quantity, Q, is calculated as follows:

$$Q = \sqrt{\frac{2K \times AVG}{h}}$$

TABLE 3-2

SERVICE LEVEL AND THE SAFETY FACTOR, Z

Service level	90%	91%	92%	93%	94%	95%	96%	97%	98%	99%	99.9%
z	1.29	1.34	1.41	1.48	1.56	1.65	1.75	1.88	2.05	2.33	3.08

If there is no variability in customer demand, the distributor would order Q items whenever inventory is at the level $L \times AVG$ since it takes L days to receive the order. However, there is variability in demand, so the distributor places an order for Q items whenever the inventory position is at the reorder level, s. Therefore, the order-up-to level is

$$S = Q + s$$

Observe that when (s, S) policies are employed, the inventory position may drop below the reorder point, in which case the (s, S) policy implies that the distributor should order enough to raise the inventory position to the order-up-to level. Evidently, this amount may be larger than Q.

Figure 3-11 illustrates the inventory level over time when this type of policy is implemented. What is the average inventory level in this policy? Observe that, between two successive orders, the minimum level of inventory is achieved right before receiving an order, while the maximum level of inventory is achieved immediately after receiving the order. The expected level of inventory before receiving the order is the safety stock

$$z \times STD \times \sqrt{L}$$

while the expected level of inventory immediately after receiving the order is

$$Q + z \times STD \times \sqrt{L}$$

Thus, the average inventory level is the average of these two values, which is equal to

$$\frac{Q}{2} + z \times STD \times \sqrt{L}$$

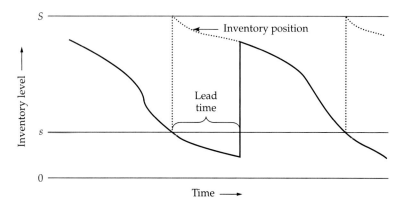

FIGURE 3-11 (s, S) policy with multiple order opportunities.

CHAPTER 3: INVENTORY MANAGEMENT AND RISK POOLING **61**

EXAMPLE 3-7

Suppose the distributor of the TV sets is trying to set inventory policies at the warehouse for one of the TV models. Assume that whenever the distributor places an order for TV sets, there is a fixed ordering cost of $4,500, which is independent of the order size. The cost of a TV set to the distributor is $250 and annual inventory holding cost is about 18 percent of the product cost. Replenishment time (i.e., lead time) is about two weeks.

Table 3-3 provides data on the number of TV sets sold in each of the last 12 months. Given that the distributor would like to ensure 97 percent service level, what is the reorder level and the order-up-to level that the distributor should use?

TABLE 3-3

HISTORICAL DATA

Month	Sept.	Oct.	Nov.	Dec.	Jan.	Feb.	Mar.	Apr.	May	June	July	Aug.
Sales	200	152	100	221	287	176	151	198	246	309	98	156

Table 3-3 implies that average monthly demand is 191.17 and the standard deviation of monthly demand is 66.53.

Since lead time is two weeks, we transform the average and the standard deviation to weekly values as follows:

$$\text{Average weekly demand} = \frac{\text{Average monthly demand}}{4.3}$$

while

$$\text{Standard deviation of weekly demand} = \frac{\text{Monthly standard deviation}}{\sqrt{4.3}}$$

These data are provided in Table 3-4. This allows us to calculate average demand during lead time and safety stock using a safety factor $z = 1.9$ (or, more precisely, 1.88) taken from Table 3-2 based on a 97 percent service level. The reorder point is simply the sum of the average demand during lead time plus the safety stock. All these data are presented in Table 3-4.

TABLE 3-4

INVENTORY ANALYSIS

Parameter	Average weekly demand	Standard deviation of weekly demand	Average demand during lead time	Safety stock	Reorder point
Value	44.58	32.08	89.16	86.20	176

To determine the order-up-to level, observe that the weekly inventory holding cost per TV set is

$$\frac{0.18 \times 250}{52} = 0.87$$

or 87 cents. This implies that the order quantity, Q, should be calculated as

$$Q = \sqrt{\frac{2 \times 4,500 \times 44.58}{0.87}} = 679$$

and hence the order-up-to level is

$$\text{Reorder point} + Q = 176 + 679 = 855$$

That is, the distributor should place an order to raise the inventory position to 855 TV sets whenever the inventory level is below or at 176 units. Finally, the average inventory level is equal to

$$\frac{679}{2} + 86.20 = 426$$

which means that, on average, the distributor keeps at the warehouse about 10 ($= 426/44.58$) weeks of supply.

3.2.6 Variable Lead Times

In many cases, the assumption that the delivery lead time to the warehouse is fixed and known in advance does not necessarily hold. Indeed, in many practical situations, the lead time to the warehouse must be assumed to be normally distributed with average lead time denoted by *AVGL* and standard deviation denoted by *STDL*. In this case, the reorder point, *s*, is calculated as follows:

$$s = AVG \times AVGL + z\sqrt{AVGL \times STD^2 + AVG^2 \times STDL^2}$$

where $AVG \times AVGL$ represents average demand during lead time, while

$$\sqrt{AVGL \times STD^2 + AVG^2 \times STDL^2}$$

is the standard deviation of demand during lead time. Thus, the amount of safety stock that has to be kept is equal to

$$z\sqrt{AVGL \times STD^2 + AVG^2 \times STDL^2}$$

As before, the order-up-to level is the sum of the reorder point and Q; that is,

$$S = Q + AVG \times AVGL + z\sqrt{AVGL \times STD^2 + AVG^2 \times STDL^2}$$

Finally, the safety factor *z* is chosen from Table 3-2.

3.2.7 Periodic Review Policy

In many real-life situations, the inventory level is reviewed periodically, at regular intervals, and an appropriate quantity is ordered after each review. For instance, the inventory level may be reviewed at the start of each month or the end of each week, and an order may be placed at that time. Since inventory levels are reviewed at a periodic interval, the fixed cost of placing an order is a sunk cost and hence can be ignored; presumably, the fixed cost was used to determine the review interval. The quantity ordered arrives after the appropriate lead time.

What inventory policy should the warehouse use in this case? Since fixed cost does not play a role in this environment, the inventory policy is characterized by one parameter, the **base-stock level.** That is, the warehouse determines a target inventory level, the base-stock level, and each review period, the inventory position is reviewed and the warehouse orders enough to raise the inventory position to the base-stock level.

What is an effective base-stock level? For this purpose, let *r* be the length of the review period—we assume that orders are placed every *r* period of time. As before, *L* is the lead time, *AVG* is the average daily demand faced by the warehouse, and *STD* is the standard deviation of this daily demand.

Observe that at the time the warehouse places an order, this order raises the inventory position to the base-stock level. This level of the inventory position should be enough to protect the warehouse against shortages until the next order arrives. Since the next order arrives after a period of $r + L$ days, the current order should be enough to cover demand during a period of $r + L$ days.

Thus, the base-stock level should include two components: average demand during an interval of $r + L$ days, which is equal to

$$(r + L) \times AVG$$

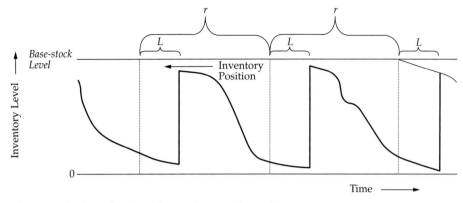

FIGURE 3-12 Inventory level in a periodic review policy.

and the safety stock, which is the amount of inventory that the warehouse needs to keep to protect against deviations from average demand during a period of $r + L$ days. This quantity is calculated as follows:

$$z \times STD \times \sqrt{r + L}$$

where z is the safety factor.

Figure 3-12 illustrates the inventory level over time when this type of policy is implemented. What is the average inventory level in this case? As before, the maximum inventory level is acheived immediately after receiving an order, while the minimum level of inventory is acheived just before receiving an order. It is easy to see that the expected level of inventory after receiving an order is equal to

$$r \times AVG + z \times STD \times \sqrt{r + L}$$

while the expected level of inventory before an order arrives is just the safety stock,

$$z \times STD \times \sqrt{r + L}$$

Hence, the average inventory level is the average of these two values, which is equal to

$$\frac{r \times AVG}{2} + z \times STD \times \sqrt{r + L}$$

EXAMPLE 3-8

We continue with the previous example and assume that the distributor places an order for TV sets every three weeks. Since lead time is two weeks, the base-stock level needs to cover a period of five weeks. Thus, average demand during that period is

$$44.58 \times 5 = 222.9$$

and the safety stock, for 97 percent service level, is

$$1.9 \times 32.08 \times \sqrt{5} = 136.3$$

Hence, the base-stock level should be $223 + 136 = 359$. That is, when the distributor places an order every three weeks, he should raise the inventory position to 359 TV sets. The average inventory level in this case equals

$$\frac{3 \times 44.58}{2} + 1.9 \times 32.08 \times \sqrt{5} = 203.17$$

which implies that, on average, the distributor keeps five ($= 203.17/44.58$) weeks of supply.

3.3 RISK POOLING

Consider the following case.

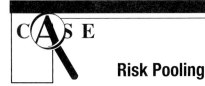

Risk Pooling

ACME, a company that produces and distributes electronic equipment in the Northeast of the United States, faces a distribution problem. The current distribution system partitions the Northeast into two markets, each of which has a single warehouse. One warehouse is located in Paramus, New Jersey, and the second is located in Newton, Massachusetts. Customers, typically retailers, receive items directly from the warehouses; in the current distribution system, each customer is assigned to a single market and receives deliveries from the corresponding warehouse.

The warehouses receive items from a manufacturing facility in Chicago. Lead time for delivery to each of the warehouses is about one week and the manufacturing facility has sufficient production capacity to satisfy any warehouse order. The current distribution strategy provides a 97 percent service level; that is, the inventory policy employed by each warehouse is designed so that the probability of a stockout is 3 percent. Of course, unfilled orders are lost to the competition and thus cannot be satisfied by future deliveries.

Since the original distribution system was designed over seven years ago, the company's newly appointed CEO has decided to review the current logistics and distribution system. ACME handles about 1,500 different products in its supply chain and serves about 10,000 accounts in the Northeast.

ACME is considering the following alternative strategy: Replace the two warehouses with a single warehouse located between Paramus and Newton that will serve all customer orders. We will refer to this proposed system as the centralized distribution system. The CEO insists that the same service level, 97 percent, be maintained regardless of the logistics strategy employed.

Obviously, the current distribution system with two warehouses has an important advantage over the single warehouse system because each warehouse is close to a particular subset of customers, decreasing delivery time. However, the proposed change also has an important advantage; it allows ACME to achieve either the same service level of 97 percent with much lower inventory or a higher service level with the same amount of total inventory.

Intuitively this is explained as follows. With random demand, it is very likely that a higher-than-average demand at one retailer will be offset by a lower-than-average demand at another. As the number of retailers served by a warehouse goes up, this likelihood also goes up. Indeed, this is precisely the third principle of all forecasts described at the beginning of Section 3.2.2: aggregate forecasts are more accurate.

How much can ACME reduce inventory if the company decides to switch to the centralized system but maintain the same 97 percent service level?

To answer that question, we need to perform a more rigorous analysis of the inventory policy that ACME should use in both the current system and the centralized system. We will explain this analysis for two specific products, Product A and Product B, although the analysis must be conducted for all products.

For both products, an order from the factory costs $60 per order and holding inventory costs are $0.27 per unit per week. In the current distribution system, the cost of transporting a product from a warehouse to a customer is, on average, $1.05 per product. It is estimated that in the centralized distribution system, the transportation cost from the central warehouse will be, on average, $1.10 per product. For this analysis, we assume that delivery lead time is not significantly different in the two systems.

Tables 3-5 and 3-6 provide historical data for Products A and B, respectively. The tables include weekly demand information for each product for the last eight weeks in each market area. Observe that Product B is a slow-moving product: the demand for Product B is fairly small relative to the demand for Product A.

Table 3-7 provides a summary of average weekly demand and the standard deviation of weekly demand for each product. It also presents the *coefficient of variation* of demand faced by each warehouse. This is defined as follows:

$$\text{Coefficient of variation} = \frac{\text{Standard deviation}}{\text{Average demand}}$$

It is important at this point to understand the difference between the standard deviation and the coefficient of variation, both of which provide a measure of variability of customer demand. Indeed, while the standard deviation measures the absolute variability of customer demands, the coefficient of variation measures variability relative to average demand. For instance, in the case of the two products analyzed here, we observe that Product A has a much larger standard deviation while Product B has a significantly larger coefficient of variation. This distinction between the two products plays an important role in the final analysis.

Finally, note that for each product the average demand faced by the warehouse in the centralized distribution system is the sum of the average demand faced by each of the existing warehouses. However, the variability faced by the central warehouse, measured either by the standard deviation or the coefficient of variation, is much smaller than the combined variabilities faced by the two existing warehouses. This has a major impact on inventory levels in the current and proposed systems. These levels, calculated as we have described in previous sections, are shown in Table 3-8.

Notice that the average inventory for Product A at the warehouse in Paramus, New Jersey, is about

$$\text{Safety stock} + \frac{Q}{2} = 88$$

TABLE 3-5

HISTORICAL DATA FOR PRODUCT A

Week	1	2	3	4	5	6	7	8
Massachusetts	33	45	37	38	55	30	18	58
New Jersey	46	35	41	40	26	48	18	55
Total	79	80	78	78	81	78	36	113

TABLE 3-6

HISTORICAL DATA FOR PRODUCT B

Week	1	2	3	4	5	6	7	8
Massachusetts	0	2	3	0	0	1	3	0
New Jersey	2	4	0	0	3	1	0	0
Total	2	6	3	0	3	2	3	0

TABLE 3-7

SUMMARY OF HISTORICAL DATA

Statistics	Product	Average demand	Standard deviation of demand	Coefficient of variation
Massachusetts	A	39.3	13.2	0.34
Massachusetts	B	1.125	1.36	1.21
New Jersey	A	38.6	12.0	0.31
New Jersey	B	1.25	1.58	1.26
Total	A	77.9	20.71	0.27
Total	B	2.375	1.9	0.81

TABLE 3-8

INVENTORY LEVELS

	Product	Average demand during lead time	Safety stock	Reorder point	Q	Order-up-to level
Massachusetts	A	39.3	25.08	65	132	197
Massachusetts	B	1.125	2.58	4	25	29
New Jersey	A	38.6	22.80	62	131	193
New Jersey	B	1.25	3	5	24	29
Central	A	77.9	39.35	118	186	304
Central	B	2.375	3.61	6	33	39

Similarly, average inventory at the Newton, Massachusetts, warehouse for the same product is about 91 units, while average inventory in the centralized warehouse is about 132 units. Thus, average inventory for Product A is reduced by about 36 percent when ACME shifts from the current system to the new, centralized system—a significant reduction in average inventory.

The average inventory for Product B is 15 at the warehouse in Paramus, 14 at the warehouse in Newton, and 20 at the centralized warehouse. In this case, ACME is going to achieve a reduction of about 43 percent in average inventory level.

The previous case illustrates **risk pooling**, an important concept in supply chain management. Risk pooling suggests that demand variability is reduced if one aggregates demand across locations because, as we aggregate demand across different locations, it becomes more likely that high demand from one customer will be offset by low demand from another. This reduction in variability allows a decrease in safety stock and therefore reduces average inventory. For example, in the centralized distribution system described above, the warehouse serves all customers, which leads to a reduction in variability measured by either the standard deviation or the coefficient of variation.

We summarize the three critical points we have made about risk pooling:

1. Centralizing inventory reduces both safety stock and average inventory in the system. Intuitively this is explained as follows. In a centralized distribution system, whenever demand from one market area is higher than average while demand in another market area is lower than average, items in the warehouse that were originally allocated for one market can be reallocated to the other. The process of reallocating inventory is not possible in a decentralized distribution system where different warehouses serve different markets.
2. The higher the coefficient of variation, the greater the benefit obtained from centralized systems; that is, the greater the benefit from risk pooling. This is explained as follows. Average inventory includes two components: one proportional to average weekly demand (Q) and the other proportional to the standard deviation of weekly demand (safety stock). Since reduction in average inventory is achieved mainly through a reduction in safety stock, the higher the coefficient of variation, the larger the impact of safety stock on inventory reduction.
3. The benefits from risk pooling depend on the behavior of demand from one market relative to demand from another. We say that demand from two markets is *positively correlated* if it is very likely that whenever demand from one market is greater then average, demand from the other market is also greater than average. Similarly, when demand from one market is smaller than average, so is demand from the other. Intuitively, the benefit from risk pooling decreases as the correlation between demand from the two markets becomes more positive.

In Chapter 5, we provide different examples of risk pooling. In that chapter, risk pooling is applied by *aggregating demand across products* or *across time*, rather than across customers as we do here.

3.4 CENTRALIZED VERSUS DECENTRALIZED SYSTEMS

The analysis in the previous section raises an important practical issue: What are the trade-offs that we need to consider in comparing centralized distribution systems with decentralized distribution systems?

Safety stock. Clearly, safety stock decreases as a firm moves from a decentralized to a centralized system. The amount of decrease depends on a number of parameters, including the coefficient of variation and the correlation between the demand from the different markets.

Service level. When the centralized and decentralized systems have the same total safety stock, the service level provided by the centralized system is higher. As before, the magnitude of the increase in service level depends on the coefficient of variation and the correlation between the demand from the different markets.

Overhead costs. Typically, these costs are much greater in a decentralized system because there are fewer economies of scale.

Customer lead time. Since the warehouses are much closer to the customers in a decentralized system, response time is much shorter (see Chapter 2).

Transportation costs. The impact on transportation costs depends on the specifics of the situation. On one hand, as we increase the number of warehouses, outbound transportation costs—the costs incurred for delivering the items from the warehouses to the customers—decrease because warehouses are much closer to the market areas. On the other hand, inbound transportation costs—the costs of shipping the products from the supply and manufacturing facilities to the warehouses—increase. Thus, the net impact on total transportation cost is not immediately clear.

3.5 MANAGING INVENTORY IN THE SUPPLY CHAIN

Most of the inventory models and examples considered so far assume a single facility (e.g., a warehouse or a retail outlet) managing its inventory in order to minimize its own cost as much as possible. In the discussion of supply contracts we analyzed multiple facilities, each of which focuses on maximizing its own profit.

In this section we consider a multifacility supply chain that belongs to a single firm. The objective of the firm is to manage inventory so as to reduce systemwide cost; thus, it is important to consider the interaction of the various facilities and the impact this interaction has on the inventory policy that should be employed by each facility.

For this purpose, consider a retail distribution system with a single warehouse serving a number of retailers. We make two important, but reasonable, assumptions:

1. Inventory decisions are made by a single decision maker whose objective is to minimize systemwide cost.
2. The decision maker has access to inventory information at each of the retailers and at the warehouse.

Under these assumptions, an inventory policy based on the so-called *echelon inventory* is an effective way to manage the system.

To understand this policy, it is necessary to introduce the concept of echelon inventory. In a distribution system, each stage or level (i.e., the warehouse or the retailers) often is referred to as an echelon. Thus, the echelon inventory at any stage or level of the system is equal to the inventory on hand at the echelon, plus all *downstream inventory*. For example, the echelon inventory at the warehouse is equal to the inventory at the warehouse, plus all of the inventory in transit to and in stock at the retailers. Similarly, the *echelon inventory position* at the warehouse is the echelon inventory at the warehouse, plus those items ordered by the warehouse that have not yet arrived minus all items that are backordered (see Figure 3-13).

This suggests the following effective approach to managing the single warehouse multiretailer system. First, the individual retailers are managed as described in Section 3.2.4, using the appropriate (s, S) inventory policy. Second, the warehouse ordering decisions are based on the echelon inventory position at the warehouse.

FIGURE 3-13 The warehouse echelon inventory.

Specifically, the reorder point, s, and order-up-to level, S, are calculated for each retailer using the approach described in Section 3.2.4. Whenever the inventory position at a retailer falls below the reorder point s, an order is placed to raise its inventory position to S. Similarly, a reorder point s and an order-up-to level S are calculated for the warehouse. In this case, however, the warehouse policy controls its echelon inventory position; whenever the echelon inventory position for the warehouse is below s, an order is placed to raise its echelon inventory position to S.

How should the reorder point associated with the warehouse echelon inventory position be calculated? In this case, the reorder point is

$$s = L^e \times AVG + z \times STD\sqrt{L^e}$$

where

$L^e = $ *echelon lead time*, defined as the lead time between the retailers and the warehouse *plus* the lead time between the warehouse and its supplier

$AVG = $ average demand across all retailers (i.e., the average of the aggregate demand)

$STD = $ standard deviation of (aggregate) demand across all retailers

EXAMPLE 3-9

Consider the TV distributor from Example 3-7. In that example, we determined the inventory policy for the warehouse. Now suppose that the warehouse supplies a group of retailers. The historical demand data provided in Table 3-3 is the aggregate demand data for the retailers. Finally, the two weeks' lead time is the echelon lead time—the time it takes an order placed by the warehouse to reach a customer. Thus, the distributor needs to ensure that a total of 176 units of inventory, or about four weeks' supply, is somewhere in the system, either in the pipeline to the warehouse, at the warehouse, in transit to the retailers, or at the retailers.

What about the retailers? In this case, we need to perform exactly the same calculations, but this time utilizing the specific demand faced by each retailer and the associated lead time from the warehouse to that retailer.

Suppose, for example, that the average weekly demand at a specific retailer is 11.6, with a standard deviation of 4.5. Furthermore, suppose that it takes one week for items to get from the warehouse to the retailer. Using the same approach as before to achieve a 97 percent service level, we find that the reorder level, s, for the retailer is 20. Thus, an order is placed whenever the retailer inventory position is 20. Obviously, if other retailers face different demand or lead times, they will have different reorder levels.

This technique can be extended to more complex supply chains—supply chains with additional levels—provided that the supply chains are under centralized control and that inventory information from each of the echelons is available to the decision maker.

3.6 PRACTICAL ISSUES

In a recent survey,[1] materials and inventory managers were asked to identify effective inventory reduction strategies. The top seven strategies in this survey are:

1. **Periodic inventory review.** In this strategy, inventory is reviewed at a fixed time interval and every time it is reviewed, a decision is made on the order size. The periodic inventory review policy makes it possible to identify slow-moving and obsolete products and allows management to continuously reduce inventory levels.
2. **Tight management of usage rates, lead times, and safety stock.** This allows the firm to make sure inventory is kept at the appropriate level. Such an inventory control process allows the firm to identify, for example, situations in which usage rates decrease for a few months. If no appropriate action is taken, this decrease in usage rates implies an increase in inventory levels over the same period of time.
3. **Reduce safety stock levels.** This can perhaps be accomplished by focusing on lead-time reduction.
4. **Introduce or enhance cycle counting practice.** This process replaces the annual inventory physical inventory count by a system where part of the inventory is counted every day, and each item is counted several times per year.
5. **ABC approach.** In this strategy, items are classified into three categories. Class A items include all high-revenue products, which typically account for about 80 percent of annual ($) sales and represent about 20 percent of inventory SKUs. Class B items include products that account for about 15 percent of annual sales, while Class C products represent low-revenue items, products whose value is no more than 5 percent of sales. Because Class A items account for the major part of the business, a high-frequency periodic review policy (e.g., a weekly review) is appropriate in this case. Similarly, a periodic review policy is applied to control Class B products, although the frequency of review is not as high as that for Class A products. Finally, depending on product value, the firm either keeps no inventory of expensive Class C products or keeps a high inventory of inexpensive Class C products.
6. **Shift more inventory or inventory ownership to suppliers.**
7. **Quantitative approaches.** These approaches are similar to those described in this chapter that focus on the right balance between inventory holding and ordering costs.

Observe that the focus in the survey was not on reducing cost but on reducing inventory levels. Indeed, in the last few years we have seen a significant effort by industry to increase the *inventory turnover ratio*, defined as follows:

$$\text{Inventory turnover ratio} = \frac{\text{Annual sales}}{\text{Average inventory level}}$$

This definition implies that an increase in inventory turnover leads to a decrease in average inventory levels. For instance, retailing powerhouse Wal-Mart has the highest inventory turnover ratio of any discount retailer. This suggests that Wal-Mart has a higher level of liquidity, smaller risk of obsolescence, and reduced investment in

---

[1] *Inventory Reduction Report*, no. 07-01 (July 2001), pp. 10–12.

TABLE 3-9			

INVENTORY TURNOVER RATIO FOR DIFFERENT MANUFACTURERS

Industry	Upper quartile	Median	Lower quartile
Electronic components and accessories	8.1	4.9	3.3
Electronic computers	22.7	7.0	2.7
Household audio and video equipment	6.3	3.9	2.5
Paper Mills	11.7	8.0	5.5
Industrial chemicals	14.1	6.4	4.2
Bakery products	39.7	23.0	12.6
Books: Publishing and printing	7.2	2.8	1.5

Source: Based on a survey conducted by Risk Management Associates.

inventory. Of course, a low inventory level in itself is not always appropriate since it increases the risk of lost sales.

Thus, the question is, what are the appropriate inventory turns that the firm should use in practice? A recent survey of industry practices suggests that the answer does change from year to year and depends, in particular, on the specific industry.[2] Indeed, the survey reports a significant increase in inventory turnover ratios in 2001: about 52.9 percent of the manufacturers participating in the survey increased their turnover. Table 3-9 provides some examples of inventory turnover in different manufacturing companies, by industry, in 2001.

3.7 FORECASTING

Throughout this chapter, we have recounted the problems with forecasting. After all, the three rules of forecasting are

1. The forecast is always wrong.
2. The longer the forecast horizon, the worse the forecast.
3. Aggregate forecasts are more accurate.

Nevertheless, forecasting is a critical tool in the management toolbox. We have seen that by correctly managing inventory, managers can make the best possible use of forecasts, in spite of the inherent difficulties of forecasting. In addition, forecasts aren't just for inventory decision making; decisions about whether to enter a particular market at all, about whether to expand production capacity, or about whether to implement a given promotional plan can all benefit from effective forecasting. In this section, we explore a variety of the techniques that can be used, separately or in combination, to create forecasts. Of course, it would be possible to write an entire book on forecasting (and many such books exist); our goal here is to introduce the different approaches to forecasting and suggest when each of these approaches is appropriate.

Although there are many different forecasting tools and methods, they can be split into four general categories (see [61]):

- **Judgment methods** involve the collection of expert opinions.
- **Market research methods** involve qualitative studies of consumer behavior.
- **Time-series methods** are mathematical methods in which future performance is extrapolated from past performance.

---

[2] *Inventory Reduction Report*, no. 03-02 (March 2002), pp. 6–10.

- **Causal methods** are mathematical methods in which forecasts are generated based on a variety of system variables.

Below, we discuss these methods in more detail.

3.7.1 Judgment Methods

Judgment methods strive to assemble the opinions of a variety of experts in a systematic way. For example, salespeople (or dealers) frequently have a good understanding of expected sales, since they are close to the market. A **sales-force composite** can be assembled that combines each salesperson's sales estimate in a logical way.

   Panels of experts can be assembled in order to reach a consensus. This approach assumes that by communicating and openly sharing information, a superior forecast can be agreed upon. These experts can be external experts, or internal experts, from a variety of functional areas within a company.

   The **Delphi method** is a structured technique for reaching a consensus with a panel of experts without gathering them in a single location. Indeed, the technique is designed to eliminate the danger of one or a few strong-willed individuals dominating the decision-making process. In the Delphi method, each member of the group of experts is surveyed for his or her opinion, typically in writing. The opinions are compiled and summarized, and each individual is given the opportunity to change his or her opinion after seeing the summary. This process is repeated until consensus is achieved.

   Recall, for example, the swimsuit production case presented throughout this chapter. In that case, a swimsuit manufacturer used a probabilistic forecast to make production and inventory decisions. This forecast consisted of several scenarios, each with an assigned probability of occurring. In all likelihood, the marketing department used one or more of the judgment methods listed above to develop this probabilistic forecast.

3.7.2 Market Research Methods

Market testing and **market surveys** can be valuable tools for developing forecasts, particularly of newly introduced products. In market testing, focus groups of potential customers are assembled and tested for their response to products, and this response is extrapolated to the entire market to estimate the demand for products. Market surveys involve gathering these data from a variety of potential customers, typically through interviews, telephone-based surveys, and written surveys.

3.7.3 Time-Series Methods

Time-series methods use a variety of past data (that is, past values of the value being predicted) to estimate future data. There are a variety of techniques that are commonly used, each of which has different advantages and disadvantages. We explore the relationship between time-series forecasting methods and the bullwhip effect in Chapter 4. Below, we discuss some common time-series methods (see [113] for more details):

   Moving average. Each forecast is the average of some number of previous demand points. The key here is to select the number of points in the moving average so that the effect of irregularities in the data is minimized. See Chapter 4 for the impact of the moving average forecast on the bullwhip effect.

   Exponential smoothing. Each forecast is a weighted average of the previous forecast and the last demand point. Thus, this method is similar to the moving average, except that it is a weighted average of all past data points, with more recent points receiving more weight.

Methods for data with trends. The previous two approaches assume that there is no trend in the data. If there is a trend, methods such as **regression analysis** and **Holt's method** are more useful, as they specifically account for trends in the data. Regression analysis fits a straight line to data points, while Holt's method combines the concept of exponential smoothing with the ability to follow a linear trend in the data.

Methods for seasonal data. A variety of techniques account for seasonal changes in demand. For example, **seasonal decomposition** methods remove the seasonal patterns from the data and then apply the approaches listed above on these edited data. Similarly, **Winter's method** is a version of exponential smoothing that accounts for trends and seasonality.

More complex methods. A variety of more complex methods have been proposed. However, these more complex methods are typically not used in practice, and indeed, there is some evidence that complex methods don't outperform more simple methods [113].

3.7.4 Causal Methods

Recall that in the time-series methods described above, forecasts are based entirely on previous values of the data being predicted. In contrast, causal methods generate forecasts based on data *other than the data being predicted*. More specifically, the forecast is a function of some other pieces of data. For example, the causal sales forecast for the next quarter may be a function of inflation, GNP, the unemployment rate, the weather, or anything besides the sales in this quarter.

3.7.5 Selecting the Appropriate Forecasting Technique

With so many forecasting techniques available, which one is appropriate for a given situation? Chambers, Mullick, and Smith (CMS), in their seminal *Harvard Business Review* article [26], pose three questions that help with this decision:

- **What is the purpose of the forecast? How is it to be used?** If gross sales estimates are sufficient, a less complex technique may be appropriate, whereas if detailed estimates are required, more advanced techniques may be necessary.
- **What are the dynamics of the system for which the forecast will be made?** Is the system sensitive to the type of economic data that would indicate that a causal model makes sense? Is the demand seasonal, or trending upwards or downwards? All of these impact the choice of forecasting tool.
- **How important is the past in estimating the future?** If the past is very important, time-series methods make sense. If significant systemwide changes render the past less important, judgment or market research methods may be indicated.

CMS also point out that at different stages of the product life cycle, different forecast techniques are appropriate. In the product development phase, market research methods may indicate the potential sales of different products and designs. In the testing and introduction phases, additional market research may be valuable, and judgment methods can be useful for predicting future demand of the products. In the rapid growth phase of the product life cycle, time-series data may be the most valuable. Finally, once a product becomes mature, time-series analysis will be valuable, as will causal methods, which predict long-term sales performance based on estimates of economic data.

Finally, the quality of forecasts can frequently be improved by combining a variety of the techniques described in this section. Georgoff and Murdick observe that "the results of combined forecasts greatly surpass most individual projections, techniques, and analysis by experts." This is particularly true since it is generally difficult to tell *a priori* which of several available forecasting techniques will work best for a given situation.

SUMMARY

Matching supply and demand in the supply chain is a critical challenge. To reduce cost and provide the required service level, it is important to take into account inventory holding and setup costs, lead time, and forecast demand. Unfortunately, the so-called *first rule* of inventory management states that *forecast demand is always wrong*. Thus, a single number, forecast demand, is not enough when determining an effective inventory policy. Indeed, the inventory management strategies described in this chapter also take into account information about demand variability.

The *second rule* of inventory management is that *the longer the forecast horizon, the worse is the forecast.* This implies that the accuracy of weekly forecast decreases as the forecast horizon increases.

The *third rule* of inventory management is that *aggregate demand information is always more accurate than disaggregate data.* That is, aggregate demand data have much smaller variability. This is exactly the basis for the risk pooling concept that enables lower inventory level without affecting service level.

Of course, although forecasting has many weaknesses, it is important to develop a forecast that is as effective as possible. There are a variety of approaches that are useful for improving forecasts.

Finally, globally optimal inventory policies, in which the best possible policy for the entire supply chain is implemented, are the best course of action. Well-designed supply contracts frequently make this global optimization possible.

DISCUSSION QUESTIONS

1. How can firms cope with huge variability in customer demand?
2. What is the relationship between service and inventory levels?
3. What is the impact of lead time, and lead time variability, on inventory levels?
4. What factors should management consider when determining a target service level?
5. Consider the (s, S) policy analyzed in Section 3.2.5. Explain why the expected level of inventory before receiving the order is

$$z \times STD \times \sqrt{L}$$

while the expected level of inventory immediately after receiving the order is

$$Q + z \times STD \times \sqrt{L}$$

6. Consider the base-stock policy analyzed in Section 3.2.7. Explain why the expected level of inventory after receiving an order is equal to

$$r \times AVG + z \times STD \times \sqrt{r + L}$$

while the expected level of inventory before an order arrives is

$$z \times STD \times \sqrt{r + L}$$

7. Consider a supply chain consisting of a single manufacturing facility, a cross-dock, and two retail outlets. Items are shipped from the manufacturing facility to the cross-dock facility and from there to the retail outlets. Let L_1 be the lead time from the factory to the cross-dock facility and L_2 be the lead time from the cross-dock facility to each retail outlet. Let $L = L_1 + L_2$. In the analysis below, we fix L and vary L_1 and L_2.

   a. Compare the amount of safety stock in two systems, one in which lead time from the cross-dock facility to a retail outlet is zero (i.e., $L_1 = L$ and $L_2 = 0$) and a second system in which the lead time from the factory to the cross-dock facility is equal to zero (i.e., $L_1 = 0$ and $L_2 = L$).

   b. To reduce safety stock, should the cross-dock facility be closer to the factory or the retail outlets? For this purpose, analyze the impact of increasing L_1, and therefore decreasing L_2, on total safety stock.

8. Suppose you are selecting a supplier. Would you prefer a supplier with a short but highly variable delivery lead time or a supplier with a longer but less variable lead time?

9. Although we typically model inventory-related costs as either fixed or variable, in the real world the situation is more complex. Discuss some inventory-related costs that are fixed in the short term but may be considered variable if a longer time horizon is considered.

10. When is a model such as *economic lot sizing* model, which ignores randomness, useful?

11. What are the penalties of facing highly variable demand? Are there any advantages?

12. In this chapter, we discuss a variety of types of supply contracts, each of which can be used to coordinate the supply chain. What are the advantages and disadvantages of each type of contract? Why would you select one over the others?

13. In Example 3-6, we discuss the revenue-sharing contract between Blockbuster Video and the movie studios. This contract has been extremely profitable for both sides. Since economists have explored revenue-sharing contracts for many years, why do you think Blockbuster and the movie studios took until 1998 to implement a revenue-sharing contract?

14. Give a specific example of risk pooling (a) across locations, (b) across time, and (c) across products.

15. When would you expect demand for a product in two stores to be positively correlated? When would you expect it to be negatively correlated?

16. Consider the first Walkman^{TM} model introduced by Sony. Discuss which forecasting approach would be most useful at the start, in the middle, and towards the end of the product life cycle. Now, consider a more recent Walkman model. How would your assessment of the appropriate forecasting techniques change?

17. **Technical question:** KLF Electronics is an American manufacturer of electronic equipments. The company has a single manufacturing facility in San Jose, California.

   KLF Electronics distributes its products through five regional warehouses located in Atlanta, Boston, Chicago, Dallas, and Los Angeles. In the current distribution system, the United States is partitioned into five major markets, each of which is served by a single regional warehouse. Customers, typically retail outlets, receive items directly from the regional warehouse in their market. That is, in the current distribution system, each customer is assigned to a single market and receives deliveries from one regional warehouse.

The warehouses receive items from the manufacturing facility. Typically, it takes about two weeks to satisfy an order placed by any of the regional warehouses. Currently, KLF provides their customers with a service level of about 90 percent.

In recent years, KLF has seen a significant increase in competition and huge pressure from their customers to improve service level and reduce costs. To improve service level and reduce costs, KLF would like to consider an alternative distribution strategy in which the five regional warehouses are replaced with a single, central warehouse that will be in charge of all customer orders. This warehouse should be one of the existing warehouses. The company CEO insists that whatever distribution strategy is used, KLF will design the strategy so that service level is increased to about 97 percent.

Answer the following three questions:

a. A detailed analysis of customer demand in the five market areas reveals that the demand in the five regions are very similar; that is, it is common that if weekly demand in one region is above average, so is the weekly demand in the other regions. How does this observation affect the attractiveness of the new system?

b. To perform a rigorous analysis, you have identified a typical product, Product A. Table 3-10 provides historical data that includes weekly demand for this product for the last 12 weeks in each of the market areas. An order (placed by a warehouse to the factory) costs $5,550 (per order), and holding inventory costs $1.25 per unit per week. In the current distribution system, the cost of transporting a product from the manufacturing facility to a warehouse is given in Table 3-11 (see the column "Inbound"). Table 3-11 also provides information about transportation cost per unit from each warehouse to the stores in its market area (see the column "Outbound"). Finally, Table 3-12 provides information about transportation costs per unit product from each existing regional warehouse to all other market areas, assuming this regional warehouse becomes the central warehouse.

TABLE 3-10

HISTORICAL DATA

Week	1	2	3	4	5	6	7	8	9	10	11	12
Atlanta	33	45	37	38	55	30	18	58	47	37	23	55
Boston	26	35	41	40	46	48	55	18	62	44	30	45
Chicago	44	34	22	55	48	72	62	28	27	95	35	45
Dallas	27	42	35	40	51	64	70	65	55	43	38	47
Los Angeles	32	43	54	40	46	74	40	35	45	38	48	56

TABLE 3-11

TRANSPORTATION COSTS PER UNIT PRODUCT

Warehouse	Inbound	Outbound
Atlanta	12	13
Boston	11.50	13
Chicago	11	13
Dallas	9	13
Los Angeles	7	13

TABLE 3-12

TRANSPORTATION COSTS PER UNIT IN CENTRALIZED SYSTEM

Warehouse	Atlanta	Boston	Chicago	Dallas	Los Angeles
Atlanta	13	14	14	15	17
Boston	14	13	8	15	17
Chicago	14	8	13	15	16
Dallas	15	15	15	13	8
Los Angeles	17	17	16	8	13

Suppose you are to compare the two systems for Product A only, what is your recommendation? To answer this question, you should compare costs and average inventory levels for the two strategies assuming demands occur according to the historical data. Also, you should determine which regional warehouse will be used as the centralized warehouse.

c. It is proposed that in the centralized distribution strategy, that is, the one with a single warehouse, products will be distributed using UPS Ground Service, which guarantees that products will arrive at the warehouse in three days (0.5 week). Of course, in this case, transportation cost for shipping a unit product from a manufacturing facility to the warehouse increases. In fact, in this case, transportation costs increase by 50 percent. Thus, for instance, shipping one unit from the manufacturing facility to Atlanta will cost $18. Would you recommend using this strategy? Explain your answer.

C A S E

Sport Obermeyer

Aspen, Colorado

Wally Obermeyer deftly balanced his office keys and a large printout of forecasting data as he wheeled his mountain bike through the front entrance of Sport Obermeyer's headquarters in Aspen, Colorado. It was a crisp November morning in 1992; Wally paused for just a moment to savor the fresh air and beauty of the surrounding mountains before dosing the door behind him.

Wally had arrived at work early to start one of the most critical tasks Sport Obermeyer, a fashion skiwear manufacturer, faced each year—committing to specific production quantities for each skiwear item the company would offer in the coming year's line. The task required carefully blending analysis, experience, intuition, and sheer speculation. This morning Sport Obermeyer would start to make firm commitments for producing its 1993–1994 line of fashion skiwear with scant information about how the market would react to the line. In fact, no clear indications had yet emerged about how end-consumers were responding to the company's current 1992–1993 line. Despite the attraction of waiting for market information, Wally knew that further procrastination would delay delivery to retailers and that late delivery would reduce the exposure consumers would have to Obermeyer products.

As usual, Obermeyer's new line offered strong designs, but the ultimate success of the line was highly dependent on how well the company was able

Source: Copyright © 1994 by the President and Fellows of Harvard College. This case was written by Janice H. Hammond and Ananth Raman of Harvard Business School.

to predict market response to different styles and colors. Feedback from retailers on the 1993–1994 line wouldn't begin to surface until the Las Vegas trade show next March, long after many of Obermeyer's products had entered production. Wally mused:

> How appropriate that our fate is always determined in Las Vegas. Like most fashion apparel manufacturers, we face a "fashion gamble" each year. Every fall we start manufacturing well in advance of the selling season, knowing full well that market trends may change in the meantime. Good gamblers calculate the odds before putting their money down. Similarly, whether we win or lose the fashion gamble on a particular ski parka depends on how accurately we predict each parka's salability.

Inaccurate forecasts of retailer demand had become a growing problem at Obermeyer: in recent years greater product variety and more intense competition had made accurate predictions increasingly difficult. Two scenarios resulted—both painful. On one hand, at the end of each season, the company was saddled with excess merchandise for those styles and colors that retailers had not purchased; styles with the worst selling records were sold at deep discounts, often well below their manufactured cost. On the other hand, the company frequently ran out of its most popular items; although popular products were clearly desirable, considerable income was lost each year because of the company's inability to predict which products would become best-sellers.

Wally sat down at his desk and reflected on the results of the day-long "Buying Committee" meeting he had organized the previous day. This year Wally had changed the company's usual practice of having the committee, which comprised six key Obermeyer managers, make production commitments based on the group's consensus. Instead, hoping to gather more complete information, he had asked each member independently to forecast retailer demand for each Obermeyer product. Now it was up to him to make use of the forecasts generated by the individuals in the group. He winced as he noted the discrepancies between different committee members' forecasts. How could he best use the results of yesterday's efforts to make appropriate production commitments for the coming year's line?

A second issue Wally faced was how to allocate production between factories in Hong Kong and China. Last year, almost a third of Obermeyer's parkas had been made in China, all by independent subcontractors in Shenzhuen. This year, the company planned to produce half of its parkas in China, continuing production by subcontractors, and starting production in a new plant in Lo Village, Guangdong. Labor costs in China were extremely low, yet Wally had some concerns about the quality and reliability of Chinese operations. He also knew that plants in China typically required larger minimum order quantities than those in Hong Kong and were subject to stringent quota restrictions by the U.S. government. How should he incorporate all of these differences into a well-founded decision about where to source each product?

Tsuen Wan, New Territories, Hong Kong

Raymond Tse, managing director, Obersport Limited, was anxiously awaiting Sport Obermeyer's orders for the 1993–1994 line. Once the orders arrived, he would have to translate them quickly into requirements for specific components and then place appropriate component orders with vendors. Any delay would cause problems: increased pressure on his relationships with vendors, overtime at his or his subcontractors' factories, or even late delivery to Sport Obermeyer.

Obersport Ltd. was a joint venture established in 1985 by Klaus Obermeyer and Raymond Tse to coordinate production of Sport Obermeyer products in the Far East. (See Figure 3-14.) Obersport was responsible for fabric and component sourcing for Sport Obermeyer's entire production in the Far East. The materials were then cut and sewn either in Raymond Tse's own "Alpine" factories or in independent subcontractors located in Hong Kong, Macau, and China. Raymond was owner and president of Alpine Ltd., which included skiwear manufacturing plants in Hong Kong as well as a recently established facility in China. Sport Obermeyer's orders represented about 80 percent of Alpine's annual production volume.

Lo Village, Guangdong, China

Raymond Tse and his cousin, Shiu Chuen Tse, gazed with pride and delight at the recently completed factory complex. Located among a wide expanse of rice paddies at the perimeter of Lo Village, the facility would eventually provide jobs, housing, and recreational facilities for more than 300 workers.

FIGURE 3-14 Map of Facilities (Hong Kong and Guangdong).

This facility was Alpine's first direct investment in manufacturing capacity in China.

Shiu Chuen had lived in Lo Village all of his life—the Tse family had resided there for generations. Raymond's parents, former landowners in the village, had moved to Hong Kong before Raymond was born, returning to the village for several years when Raymond was a young boy during the Japanese occupation of Hong Kong in World War II. In 1991, Raymond Tse had visited Lo Village for the first time in over 40 years. The villagers were delighted to see him. In addition to their personal joy at seeing Raymond, they hoped to convince him to bring some of his wealth and managerial talent to Lo Village. After discussions with people in the community, Raymond decided to build the factory, so far investing over US$1 million in the facility.

Working with Alpine's Hong Kong management, Shiu Chuen had hired 200 workers for the factory's first full year of operation. The workers had come from the local community as well as distant towns in neighboring provinces; most had now arrived and were in training in the plant. Shiu Chuen hoped he had planned appropriately for the orders Alpine's customers would assign to the plant this year; planning had been difficult since demand, worker skill levels, and productivity levels were all hard to predict.

SPORT OBERMEYER, LTD.

Sport Obermeyer's origins traced to 1947, when Klaus Obermeyer emigrated from Germany to the United States and started teaching at the Aspen Ski School. On frigid, snowy days Klaus found many of his students cold and miserable due to the impractical clothing they wore—garments both less protective and less stylish than those skiers wore in his native Germany.

During summer months, Klaus began to travel to Germany to find durable, high-performance ski clothing and equipment for his students. An engineer by training, Klaus also designed and introduced a variety of skiwear and ski equipment products; he was credited with making the first goose-down vest out of an old down comforter, for example, in the 1950s. In the early 1980s, he popularized the "ski brake," a simple device replacing cumbersome "run-away straps"; the brake kept skis that had fallen off skiers from plunging down the slopes. Over the years, Sport Obermeyer developed into a preeminent competitor in the U.S. skiwear market: estimated sales in 1992 were $32.8 million. The company held a commanding 45 percent share of the children's skiwear market and an 11 percent share of the adult skiwear market. Columbia Sportswear was a lower-price, high-volume-per-style competitor whose sales had increased rapidly during the previous three years. By 1992 Columbia had captured about 23 percent of the adult ski-jacket market.

Obermeyer offered a broad line of fashion ski apparel, including parkas, vests, ski suits, shells, ski pants, sweaters, turtlenecks, and accessories. Parkas were considered the most critical design component of a collection; the other garments were fashioned to match their style and color.

Obermeyer products were offered in five different "genders": men's, women's, boys', girls', and preschoolers'. The company segmented each "gender" market according to price, type of skier, and how "fashion-forward" the market was. For example, the company divided its adult male customers into four types, dubbed Fred, Rex, Biege, and Klausie. A Fred was the most conservative of the four types; Freds had a tendency to buy basic styles and colors and were likely to wear the same outfit over multiple seasons. High-tech Rex was an affluent, image-conscious skier who liked to sport the latest technologies in fabrics, features, and ski equipment. In contrast, Biege was a hard-core mountaineering-type skier who placed technical performance above all else and shunned any nonfunctional design elements. A Klausie was a flamboyant, high-profile skier or snowboarder who wore the latest styles, often in bright colors such as neon pink or lime green.

Within each "gender," numerous styles were offered, each in several colors and a range of sizes. Figure 3-15 shows how the variety of Obermeyer's women's parkas had changed over time, including the total number of stockkeeping units Obermeyer offered during the preceding 16-year period, as well as the average number of styles, colors per style, and sizes per style-color combination offered.

Obermeyer competed by offering an excellent price/value relationship, where value was defined as both functionality and style, and targeted the middle to high end of the skiwear market. Unlike some of its competitors who made outerwear for both skiing and casual "street wear," Obermeyer sold the vast majority (over 85 percent) of its products to customers for use while skiing. Functionality was critical to the serious skier: products had to be warm and waterproof, yet not constrain the skier's ability to move his or her arms and legs freely.

Management believed that the effective implementation of its product strategy relied on several logistics-related activities, including delivering matching collections of products to retailers at the same time (to allow consumers to view and purchase coordinated items at the same time) and delivering products to retail stores early in the selling season (to maximize the number of "squarefootage days" products were available at retail).

Management Approach

Throughout the company's history, Klaus Obermeyer had been actively involved in company management. Klaus believed that a company should run "free of tension." Klaus's personal philosophy was at the core of his management style; in both his personal life and his professional life he sought to "achieve harmony." He observed:

> We're blending with the forces of the market rather than opposing them. This leads to conflict resolution. If you oppose a force, you get conflict escalation. It is not money, it is not possessions, it is not market share. It is to be at peace with your surroundings.

In accordance with his philosophy, Klaus believed that the skiwear industry should be left to people who were "comfortable with an uncertain bottom line." Klaus's management style emphasized trust in people and providing value to customers. He believed many aspects of the business fell into the artistic realm; in making decisions, one should be guided by one's judgment and intuition. In his joint venture with Raymond Tse, Klaus relied on his trust of Raymond and had always left production and investment decisions to Raymond.

Although Klaus was the "heart and soul" of the company, other members of the family had played key roles in the company's growth as well. Klaus's wife, Nome, a successful designer, was actively involved in developing new products for the company. In Klaus's judgment, Nome had a "feel" for fashion—Klaus

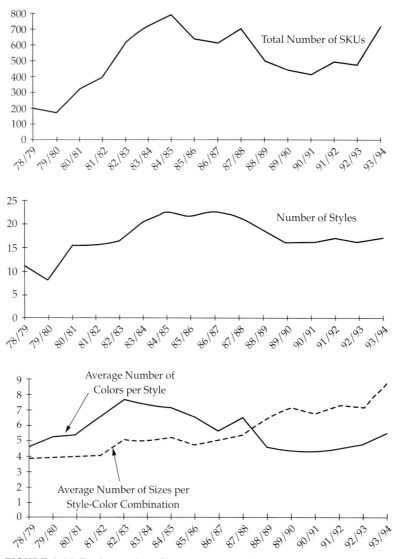

FIGURE 3-15 Product variety, Obermeyer women's parkas.
Note:
An example of a "style" is a Stardust parka.
An example of a "style-color combination" is a red Stardust parka.
An example of an "SKU" (stockkeeping unit) is a size 8, petite, red Stardust parka.

had relied heavily on her judgment in assessing the relative popularity of various designs.

In recent years, Klaus's son Wally had become actively involved in managing the company's internal operations. After completing high school, Wally combined working part time for the company with ski-patrolling on Aspen Mountain for six years, before entering college in 1980. After graduating from the Harvard Business School in 1986, Wally initially

focused his efforts on developing a hydro-electric power-generating plant in Colorado. By 1989, the power plant was established and required less day-to-day involvement. He joined Sport Obermeyer full time in 1989 as vice president.

As is often the case, the company founder and his MBA son had different management approaches: Wally relied more heavily on formal data-gathering and analytical techniques, whereas Klaus took a more intuitive style that was heavily informed by his extensive industry experience.

THE ORDER CYCLE

Sport Obermeyer sold its products primarily through specialty ski-retail stores, located either in urban areas or near ski resorts. Obermeyer also served a few large department stores (including Nordstrom) and direct mail retailers (including REI). In the United States, most retail sales of skiwear occurred between September and January, with peak sales occurring in December and January. Most retailers requested full delivery of their orders prior to the start of the retail season; Sport Obermeyer attempted to deliver coordinated collections of its merchandise into retail stores by early September. Nearly two years of planning and production activity took place prior to the actual sale of products to consumers. (See Table 3-13.)

The Design Process

The design process for the 1993–1994 line began in February 1992, when Obermeyer's design team and senior management attended the annual international outdoorswear show in Munich, Germany, where they viewed current European offerings. "Europe is more fashion-forward than the United States," Klaus noted. "Current European styles are often good indicators of future American fashions." In addition, each year, a major trade show for ski equipment and apparel was held in Las Vegas. The March 1992 Las Vegas show had provided additional input to the design process for the 1993–1994 line. By May 1992, the design concepts were finalized; sketches were sent to Obersport for prototype production in July. Prototypes were usually made from leftover fabric from the previous year since the prototype garments would be used only internally by Obermeyer management for decision-making purposes. Obermeyer refined the designs based on the prototypes and finalized designs by September 1992.

Sample Production

As soon as designs were finalized, Obersport began production of sample garments—small quantities of each style-color combination for the sales force to show to retailers. In contrast to prototypes, samples were made with the actual fabric to be used for final production; dyeing and printing subcontractors were willing to process small material batches for sample-making purposes. Sales representatives started to show samples to retailers during the week-long Las Vegas show, typically held in March, and then took them to retail sites throughout the rest of the spring.

Raw Material Sourcing and Production

Concurrent with sample production, Obersport determined fabric and component requirements for Obermeyer's initial production order (typically about half of Obermeyer's annual production) based on Obermeyer's bills of material. It was important that Obersport place dyeing/printing instructions and component orders quickly since some suppliers' lead times were as long as 90 days. Cutting and sewing of Obermeyer's first production order would begin in February 1993.

Retailer Ordering Process

During the Las Vegas trade show, most retailers placed their orders; Obermeyer usually received orders representing 80 percent of its annual volume by the week following the Las Vegas show. With this information in hand, Obermeyer could forecast its total demand with great accuracy (see Figure 3-16). After completing its forecast, Obermeyer placed its second and final production order. The remainder of retailers' regular (nonreplenishment) orders were received in April and May. As noted below, retailers also placed replenishment orders for popular items during the peak retail sales season.

Shipment to Obermeyer Warehouse

During June and July, Obermeyer garments were transported by ship from Obersport's Hong Kong warehouse to Seattle, from which they were trucked to Obermeyer's Denver warehouse. (Shipment took approximately six weeks.) Most goods produced in August were air-shipped to Denver to ensure timely delivery to retailers. In addition, for goods manufactured in China, air freighting was often essential due to strict quota restrictions in certain product categories. The U.S. government limited the number of units that could be imported from China into the United States. Government officials at the U.S. port of entry reviewed imports; products violating quota restrictions were sent back to the country of origin. Since quota restrictions were imposed on the total amount of a product category all companies imported from China, individual companies often rushed to get

TABLE 3-13

PLANNING AND PRODUCTION CYCLE, OBERMEYER 1993–1994 LINE

Month	Design activities	Order receipt and production planning	Materials management	Production	Retail activities
Jan 92					
Feb 92	Design process begins				
Mar 92	Las Vegas show for 92–93.				
Apr 92					
May 92	Concepts finalized				
Jun 92					
Jul 92	Sketches sent to Obersport		Order greige fabric		
Aug 92				Prototype production	
Sep 92	Designs finalized			Prototype production	
Oct 92				Sample production	
Nov 92		Place *first* production order with Obersport	Receive first order • Calculate fabric and component requirements • Order components • Place print/dye orders	Sample production	
Dec 92				Sample production	
Jan 93			Chinese New Year vac.	Chinese New Year vac.	
Feb 93				Full-scale production	
Mar 93		Las Vegas Show for 93–94 line (80% of retailers' initial orders received) Place *second* production order with Obersport	Receive second order • Calculate fabric and component requirements • Order components • Place print/dye orders	Full-scale production	
Apr 93		Additional retailer orders received		Full-scale production	
May 93		Additional retailer orders received		Full-scale production	
Jun 93		Additional retailer orders received		Full-scale production Ship finished goods	
Jul 93				Full-scale production Ship finished goods	
Aug 93				Full-scale produciton Air freight finished goods	93–94 line delivered to retail
Sep 93					Retail selling period
Oct 93					Retail selling period
Nov 93					Retail selling period
Dec 93		Retailer replenishment orders received			Peak retail selling period
Jan 94		Retailer replenishment orders received			Peak retail selling period
Feb 94		Retailer replenishment orders received			Retail selling period
Mar 94					Retail selling period
Apr 94					Retail selling period

Initial Forecast

Each data point represents the forecast and actual season sales for a particular parka (at the style-color level). For example, parka A had an initial forecast of 2,500 units and season sales of 510 units.

Updated Forecast, Incorporating First 20% of Sales Data

After observing 20% of demand, the revised forecast for parka A was 575 units.

Final Forecast, Incorporating First 80% of Sales Data

After observing 80% of demand, the final forecast for parka A was 500 units.

FIGURE 3-16 How demand forecasts improve with increasing information.

their products into the country before other firms had "used up" the available quota.

Shipment to Retail; Retail Replenishment Orders

Toward the end of August, Obermeyer shipped orders to retailers via small-package carriers such as UPS and RPS. Retail sales built gradually during September, October, and November, peaking in December and January. By December or January, retailers who identified items of which they expected to sell more than they currently had in stock often requested replenishment of those items from Obermeyer. This demand was filled if Obermeyer had the item in stock.

By February Obermeyer started to offer replenishment items to retailers at a discount. Similarly, retailers started marking down prices on remaining stock in an attempt to clear their shelves by the end of the season. As the season progressed, retailers offered deeper discounts; items remaining at the end of the season were held over to the following year and sold at a loss. Obermeyer used a variety of methods to liquidate inventory at year-end, including selling large shipping containers of garments well below manufacturing cost to markets in South America and engaging in barter trade (for example, trading parkas in lieu of money for products or services used by the company, such as hotel rooms or air flights).

THE SUPPLY CHAIN

Obermeyer sourced most of its outerwear products through Obersport. (See Figure 3-17.) In recent years, Wally had worked with Obersport to "pre-position" (purchase prior to the season and hold in inventory) greige fabric[3] as part of a wider effort to cope with manufacturing lead times. To preposition the fabric, Obermeyer would contract with fabric suppliers to manufacture a specified amount of fabric of a given type each month; Obermeyer would later specify how it wanted the fabric to be dyed and/or printed.

Obermeyer had to take possession of all fabric it contracted for, whether or not it was actually needed. Different types of fabrics were purchased for use as shell (outer) fabric and lining fabric. Approximately 10 types of shell fabrics were required each year. Obersport purchased shell fabric from vendors in the United States, Japan, Korea, Germany, Austria, Taiwan, and Switzerland. Lining fabric was sourced primarily from Korea and Taiwan. (Table 3-14 provides information on lead times, variety, and other aspects of component sourcing.)

Each greige fabric would later be dyed and/or printed as necessary; each shell fabric was typically offered in 8 to 12 colors and prints. Prior to the start of the season, Obersport would work with its subcontractors to prepare a small batch for each color that was required in a given fabric. The preparation of each such "lab-dip" took two weeks; the procedure at times had to be repeated if the quality of the lab-dip was not found to be satisfactory by Obermeyer managers or designers. In addition, Obersport worked with its printing subcontractors to develop "screens" that would be used to print patterns on fabric. This procedure took six weeks.

Most other tasks were performed only after the production quantities planned by Sport Obermeyer were known. Immediately after receiving production instructions from Sport Obermeyer, Obersport asked subcontractors to dye or print fabric. A typical adult's parka, for example, required 2.25 to 2.5 yards of 60" width shell fabric. The consumption of fabric was slightly less for kids' or preschoolers' parkas. Dyeing subcontractors required a lead time of 45–60 days and a minimum order quantity of 1,000 yards. Printing subcontractors required a minimum of 3,000 yards; printing lead times were also 45–50 days.

Obermeyer products used insulation materials and a variety of other components in addition to shell and lining fabric. Each parka, for example, needed around two yards of insulation material. Insulation materials (with the exception of goose-down insulation,

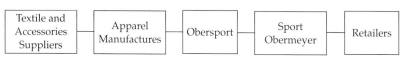

FIGURE 3-17 The supply chain.

---

[3]Greige fabric is a fabric that has been woven or knitted but not yet dyed or printed.

TABLE 3-14

PROCUREMENT INFORMATION FOR OBERMEYER'S PARKA COMPONENTS

Component	Variety	Country of origin	Procurement lead time	Minimums	Usage per parka	Avg. % of total parka material cost
Greige Shell Fabric	10	Japan, USA, Switzerland, Germany, Austria, Korea, Taiwan	45–90 days	5,000–10,000 yards	2.2–2.5 yards per adult parka 1.5–2 yards per child's parka	30
Finishing of Shell Fabric	8–12 color-prints per fabric	Finishing takes place in country of origin (see above)	Dyeing or Printing: 45–60 days	Dyeing: 1,000 yards Printing: 3,000 yards per design, at least 1,000 yards per color in any design	2.25–2.5 yards per adult parka 1.5–2 yards per child's parka	13
Finished Lining Fabric	6	Nylon: Korea, Taiwan Fleece: Korea, Taiwan, USA	45–60 days	600–1,000 yards	2–2.25 yards per adult parka 1.25–1.75 yards per child's parka	13
Insulation	3–4 different weights used (from 80–240 grams/meter)	Hong Kong, Korea, Taiwan, China	2–3 weeks	50–100 yards	~2 yards per adult parka ~1.2–1.5 yards per child's parka	16
Zippers	400 standard tape colors 4 teeth gauges 4–5 teeth colors 2–3 teeth materials 5–6 slider types	Hong Kong, Japan	Standard (from Hong Kong): 60 days Custom (from Japan): 90+ days,	500 yards (standard colors) 1,000 yards (custom colors)	~1 yard	12
Thread	80 colors	Hong Kong	30 days	5,000 yards	2,000–3,000 yards	2
Logo Patches, Drawcords, Hang Tags, etc.	various	Mostly from Hong Kong	15–30 days	various	various	10
Snaps (undyed)	10	Germany, Italy, Hong Kong	1–2 months	1,000 pieces	5–10 pieces	3
Dyeing of Snaps	50 colors	Hong Kong	15–30 days	1,000 pieces per color	5–10 pieces	1
						100

which was purchased in China and Korea) were purchased from DuPont, whose licensees in Hong Kong, Taiwan, Korea, and China could provide them within two weeks. At the beginning of each year, Obersport gave DuPont an estimate of its annual requirement for each type of insulation.

Obersport also had to ensure the availability of a variety of other components such as D-rings, buckles, snaps, buttons, zippers, pull-strings with attached castings, and various labels and tags. Buckles, D-rings, pull-strings, and buttons were procured locally in Hong Kong and had a 15- to 30-day lead time. Many snaps were purchased from German vendors; since snap lead times were long, Obersport kept an inventory of snaps and dyed them locally as needed. Labels and tags had short lead times and were relatively inexpensive; Obersport generally carried excess stock of these materials.

Most zippers were purchased from YKK, a large Japanese zipper manufacturer. Obersport used a wide variety of zipper types each year. Zippers varied by length, tape color, and slider shape as well as the gauge, color, and material of the zipper teeth. Approximately 60 percent of Obersport's zipper requirements were sourced from YKK's Hong Kong factory, where standard zippers were manufactured. The lead time for these zippers was 60 days. The remainder was nonstandard zippers, which were sourced from Japan with at least 90-day lead times—sometimes longer. YKK required a minimum order quantity of 500 yards if the dyeing color was a standard color from its catalog; if not, the minimum order quantity was 1,000 yards. All production materials were received by Obersport; materials for any given style were then collected and dispatched to the factory where the particular style was to be cut and sewn. Obermeyer products were produced in a number of different factories in Hong Kong and China.

Cut and Sew

A typical Obermeyer product required many cutting and sewing steps. (Table 3-15 shows the sequence of sewing operations for the Rococo parka.) The allocation of operations to workers differed from one factory to another depending on the workers' level of skill and the degree of worker cross-training. Workers in Hong Kong worked about 50 percent faster than their Chinese counterparts. In addition to being more highly skilled, Hong Kong workers were typically trained in a broader range of tasks. Thus, a

parka line in Hong Kong that required 10 workers to complete all operations might require 40 workers in China. Longer production lines in China led to greater imbalance in these lines; hence, a Hong Kong sewer's actual output during a given period of time was nearly twice that of a Chinese worker. (See Table 3-16 for a comparison of Hong Kong and China operations. The cost components of the Rococo parka, which was produced in Hong Kong, are shown in Table 3-17. Table 3-18 shows the estimated cost of producing the Rococo in China. Obermeyer sold the Rococo parka to retailers at a wholesale price of $112.50; retailers then priced the parka at $225.)

Workers were paid on a piece-rate basis in both China and Hong Kong: the piece rate was calculated to be consistent with competitive wage rates in the respective communities. Wages in China were much lower than in Hong Kong; an average sewer in a Guangdong sewing factory earned US$0.16 per hour compared with US$3.84 per hour in the Alpine factory in Hong Kong.

Workers in Hong Kong were also able to ramp up production faster than the Chinese workers. This ability, coupled with shorter production lines, enabled the Hong Kong factory to produce smaller order quantities efficiently. For parkas, the minimum production quantity for a style was 1,200 units in China and 600 units in Hong Kong.

Obermeyer produced about 200,000 parkas each year. The maximum capacity available to the company for cutting and sewing was 30,000 units a month; this included the production capacity at all factories available to make Sport Obermeyer products.

Obersport was responsible for monitoring production and quality at all subcontractor factories. Workers from Obersport inspected randomly selected pieces from each subcontractor's production before the units were shipped to the United States.

PRODUCTION PLANNING

Wally's immediate concern was to determine an appropriate production commitment for the first half of Obermeyer's projected demand for the 1993–1994 season. He had estimated that Obermeyer earned 24 percent of wholesale price (pre-tax) on each parka it sold, and that units left unsold at the end of the season were sold at a loss that averaged 8 percent of wholesale price. Thus, for example, on a parka style such as the Rococo, which had a wholesale selling

TABLE 3-15

SAMPLE—PARKA ASSEMBLY OPERATIONS FOR THE ROCOCO WOMEN'S PARKA

	HK$/Piece	Operation
1	$0.05	Male belt loop ($\times$1).
2	$0.20	Sew front shoulder seam with invisible stitching. Quilt all over: lining ($\times$5), front placket ($\times$1), and collar ($\times$2).
3	$0.50	Invisible-stitch front bellow facing ($\times$2).
4	$0.50	Double top-stitch front bellow facing ($\times$2).
5	$0.70	Zig-zag stitch front bellow seam ($\times$2).
6	$2.40	Set double-jetted zipped pocket ($\times$2) and insert D-ring ($\times$1).
7	$0.25	Five-stitch overlock pocket bag ($\times$2).
8	$1.00	Invisible-stitch the bottom facing of bellow, sew front shoulder pleat ($\times$2), insert front body facing.
9	$0.40	$\frac{1}{4}''$ double stitch the front and back shoulder seam ($\times$4).
10	$0.30	Single top stitch (the middle of double top-stitching) the front and back shoulder seam ($\times$4).
11	$4.50	Turn over the body and attach collar, sew zipper; invisible-stitch bottom and sleeve opening, leave a small opening at the bottom of left front zipper.
12	$1.00	$\frac{1}{4}''$ double stitch the front zipper seam from bottom to collar top.
13	$0.50	Invisible stitch the back bellow seam ($\times$2).
14	$0.50	$\frac{1}{4}''$ double stitch the back bellow seam.
15	$0.70	Zig-zag stitch back bellow seam ($\times$2).
16	$1.00	Join under facing of back bellow seam with invisible stitching ($\times$2). Join front and back shoulder seam with invisible stitching ($\times$4).
17	$0.50	Close side seam with invisible stitching, match seaming ($\times$6).
18	$0.25	Three-stitch overlook the side seam.
19	$1.00	Sew sleeve opening, bottom hem with invisible stitching.
20	$0.80	Invisible stitch front placket seam, then $\frac{1}{4}''$ double top-stitch the placket seam.
21	$1.10	Invisible stitch the sleeve seam ($\times$4); invisible stitch sleeve panel seam, sew pleats at sleeve panel seam ($\times$2).
22	$0.90	$\frac{1}{4}''$ double top-stitch raglan sleeve seam and sleeve panel seam ($\times$6).
23	$0.70	Single lockstitch raglan sleeve seam and sleeve panel seam, double stitch the center of sleeve panel seam ($\times$6).
24	$0.70	Invisible stitch the armhole seam ($\times$2), match the notch of armhole seam ($\times$2).
25	$0.50	Double stitch armhole seam ($\times$2).
26	$0.40	Single lockstitch raglan sleeve seam and sleeve panel seat, double stitch the center of sleeve panel seam ($\times$6).
27	$0.60	Single lockstitch to close bottom hem facing ($\times$1), insert the drawstring to bottom hem.
28	$0.60	Invisible stitch sleeve opening, insert/sew elastic to sleeve opening ($\times$2).
29	$1.00	Sew collar facing ($\times$1), invisible stitch the collar top, close bottom of collar, insert belt loop, change thread.
30	$0.25	$\frac{1}{4}''$ double needle stitch at middle part of placket ($\times$1).
31	$0.35	Zig-zag stitch at the center of double needle stitch at placket ($\times$1).
32	$0.80	Running stitch to close the end of filled placket ($\times$1).
33	$0.20	Sew main label, and insert the label at side seam, and then sew size label.
34	$0.80	Sew the inside pocket: pocket with zipper at left, pocket with velcro at right.
35	$0.20	Set front facing with $\frac{1}{16}''$ edge stitching ($\times$2).
36	$1.70	3 stitch overlock lining pocket bag ($\times$2).
37	$1.60	Sew triangular stitching at ends of zipper facing, invisible stitch at zipper facing seam, turn out and $\frac{1}{16}''$ edge-stitching ($\times$1).
38	$1.30	Sew 13 top stitching at the lining body.
39	$1.40	Five stitch overlock the lining body.
40	$0.80	Set shoulder pad ($\times$2).

Total Average Labor Cost for the Rococo parka = HK$78. (Column does not add—some operations were performed multiple times to completely assemble one parka.)
*For this parka, the subcomponents described in steps 1 and 2 were completed by outside subcontractors.

TABLE 3-16

COMPARISON OF OPERATIONS IN HONG KONG AND CHINA

Topic	Hong Kong	China
Hourly Wage	HK$30	RMB 0.91
Exchange Rate	HK$7.8 = US$1	RMB (Renminbi) 5.7 = US$1
Working Hours	8 hours/day, 6 days/week	9 hours/day, 6.5 days/week
	⇒ Total = 48 hours/week	⇒ Total = 58.5 hours/week
	Maximum overtime allowed = 200 hours/year	During peak production periods, workers work 13 hours/day, 6.5 days/week
Weekly (Nonpeak) Output/Worker	19 parkas	12 parkas
Actual labor content per parka (including repair work)	~2.35 hours	~3.6 hours
Paid labor time per parka (including repair work)	~2.53 hours/parka	~4.88 hours/parka
Labor Cost/Garment	HK$75.6	RMB 4.45
Line Configuration	10–12 people/line	40 people/line
Training	Cross-trained	Trained for single operation only
Minimum Order Quantity	600 units in same style	1,200 units in same style
Repair Rate	1–2%	~10%

Challenges	• Wage Rate
	• Workforce:
	  • Low unemployment (~2%)
	  • Younger workers prefer office jobs
		• Workforce:
		  • Less quality and cleanliness conscious
		  • Training requirements

TABLE 3-17

COST INFORMATION FOR ROCOCO PARKA (MADE IN HONG KONG)

Obermeyer Landed Cost	
Cost FOB Obersport[a]	$49.90
Agent's Fee (to Obersport, 7%)	$3.49
Freight (Ocean Carrier)[b]	$1.40
Duty, Insurance, and Miscellaneous	$5.29
Total Landed Cost	**$60.08**
Cost FOB Obersport:	
Material	$30.00
Labor	$10.00
Hong Kong Quota, Obersport Profit and Overhead	$9.90
Total	$49.90

All figures in US Dollars.
[a]FOB (free on board) Obersport means that Obermeyer paid for freight and owned the products while they were in-transit.
[b]If transportation by air, cost would be approximately $5.00 per parka.

price of $112.50, Obermeyer's expected profit on each parka sold was approximately 24%($112.50) = $27, and its expected loss on each parka left unsold was approximately 8%($112.50) = $9.

A Sample Problem

To build his intuition about how to make production decisions, he decided to look at a smaller version of the company's problem. He looked at the Buying

TABLE 3-18

ESTIMATED COST INFORMATION FOR ROCOCO PARKA (IF ASSEMBLED IN CHINA)

Obermeyer Landed Cost

Cost FOB Obersport[a]	$42.64
Agent's Fee (to Obersport, 7%)	$2.98
Freight (Ocean Carrier)[b]	$1.40
Duty, Insurance, and Miscellaneous	$4.90
Total Landed Cost	**$51.92**

Cost FOB Obersport:

Material	$30.00
Labor	$0.78
Transportation within China and China Overhead	$2.00
China Quota, Obersport Profit and Overhead	$9.90
Total	$42.68

All figures in US Dollars.
[a]FOB (free on board) Obersport means that Obermeyer paid for freight and owned the products while they were in-transit.
[b]If transportation by air, cost would be approximately $5.00 per parka.

TABLE 3-19

SAMPLE BUYING COMMITTEE FORECASTS, 10 STYLES OF WOMEN'S PARKAS

Style	Price[a]	Individual forecasts						Average forecast	Standard deviation	2×standard deviation
		Laura	Carolyn	Greg	Wendy	Tom	Wally			
Gail	$110	900	1,000	900	1,300	800	1,200	1,017	194	388
Isis	$99	800	700	1,000	1,600	950	1,200	1,042	323	646
Entice	$80	1,200	1,600	1,500	1,550	950	1,350	1,358	248	496
Assault	$90	2,500	1,900	2,700	2,450	2,800	2,800	2,525	340	680
Teri	$123	800	900	1,000	1,100	950	1,850	1,100	381	762
Electra	$173	2,500	1,900	1,900	2,800	1,800	2,000	2,150	404	807
Stephanie	$133	600	900	1,000	1,100	950	2,125	1,113	524	1,048
Seduced	$73	4,600	4,300	3,900	4,000	4,300	3,000	4,017	556	1,113
Anita	$93	4,400	3,300	3,500	1,500	4,200	2,875	3,296	1,047	2,094
Daphne	$148	1,700	3,500	2,600	2,600	2,300	1,600	2,383	697	1,394
Totals		20,000	20,000	20,000	20,000	20,000	20,000	20,000		

[a] Obermeyer's wholesale price.
Note:
Laura Kornashiewicz was marketing director; Carolyn Gray was customer service manager; Greg Hunter was production manager; Wendy Hemphill was production Coordinator; Tom Tweed was a sales representative; Wally Obermeyer was vice president.

Committee's forecasts for the sample of 10 women's parkas[4] (see Table 3-19.) Since these 10 styles represented about 10 percent of Obermeyer's total demand, to make this smaller version representative of the larger problem, he assumed he had cutting and sewing capacity of 3,000 units per month (10 percent of actual capacity) during the seven-month production period.

Using these assumptions, Wally needed to commit 10,000 units for the first phase of production. The remaining 10,000 units could be deferred until after the Las Vegas show.

Wally studied the Buying Committee's forecasts, wondering how he could estimate the risk associated with early production of each style. Was there

---

[4]When the Buying Committee convened, Wally had asked each member to forecast sales so that each member's total forecast summed to a specified aggregate figure (for parkas, 200,000 units). Similarly, the forecasts in the sample problem had been scaled to sum to 20,000 units.

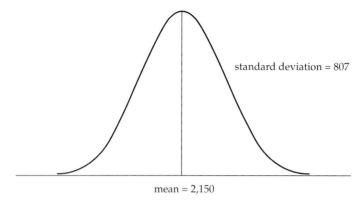

standard deviation = 807

mean = 2,150

FIGURE 3-18 Forecast distribution for the Electra parka.

some way he could use the differences among each member's forecast as a measure of demand uncertainty? An examination of demand from previous years indicated that forecast accuracy was the highest for those styles for which the Buying Committee had the highest level of agreement. (Technically, he found that the standard deviation of demand for a style was approximately twice the standard deviation of the Buying Committee's forecasts for that style.) With this in mind, he constructed a forecast distribution for each style as a normal random variable with the mean equal to the average of the Buying Committee member's forecasts and standard deviation twice that of the Buying Committee's forecasts (see Figure 3-18).

Where to Produce

To complete the planning decision, Wally would also need to decide which styles to make in Hong Kong and which would be better to produce in China. This year, Obermeyer expected to produce about half of all its products in China. Longer term, Wally wondered whether producing in China would constrain Obermeyer's ability to manage production and inventory risks. Would China's larger minimum order sizes limit the company's ability to increase the range of products it offered or to manage inventory risk? Was Obermeyer's trend toward increased production in

China too risky given the uncertainty in China's trade relationship with the United States?

CASE DISCUSSION QUESTIONS

1. Using the sample data given in Table 3-19, make a recommendation for how many units of each style Wally should make during the initial phase of production. Assume that all of the 10 styles in the sample problem are made in Hong Kong and that Wally's initial production commitment must be at least 10,000 units. Ignore price differences among styles in your initial analysis.
2. Can you come up with a measure of risk associated with your ordering policy? This measure should be quantifiable.
3. Repeat your methodology and assume now that all 10 styles are made in China. What is the difference (if any) between the two initial production commitments?
4. What operational changes would you recommend to Wally to improve performance?
5. How should Wally think (both short-term and long-term) about sourcing in Hong Kong versus China? What kind of sourcing policy do you recommend?

CHAPTER 4

The Value of Information

Barilla SpA (A)

Giorgio Maggiali was becoming increasingly frustrated. As director of logistics for the world's largest pasta producer, Barilla SpA (Societa per Azioni translates as "Society for Stockholders" and is interpreted as "Inc."), Maggiali was acutely aware of the growing burden that demand fluctuations imposed on the company's manufacturing and distribution system. Since his appointment in 1988 as Director of Logistics, he had been trying to make headway on an innovative idea proposed by Brando Vitali, who had served as Barilla's director of logistics before Maggiali. The idea, which Vitali called just-in-time distribution (JITD), was modeled after the popular "just-in-time" manufacturing concept. In essence, Vitali proposed that, rather than follow the traditional practice of delivering product to Barilla's distributors on the basis of whatever orders those distributors placed with the company, Barilla's own logistics organization would instead specify the "appropriate" delivery quantities—those that would more effectively meet the end consumer's needs yet also would distribute the workload on Barilla's manufacturing and logistics systems more evenly.

For two years Maggiali, a strong supporter of Vitali's proposal, had tried to implement the idea, but now, in the spring of 1990, little progress had been made. It seemed that Barilla's customers were simply unwilling to give up their authority to place orders as they pleased; some were even reluctant to provide the detailed sales data upon which Barilla could make delivery decisions and improve its demand forecasts. Perhaps more disconcerting was the internal resistance from Barilla's own sales and marketing organizations, which saw the concept as infeasible or dangerous, or both. Perhaps it was time to discard the idea as simply unworkable. If not, how might Maggiali increase the chances that the idea would be accepted?

COMPANY BACKGROUND

Barilla was founded in 1875 when Pietro Barilla opened a small shop in Parma, Italy, on Via Vittorio Emanuele. Adjoining the shop was the small "laboratory" Pietro used to make the pasta and bread products he sold in his store. Pietro's son Ricardo led the company through a significant period of growth and, in the 1940s, passed the company to his own sons, Pietro and Gianni. Over time Barilla evolved from its modest beginnings into a large, vertically integrated corporation with flour mills, pasta plants, and bakery-product factories located throughout Italy.

In a crowded field of more than 2,000 Italian pasta manufacturers, Pietro and Gianni Barilla differentiated their company with a high-quality product supported by innovative marketing programs. Barilla

Source: Copyright © 1994 by the President and Fellows of Harvard College. This case was written by Janice H. Hammond of Harvard Business School.

revolutionized the Italian pasta industry's market-ing practices by creating a strong brand name and image for its pasta, selling pasta in a sealed card-board box with a recognizable color pattern rather than in bulk, and investing in large-scale advertis-ing programs. In 1968, to support the double-digit sales growth the company had experienced during the 1960s, Pietro and Gianni Barilla began construction of a 125-million-square-meter state-of-the-art pasta plant in Pedrignano, a rural town 5 km outside Parma.

The cost of this massive facility—the largest and most technologically advanced pasta plant in the world—drove the Barillas deeply into debt. In 1971 the brothers sold the company to the U.S. multi-national firm W. R. Grace, Inc. Grace brought additional capital investment and professional man-agement practices to the company and launched an important new Mulino Bianco ("White Mill") line of bakery products. Throughout the 1970s, facing diffi-cult economic conditions and new Italian legislation that both capped retail pasta prices and increased the cost-of-living allowances for employees, Grace strug-gled to make its Barilla acquisition pay off. In 1979, Grace sold the company back to Pietro Barilla, who by then had secured the necessary funds to purchase it.

The capital investments and organizational changes that Grace had brought to Barilla, combined with improving market conditions, helped Pietro Barilla launch a successful return to the company. During the 1980s, Barilla enjoyed an annual growth rate of over 21 percent (see Table 4-1). Growth was realized through the expansion of existing businesses, both in Italy and other European countries, as well as through acquisition of new, related businesses.

By 1990 Barilla had become the largest pasta manufacturer in the world, making 35 percent of the pasta sold in Italy and 22 percent of the pasta sold in Europe. Barilla's share in Italy comprised its three brands: The traditional Barilla brand represented 32 percent of the market; the remaining 3 percent of market share was divided between its Voiello brand (a traditional Neapolitan pasta competing in the high-priced segment of the semolina pasta market) and its Braibanti brand (a high-quality, traditional Parmesan pasta made from eggs and semolina). About half of Barilla's pasta was sold in northern Italy and half in the south, where Barilla held a smaller share of the market than in the north but where the market was larger. In addition, Barilla held a 29 percent share of the Italian bakery products market.

TABLE 4-1

BARILLA SALES, 1960–1991

Year	Barilla sales (lire in billions*)	Italian wholesale price index
1960	15	10.8
1970	47	41.5
1980	344	57.5
1981	456	67.6
1982	609	76.9
1983	728	84.4
1984	1,034	93.2
1985	1,204	100.0
1986	1,381	99.0
1987	1,634	102.0
1988	1,775	106.5
1989	2,068	121.7
1990[†]	2,390	126.0

*In 1990, 1,198 lire = US$1.00.
[†]1990 figures are estimates.
Source: Based on company documents and *International Finan-cial Statistics Yearbook, International Monetary Fund.*

In 1990 Barilla was organized into seven divi-sions: three pasta divisions (Barina, Voiello, and Braibanti), the Bakery Products Division (manufac-turing medium- to long-shelf-life bakery products), the Fresh Bread Division (manufacturing very-short-shelf-life bakery products), the Catering Division (distributing cakes and frozen croissants to bars and pastry shops), and the International Division. Barilla's corporate headquarters were located adjacent to the Pedrignano pasta plant.

INDUSTRY BACKGROUND

The origins of pasta are unknown. Some believe it originated in China and was first brought to Italy by Marco Polo in the 13th century. Others claim that pasta's origins were rooted in Italy, citing as proof a bas relief on a third-century tomb located near Rome that depicts a pasta roller and cutter. "Regardless of its origins," Barilla marketing literature pronounced, "since time immemorial, Italians have adored pasta." Per capita pasta consumption in Italy averaged nearly 18 kilos per year, greatly exceeding that of other western European countries (see Table 4-2). There was limited seasonality in pasta demand—for exam-ple, special pasta types were used for pasta salads in the summer while egg pasta and lasagna were very popular for Easter meals.

TABLE 4-2

PER CAPITA CONSUMPTION OF PASTA AND BAKERY PRODUCTS, IN KILOGRAMS, 1990

Country	Bread	Breakfast cereals	Pasta	Biscuits
Belgium	85.5	1.0	1.7	5.2
Denmark	29.9	3.7	1.6	5.5
France	68.8	0.6	5.9	6.5
Germany (West)	61.3	0.7	5.2	3.1
Greece	70.0		6.2	8.0
Ireland	58.4	7.7		17.9
Italy	130.9	0.2	17.8	5.9
Netherlands	60.5	1.0	1.4	2.8
Portugal	70.0		5.7	4.6
Spain	87.3	0.3	2.8	5.2
United Kingdom	43.6	7.0	3.6	13.0
Average	70.3	2.5	5.2	7.1

Adapted from *European Marketing Data and Statistics* 1992, Euromonitor Plc 1992, p. 323.

In the late 1980s the Italian pasta market as a whole was relatively flat, growing less than 1 percent per year. By 1990 the Italian pasta market was estimated at 3.5 trillion lire. Semolina pasta and fresh pasta were the only growth segments of the Italian pasta market. In contrast, the export market was experiencing record growth; pasta exports from Italy to other European countries were expected to rise as much as 20 to 25 percent per year in the early 1990s. Barilla's management estimated that two-thirds of this increase would be attributed to the new flow of exported pasta to eastern European countries seeking low-priced basic food products. Barilla managers viewed the eastern European market as an excellent export opportunity, with the potential to encompass a full range of pasta products.

PLANT NETWORK

Barilla owned and operated an extensive network of plants located throughout Italy (see Table 4-3 and Figure 4-1), including large flour mills, pasta plants, and fresh bread plants, as well as plants producing specialty products such as panettone (Christmas cake) and croissants. Barilla maintained state-of-the-art research and development (R&D) facilities and a pilot production plant in Pedrignano for developing and testing new products and production processes.

TABLE 4-3

BARILLA PLANT LOCATIONS AND PRODUCTS MANUFACTURED, 1989

Index	Plant location	Products
1	Bribanti	Pasta
2	Cagliari	Pasta
3	Foggia	Pasta
4	Matera	Pasta
5	Pedrignano	Pasta, noodles, biscuits
6	Viale Barilla	Tortellini, noodles, fresh pasta
7	Caserta	Pasta, rusks, breadsticks
8	Grissin Bon	Breadsticks
9	Rubbiano	Rusks, breadsticks
10	Milano	Panettone, cakes, croissants
11	Pomezia	Croissants
12	Mantova	Biscuits, cakes
13	Melfi	Snacks
14	Ascoli	Snacks, sliced loafs
15	Rodolfi	Sauces
16	Altamura	Flour mill
17	Castelplanio	Flour mill
18	Ferrara	Flour mill
19	Matera	Flour mill
20	Termoli	Flour mill
21	Milano	Fresh bread
22	Milano	Fresh bread
23	Altopascio	Fresh bread
24	Padova	Fresh bread
25	Torino	Fresh bread

▲ CDC
★ Company headquarters
● Refers to Table 4-3 index

FIGURE 4-1 Map of Barilla plant locations and products manufactured.

Pasta Manufacturing

The pasta-making process is similar to the process by which paper is made. In Barilla plants, flour and water (and for some products, eggs and/or spinach meal) were mixed to form dough, which was then rolled into a long, thin continuous sheet by sequential pairs of rollers set at increasingly closer tolerances. After being rolled to the desired thickness, the dough sheet was forced through a bronze extruding die screen; the die's design gave the pasta its distinctive shape. After passing through the extruder, Barilla workers cut the pasta to a specified length. The cut pieces were then hung over dowels (or placed onto trays) and moved slowly through a long tunnel kiln that snaked across the factory floor. The temperature and humidity in the kiln were precisely specified for each size and shape of pasta and had to be tightly controlled to ensure a high-quality product. To keep changeover costs low and product quality high, Barilla followed a carefully chosen production sequence that minimized the incremental changes in kiln temperature and humidity between pasta shapes. After completing the four-hour drying process, the pasta was weighed and packaged.

At Barilla, raw ingredients were transformed into packaged pasta on fully automated 120-meter-long production lines. In the Pedrignano plant, the largest and most technologically advanced of Barilla's plants, 11 lines produced 9,000 quintals (900,000 kilos) of pasta each day. Barilla employees used bicycles to travel within this enormous facility.

Barilla's pasta plants were specialized by the type of pasta produced in the plant. The primary distinctions were based on the consumption of the pasta—for example, whether it was made with or without eggs or spinach and whether it was sold as dry or fresh pasta. All of Barilla's pasta was made with flour ground from *grano duro* (high protein "hard" wheat), the highest-quality flour for making traditional pasta products. Semolina, for example, is a finely ground durum wheat flour. Barilla used flours made from *grano tenero* (tender wheat), such as farina, for more delicate products such as egg pasta and bakery products. Barilla's flour mills ground flour from both types of wheat.

Even within the same family of pasta products, individual products were assigned to plants based on the size and shape of the pasta. "Short" pasta products, such as macaroni or fusilli, and "long" products, such as spaghetti or capellini, were made in separate facilities because of the different sizes of equipment required.

CHANNELS OF DISTRIBUTION

Barilla divided its entire product line into two general categories:

- "Fresh" products, including fresh pasta products, which had 21-day shelf lives, and fresh bread, which had a one-day shelf life.
- "Dry" products, including dry pasta, and longer shelf-life bakery products such as cookies, biscuits, flour, bread sticks, and dry toasts. Dry products represented about 75 percent of Barilla's sales and had either "long" shelf lives of 18 to 24 months (e.g., pasta and dried toasts) or "medium" shelf lives of 10 to 12 weeks (e.g., cookies). In total, Barilla's "dry" products were offered in some 800 different packaged stockkeeping units (SKUs). Pasta was made in 200 different shapes and sizes and was offered in more than 470 different packaged SKUs. The most popular pasta products were offered in a variety of packaging options; for example, at any one time Barilla's #5 spaghetti might be offered in a 5-kg package, a 2-kg package, a 1-kg package with a northern Italian motif, a 2-kg package with a southern Italian motif, a 0.5-kg "northern-motif" package, a 0.5-kg "southern-motif" package, a display pallet, and a special promotional package with a free bottle of Barilla pasta sauce.

Most Barilla products were shipped from the plants in which they were made to one of two Barilla central distribution centers (CDCs): the northern CDC in Pedrignano or the southern CDC on the outskirts of Naples. See Figure 4-2. (Certain products, such as fresh bread, did not flow through the CDCs.) Other fresh products were moved quickly through the distribution system; fresh product inventory was typically held only three days in each of the CDCs. In contrast, each CDC held about a month's worth of dry product inventory.

Barilla maintained separate distribution systems for its fresh and dry products because of their differences in perishability and retail service requirements. Fresh products were purchased from the two CDCs by independent agents (*concessionari*) who then channeled the products through 70 regional

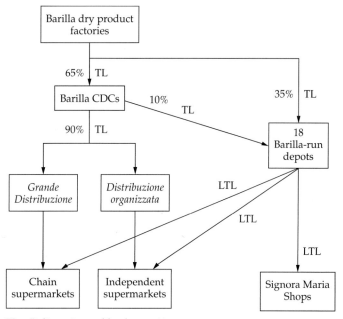

TL = Delivery in truckload quantities.
LTL = Delivery in less-than-truckload quantities.

Note: Shipping percentages are based on product weight.

FIGURE 4-2 Barilla distribution patterns.

warehouses located throughout Italy. Nearly two-thirds of Barilla's dry products were destined for supermarkets; these products were shipped first to one of Barilla's CDCs, where they were purchased by distributors. The distributors in turn shipped the product to supermarkets. Brando Vitali's JITD proposal focused solely on dry products sold through distributors. The remainder of the dry products was distributed through 18 small Barilla-owned warehouses, mostly to small shops.

Barilla products were distributed through three types of retail outlets: small independent grocers, supermarket chains, and independent supermarkets. In sum, Barilla estimated that its products were offered in 100,000 retail outlets in Italy alone.

1. **Small independent shops.** Small shops were more prevalent in Italy than in other western European countries. Through the late 1980s the Italian government had supported small grocers (often referred to as "Signora Maria" shops) by restricting the number of licenses provided to operate large supermarkets. However, in the early 1990s

the number of supermarkets began to grow as governmental restrictions abated.

Approximately 35 percent of Barilla's dry products (30 percent in the north of Italy and 40 percent in the south) were distributed from Barilla's internally owned regional warehouses to small independent shops, which typically held over two weeks of inventory at the store level. Small shop owners purchased products through brokers who dealt with Barilla purchasing and distribution personnel.

2. **Supermarkets.** The remaining dry products were distributed through outside distributors to supermarkets—70 percent to supermarket chains and 30 percent to independent supermarkets. A supermarket typically held from 10 to 12 days of dry product inventory within the stores, and on average carried a total of 4,800 dry product SKUs. Although Barilla offered many pasta products in multiple types of packages, most retailers would carry a product in only one (and at most two) packaging options.

Dry products destined for a supermarket chain were distributed through the chain's own distribution organization, known as a *grande distribuzione* ("grand distributor"), or GD; those destined for independent supermarkets were channeled through a different set of distributors known as *distribuzione organizzata* ("organized distributors"), or DOs. A DO acted as a central buying organization for a large number of independent supermarkets. Most DOs had regional operations, and the retailers they served usually got their products from only a single DO.

Due to regional preferences and differences in retail requirements, a typical distributor might distribute 130 of Barilla's 800 dry product SKUs. Most distributors handled products coming from about 200 different suppliers; of these, Barilla typically would be the largest in terms of the physical volume of products purchased. Distributors typically carried from 7,000 to 10,000 SKUs in total. However, their strategies varied. For example, one of Barilla's largest DOs, Cortese, carried only 100 of Barilla's dry products and carried a total of only 5,000 SKUs.

Both GDs and DOs purchased products from the Barilla CDCs, maintained inventory in their own warehouses, and then filled supermarket orders from their warehouse inventory. A distributor's warehouse typically held a two-week supply of Barilla dry products in inventory.

Many supermarkets placed daily orders with distributors; the store manager would walk up and down the store aisles and note each product that needed to be replenished and the number of boxes required (more sophisticated retailers used handheld computers to record order quantities as they checked the shelves). The order would then be transmitted to the store's distributor; orders were typically received at the store 24 to 48 hours after receipt of the order at the distribution center.

SALES AND MARKETING

Barilla enjoyed a strong brand image in Italy. Its marketing and sales strategy was based upon a combination of advertising and promotions.

Advertising

Barilla brands were heavily advertised. Advertising copy differentiated Barilla pasta from basic commodity "noodles" by positioning the brand as the highest quality, most sophisticated pasta product available.

One ad campaign was built on the phrase: "Barilla: a great collection of premium Italian pasta." The "collection" dimension was illustrated by showing individual uncooked pasta shapes against a black background, as though they were jewels, evoking a sense of luxury and sophistication. Unlike other pasta manufacturers, Barilla avoided images of traditional Italian folklore, preferring modern, sophisticated settings in major Italian cities.

Advertising themes were supported by sponsorships of well-known athletes and celebrities. For example, Barilla engaged tennis stars Steffi Graf to promote Barilla products in Germany and Stefan Edberg in the Scandinavian countries. Luminaries such as actor Paul Newman were also used to promote Barilla products. In addition, Barilla advertising focused on developing and strengthening loyal relationships with Italian families by using messages such as "Where there is Barilla, there is a home."

Trade Promotions

Barilla's sales strategy relied on the use of trade promotions to push its products into the grocery distribution network. A Barilla sales executive explained the logic of the promotion-based strategy:

> We sell to a very old-fashioned distribution system. The buyers expect frequent trade promotions, which they then pass along to their own customers. So a store will know right away if another store is buying Barilla pasta at a discount. You have to understand how important pasta is in Italy. Everyone knows the price of pasta. If a store is selling pasta at a discount one week, consumers notice the reduced price immediately.

Barilla divided each year into 10 or 12 "canvass" periods, typically four to five weeks in length, each corresponding to a promotional program. During any canvass period, a Barilla distributor could buy as many products as desired to meet current and future needs. Incentives for Barilla sales representatives were based on achieving the sales targets set for each canvass period. Different product categories were offered during different canvass periods, with the discount depending on the margin structure of the category. Typical promotional discounts were 1.4 percent for semolina pasta, 4 percent for egg pasta, 4 percent for biscuits, 8 percent for sauces, and 10 percent for breadsticks.

Barilla also offered volume discounts. For example, Barilla paid for transportation, thus providing incentives of 2 to 3 percent for orders in full truck-load quantities. In addition, a sales representative might offer a buyer a 1,000 lire per carton discount (representing a 4 percent discount) if the buyer purchased a minimum of three truckloads of Barilla egg pasta.

Sales Representatives

Barilla sales representatives serving DOs spent an estimated 90 percent of their time working at the store level. In the store, sales reps helped merchandise Barilla products and set up in-store promotions; took note of competitive information, including competitors' prices, stockouts, and new product introductions; and discussed Barilla products and ordering strategies with store management. In addition, each sales rep spent a half day in a regularly scheduled weekly meeting with the distributor's buyer, helping the distributor place its weekly order, explaining promotions and discounts, and settling problems such as returns and deletions associated with the last delivery. Each rep carried a portable computer for inputting distributor orders. The rep also would spend a few hours a week at the CDC, discussing new products and prices, covering problems concerning the previous week's deliveries, and settling disputes about different discounts and deal structures.

In contrast, a very small sales force served the GDs. The GD sales force rarely visited GD warehouses and usually sent their orders to Barilla via fax.

DISTRIBUTION

Distributor Ordering Procedures

Most distributors—GDs and DOs alike—checked their inventory levels and placed orders with Barilla once a week. Barilla products would then be shipped to the distributor over the course of the week that started 8 days after the order was placed and ended 14 days after the order was placed—the average lead time was 10 days. For example, a large distributor that ordered every Tuesday might order several truckloads to be delivered from the following Wednesday through the following Tuesday (see below). Distributors' sales volumes varied; small distributors might order only one truckload a week, whereas the largest warranted deliveries of as many as five truckloads a week.

Most distributors used simple periodic review inventory systems. For example, a distributor might review inventory levels of Barilla products each Tuesday; the distributor would then place orders for those products whose levels fell below the reorder level. Nearly all of the distributors had computer-supported ordering systems, but few had forecasting systems or sophisticated analytical tools for determining order quantities.

Impetus for the JITD Program

As the 1980s progressed, Barilla increasingly felt the effects of fluctuating demand. Orders for Barilla dry products often swung wildly from week to week (see Figure 4-3). Such extreme demand variability strained

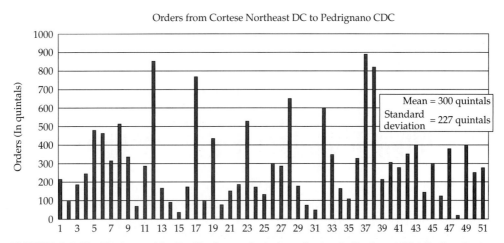

FIGURE 4-3 Weekly demand for Barilla dry products from Cortese's Northeast Distribution Center to the Pedrignano CDC, 1989.

Barilla's manufacturing and logistics operations. For example, the specific sequence of pasta production necessitated by the tight heat and humidity specifications in the tunnel kiln made it difficult to quickly produce a particular pasta that had been sold out owing to unexpectedly high demand. On the other hand, holding sufficient finished goods inventories to meet distributors' order requirements was extremely expensive when weekly demand fluctuated so widely and was so unpredictable.

Some manufacturing and logistics personnel favored asking distributors or retailers to carry additional inventory to check the fluctuation in distributors' orders, noting that with their current inventory levels, many distributors' service levels to the retailers were unacceptable (see Figure 4-4 for sample distributor inventory levels and stockout rates). Others felt that the distributors and retailers were already carrying too much inventory. In the late 1980s a Barilla logistics manager discussed retail inventory pressure:

> Our customers are changing. And do you know why they are changing? As I see it, they are realizing they do not have enough room in their stores and warehouses to carry the very large inventories manufacturers would like them to. Think of shelf space in retail outlets. You cannot easily increase it. Yet manufacturers are continuously introducing new products, and they want retailers to display each product on the fronts of their shelves! That would be impossible even if supermarkets were made from rubber![1]

Distributors felt similar pressure to increase the inventory of items they already stocked and to add items they currently did not carry.

FIGURE 4-4 Sample stockout and inventory levels, Cortese's Northeast Distribution Center, 1989.

---

[1] Claudia Ferrozzi, *The Pedrignano Warehouse* (Milan: GEA, 1988).

In 1987 Brando Vitali, then Barilla's director of logistics, had expressed strong feelings about finding an alternative approach to order fulfillment. At that time, he noted, "Both manufacturers and retailers are suffering from thinning margins; we must find a way to take costs out of our distribution channel without compromising service." Vitali was seen as a visionary whose ideas stretched beyond the day-to-day details of a logistics organization. He envisioned an approach that would radically change the way in which the logistics organization managed product delivery. In early 1988 Vitali explained his plan:

I envision a simple approach: rather than send product to the distributors according to their internal planning processes, we should look at all of the distributors' shipment data and send only what is needed at the stores—no more, no less. The way we operate now it's nearly impossible to anticipate demand swings, so we end up having to hold a lot of inventory and do a lot of scrambling in our manufacturing and distribution operations to meet distributor demand. And even so, the distributors don't seem to do such a great job servicing their retailers. Look at the stockouts (see Figure 4-4) these DOs have experienced in the last year. And that's despite their holding a couple of weeks of inventory.

In my opinion, we could improve operations for ourselves and our customers if we were responsible for creating the delivery schedules. We'd be able to ship product only as it is needed, rather than building enormous stocks in both of our facilities. We could try to reduce our own distribution costs, inventory levels, and ultimately our manufacturing costs if we didn't have to respond to the volatile demand patterns of the distributors.

We have always had the mentality that orders were an unchangeable input into our process and therefore that one of the most important capabilities we needed to achieve was flexibility to respond to those inputs. But in reality, demand from the end consumer is the input and I think that we should be able to manage the input filter that produces the orders.

How would this work? Every day each distributor would provide us data on what Barilla products it had shipped out of its warehouse to retailers during the previous day, as well as the current stock level for each Barilla SKU. Then we could look at all of the data and make replenishment decisions based on our own forecasts. It would be similar to using point-of-sale data from retailers—we would just be responding to see-through information one step behind the retailer. Ideally, we would use actual retail sell-through data, but that's hard to come by given the structure of our distribution channel and the fact that most grocers in Italy aren't equipped yet with the necessary bar-code scanners and computer linkages.

Of course, it's not quite as simple as that. We need to improve our own forecasting systems so we can make better use of the data that we receive. We'll also need to develop a set of decision rules that we can use to determine what to send after we've made a new forecast.

Vitali's proposal, "just-in-time distribution," met with significant resistance within Barilla. The sales and marketing organizations were particularly vocal in their opposition to the plan. A number of sales representatives felt their responsibilities would be diminished if such a program were put in place. A range of concerns was expressed from the bottom to the top of the sales organization. The following remarks were heard from Barilla sales and marketing personnel:

- "Our sales levels would flatten if we put this program in place."
- "We run the risk of not being able to adjust our shipments sufficiently quickly to changes in selling patterns or increased promotions."
- "It seems to me that a pretty good part of the distribution organization is not yet ready to handle such a sophisticated relationship."
- "If space is freed up in our distributors' warehouses when inventories of our own product decrease, we run the risk of giving our competitors more distributor shelf space. The distributors would then push our competitors' product more than our own, since once something is bought it must be sold."
- "We increase the risk of having our customers stock out of our product if we have disruption in our supply process. What if we have a strike or some other disturbance?"
- "We wouldn't be able to run trade promotions with JITD. How can we get the trade to push Barilla product to retailers if we don't offer some sort of incentive?"
- "It's not clear that costs would even be reduced. If a DO decreases its stock, we at Barilla may have to increase our own inventory of those products for which we cannot change production schedules due to our lack of manufacturing flexibility."

Vitali countered the concerns of the sales organization:

I think JITD should be considered a selling tool, rather than a threat to sales. We're offering the customer additional service at no extra cost. In addition, the program will improve Barilla's visibility with the trade and make distributors more dependent on us—it should improve the relationships between Barilla and the distributors rather than harm them. And what's more, the information regarding the supply at the distributors' warehouses provides us with objective data that would permit us to improve our own planning procedures.

Giorgio Maggiali, head of materials management for Barilla's fresh products group, was appointed director of logistics in late 1988 when Vitali was promoted to head one of the company's new divisions. Maggiali was a hands-on manager, known for his orientation to action. Shortly after his appointment, Maggiali appointed a recent college graduate, Vincenzo Battistini, to help him develop and implement the JITD program.

Maggiali recounted his frustrations in implementing the JITD program:

> In 1988 we developed the basic ideas for the approach we wanted to use and tried to convince several of our distributors to sign on. They weren't even interested in talking about it; the manager of one of our largest distributors pretty much summed up a lot of the responses we had when he cut off a conversation saying, "Managing stock is my job; I don't need you to see my warehouse or my figures. I could improve my inventory and service levels myself if you would deliver my orders more quickly. I'll make you a proposal—I'll place the order and you deliver within 36 hours." He didn't understand that we just can't respond to wildly changing orders without more notice than that.

Another distributor expressed concerns about becoming too closely linked to Barilla. "We would be giving Barilla the power to push product into our warehouses just so Barilla can reduce its costs." Still another asked, "What makes you think that you could manage my inventories any better than I can?"

We were finally able to convince a couple of our distributors to have in-depth discussions about the JITD proposal. Our first discussion was with Marconi, a large, fairly old-fashioned GD. First Battistini and I visited Marconi's logistics department and presented our plan. We made it clear that we planned to provide them with such good service that they could both decrease their inventories and improve their fill rate to their stores. The logistics group thought it sounded great and was interested in conducting an experimental run of the program. But as soon as Marconi's buyers heard about it, all hell broke loose. First the buyers started to voice their own concerns; then, after talking to their Barilla sales reps, they started to repeat some of our own sales department's objections as well. Marconi finally agreed to sell us the data we wanted, but otherwise things would continue as before with Marconi making decisions about replenishment quantities and timing. This clearly wasn't the type of relationship we were looking for, so we talked to other distributors, but they weren't much more responsive.

We need to regroup now and decide where to go with JITD. Is this type of program feasible in our environment? If so, what kind of customer should we target? And how do we convince them to sign up?

The Barilla case raises two important issues:

- Variations in distributors' order patterns have caused severe operational inefficiencies and cost penalties for Barilla. The extreme variability in orders that Barilla receives is surprising considering the distribution of demand for pasta in Italy. Indeed, while variability in aggregate demand for pasta is quite small, orders placed by the distributors have a huge variability.
- In the proposed JITD strategy, Barilla will be in charge of the channel between the CDCs and the distributors and decide on the timing and size of shipments to its distributors. Thus, unlike traditional supply chains in which distributors place orders and manufacturers try to satisfy these orders as much as possible, in JITD "Barilla's own logistics organization would specify the appropriate delivery quantities—those that would more effectively meet the end consumer's needs yet would also more evenly distribute the workload on Barilla's manufacturing and logistics systems." In the last few years, such a strategy has been referred to as *vendor managed inventory* (*VMI*).

By the end of this chapter, you should be able to answer the following questions:

- What are the reasons for the increase in variability in Barilla's supply chain?
- How can the firm cope with the increase in variability?
- What is the impact of transferring demand information across the supply chain?

- Can the VMI strategy solve the operational problems faced by Barilla?
- How can the supply chain meet conflicting goals of different partners and facilities?

4.1 INTRODUCTION

We live in the "Information Age." Data warehouses, web services, XML, wireless, the Internet, and portals are just a few of the technologies dominating the business page of the daily newspaper. In Chapter 11, we examine these technologies in detail and look at the issues surrounding their implementation. In this chapter, we consider the value of using any type of information technology; we deal specifically with the potential availability of more and more information throughout the supply chain and the implications this availability has on effective design and management of the integrated supply chain.

The implications of this abundance of available information are enormous. The supply chain pundits and consultants like to use the phrase, *In modern supply chains, information replaces inventory.* We don't dispute this idea, but its meaning is vague. After all, at some point the customer needs products, not just information! Nevertheless, information changes the way supply chains can and should be effectively managed, and these changes may lead to, among other things, lower inventories. Indeed, our objective in this chapter is to characterize how information affects the design and operation of the supply chain. We show that by effectively harnessing the information now available, one can design and operate the supply chain much more efficiently and effectively than ever before.

It should be apparent to the reader that having accurate information about inventory levels, orders, production, and delivery status throughout the supply chain should not make the managers of a supply chain less effective than if this information were not available. After all, they could choose to ignore it. As we will see, however, this information provides a tremendous opportunity to improve the way the supply chain is designed and managed. Unfortunately, using this information effectively does make the design and management of the supply chain more complex because many more issues must be considered.

We argue here that this abundant information

- Helps reduce variability in the supply chain.
- Helps suppliers make better forecasts, accounting for promotions and market changes.
- Enables the coordination of manufacturing and distribution systems and strategies.
- Enables retailers to better serve their customers by offering tools for locating desired items.
- Enables retailers to react and adapt to supply problems more rapidly.
- Enables lead time reductions.

The chapter is based on the seminal work in [90] and [91] as well as the recent work in [28] and [30]. In the next section, we follow the review article [29].

4.2 THE BULLWHIP EFFECT

In recent years many suppliers and retailers have observed that while customer demand for specific products does not vary much, inventory and back-order levels fluctuate considerably across their supply chain. For instance, in examining the demand for Pampers disposal diapers, executives at Procter & Gamble noticed an interesting phenomenon.

FIGURE 4-5 The supply chain.

As expected, retail sales of the product were fairly uniform; there is no particular day or month in which the demand is significantly higher or lower than any other. However, the executives noticed that distributors' orders placed to the factory fluctuated much more than retail sales. In addition, P&G's orders to its suppliers fluctuated even more. This increase in variability as we travel up in the supply chain is referred to as the *bullwhip effect*.

Figure 4-5 illustrates a simple four-stage supply chain: a single retailer, a single wholesaler, a single distributor, and a single factory. The retailer observes customer demand and places orders to the wholesaler. The wholesaler receives products from the distributor, who places orders to the factory. Figure 4-6 provides a graphical representation of orders, as a function of time, placed by different facilities. The figure clearly shows the increase in variability across the supply chain.

To understand the impact of the increase in variability on the supply chain, consider the second stage in our example, the wholesaler. The wholesaler receives orders from the retailer and places orders to his supplier, the distributor. To determine these order quantities, the wholesaler must forecast the retailer's demand. If the wholesaler does not have access to the customer's demand data, he must use orders placed by the retailer to perform his forecasting.

Since variability in orders placed by the retailer is significantly higher than variability in customer demand, as Figure 4-6 shows, the wholesaler is forced to carry more safety stock than the retailer or else to maintain higher capacity than the retailer in order to meet the same service level as the retailer.

This analysis can be carried over to the distributor as well as the factory, resulting in even higher inventory levels and therefore higher costs at these facilities.

Consider, for example, a simple widget supply chain. A single factory, Widget-Makers Inc., supplies a single retailer, the WidgetStore. Average annual widget demand at the WidgetStore is 5,200 units, and shipments are made from WidgetMakers to the

FIGURE 4-6 The increase in variability in the supply chain.

store each week. If the variability in orders placed by the WidgetStore is low, so that the shipment every week is about 100 units, WidgetMakers' production capacity and weekly shipping capacity need be only about 100 units. If weekly variability is very high, so that during certain weeks WidgetMakers must make and ship 400 units and some weeks no units at all, it is easy to see that production and shipping capacity must be much higher and that some weeks this capacity will be idle. Alternatively, WidgetMakers could build up inventory during weeks with low demand and supply these items during weeks with high demand, thus increasing inventory holding costs.

Thus, it is important to identify techniques and tools that will allow us to control the bullwhip effect; that is, to control the increase in variability in the supply chain. For this purpose, we need to first understand the main factors contributing to the increase in variability in the supply chain.

1. *Demand forecasting*. Traditional inventory management techniques (see Chapter 3) practiced at each level in the supply chain lead to the bullwhip effect. To explain the connection between forecasting and the bullwhip effect, we need to revisit inventory control strategies in supply chains. As discussed in Chapter 3, an attractive policy used in practice by each stage of the supply chain is the *min-max inventory policy*. Here, whenever the inventory position at a facility is less than a given number, referred to as the *reorder point*, the facility raises its inventory level up to a given target level, called the *order-up-to level*.

   The reorder point is typically set equal to the average demand during lead time plus a multiple of the standard deviation of demand during lead time. The latter quantity is referred to as *safety stock*. Typically, managers use *standard forecast smoothing techniques* to estimate average demand and demand variability. An important characteristic of all forecasting techniques is that as more data are observed, the more we modify the estimates of the mean and the standard deviation (or variability) in customer demands. Since safety stock, as well as the order-up-to level, strongly depends on these estimates, the user is forced to change order quantities, thus increasing variability.

2. *Lead time*. It is easy to see that the increase in variability is magnified with increasing lead time. For this purpose, recall from Chapter 3 that to calculate safety stock levels and reorder points, we in effect multiply estimates of the average and standard deviation of the daily customer demands by the lead time. Thus, with longer lead times, a small change in the estimate of demand variability implies a significant change in safety stock and reorder level, leading to a significant change in order quantities. This of course leads to an increase in variability.

3. *Batch ordering.* The impact of batch ordering is quite simple to understand. If the retailer uses batch ordering, as happens when using a min-max inventory policy, then the wholesaler will observe a large order, followed by several periods of no orders, followed by another large order, and so on. Thus, the wholesaler sees a distorted and highly variable pattern of orders.

   It is useful to remind the reader that firms use batch ordering for a number of reasons. First, as pointed out in Chapter 3, a firm that is faced with fixed ordering costs needs to apply the min-max inventory policy, which leads to batch ordering. Second, as transportation costs become more significant, retailers may order quantities that allow them to take advantage of transportation discounts (e.g., full truckload quantities). This may lead to some weeks with large orders, and some with no orders at all. Finally, the quarterly or yearly sales quotas or incentives observed in many businesses can also result in unusually large orders observed on a periodic basis.

4. *Price fluctuation.* Price fluctuation can also lead to the bullwhip effect. If prices fluctuate, retailers often attempt to *stock up* when prices are lower. This is accentuated by the prevailing practice in many industries of offering promotions and discounts at certain times or for certain quantities.

5. *Inflated orders.* Inflated orders placed by retailers during shortage periods tend to magnify the bullwhip effect. Such orders are common when retailers and distributors suspect that a product will be in short supply, and therefore anticipate receiving supply proportional to the amount ordered. When the period of shortage is over, the retailer goes back to its standard orders, leading to all kinds of distortions and variations in demand estimates.

4.2.1 Quantifying the Bullwhip Effect[2]

So far, we have discussed factors contributing to the increase in variability in the supply chain. To better understand and control the bullwhip effect, we also would find it useful to *quantify* the bullwhip effect; that is, quantify the increase in variability that occurs at every stage of the supply chain. This would be useful not only to demonstrate the magnitude of the increase in variability, but also to show the relationship between the forecasting technique, the lead time, and the increase in variability.

To quantify the increase in variability for a simple supply chain, consider a two-stage supply chain with a retailer who observes customer demand and places an order to a manufacturer. Suppose that the retailer faces a fixed lead time, so that an order placed by the retailer at the end of period t is received at the start of period $t + L$. Also, suppose the retailer follows a simple periodic review policy (see Chapter 3) in which the retailer reviews inventory every period and places an order to bring its inventory level up to a target level. Observe that in this case the review period is one.

---

[2]This section can be skipped without loss of continuity.

Hence, as discussed in Chapter 3, Section 3.2.7, the order-up-to point is calculated as

$$L \times AVG + z \times STD \times \sqrt{L}$$

where *AVG* and *STD* are the average and standard deviation of daily (or weekly) customer demand. The constant z is the safety factor and is chosen from statistical tables to ensure that the probability of stockouts during lead time is equal to the specified level of service.

To implement this inventory policy, the retailer must estimate the average and standard deviation of demand based on its observed customer demand. Thus, in practice, the order-up-to point may change from day to day according to changes in the current estimate of the average and the standard deviation.

Specifically, the order-up-to point in period t, y_t, is estimated from the observed demand as

$$y_t = \hat{\mu}_t L + z\sqrt{L}S_t$$

where $\hat{\mu}_t$ and S_t are the estimated average and standard deviation of daily customer demand at time t.

Suppose the retailer uses one of the simplest forecasting techniques: the moving average. In other words, in each period the retailer estimates the mean demand as an average of the previous p observations of demand. The retailer estimates the standard deviation of demand in a similar manner. That is, if D_i represents customer demand in period i, then

$$\hat{\mu}_t = \frac{\sum_{i=t-p}^{t-1} D_i}{p}$$

and

$$S_t^2 = \frac{\sum_{i=t-p}^{t-1} (D_i - \hat{\mu}_t)^2}{p-1}$$

Note that the expressions above imply that in every period the retailer calculates a new mean and standard deviation based on the p most recent observations of demand. Then, since the estimates of the mean and standard deviation change every period, the target inventory level will also change in every period.

In this case, we can quantify the increase in variability; that is, we can calculate the variability faced by the manufacturer and compare it to the variability faced by the retailer. If the variance of the customer demand seen by the retailer is $Var(D)$, then the variance of the orders placed by that retailer to the manufacturer, $Var(Q)$, relative to the variance of customer demand satisfies

$$\frac{Var(Q)}{Var(D)} \geq 1 + \frac{2L}{p} + \frac{2L^2}{p^2}$$

Figure 4-7 shows the lower bound on the increase in variability as a function of p for various values of the lead time, L. In particular, when p is large and L is small, the bullwhip effect due to forecasting error is negligible. The bullwhip effect is magnified as we increase the lead time and decrease p.

For instance, suppose the retailer estimates the mean demand based on the last five demand observations, that is, $p = 5$. Suppose also that an order placed by the retailer at the end of period t is received at the start of period $t + 1$. This implies that the lead time (more precisely the lead time plus the review period) equals 1, that is, $L = 1$. In

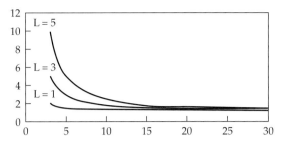

FIGURE 4-7 A lower bound on the increase in variability given as a function of *p*.

this case the variance of the orders placed by the retailer to the manufacturer will be at least 40 percent larger than the variance of the customer demand seen by the retailer, that is,

$$\frac{Var(Q)}{Var(D)} \geq 1.4$$

Next consider the same retailer, but now assume, as is the case in the retail industry, that the retailer uses 10 demand observations (i.e., $p = 10$) to estimate the mean and standard deviation of demand. Then the variance of the orders placed by the retailer to the manufacturer will be at least 1.2 times the variance of the customer demand seen by the retailer. In other words, by increasing the number of observations used in the moving average, the retailer can significantly reduce the variability of the orders it places to the manufacturer.

4.2.2 The Impact of Centralized Information on the Bullwhip Effect

One of the most frequent suggestions for reducing the bullwhip effect is to centralize demand information within a supply chain, that is, to provide each stage of the supply chain with complete information on the actual customer demand. To understand why centralized demand information can reduce the bullwhip effect, note that if demand information is centralized, each stage of the supply chain can use the actual customer demand data to create more accurate forecasts, rather than relying on the orders received from the previous stage, which can vary significantly more than the actual customer demand.

In this subsection, we consider the value of sharing customer demand information within a supply chain. For this purpose, consider again the initial four-stage supply chain, described in Figure 4-5, with a single retailer, wholesaler, distributor, and factory. To determine the impact of centralized demand information on the bullwhip effect, we distinguish between two types of supply chains: one with centralized demand information and a second with decentralized demand information. These systems are described below.

Supply Chain with Centralized Demand Information In the first type of supply chain, the *centralized supply chain*, the retailer, or the first stage in the supply chain, observes customer demand, forecasts the mean demand using a moving average with *p* demand observations, finds his target inventory level based on the forecast mean demand, and places an order to the wholesaler. The wholesaler, or the second stage of the supply chain, receives the order along with the retailer's forecast mean demand, uses this forecast to determine its target inventory level, and places an order to the distributor. Similarly, the distributor, or the third stage of the supply chain, receives the order along with the retailer's forecast mean demand, uses this forecast to determine its target inventory level, and places an order to the fourth stage of the supply chain, the factory.

In this centralized supply chain, each stage of the supply chain receives the retailer's forecast mean demand and follows an order-up-to inventory policy based on this mean demand. Therefore, in this case we have centralized the demand information, the forecasting technique, and the inventory policy.

Following the analysis above, it is not difficult to show that the variance of the orders placed by the kth stage of the supply chain, $Var(Q^k)$, relative to the variance of the customer demand, $Var(D)$, is just

$$\frac{Var(Q^k)}{Var(D)} \geq 1 + \frac{2\sum_{i=1}^{k} L_i}{p} + \frac{2\left(\sum_{i=1}^{k} L_i\right)^2}{p^2}$$

where L_i is the lead time between stage i and stage $i + 1$. That is, the lead time L_i implies that an order placed by facility i at the end of period t arrives at that facility at the beginning of period $t + L_i$. For example, if an order placed by the retailer to the wholesaler at the end of period t arrives at the beginning of period $t + 2$, then $L_1 = 2$. Similarly, if the lead time from the wholesaler to the distributor is two periods, then $L_2 = 2$, and if the lead time from the distributor to the factory is also two periods, then $L_3 = 2$. In this case, the total lead time from the retailer to the factory is

$$L_1 + L_2 + L_3 = 6 \text{ periods}$$

This expression for the variance of the orders placed by the kth stage of the supply chain is very similar to the expression for the variability of the orders placed by the retailer given in the previous section, with the single stage lead time L replaced by the k stage lead time $\sum_{i=1}^{k} L_i$. Thus, we see that *the variance of the orders placed by a given stage of a supply chain is an increasing function of the total lead time between that stage and the retailer.* This implies that the variance of the orders becomes larger as we move up the supply chain, so that the orders placed by the second stage of the supply chain are more variable than the orders placed by the retailer (the first stage) and the orders placed by the third stage will be more variable than the orders placed by the second stage, and so on.

Decentralized Demand Information   The second type of supply chain that we consider is the *decentralized supply chain*. In this case the retailer does not make its forecast mean demand available to the remainder of the supply chain. Instead, the wholesaler must estimate the mean demand based on the orders received from the retailer.

Again we assume that the wholesaler uses a moving average with p observations— these are the latest p orders placed by the retailer—to forecast the mean demand. It then uses this forecast to determine the target inventory level and places an order to the supplier, the distributor. Similarly, the distributor uses a moving average with p observations of the orders placed by the wholesaler to forecast the mean and standard deviation of demand and uses these forecasts to determine the target inventory level. The distributor's target level is used to place orders to the fourth stage of the supply chain.

It turns out that in this system the variance of the orders placed by the kth stage of the supply chain, $Var(Q^k)$, relative to the variance of the customer demand, $Var(D)$, satisfies

$$\frac{Var(Q^k)}{Var(D)} \geq \prod_{i=1}^{k} \left[1 + \frac{2L_i}{p} + \frac{2L_i^2}{p^2} \right]$$

where, as before, L_i is the lead time between stages i and $i+1$.

Note that this expression for the variance of the orders placed by the kth stage of the supply chain is very similar to the expression for the variability of orders placed by the retailer in the centralized case, but now the variance increases multiplicatively at each stage of the supply chain. Again the variance of the orders becomes larger as we move up the supply chain so that the orders placed by the wholesaler are more variable than the orders placed by the retailer.

Managerial Insights on the Value of Centralized Information   We have already seen that for either type of supply chain, centralized or decentralized, the variance of the order quantities becomes larger as we move up the supply chain so that the orders placed by the wholesaler are more variable than the orders placed by the retailer, and so on. The difference in the two types of supply chains is in terms of how much the variability grows as we move from stage to stage.

The results above indicate that the variance of the orders grows additively in the total lead time for the centralized supply chain, while the increase is multiplicative for the decentralized supply chain. In other words, a decentralized supply chain, in which only the retailer knows the customer demand, can lead to significantly higher variability than a centralized supply chain, in which customer demand information is available at each stage of the supply chain, particularly when lead times are large. We therefore conclude that *centralizing demand information can significantly reduce the bullwhip effect.*

This reduction is illustrated nicely in Figure 4-8, which shows the ratio between variability of orders placed by stage k, for $k = 3$ and $k = 5$, and variability of customers' demands for the centralized and decentralized systems when $L_i = 1$ for each i. It also shows the ratio between variability in orders placed by the retailer and variability in customers' demands ($k = 1$).

Thus, it is now clear that by sharing demand information with each stage of the supply chain, we can significantly reduce the bullwhip effect. Indeed, when demand information is centralized, each stage of the supply chain can use the actual customer

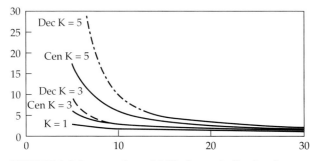

FIGURE 4-8 Increase in variability for centralized and decentralized systems.

demand data to estimate the average demand. On the other hand, when demand information is not shared, each stage must use the orders placed by the previous stage to estimate the average demand. As we have already seen, these orders are more variable than the actual customer demand data, and thus the forecasts created using these orders are more variable, leading to more variable orders.

Finally, it is important to point out that the bullwhip effect exists even when demand information is completely centralized and all stages of the supply chain use the same forecasting technique and inventory policy. In other words, if every stage of the supply chain follows a simple order-up-to policy and if each stage uses the same customer demand data and forecasting technique to predict the expected demand, then we will still see the bullwhip effect. However, the analysis indicates that if information is not centralized—that is, if each stage of the supply chain is not provided with customer demand information—then the increase in variability can be significantly larger. Thus, we conclude that *centralizing demand information can significantly reduce, but will not eliminate, the bullwhip effect.*

4.2.3 Methods for Coping with the Bullwhip Effect

Our ability to identify and quantify the causes of the bullwhip effect lead to a number of suggestions for reducing the bullwhip effect or for eliminating its impact. These include reducing uncertainty, reducing the variability of the customer demand process, reducing lead times, and engaging in strategic partnerships. These issues are discussed briefly below.

1. *Reducing uncertainty.* One of the most frequent suggestions for decreasing or eliminating the bullwhip effect is to reduce uncertainty throughout the supply chain by centralizing demand information, that is, by providing each stage of the supply chain with complete information on actual customer demand. The results presented in the previous subsection demonstrate that centralizing demand information can reduce the bullwhip effect.

   Note, however, that even if each stage uses the same demand data, each may still employ different forecasting methods and different buying practices, both of which may contribute to the bullwhip effect. In addition, the results presented in the previous subsection indicate that even when each stage uses the same demand data, the same forecasting method, and the same ordering policy, the bullwhip effect will continue to exist.

2. *Reducing variability.* The bullwhip effect can be diminished by reducing the variability inherent in the customer demand process. For example, if we can reduce the variability of the customer demand seen by the retailer, then even if the bullwhip effect occurs, the variability of the demand seen by the wholesaler will also be reduced.

   We can reduce the variability of customer demand through, for example, the use of an "everyday low pricing" (EDLP) strategy. When a retailer uses EDLP, it offers a product at a single consistent price, rather than offering a regular price with periodic price promotions. By eliminating price promotions, a retailer can eliminate many of the dramatic shifts in demand that occur along with these promotions. Therefore, everyday low pricing strategies can lead to much more stable—that is, less variable—customer demand patterns.

3. *Lead-time reduction.* The results presented in the previous subsections clearly indicate that lead times serve to magnify the increase in variability due to demand

forecasting. We have demonstrated the dramatic effect that increasing lead times can have on the variability at each stage of the supply chain. Therefore, lead-time reduction can significantly reduce the bullwhip effect throughout a supply chain.

Observe that lead times typically include two components: order lead times (i.e., the time it takes to produce and ship the item) and information lead times (i.e., the time it takes to process an order). This distinction is important since order lead times can be reduced through the use of cross-docking while information lead time can be reduced through the use of electronic data interchange (EDI).

4. *Strategic partnerships.* The bullwhip effect can be eliminated by engaging in any of a number of strategic partnerships. These strategic partnerships change the way information is shared and inventory is managed within a supply chain, possibly eliminating the impact of the bullwhip effect. For example, in vendor managed inventory (VMI, see Chapter 6), the manufacturer manages the inventory of its product at the retailer outlet, and therefore determines for itself how much inventory to keep on hand and how much to ship to the retailer in every period. Therefore, in VMI the manufacturer does not rely on the orders placed by a retailer, thus avoiding the bullwhip effect entirely.

Other types of partnerships are also applied to reduce the bullwhip effect. The previous analysis indicates, for example, that centralizing demand information can dramatically reduce the variability seen by the upstream stages in a supply chain. Therefore, it is clear that these upstream stages would benefit from a strategic partnership that provides an incentive for the retailer to make customer demand data available to the rest of the supply chain. See Chapter 6 for a detailed discussion.

4.3 EFFECTIVE FORECASTS

Information leads to more effective forecasts. The more factors that predictions of future demand can take into account, the more accurate these predictions can be. See Chapter 3 for a more detailed discussion of forecasts.

For example, consider retailer forecasts. These are typically based on an analysis of previous sales at the retailer. However, future customer demand is clearly influenced by such issues as pricing, promotions, and the release of new products. Some of these issues are controlled by the retailer, but some are controlled by the distributor, wholesaler, manufacturer, or competitors. If this information is available to the retailer's forecasters, the forecasts obviously will be more accurate.

Similarly, distributor and manufacturer forecasts are influenced by factors under retailer control. For example, the retailer may design promotions or set pricing. Also, the retailer may introduce new products into the stores, altering demand patterns.

In addition, because a manufacturer or distributor has fewer products to consider than the retailer, he may have more information about these products. For example, sales may be closely tied to some event. If a retailer is aware of this, he can increase inventories or raise prices to take advantage of this fact.

For all of these reasons, many supply chains are moving toward cooperative forecasting systems. In these supply chains, sophisticated information systems enable an iterative forecasting process, in which all of the participants in the supply chain collaborate to arrive at an agreed-upon forecast. This implies that all components of the supply chain share and use the same forecasting tool, leading to a decrease in the bullwhip effect (see Chapter 11, Section 11.4.6).

EXAMPLE 4-1

In fall 1996 Warner-Lambert, the consumer goods manufacturer, and Wal-Mart, the department store, began a pilot study of the collaborative planning, forecasting, and replenishment (CPFR) system. This software system facilitates collaboration in forecasting efforts between retailers and manufacturers. CPFR makes it easy to exchange drafts of forecasts as well as details of future sales promotions and past sales trends. The software "makes it easy for each side to review related messages and append new ones." Other companies, including Procter & Gamble, intend to adopt the CPFR system, and software companies intend to launch competing versions of this software. These systems go under the general name of *collaborative systems* [156].

4.4 INFORMATION FOR THE COORDINATION OF SYSTEMS

Within any supply chain are many systems, including various manufacturing, storage, transportation, and retail systems. We have seen that managing any one of these systems involves a series of complex trade-offs. For example, to efficiently run a manufacturing operation, setup and operating costs must be balanced with the costs of inventory and raw materials. Similarly, we have seen in Chapter 3 that inventory level is a delicate balance between holding costs, order setup costs, and required service level. We have also seen in Chapter 3 that there is a balance between inventory costs and transportation costs, because transportation typically involves quantity discounts of one type or another.

However, all of these systems are connected. Specifically, the outputs from one system within the supply chain are the inputs to the next system. For example, the outputs from the manufacturing operation may be the inputs to a transportation or storage system, or both. Thus, trying to find the best set of trade-offs for any one stage isn't sufficient. We need to consider the entire system and coordinate decisions.

This will be true whether or not there is a common owner for several of the systems in the supply chain. If there is, it is clearly in this owner's best interest to ensure that the overall cost is reduced, although this could lead to an increase in costs in one system if larger decreases occur elsewhere. Even if there is no common owner, however, the various systems still need some kind of coordination to operate effectively. The issue, of course, is whose best interest is it to reduce *overall* system cost and how will these savings be shared among the system owners?

To explain this, observe that when the system is not coordinated—that is, each facility in the supply chain does what is best for that facility—the result, as we discussed in Chapter 1, is *local optimization*. Each component of the supply chain optimizes its own operation without due respect to the impact of its policy on other components in the supply chain.

The alternative to this approach is *global optimization*, which implies that one identifies what is best for the entire system. In this case, two issues need to be addressed:

1. Who will optimize?
2. How will the savings obtained through the coordinated strategy be split between the different supply chain facilities?

These issues can be addressed in various ways. For example, in Chapter 3 we discuss the use of supply contracts, and in Chapter 6 we discuss these issues as part of a detailed discussion on strategic partnerships.

To coordinate these facets of the supply chain, information must be available. Specifically, the knowledge of production status and costs, transportation availability and quantity discounts, inventory costs, inventory levels, and various capacities and customer demand is necessary to coordinate systems, especially in cost-effective ways.

4.5 LOCATING DESIRED PRODUCTS

There is more than one way to meet customer demand. Typically, for a make-to-stock system, we think of meeting customer demand from retail inventory if at all possible. However, there are other ways to meet customer demand.

For example, suppose you go to a retailer to buy a large appliance and it is not available. Perhaps you will go to the retailer's competitor down the street. But what if the retailer searches a database and promises to have the item delivered to your house within 24 hours. You will probably feel like you've received great customer service, even though the retailer is out of stock of the item you wanted. Thus, being able to locate and deliver goods is sometimes as effective as having them in stock. But if the goods are located at the retailer's competitor, it is not clear whether this competitor would be willing to transfer the item. We discuss these kinds of issues in detail in Chapter 6, Section 6.5, "Distributor Integration."

4.6 LEAD-TIME REDUCTION

The importance of lead-time reduction cannot be overstated. It typically leads to

1. The ability to quickly fill customer orders that can't be filled from stock.
2. Reduction in the bullwhip effect.
3. More accurate forecasts due to a decreased forecast horizon.
4. Reduction in finished goods inventory levels (see Chapter 3). This is true because one can stock raw materials and packaging material (or subassembly) inventories to reduce finished goods cycle time.

For all of these reasons, many firms are actively searching for suppliers with shorter lead times, and many potential customers consider lead time a very important criterion for vendor selection.

Much of the manufacturing revolution of the past 20 years led to reduced lead times; see [71]. Similarly, in Chapter 5 we will discuss distribution network designs that reduce lead times; these designs can exist only because of the availability of information about the status of the entire supply chain. However, as discussed earlier, effective information systems (e.g., EDI) cut lead times by reducing that portion of the lead time linked to order processing, paperwork, stock picking, transportation delays, and so on. Often these can be a substantial portion of the lead time, especially if there are many different stages in the supply chain and this information is transmitted one stage at a time. Clearly, if a retailer order *rapidly* propagates up the supply chain through the tiers of suppliers as far back as is necessary to meet the order, lead time can be greatly reduced.

Similarly, transferring point-of-sale (POS) data from the retailer to its supplier can help reduce lead times significantly because the supplier can anticipate an incoming order by studying POS data. These issues are covered in depth in Chapter 6, where we discuss strategic partnering between retailers and suppliers.

4.7 INFORMATION AND SUPPLY CHAIN TRADE-OFFS

As observed in Chapter 1, a major challenge in supply chain management is replacing sequential planning processes with global optimization. In sequential planning, each stage of the supply chain optimizes its profit with no regard to the impact of its decisions on other supply chain stages. In contrast, in global optimization the objective is to **coordinate** supply chain activities so as to maximize **supply chain performance.**

Unfortunately, as we discuss in detail below, the managers of different stages in the supply chain have conflicting goals, and it is exactly these conflicts that necessitate the integration and coordination of the different stages in the supply chain. Even within one stage, trade-offs have to be made between reducing inventory or transportation costs, or between increasing product variety or reducing inventory levels.

By carefully using the available information, the supply chain can move toward global optimization, and as a result reduce systemwide cost while accounting for these conflicting goals and various trade-offs. This is easier to do in a centralized system, but even in a decentralized system it may be necessary to find incentives to bring about the integration of supply chain facilities.

4.7.1 Conflicting Objectives in the Supply Chain[3]

We begin with the raw material suppliers. To operate and plan efficiently, these suppliers would like to see stable volume requirements, with little variation in the mix of required materials. In addition, they prefer flexible delivery times, so that they can deliver efficiently to more than one customer. Finally, most suppliers would like to see large volume demands, so that they can take advantage of economies of scope and scale.

Manufacturing management also has its own wish list. High production costs frequently limit the number of expensive changeovers as well as quality problems that may occur at the start of production runs. Typically, manufacturing management wants to achieve high productivity through production efficiencies, leading in turn to low production costs. These goals are facilitated if the demand pattern is known far into the future and has little variability.

The materials, warehousing, and outbound logistics management also have lists of criteria. These include minimizing transportation costs by taking advantage of quantity discounts, minimizing inventory levels, and quickly replenishing stock.

Finally, to satisfy their customers, retailers need short order lead times and efficient and accurate order delivery. The customers in turn demand in-stock items, enormous variety, and low prices.

4.7.2 Designing the Supply Chain for Conflicting Goals

In the past, for some of these goals to be met, others had to be sacrificed. The supply chain was viewed as a set of trade-offs that had to be made. Typically, high inventory levels and shipping costs, and less product variety, enabled manufacturers and retailers to come closer to meeting their goals. At the same time, customers' expectations were not as high as they are today. As we know, these expectations have increased dramatically in recent times as customers demand high variety and low cost, even as increased pressure to control inventory and transportation costs has also become prevalent. Fortunately, the large amount of information now available allows supply chains to be designed so that they come closer to meeting all of these apparently conflicting goals. In effect, some of the trade-offs that were considered several years ago to be inherent in any supply chain may not be trade-offs at all.

In the following subsections, we discuss many of these perceived trade-offs and how, through the use of advanced information technology and creative network design, they

---

[3]This section is based on the recent work of Lee and Billington [89].

don't have to be trade-offs at all in a modern supply chain—or, at the very least, their impact can be reduced.

The Lot Size–Inventory Trade-Off As we have seen, manufacturers would like to have large lot sizes. Per unit setup costs are reduced, manufacturing expertise for a particular product increases, and processes are easier to control. Unfortunately, typical demand doesn't come in large lot sizes, so large lot sizes lead to high inventory. Indeed, much of the focus of the "manufacturing revolution" of the 1980s involved switching to manufacturing systems with smaller lot sizes.

Setup time reduction, Kanban and CONWIP (constant work in progress) systems, and other "modern manufacturing practices" were typically geared toward reducing inventories and improving system responsiveness. Although traditionally viewed in a manufacturing context, this approach to manufacturing has implications across the entire supply chain. Retailers and distributors would like short delivery lead times and wide product variety to respond to the needs of their customers. These advanced manufacturing systems make it possible for manufacturers to meet these needs by enabling them to respond more rapidly to customer needs.

This is especially true if information is available to ensure that the manufacturer has as much time as possible to react to the needs of downstream supply chain members. Similarly, if distributors or retailers have the ability to observe factory status and manufacturer inventory, they can quote lead times to customers more accurately. In addition, these systems enable retailers and distributors to develop an understanding of, and confidence in, the manufacturers' ability. This confidence allows the distributors and retailers to reduce the inventory they hold in anticipation of manufacturing problems.

The Inventory–Transportation Cost Trade-Off There is a similar trade-off between inventory and transportation costs. To see this, we need to review the nature of transportation costs, which we explored in more detail in Chapter 2. First, consider a company that operates its own fleet of trucks. Each truck has some fixed cost of operation (e.g., depreciation, driver time) and some variable cost (e.g., gas). If a truck is always full when it makes a delivery, the cost of operating the truck is spread out over the largest possible number of items. Since, in the end, the same total number of goods is always delivered (more or less equal to customer demand), carrying full truckloads minimizes transportation costs.

Similarly, if an outside firm is used for shipping, the firm typically provides quantity discounts. Also, it is usually cheaper to ship in quantities of full truckloads (TL shipping) than partial (less than) truckloads (LTL shipping). Thus, in this case too, operating full trucks minimizes transportation costs.

In many cases, however, demand is in units of far less than a single truckload. Thus, when items are delivered in full truckloads, they typically have to wait for longer periods of time before they are consumed, leading to higher inventory costs.

Unfortunately, this trade-off can't be eliminated completely. However, we can use advanced information technology to reduce this effect. For example, advanced production control systems can be used to manufacture items as late as possible to ensure full truckloads. Similarly, distribution control systems may allow a materials manager to combine shipments of different products from warehouses to stores in order to fill trucks. This requires knowledge of orders and demand forecasts, as well as supplier delivery schedules. Cross-docking, described earlier in the chapter, also helps to control this trade-off by allowing the retailer to combine shipments from many different manufacturers onto one truck destined for a particular location.

Indeed, recent advances in decision-support systems allow the supply chain to find the appropriate balance between transportation and inventory costs by taking into account all aspects of the supply chain. Regardless of the transportation strategy selected, competition in the transportation industry will force costs down. This effect is enhanced by advanced transportation modes and carrier selection programs that ensure that the most cost-effective approach is used for each particular delivery, lowering overall transportation costs.

The Lead Time–Transportation Cost Trade-Off   Total lead time is made up of time devoted to processing orders, to procuring and manufacturing items, and to transporting items between the various stages of the supply chain. As we mentioned above, transportation costs are lowest when large quantities of items are transported between stages of the supply chain. However, lead times can often be reduced if items are transported immediately after they are manufactured or arrive from suppliers. Thus, there is a trade-off between holding items until enough accumulate to reduce transportation costs and shipping them immediately to reduce lead time.

Again, this trade-off cannot be completely eliminated, but information can be used to reduce its effect. Transportation costs can be controlled as described in the previous section, reducing the need to hold items until a sufficient number accumulate. In addition, improved forecasting techniques and information systems reduce the other components of lead time, so that it may not be essential to reduce the transportation component.

The Product Variety–Inventory Trade-Off   Evidently product variety greatly increases the complexity of supply chain management. Manufacturers that make a multitude of different products with smaller lot sizes find their manufacturing costs increase and their manufacturing efficiency decreases. To maintain the same lead times as a company may have had with fewer products, smaller amounts will probably be shipped so warehouses will need to hold a larger variety of products; thus, increasing product variety increases both transportation and warehousing costs. Finally, because it is usually difficult to accurately forecast the demand for each product, because all are competing for the same customers, higher inventory levels must be maintained to ensure the same service level.

The main issue that a firm supplying a variety of products needs to address is how to match supply and demand effectively. For instance, consider a manufacturer of winter ski jackets. Typically, 12 months before the selling season the firm introduces a number of designs that it will sell in the winter. Unfortunately, it is not clear how many ski jackets to produce from each design; therefore, it is not clear how to plan production.

One way to support the required product variety efficiently is to apply the concept called *delayed differentiation*, which we will discuss in Chapter 5, Section 5.2, and Chapter 9. In a supply chain in which delayed differentiation is utilized, *generic products* are shipped as far as possible down the supply chain before variety is added. This could mean that a single product is received in the distribution center, and there it is modified or customized according to customer demand as seen by the warehouse.

Observe that by doing so, we are again using the concept of risk pooling introduced in Chapter 3. Indeed, by shipping a generic product to the warehouses, we have aggregated customer demand across all products. As we have seen, this implies a more accurate demand forecast with a much smaller variability, leading to reduced safety stock. This process of aggregating across products is similar to the process of aggregating across retailers (see Chapter 3).

Delayed differentiation is one example of *design for logistics*, a concept we will discuss in much more detail in Chapter 9.

The Cost–Customer Service Trade-Off   All of these trade-offs are examples of the cost–customer service trade-off. Reducing inventories, manufacturing costs, and transportation costs typically comes at the expense of customer service. In the preceding subsections, we have seen that the level of customer service can be maintained while decreasing these costs by using information and appropriate supply chain designs. Implicitly, we have defined customer service as the ability of a retailer to meet a customer's demand from stock.

Of course, customer service could mean the ability of a retailer to meet a customer's demand quickly. We have discussed how transshipping may make this possible without increasing inventory. In addition, direct shipping from warehouses to the homes of retail customers is another way to achieve this. For example, Sears delivers a large proportion of the large appliances that it sells directly from warehouses to the end customer. This controls inventory cost at retail stores and allows warehouses to take direct advantage of risk pooling effects. For this kind of system to work, information about warehouse inventories must be available at the stores, and order information should be rapidly transmitted to the warehouse. This is just one example of a system in which available information and appropriate supply chain design lead to decreased costs and increased service. In this case, costs are lower when the inventory is stored in a centralized warehouse than when there is a larger inventory in the store. At the same time customer service is improved because customers have a larger inventory to choose from and appliances are immediately delivered to their homes.

Finally, it is important to point out that so far we have emphasized how supply chain technology and management can be applied to increase customer service levels *defined in some traditional sense* and reduce costs. However, advanced supply chain management techniques and information systems could be used to give customers a kind of service that they have never been able to realize before, and for which suppliers could charge a premium. One such example is the concept of *mass customization*, which involves delivering highly personalized goods and services to customers at reasonable prices and at high volume. Although this may not have been economically feasible in the past, improving logistics and information systems now makes this possible. The concept of mass customization is explained in more detail in Chapter 9.

SUMMARY

The bullwhip effect suggests that variability in demand increases as one moves up in the supply chain. This increase in variability causes significant operational inefficiencies (e.g., it forces every facility in the supply chain to increase inventory significantly). Indeed, in [90] the authors estimate that in certain industries, such as the pharmaceutical industry, this distorted information can cause the total inventory in the supply chain to exceed 100 days of supply. Thus, it is important to identify strategies to efficiently cope with the bullwhip effect. In this chapter, we have identified specific techniques to "counteract" the bullwhip effect, one of which is information sharing, that is, centralized demand information.

Finally, we looked at the interaction of various supply chain stages. Typically, operating a supply chain is viewed as a series of trade-offs both within and between the different stages. We concluded that information is the key enabler of integrating the different supply chain stages and discussed how information can be used to reduce the necessity of many of these trade-offs. Chapter 5 provides more information on this and related topics.

DISCUSSION QUESTIONS

1. Answer these questions about the Barilla case study:
   a. Diagnose the underlying causes of the difficulties that the JITD program was created to solve. What are the benefits of this program?
   b. What conflicts or barriers internal to Barilla does the JITD program create? What causes these conflicts? As Giorgio Maggiali, how would you deal with this?
   c. As one of Barilla's customers, what would your response to JITD be? Why?
   d. In the environment in which Barilla operated in 1990, do you believe JITD would be feasible? Effective? If so, which customers would you target next? How would you convince them that the JITD program was worth trying? If not, what alternatives would you suggest to combat some of the difficulties that Barilla's operating system faces?

2. Discuss how each of the following helps to alleviate the bullwhip effect:
   a. E-commerce and the Internet.
   b. Express delivery.
   c. Collaborative forecasts.
   d. Everyday low pricing.
   e. Vendor-managed inventory (VMI).
   f. Supply contracts.

3. What are the advantages to retailers of sharing inventory? For instance, suppose you go to a car dealer to find a blue model, and he doesn't have that model in stock. Typically, he will obtain the model from another local dealer. What are the disadvantages to the retailer?

4. Discuss five ways that the lead times within a supply chain can be reduced.

5. Consider the supply chain for breakfast cereal. Discuss the competing objectives of the farmers who make the raw materials, the manufacturing division of the company that makes the cereal, the logistics division of the company that makes the cereal, the marketing division of the company that makes the cereal, the distribution arm of the grocery chain that sells the cereal, and the manager of an individual grocery store that sells the cereal.

CHAPTER 5

Supply Chain Integration

Modern Book Distribution, Inc.

Richard Guy, CEO of Modern Book Distribution, Inc. (MBD), scanned the "Executive Summary" of the consulting report he had just received. Guy saw the report was filled with the latest buzzwords and hot concepts:

Establish cross-docking facilities for high-volume deliveries to large customers ... centralize storage operations to decrease safety stock levels ... leverage point-of-sale data to move toward a pull distribution strategy ...

Guy was familiar with all of these phrases and concepts at a superficial level, of course—anybody who occasionally picked up *The Wall Street Journal* or *Business Week* would be. He was less sure, however, if the consultants were trying to dazzle him with fads or if the kind of radical operating changes that were being proposed in the report would help to position MBD for the future.

Founded 80 years ago, MBD had been for many years one of the largest book distributors in the country. From its seven regional warehouses, MBD services major bookstore chains and smaller independent booksellers throughout the country. The company had continuously strived to improve its service levels and operating efficiency, and it was considered the most efficient book distributor in the industry. Using advanced forecasting techniques to control inventory levels and technologically advanced warehouses to control operating expenses, MBD shipped virtually all of the orders it received within two days from its stock of nearly 500,000 books, the largest in the industry.

The bookselling industry, however, had been changing dramatically, and Guy realized that MBD would have to make changes to remain a book distributing powerhouse. In particular, two relatively new types of retailers were becoming more and more dominant in the industry: large superstores and online booksellers. Both of these categories of retailers presented new and unique challenges to their distributors.

In the past MBD had interacted primarily with the superstores through large regional distribution centers (DCs) that the superstores maintained. In general, MBD had shipped to the DCs consolidated orders of many different titles bound ultimately for many different stores. As these superstores learned from the experiences of large retailers in other industries, they started to demand new kinds of services from their distributors. For example, some retailers had started to strongly encourage MBD to ship directly to stores, bypassing the DCs. In addition, as the industry consolidated, these huge superstores were developing more leverage with their distributors. They used this leverage to force the distributors to accept lower and lower margins.

On-line booksellers presented an entirely different set of challenges to Guy and the managers at MBD. Initially, these retailers kept no inventory at

---

Source: MBD is a fictional company. This case is loosely based on the experiences of several companies in this industry.

hand. Instead, they took orders and relayed them to distributors like MBD, who delivered the books to the retailers for repackaging and shipment. Recently, the large on-line retailers had started moving toward a new business model: they established their own distribution centers where they kept inventory and handled packaging and shipment of books directly to the end customers.

Guy realized that these industry changes could provide opportunities and challenges for his company. In particular, the new business model developed by some of the on-line retailers, in which they established their own warehouses, may cut MBD's profit margins. Clearly, if MBD was to maintain its reputation as one of the nation's leading book distributors, it would have to start doing things differently.

Furthermore, he had the consultant's report, filled with recommendations and designs for new distribution systems. Guy knew that he and his management team would have to develop an understanding of these issues in order to properly assess the consultant's suggestions. As he prepared for the next day's meeting, Guy made a list of many questions:

- What is the impact of the Internet on the business strategy used by the superstores and the on-line sellers? In particular, are on-line retailers going to keep inventory of most book categories in their distribution centers?
- How can MBD use the Internet to better serve their customers, the superstores, and the on-line sellers?
- Should MBD encourage retailers to make point-of-sale (POS) data available? What is the value of these data? How can they be used effectively?
- Should MBD establish more regional warehouses? Should it eliminate some warehouses and become more centralized? Was cross-docking really a viable strategy for book distributors?
- Should MBD encourage customers to utilize direct shipping services? Should it discourage them?

By the end of this chapter, you should be able to answer the following questions:

- What is the impact of the Internet on the supply chain strategy employed by the traditional retailers and the on-line stores? In particular, what is the impact on distribution and fulfillment strategies?
- What is a push strategy? A pull strategy? A push–pull strategy? Should MBD implement one of these strategies? What would it require? What is the impact? What would it cost?
- What distribution strategies are appropriate for MBD's businesses? What questions should MBD management ask when assessing these strategies?
- How can MBD benefit from changes in the book distribution industry?
- What are the advantages to MBD in having fewer warehouses and a more centralized operation? More warehouses and a more decentralized operation?

5.1 INTRODUCTION

In Chapter 1, we observed that supply chain management revolves around *efficient integration of suppliers, manufacturers, warehouses, and stores.* The challenge in supply chain integration, of course, is to coordinate activities across the supply chain so that the enterprise can improve performance: reduce cost, increase service level, reduce the bullwhip effect, better utilize resources, and effectively respond to changes in the market place. As many companies have recently realized, these challenges are met not only by coordinating production, transportation, and inventory decisions, but, more generally, by integrating the **front-end** of the supply chain, customer demand, to the **back-end** of the supply chain, the production and manufacturing portion of the supply chain. The objective of this chapter is to illustrate the opportunities and the challenges associated with supply chain integration. We consider

- Various supply chain strategies, including push, pull, and a relatively new paradigm, the push–pull strategy.

- A framework for matching products and industries with supply chain strategies.
- Demand-driven supply chain strategies.
- The impact of the Internet on supply chain integration.
- Effective distribution strategies.

Obviously, the availability of information plays an important role in supply chain integration. In some cases, the supply chain must be designed to make this information available. In other cases, the supply chain strategy must be designed to *take advantage* of information that is already available. And in many cases, an expensive network must be designed to compensate for the lack of information.

5.2 PUSH, PULL, AND PUSH–PULL SYSTEMS

Traditional supply chain strategies are often categorized as push or pull strategies. Probably, this stems from the manufacturing revolution of the 1980s, in which manufacturing systems were divided into these categories. Interestingly, in the last few years, a number of companies have employed a hybrid approach, the push–pull supply chain paradigm. In this section, we explain each one of the strategies.

5.2.1 Push-Based Supply Chain

In a *push-based supply chain*, production and distribution decisions are based on long-term forecasts. Typically, the manufacturer bases demand forecasts on orders received from the retailer's warehouses. It therefore takes much longer for a push-based supply chain to react to the changing marketplace, which can lead to

- The inability to meet changing demand patterns.
- The obsolescence of supply chain inventory as demand for certain products disappears.

In addition, we saw in Chapter 4 that the variability of orders received from the retailers and the warehouses is much larger than the variability in customer demand, due to the bullwhip effect. This increase in variability leads to

- Excessive inventories due to the need for large safety stocks (see Chapter 3).
- Larger and more variable production batches.
- Unacceptable service levels.
- Product obsolescence.

Specifically, the bullwhip effect leads to inefficient resource utilization, because planning and managing are much more difficult. For instance, it is not clear how a manufacturer should determine production capacity. Should it be based on peak demand, which implies that most of the time the manufacturer has expensive resources sitting idle, or should it be based on average demand, which requires extra—and expensive—capacity during periods of peak demand? Similarly, it is not clear how to plan transportation capacity: based on peak demand or average demand. Thus, in a push-based supply chain, we often find increased transportation costs, high inventory levels, and/or high manufacturing costs, due to the need for emergency production changeovers.

5.2.2 Pull-Based Supply Chain

In a *pull-based supply chain*, production and distribution are demand driven so that they are coordinated with true customer demand rather than forecast demand [9]. In a pure pull system, the firm does not hold any inventory and only responds to *specific* orders. This is enabled by fast information flow mechanisms to transfer information about customer demand (e.g., POS data) to the various supply chain participants. Pull systems are intuitively attractive since they lead to

- A decrease in lead times achieved through the ability to better anticipate incoming orders from the retailers.
- A decrease in inventory at the retailers since inventory levels at these facilities increase with lead times (see Chapter 3).
- A decrease in variability in the system and, in particular, variability faced by manufacturers (see the discussion in Section 4.2.2) due to lead-time reduction.
- Decreased inventory at the manufacturer due to the reduction in variability.

EXAMPLE 5-1

A major apparel manufacturer recently changed its supply chain strategy to a pull-based system. Retailers order from this manufacturer about once a month, but transfer POS data much more frequently, for example daily or weekly. These data allow the manufacturer to continuously adjust production quantities according to true customer demand.

Thus, in a pull-based supply chain, we typically see a significant reduction in system inventory level, enhanced ability to manage resources, and a reduction in system costs when compared with the equivalent push-based system.

On the other hand, pull-based systems are often difficult to implement when lead times are so long that it is impractical to react to demand information. Also, in pull-based systems, it is frequently more difficult to take advantage of economies of scale in manufacturing and transportation since systems are not planned far ahead in time.

These advantages and disadvantages of push and pull supply chains have led companies to look for a new supply chain strategy that takes advantage of the best of both. Frequently, this is a **push–pull** supply chain strategy.

5.2.3 Push–Pull Supply Chain

In a *push–pull* strategy, some stages of the supply chain, typically the initial stages, are operated in a push-based manner while the remaining stages employ a pull-based strategy. The interface between the push-based stages and the pull-based stages is known as the **push–pull boundary.**

To better understand this strategy, consider the **supply chain time line**, that is, the time that elapses between procurement of raw material, that is, the beginning of the time line, and the delivery of an order to the customer, that is, the end of the time line. The push–pull boundary is located somewhere along the time line and it indicates the point in time when the firm switches from managing the supply chain using one strategy, typically a push strategy, to managing it using a different strategy, typically a pull strategy. This is illustrated in Figure 5-1.

Consider a PC manufacturer who builds to stock and thus makes all production and distribution decisions based on forecast. This is a typical push system. By contrast, an example of a push–pull strategy is one in which the manufacturer builds to order. This implies that component inventory is managed based on forecast, but final assembly is in response to a specific customer request. Thus, the push portion of the manufacturer's supply chain is that portion prior to assembly, while the pull part of the supply chain starts with assembly and is performed based on actual customer demand. The push–pull boundary is at the beginning of assembly.

Observe that in this case the manufacturer takes advantage of the fact that *aggregate forecasts are more accurate* (see Chapter 3). Indeed, demand for a component is an

FIGURE 5-1 Push–pull supply chains.

aggregation of demand for all finished products that use this component. Since aggregate forecasts are more accurate, uncertainty in component demand is much smaller than uncertainty in finished goods demand and this leads to safety stock reduction. Dell Computers has used this strategy very effectively and is an excellent example of the impact of the push–pull strategy on supply chain performance.

Postponement, or delayed differentiation in product design (see Chapter 9), is also an excellent example of a push–pull strategy. In postponement, the firm designs the product and the manufacturing process so that decisions about which specific product is being manufactured can be delayed as long as possible. The manufacturing process starts by producing a generic or family product, which is differentiated to a specific end-product when demand is revealed. The portion of the supply chain prior to product differentiation is typically operated using a push-based strategy. In other words, the generic product is built and transported based on a long-term forecast. Since demand for the generic product is an aggregation of demand for all its corresponding end-products, forecasts are more accurate and thus inventory levels are reduced. In contrast, customer demand for a specific end-product typically has a high level of uncertainty and thus product differentiation occurs only in response to individual demand. Thus, the portion of the supply chain starting from the time of differentiation is pull-based.

5.2.4 Identifying the Appropriate Supply Chain Strategy

What is the appropriate supply chain strategy for a particular product? Should the firm use a push-based supply chain strategy, a pull-based strategy, or a push–pull strategy? Figure 5-2 provides a framework for matching supply chain strategies with products and industries. The vertical axis provides information on uncertainty in customer demand, while the horizontal axis represents the importance of economies of scale, either in production or distribution.

Everything else being equal, higher demand uncertainty leads to a preference for managing the supply chain based on realized demand: a pull strategy. Alternatively, smaller demand uncertainty leads to an interest in managing the supply chain based on a long-term forecast: a push strategy.

Similarly, everything else being equal, the higher the importance of economies of scale in reducing cost, the greater the value of aggregating demand, and thus the greater the importance of managing the supply chain based on long-term forecast, a push-based strategy. If economies of scale are not important, aggregation does not reduce cost, so a pull-based strategy makes more sense.

In Figure 5-2, we partition the region spanned by these two dimensions into four boxes. Box I represents industries (or, more precisely, products) that are characterized

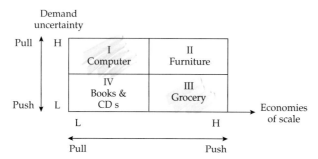

FIGURE 5-2 Matching supply chain strategies with products.

by high uncertainty and by situations in which economies of scale in production, assembly, or distribution are not important, such as the computer industry. Our framework suggests that a pull-based supply chain strategy is appropriate for these industries and products. This is exactly the strategy employed by Dell Computers.

Box III represents products that are characterized by low demand uncertainty and important economies of scale. Products in the grocery industry such as beer, pasta, and soup belong to that category. Demand for these products is quite stable, while reducing transportation cost by shipping full truckloads is critical for controlling supply chain cost. In this case, a pull strategy is not appropriate. Indeed, a traditional, push-based retail strategy is appropriate, because managing inventory based on long-term forecasts does not increase inventory holding costs while delivery costs are reduced by leveraging economies of scale.

Boxes I and III represent situations in which it is relatively easy to identify an efficient supply chain strategy. In the remaining two cases, there is a mismatch between the strategies suggested by the two attributes, uncertainty and the importance of economies of scale. Indeed, in these boxes uncertainty "pulls" the supply chain towards one strategy, while economies of scale "push" the supply chain in a different direction.

For instance, box IV represents products characterized by low demand uncertainty, indicating a push-based supply chain, and low economies of scale, suggesting a pull-based supply chain strategy. Many high-volume/fast-moving books and CDs fall in this category. In this case, a more careful analysis is required, since both traditional retail push strategies and more innovative push–pull strategies may be appropriate, depending on the specific costs and uncertainties. We discuss this choice in more detail in Section 5.4.

Finally, box II represents products and industries for which uncertainty in demand is high while economies of scale are important in reducing production and/or delivery costs. The furniture industry is an excellent example of this situation. Indeed, a typical furniture retailer offers a large number of similar products distinguished by shape, color, fabric, and so forth, and as a result demand uncertainty is very high. Unfortunately, these are bulky products and hence delivery costs are also high.

Thus, in this case, there is a need to distinguish between the production and the distribution strategies. The production strategy has to follow a pull-based strategy since it is impossible to make production decisions based on long-term forecasts. On the other hand, the distribution strategy needs to take advantage of economies of scale in order to reduce transportation cost. This is exactly the strategy employed by many retailers that do not keep any inventory of furniture. When a customer places an order, it is sent to the manufacturer, who orders the fabric and produces to order. Once the product is ready, it is shipped, typically using truckload carriers, together with many other products to the retail store and from there to the customer. For this purpose, the manufacturer typically has a fixed delivery schedule and this is used to aggregate all products that are delivered to stores in the same region, thus reducing transportation costs due to economies of scale. Hence, the supply chain strategy followed by furniture manufacturers is, in some sense, a **pull–push** strategy where production is done based on realized demand, a pull strategy, while delivery is according to a fixed schedule, a push strategy.

The automobile industry is another example of the conditions of box II. A typical car manufacturer offers a large number of similar products distinguished by functionality, motor power, shape, color, number of doors, sports wheels, and so forth, and as a result demand uncertainty for a particular configuration is very high. Delivery costs are quite high as well. Traditionally, this industry has employed a push-based supply chain strategy, building inventory for the dealer distribution systems. Thus, the automobile industry does not currently follow the model developed in Figure 5-2.

Recently, however, GM announced a dramatic vision for restructuring the way it is designing, building, and selling its products [167]. The goal to allow customers to customize and order cars on-line and have the cars delivered *to the customer's door* in less than 10 days. GM is moving exactly in the direction predicted by our model, toward a build-to-order strategy.

Unfortunately, lead times in the automobile industry are currently long: 50 to 60 days on average. To achieve its vision, GM has to redesign the entire supply chain, including the way it partners with suppliers, the way it manufactures products, and the way it distributes products. Reducing lead times to 10 days or below may also require a significant reduction in the number of options and configurations offered to buyers.

5.2.5 Implementing a Push–Pull Strategy

The framework developed in the previous section attempts to characterize the appropriate level of pull and push for different products. For instance, a high degree of pull is appropriate for products that belong to box I. Of course, achieving the design of the pull system depends on many factors, including product complexity, manufacturing lead times, and supplier–manufacturer relationships. Similarly, there are many ways to implement a push–pull strategy, depending on the location of the push–pull boundary. For instance, Dell locates the push–pull boundary at the assembly point, while furniture manufacturers locate the boundary at the production point.

EXAMPLE 5-2

Consider the automobile industry, known for its long transportation lead times. Prior to its latest effort to implement a make-to-order strategy, there were previous attempts to implement a push–pull strategy. In 1994, GM announced the establishment of a regional distribution center in Orlando, Florida, where an inventory of about 1,500 Cadillacs was maintained. Dealers could order cars they did not have in their lot from the distribution center, and the cars would be delivered within 24 hours. Thus, GM was attempting to employ a push–pull strategy in which inventory at its regional distribution center was managed based on long-term forecasts while delivery to dealers was based on realized demand. Thus, the push–pull boundary was located at the manufacturer's distribution center.

As discussed in Chapter 10, two major issues contributed to the failure of this strategy. First, the regional warehouse shifted inventory costs from the dealers to GM, since it allowed dealers to reduce inventory levels. Second, the regional distribution center equalized small and large dealers. If all dealers have access to the regional warehouse, then there is no difference between small and large dealers. Thus, it is difficult to see why large dealers would be interested in participating in such an arrangement.

The discussion so far suggests that the push strategy is applied to that portion of the supply chain where demand uncertainty is relatively small and thus managing this portion based on long-term forecast is appropriate. On the other hand, the pull strategy is applied to the portion of the supply chain time line where uncertainty is high, and hence it is important to manage this portion based on realized demand. This distinction between the two portions of the supply chain has an important impact on the objectives of the supply chain strategy, as well as on organizational skills required to manage the system effectively.

Since uncertainty in the push portion of the supply chain is relatively small, service level is not an issue, so the focus can be on **cost minimization**. In addition, this portion of the supply chain is characterized not only by low demand uncertainty and economies of scale in production and/or transportation, but also by long lead times and complex supply chain structures, including product assembly at various levels. Thus, cost minimization is achieved by better utilizing resources such as production and distribution capacities while minimizing inventory, transportation, and production costs.

On the other hand, the pull portion of the supply chain is characterized by high uncertainty, simple supply chain structure, and a short cycle time. Hence, the focus here is on service level. Specifically, high service level is achieved by deploying a **flexible** and **responsive** supply chain, that is, a supply chain that can adapt quickly to changes in customer demand.

This implies that different processes need to be used in different portions of the supply chain. Since the focus in the pull part of the supply chain is on service level, **order fulfillment** processes are typically applied. Similarly, since the focus of the push part of the supply chain is on cost and resource utilization, supply chain **planning** processes are used here to develop an effective strategy for the next few weeks or months. In Chapter 12, we provide a detailed discussion of supply chain master planning. Table 5-1 summerizes the characteristics of the push and pull portions of the supply chain.

EXAMPLE 5-3

Consider a supplier of fashion skiwear such as Sport Obermeyer [53]. Every year the company introduces many new designs, or products, for which forecast demand is highly uncertain. One strategy used successfully by Sport Obermeyer involves distinguishing between high-risk and low-risk designs. Low-risk products, that is, those for which uncertainty and price are low, are produced in advance using long-term forecasts and focusing on cost minimization, a push-based strategy. But decisions on production quantities for high-risk products are delayed until there is a clear market signal on customer demand for each style, a pull strategy. Since fabric lead times are long, the manufacturer typically orders fabric for high-risk products well in advance of receiving information about market demand, based only on long-term forecasts.

In this case, the manufacturer takes advantage of the same principle applied by Dell Computers: that aggregate forecasts are more accurate. Since demand for fabrics is an aggregation of demand for all products that use that fabric, demand uncertainty is low and thus fabric inventory is managed based on push strategy. Thus, Sport Obermayer uses a push–pull strategy for the high-risk products and a push strategy for the low-risk products.

Notice that the push portion and the pull portion of the supply chain interact only at the push–pull boundary. This is the point along the supply chain time line where there is a need to coordinate the two supply chain strategies, typically through **buffer inventory**. However, this inventory plays a different role in each portion. In the push portion, buffer inventory at the boundary is part of the output generated by the tactical planning process, while in the pull part it represents the input to the fulfillment process.

TABLE 5-1

**CHARACTERISTICS OF THE PUSH AND PULL
PORTIONS OF THE SUPPLY CHAIN**

Portion	Push	Pull
Objective	Minimize cost	Maximize service level
Complexity	High	Low
Focus	Resource allocation	Responsiveness
Lead time	Long	Short
Processes	Supply chain planning	Order fulfillment

Thus, the interface between the push portion of the supply chain and the pull portion of the supply chain is forecast demand. This forecast, which is based on historical data obtained from the pull portion, is used to drive the supply chain planning process and determines the buffer inventory.

5.3 DEMAND-DRIVEN STRATEGIES

The framework we have developed in this chapter requires integrating demand information into the supply chain planning process. This information is generated by applying two different processes:

- **Demand forecast:** A process in which historical demand data are used to develop long-term estimates of expected demand, that is, forecasts (see Chapter 3 for details).
- **Demand shaping:** A process in which the firm determines the impact of various marketing plans such as promotion, pricing discounts, rebates, new product introduction, and product withdrawal on demand forecasts.

Of course, in either case, the forecast is not completely accurate, and hence an important output from the demand-forecast and demand-shaping processes is an estimate of the **accuracy** of the forecast, the so-called **forecast error**, measured according to its **standard deviation**. This information provides insight into the likelihood that demand will be higher (or lower) than the forecast.

High demand forecast error has a detrimental impact on supply chain performance, resulting in lost sales, obsolete inventory, and inefficient utilization of resources. Can the firm employ supply chain strategies to increase forecast accuracy and thus decrease forecast error? We identify the following approaches:

- Select the push–pull boundary so that demand is aggregated over one or more of the following dimensions:
  —Demand is aggregated across products.
  —Demand is aggregated across geography.
  —Demand is aggregated across time.
  The objective is clear. Since aggregate forecasts are more accurate, the result is improved forecast accuracy.
- Use market analysis and demographic and economic trends to improve forecast accuracy (see Chapter 3 for details).
- Determine the optimal assortment of products by store so as to reduce the number of SKUs competing in the same market. Indeed, we are familiar with a large retailer who used to keep in each store more than 30 different types of garbage cans. It

was relatively easy to predict aggregate demand across all SKUs in the garbage can category, but very difficult to predict demand for an individual SKU.

- Incorporate collaborative planning and forecasting processes with your customers so as to achieve a better understanding of market demand, impact of promotions, pricing events, and advertising.

At the end of the demand planning process, the firm has a demand forecast by SKU by location. The next step is to analyze the supply chain and see if it can support these forecasts. This process, called **supply and demand management**, involves matching supply and demand by identifying a strategy that minimizes total production, transportation, and inventory costs, or a strategy that maximizes profits. Along the way, the firm also determines the best way to handle volatility and risks in the supply chain. We describe this tactical planning process in Chapter 12.

Of course, demand planning and tactical planning impact each other. Thus, an iterative process must be used to identify

- The best way to allocate marketing budgets and associated supply and distribution resources.
- The impact of deviations from forecast demand.
- The impact of changes in supply chain lead times.
- The impact of competitors' promotional activities on demand and supply chain strategies.

The importance of the iterative process is demonstrated by the following example.

EXAMPLE 5-4

A classic example of the perils of not including supply chain analysis in market plans is the story of Campbell's Soup's winter promotion. In one unfortunate season, the marketing department decided to promote chicken noodle soup in the winter. Of course, there is a seasonal spike in the demand for soup in winter anyway. By itself, this seasonal spike requires preparing and storing chicken and ingredients in huge quantities in the spring and fall in order to meet the demand. In addition, due to the promotion, production had to start early and use overtime capacity in order to meet the demand. Unfortunately, the cost of the excess production and inventory requirements far exceeded the revenue from the promotions [32].

5.4 THE IMPACT OF THE INTERNET ON SUPPLY CHAIN STRATEGIES

The influence of the Internet and e-commerce on the economy in general, and business practice in particular, has been tremendous. Changes are happening rapidly. For instance, the direct-business model employed by industry giants such as Dell Computers and Amazon.com enables customers to order products over the Internet and thus allows companies to sell their products without relying on third-party distributors. Similarly, business-to-business e-commerce, which is predicted by Forrester Research to skyrocket from $43 billion in 1998 to $1.3 trillion in 2003, promises convenience and cost reduction.

In parallel, the Internet and the emerging e-business models have produced expectations that many supply chain problems will be resolved merely by using these new technology and business models. E-business strategies were supposed to reduce cost, increase service level, and increase flexibility and, of course, profits, albeit sometime in the future. In reality, these expectations have frequently gone unmet, as many of the new e-businesses have not been successful. In many cases, the downfall of some of the highest-profile Internet businesses has been attributed to their logistics strategies. Several examples follow.

EXAMPLE 5-5

The furniture industry seemed ripe for modernization and e-business when executives from living.com purchased Shaw Furniture Gallery, the 10th largest furniture store in North Carolina, in March of 1999. The purchase was intended to provide living.com with access to top-line furniture manufacturers. After an investment of $70 million in capital and a spot as the exclusive Amazon.com furniture link, living.com declared bankruptcy on August 29, 2000. Reasons for the failure included the investment in a new information system that did not function correctly and the switch to a carrier that had no experience with furniture delivery, leading to a stunning 30 percent return rate.

EXAMPLE 5-6

Furniture.com, launched in January 1999, offered thousands of products from many furniture makers, although only few brand names. The company had $22 million in sales in the first nine months of 2000 and one million visitors a month to its website. Its recent (November 6, 2000) downfall was due to logistics details, and, in particular, inefficient delivery processes. Initially, Furniture.com used carriers to ship its products from a central warehouse to the customers. Since transportation costs were too high, the firm formed an alliance with six regional distributors. Unfortunately, these relationships were hard to maintain and left many problems unsolved, including handling of repairs and returns.

EXAMPLE 5-7

Founded in 1989, Peapod is based in Skokie, Illinois, and is considered one of America's leading on-line grocers. As a highly experienced on-line grocer, the company serves more than 130,000 customers. In 1999, Peapod had sales of $73 million and generated a loss of $29 million. Peapod's mounting losses and inability to secure additional funding resulted in a buyout of a majority of its stock in April 2000 by Royal Ahold, the international food company. Peapod thus escaped the fate of Shoplink.com, Streamline.com, and Priceline's WebHouse Club, all of which have recently left the on-line grocery business. These failures are generally attributed to high delivery costs.

EXAMPLE 5-8

What started in 1995 as Earth's biggest bookstore is rapidly becoming Earth's biggest store. Amazon.com's main site offers millions of books, CDs, DVDs, videos, toys, tools, and electronics. In addition, Amazon.com conducts auctions for items ranging from art to real estate and provides schedulers, address books, and on-line greeting cards. Amazon also owns stakes in on-line sellers of pet supplies, prescription drugs, cars, groceries, and more. Although Amazon.com has become a model for Internet companies by placing market share ahead of profits and making acquisitions funded by its meteoric market capitalization, it has yet to make a profit. In 1996 the company had $16M in sales and a $6M loss; in 1999 it had $1.6B in sales and a $720M loss; in 2000 it had $2.7B in sales and a $1.4B loss, hardly a financial success story.

Some companies, of course, are extremely successful in developing new business models that allow them to increase profits significantly and capture a sizeable market share. These companies use the Internet as the driver of business change.

EXAMPLE 5-9

According to the Stern Stewart EVA 1000 database, Dell Computers has outperformed the competition by over 3,000 percent in terms of shareholder growth over the eight-year period 1988 to 1996. This example is important in our discussion since competition in the PC industry is not based on new technology. Indeed, most PC manufacturers use the same technology, the so-called Wintel standard. Competition in the PC industry is based primarily on price and service level. Dell's success is attributed to its virtual integration, a strategy that blurs the traditional boundaries between suppliers, manufacturers, and end users. Dell's decision to sell computers built from components produced by other manufacturers has relieved the firm of the burdens of owning assets, doing research and development, and managing a large workforce. At the same time, Dell only produces to order, and thus keeps no finished goods inventory. These business decisions have allowed Dell to grow much faster than its competition and maintain only eight days of inventory.

Despite its downturn in 2001 and the write-off of $2.25B in excess inventory, Cisco is a good model of a company that makes innovative use of the Internet.

EXAMPLE 5-10

According to Peter Solvik, who is CIO of Cisco, "Cisco's Internet-based business model has been instrumental in its ability to quadruple in size from 1994 to 1998 ($1.3 billion to over $8 billion), hire approximately 1,000 new employees per quarter while increasing their productivity, and save $560M annually in business expenses." Over 80 percent of Cisco's customer business is performed over the Internet, and this is only a small part of the entire picture. Indeed, to differentiate itself from the competition in what is essentially a commodity business, Cisco acquires companies that have leading technology and integrates these companies rapidly with its systems. It also sells network solutions, not just components, to its customers. This requires coordination of hardware, software, and service components in many sales. The ability to provide these services and integrate comes from Cisco's single-enterprise system. This system provides the backbone for all activities in the company and not only connects customers and employees but also chip manufacturers, component distributors, contract manufacturers, logistics companies, and systems integrators. These participants can perform like one company because they all rely on the same web-based data sources. All of Cisco's suppliers see the same demand and do not rely on their own forecasts based on information flowing from multiple points in the supply chain. Cisco also built a dynamic replenishment system to help reduce supplier inventory. Cisco's average turns in 1999 were 10, compared with an average of 4 for competitors. Inventory turns for commodity items are even more impressive: they reach 25–35 turns a year.

The previous examples raise an important question: Why is it that, in some cases, these new business models fail, while, in other cases, they are incredibly successful? If Dell and Cisco can use the Internet to develop such effective business models, what inhibits other firms from adopting similar techniques?

To answer this question, we require a better understanding of Internet-based supply chain strategies.

5.4.1 What Is E-Business?

To better understand the impact of the Internet on supply chains, we start by introducing our definition of e-business and e-commerce.

E-business is a collection of business models and processes motivated by Internet technology and focusing on improvement of extended enterprise performance.

E-commerce is the ability to perform major commerce transactions electronically.

These definitions lead to several observations. First, e-commerce is only part of e-business. Second, Internet technology is the force behind the business change. Finally, the focus in e-business is on the extended enterprise, that is, intra-organizational, business-to-consumer (B2C), and business-to-business (B2B) transactions. B2C refers to businesses that are "direct to customer," especially retail activities over the Internet, and includes products, insurance, banking, and so forth. B2B refers to business conducted over the Internet predominantly between businesses. This includes both the currently ubiquitous exchanges, as well as collaboration with suppliers and vendors to achieve common goals.

Many companies have recognized that the Internet can have a huge impact on supply chain performance. Indeed, these companies have observed that the Internet can help them move away from the traditional push strategies employed by most supply chains. Initially, the move was toward a pull strategy, but, eventually, many companies ended up with a push–pull supply chain.

5.4.2 The Grocery Industry

Consider the grocery industry. A typical supermarket employs a push-based strategy where inventory at the warehouses and stores is based on a forecast. When Peapod was founded 11 years ago, the idea was to establish a pure pull strategy with no inventory and no facilities. When a customer ordered groceries, Peapod would pick the products at a nearby supermarket. This strategy had significant service problems since stockout rates were very high (about 8 to 10 percent). In the last few years, Peapod has changed its business model to a push–pull strategy by setting up a number of warehouses; stockout rates are now less than 2 percent. Observe that in this case, the push part is the portion of the Peapod supply chain prior to satisfying customer demand and the pull part starts from a customer order. Also note that since a Peapod warehouse covers a large geographical area, clearly larger than the one covered by an individual supermarket, demand is aggregated over many customers and locations, resulting in better forecasts and inventory reduction.

Of course, in the on-line grocery industry there are other challenges, including reducing transportation costs and responding in a very short period of time, that is, typically within 12 hours in a tight delivery window. Unfortunately, no current on-line grocers have the density of customers that will allow them to control transportation costs, and therefore compete successfully with traditional supermarkets. This is the reason why most on-line grocers have failed. Indeed, the framework developed in the previous section suggests that this industry is characterized by low level of demand uncertainty for many products and high economies of scale in transportation cost, implying that a push-based strategy is more appropriate.

5.4.3 The Book Industry

The book industry is another excellent example of the evolution of supply chain strategies from push to pull and then to push–pull. Until recently, Barnes and Noble had a typical push supply chain. When Amazon.com was established about six years ago, their supply chain was a pure pull system with no warehouses and no stock. Indeed, at that time Ingram Book Group supplied most of Amazon's customer demand.

Ingram Book can aggregate across many customers and suppliers and take advantage of economies of scale. Thus, the pull model employed by Amazon.com was an appropriate strategy when Amazon.com was building its brand name. As volume and demand increased, two issues became clear. First, Amazon.com's service level was affected by Ingram Book's distribution capacity, which was shared by many booksellers. Indeed, during periods of peak holiday demand, Amazon.com could not meet its service level goals. Second, using Ingram Book in the first few years allowed Amazon.com to avoid inventory costs but significantly reduced profit margins. As demand increased, it became evident that Ingram Book did not provide any advantage for many of the book categories, because Amazon.com's ability to aggregate across large geographical areas allowed the company to reduce uncertainties and hence inventory costs by itself, without using a distributor.

As Amazon.com discovered these issues, the company changed its philosophy, and now Amazon.com has several warehouses around the country where most of the titles are stocked. Thus, inventory at the warehouses is managed based on a push strategy, while demand is satisfied based on individual requests, a pull strategy.

5.4.4 The Retail Industry

The retail industry was in general late to respond to competition from virtual stores and to recognize the opportunities provided by the Internet. Recently, however, the landscape has changed, as many so called brick-and-mortar companies are adding an Internet shopping component to their offering. Enter click-and-mortar giants Wal-Mart, Kmart, Target, and Barnes and Noble, among others. These retailers recognize the advantage they have over pure Internet companies. Indeed, they already have the distribution and warehousing infrastructure in place. Thus, they have established virtual retail stores, serviced by their existing warehousing and distribution structures.

As a result of going on-line, click-and-mortar firms have changed their approach to stocking inventory. High-volume, fast-moving products, whose demand can be accurately matched with supply based on long-term forecasts, are stocked in stores, while low-volume, slow-moving products are stocked centrally for on-line purchasing. The low-volume products have highly uncertain demand levels, and thus require high levels of safety stock. Centralized stocking reduces uncertainties by aggregating demand across geographical locations, and thus reduces inventory levels. The analysis implies that these retailers use a push strategy for high volume, fast-moving products and a push-pull strategy for low volume, slow-moving products.

Of course, the move from brick-and-mortar to click-and-mortar is not an easy one, and may require skills that the brick-and-mortar companies don't have.

EXAMPLE 5-11

Wal-Mart has always prided itself on its distribution operations. Thus, it was a huge surprise when the company announced that it planned to hire an outside firm to handle order fulfillment and warehousing for its on-line store, Wal-Mart.com, which the retailer launched in the fall of 1999. Fingerhut Business Services filled orders behind the scenes at Wal-Mart's cyberstore. Indeed, with a background in handling individual orders, Fingerhut has emerged as a major provider of third-party distribution services to other retailers and e-tailers interested in home delivery. Fingerhut provided Internet order fulfillment, warehousing, shipment, payment processing, customer service, and merchandise returns for Wal-Mart.com when the service was launched.

5.4.5 Impact on Transportation and Fulfillment

This review of the evolution of supply chain strategies in various industries suggests the following insight: The Internet and the associated new supply chain paradigms introduce a shift in fulfillment strategies: from cases and bulk shipments to single items and smaller-size shipments, and from shipping to a small number of stores to serving highly geographically dispersed customers. This shift has also increased the importance and the complexity of reverse logistics.

Table 5-2 summarizes the impact of the Internet on fulfillment strategies. Specifically, the new developments in supply chain strategies are very good news for the

TABLE 5-2

TRADITIONAL FULFILLMENT VERSUS E-FULFILLMENT

	Traditional fulfillment	E-fulfillment
Supply chain strategy	Push	Push–pull
Shipment	Bulk	Parcel
Reverse logistics	Small part of the business	Important and highly complex
Delivery destination	Small number of stores	Large number of geographically disperesed customers
Lead times	Relatively long	Relatively short

parcel and LTL industries. Both pull and push–pull systems rely heavily on individual (e.g., parcel) shipments rather than bulk shipments. This is especially true in the business-to-consumer area, where a new term has been coined: e-fulfillment.

Another impact of e-fulfillment on the transportation industry is the significant increase in reverse logistics. Indeed, in the business-to-consumer arena, e-fulfillment typically means that the supplier needs to handle many returns, each of which consists of a small shipment. This is true, since on-line retailers need to build customer trust through generous return terms. Parcel shipping is already set up to handle these returns, a major issue in B2C and in many cases in B2B commerce. This is a challenge for the LTL industry, which traditionally has not been very involved in door-to-door services.

E-fulfillment logistics requires short lead time, the ability to serve globally dispersed customers, and the ability to reverse the flow easily from B2C to C2B. Only parcel shipping can do all that. Indeed, one important advantage of the parcel industry is the existence of an excellent information infrastructure that enables real-time tracking. Thus, the future looks promising for the parcel shipping industry and, in particular, for those carriers and consolidators who work to modify their own systems in order to integrate it with their customers' supply chains.

5.5 DISTRIBUTION STRATEGIES

We now consider the portion of the supply chain beginning with the manufacturer and supplier and continuing, in the case of retail goods, to the the retailer. Typically, three distinct outbound distribution strategies are utilized:

1. **Direct shipment.** In this strategy, items are shipped directly from the supplier to the retail stores without going through distribution centers.
2. **Warehousing.** This is the classical strategy in which warehouses keep stock and provide customers with items as required.
3. **Cross-docking.** In this strategy, items are distributed continuously from suppliers through warehouses to customers. However, the warehouses rarely keep the items for more than 10 to 15 hours.

We have already discussed traditional warehousing strategies in some depth in Chapter 3. Here we describe direct shipment and cross-docking.

5.5.1 Direct Shipment

Direct shipment strategies exist to bypass warehouses and distribution centers. Employing direct shipment, the manufacturer or supplier delivers goods directly to retail stores. The advantages of this strategy are that

- The retailer avoids the expenses of operating a distribution center.
- Lead times are reduced.

This type of distribution strategy also has a number of important disadvantages:

- Risk-pooling effects, which we described in Chapter 3, are negated because there is no central warehouse.
- The manufacturer and distributor transportation costs increase because it must send smaller trucks to more locations.

For these reasons, direct shipment is common when the retail store requires fully loaded trucks, which implies that the warehouse does not help in reducing transportation cost. It is most often mandated by powerful retailers or used in situations where lead time is critical. Sometimes, the manufacturer is reluctant to be involved with direct shipping but may have no choice in order to keep the business. Direct shipment is also prevalent in the grocery industry, where lead times are critical because of perishable goods.

EXAMPLE 5-12

JCPenney has successfully implemented a direct shipping strategy. JCPenney sells general merchandise through nearly a thousand stores and millions of catalogs. With 200,000 items from more than 20,000 suppliers, managing the flow of goods is a formidable task. Each individual store retains total accountability for sales, inventory, and profit and is responsible for sales forecasts and releasing orders. Orders are communicated to buyers who coordinate the shipment with distribution personnel to ensure quick response, and an internal control and tracking system is used to monitor the flow of materials. In most cases, products are shipped directly to Penney's stores.

5.5.2 Cross-Docking

Cross-docking is a strategy that Wal-Mart made famous. In this system, warehouses function as inventory coordination points rather than as inventory storage points. In typical cross-docking systems, goods arrive at warehouses from the manufacturer, are transferred to vehicles serving the retailers, and are delivered to the retailers as rapidly as possible. Goods spend very little time in storage at the warehouse—often less than 12 hours. This system limits inventory costs and decreases lead times by decreasing storage time.

Of course, cross-docking systems require a significant start-up investment and are very difficult to manage:

1. Distribution centers, retailers, and suppliers must be linked with advanced information systems to ensure that all pickups and deliveries are made within the required time windows.
2. A fast and responsive transportation system is necessary for a cross-docking system to work.
3. Forecasts are critical, necessitating the sharing of information.
4. Cross-docking strategies are effective *only* for large distribution systems in which a large number of vehicles are delivering and picking up goods at the cross-dock facilities at any one time. In such systems, there is enough volume every day to allow

shipments of fully loaded trucks from the suppliers to the warehouses. Since these systems typically include many retailers, demand is sufficient so items that arrive at the cross-docking facilities can be delivered immediately to the retail outlets in full truckload quantities.

EXAMPLE 5-13

The tremendous market growth of Wal-Mart over the past 15 to 20 years highlights the importance of an effective strategy that coordinates inventory replenishment and transportation policies [145]. Over this time period Wal-Mart developed into the largest and highest-profit retailer in the world. A number of major components in Wal-Mart's competitive strategy were critical to its success, but perhaps the most important has been its enthusiastic use of cross-docking. Wal-Mart delivers about 85 percent of its goods utilizing cross-docking techniques, as opposed to about 50 percent for Kmart. To facilitate cross-docking, Wal-Mart operates a private satellite communications system that sends point-of-sale (POS) data to all of its vendors, allowing them to have a clear picture of sales at all of its stores. In addition, Wal-Mart has a dedicated fleet of 2,000 trucks and, on average, stores are replenished twice a week. Cross-docking enables Wal-Mart to achieve economies of scale by purchasing full truckloads. It reduces the need for safety stocks and has cut the cost of sales by 3 percent compared to the industry average, a major factor explaining Wal-Mart's large profit margins.

Very few major retailers utilize one of these strategies exclusively. Typically, different approaches are used for different products, making it necessary to analyze the supply chain and determine the appropriate approach to use for a particular product or product family.

To evaluate these concepts we proceed with a simple question: What are the factors that influence distribution strategies? Obviously, customer demand and location, service level, and costs, including transportation and inventory costs, all play a role. It is important to note the interplay of inventory and transportation costs (see Chapter 3). Both transportation and inventory costs depend on shipment size, but in opposite ways. Increasing lot sizes reduces the delivery frequency and enables the shipper to take advantage of price breaks in shipping volume, therefore reducing transportation costs. However, large lot sizes increase inventory cost per item because items remain in inventory for a longer period of time until they are consumed.

Demand variability also has an impact on the distribution strategy. Indeed, as we observed in Chapter 3, demand variability has a huge impact on cost; the larger the variability, the more safety stock needed. Thus, stock held at the warehouses provides protection against demand variability and uncertainty, and due to *risk pooling*, the more warehouses a distributor has, the more safety stock is needed. On the other hand, if the warehouses are not used for inventory storage, as in the cross-docking strategy, or if there are no warehouses at all, as in direct shipping, more safety stock is required in the distribution system. This is true because in both cases *each store* needs to keep enough safety stock. This effect is mitigated, however, by distribution strategies that enable better demand forecasts and smaller safety stocks, and transshipment strategies, described below. Any assessment of different strategies must also consider lead time and volume requirements, as well as the capital investment involved in the various alternatives.

Table 5-3 summarizes and compares the three distribution strategies discussed in this subsection. The inventory-at-warehouses strategy refers to the classical distribution strategy in which inventory is kept at the warehouses. The allocation row in the table refers to the point at which the allocation of different products to different retail outlets

TABLE 5-3			

DISTRIBUTION STRATEGIES

Strategy → Attribute ↓	Direct shipment	Cross-docking	Inventory at warehouses
Risk pooling			Take advantage
Transportation costs		Reduced inbound costs	Reduced inbound costs
Holding costs	No warehouse costs	No holding costs	
Allocation		Delayed	Delayed

needs to be made. Clearly, in direct shipment, allocation decisions have to be made earlier than in the other two, so forecast horizons need to be longer.

5.5.3 Transshipment

The growth of rapid transportation options and advanced information systems has made transshipment an important option to consider when selecting supply chain strategies. By *transshipment*, we mean the shipment of items between different facilities *at the same level in the supply chain* to meet some immediate need.

Most often, transshipment is considered at the retail level. As we mentioned above, transshipment capability allows the retailer to meet customer demand from *the inventory of other retailers*. To do this, the retailer must know what other retailers have in inventory and must have a rapid way to ship the items either to the store where the customer originally tried to make the purchase or to the customer's home. These requirements can be met only with advanced information systems, which allow a retailer to see what other retailers have in stock and facilitate rapid shipping between retailers.

It is easy to see that if the appropriate information systems exist, shipment costs are reasonable, and all of the retailers have the same owner, transshipment makes sense. In this case, the system is effectively taking advantage of the risk-pooling concept, even if no central warehouse exists, because one can view inventory in different retail outlets as part of a large, single pool.

Retailers that are independently owned and operated may want to avoid transshipment because they will be helping their competitors. In Chapter 6, we consider the issues associated with *distributor integration*, in which independent distributors cooperate in various ways, including transshipment of needed goods.

5.6 CENTRALIZED VERSUS DECENTRALIZED CONTROL

In a centralized system, decisions are made at a central location for the entire supply network. Typically, the objective is to minimize the total cost of the system subject to satisfying some service-level requirements. This is clearly the case when the network is owned by a single entity, but it is also true in a centralized system that includes many different organizations. In this case, the savings, or profits, need to be allocated across the network using some contractual mechanism. We have already seen that centralized control leads to global optimization. Similarly, in a decentralized system, each facility identifies its most effective strategy without considering the impact on the other facilities in the supply chain. Thus, a decentralized system leads to local optimization.

It is easy to see that, theoretically, a centralized distribution network will be at least as effective as a decentralized one because the centralized decision makers can make all of the decisions that decentralized decision makers would make, but also have the option of considering the interplay of decisions made at different locations in the supply network.

In a logistics system in which each facility can access only its own information, a centralized strategy is not possible. With advances in information technologies, however, all facilities in a centralized system can have access to the same data. Indeed, in Chapter 11 we discuss the concept of *single point of contact*. In this case, information can be accessed from anywhere in the supply chain and is the same no matter what mode of inquiry is used or who is seeking the information. Thus, centralized systems allow the sharing of information and, more importantly, the utilization of this information in ways that reduce the bullwhip effect (see Chapter 4) and improve forecasts. Finally, they allow the use of coordinated strategies across the entire supply chain—strategies that reduce systemwide costs and improve service levels.

Sometimes, of course, a system cannot be centralized "naturally." The retailers, manufacturers, and distributors might all have different owners and different objectives. In these cases, it is often helpful to form partnerships to approach the advantages of a centralized system. We discuss these kinds of partnerships in Chapter 6. Also, detailed supply contracts can be useful, and we discuss these in more detail in Chapter 3.

5.7 CENTRAL VERSUS LOCAL FACILITIES

Another critical decision in supply chain design involves whether to use centralized or local production and warehousing facilities. We discussed certain elements of this decision in Chapter 2. Here we summarize additional important considerations:

Safety stock. Consolidating warehouses allows the vendor to take advantage of risk pooling. In general, this means that the more centralized an operation is, the lower are the safety stock levels.

Overhead. Economies of scale suggest that operating a few large central warehouses leads to lower total overhead cost relative to operating many smaller warehouses.

Economies of scale. In many manufacturing operations, economies of scale can be realized if manufacturing is consolidated. It is often much more expensive to operate many small manufacturing facilities than to operate a few large facilities with the same total capacity.

Lead time. Lead time to market can often be reduced if a large number of warehouses are located closer to the market areas.

Service. This depends on how *service* is defined. As we indicated above, centralized warehousing enables the utilization of risk pooling, which means that more orders can be met with a lower total inventory level. On the other hand, shipping time from the warehouse to the retailer will be longer.

Transportation costs. Transportation costs are directly related to the number of warehouses used. As the number of warehouses increases, transportation costs between the production facilities and the warehouses also increase because total distance traveled is greater and, more importantly, quantity discounts are less likely to apply. However, transportation costs from the warehouses to the retailers are likely to fall because the warehouses tend to be much closer to the market areas.

Of course, it is possible that in an effective distribution strategy, some products will be stored in a central facility while others will be kept in various local warehouses. For instance, very expensive products with low customer demand may be stocked at a central warehouse while low-cost products facing high customer demand may be stocked at many local warehouses. In addition, the use of centralized or local production and warehousing facilities is not necessarily an either-or decision. There are degrees of local and centralized operation, with varying degrees of the advantages and disadvantages listed above. Finally, advanced information systems help each type of system maintain some of the advantages of the other type. For example, lead times from central warehouses and safety stock for local warehouses can be reduced.

SUMMARY

In recent years many companies have improved performance, reducing cost, increasing service levels, reducing the bullwhip effect, and improving responsiveness to changes in the marketplace, by integrating the supply chain. In many cases, this was facilitated by the implementation of push–pull strategies and by a focus on demand-driven strategies. In particular, the Internet has created the opportunity to revolutionize supply chain strategies. Indeed, the success of giants such as Dell Computers and Cisco and the significant market capitalization of newly established companies such as Amazon.com can be attributed to sophisticated Internet-based supply chain strategies.

At the same time, the collapse of many Internet companies sends an alarming message that e-business presents not only opportunities but also great challenges. Key to these challenges is the ability to identify the appropriate supply chain strategy for a particular company and individual products. Indeed, the premise on which many of the Internet companies were built, that in the new economy there is no need for either physical infrastructure or inventory, has in many cases been disastrous. The new supply chain paradigm, push–pull strategy, advocates holding inventory, although it pushes the inventory upstream in the supply chain.

Of course, even traditional firms need to have an effective distribution strategy. Depending on the details of the situation, traditional warehouse, cross-docking, direct shipment, and transshipment can all be effective tools for managing inventory and distribution costs.

DISCUSSION QUESTIONS

1. Discuss the advantages of a push-based supply chain. What about a pull-based supply chain?
2. What is an example of a product with a primarily push-based supply chain? A product with a primarily pull-based supply chain?
3. What are the advantages of moving the push–pull boundary earlier in a supply chain? What about later?
4. Amazon.com, Peapod, Dell, and many furniture manufacturers use push–pull supply chain strategies. Describe how each of these companies takes advantage of the risk-pooling concept.
5. Discuss some additional examples of each of the four categories in Figure 5-2.
6. Is it possible for the appropriate supply chain (push, pull, or push–pull) to change during a product's life cycle? If not, explain why? If it is possible, what are some specific examples of products for which the appropriate supply chain changed?
7. Is e-fulfillment a new concept? What is the difference between on-line and catalog selling? Consider, for instance, Land's End, a company that has both channels.

8. Explain how demand for a product like televisions can be shaped? How does this compare to the ways in which demand for a product like canned soup can be shaped?

9. Other than the examples listed in Section 5.4, what are some more examples of failed Internet supply chain strategies? Successful Internet supply chain strategies?

10. Consider a large discount store. Discuss some products and suppliers for which the discount store should use a cross-docking strategy, some products and suppliers better suited to a direct shipment strategy, and, finally, some products and suppliers for which the discount store should utilize a direct shipment strategy.

11. Answer these questions about the case at the beginning of this chapter:
    a. Should MBD implement a push strategy? A pull strategy? A push–pull strategy? What would it require? What is the impact?
    b. What distribution strategies are appropriate for MBD's businesses? What questions should MBD management ask when assessing these strategies?
    c. How can MBD benefit from changes in the book distribution industry?
    d. What are the advantages to MBD in having fewer warehouses and a more centralized operation? More warehouses and a more decentralized operation?

C A S E

The Great Inventory Correction

John Chambers likened it to a 100-year flood, although the problem was dearth, not plenitude. The swift evaporation of technology demand that began in the latter part of 2000 was indeed exceptional, as the CEO of Cisco Systems famously suggested. Chipmakers and PC companies suddenly found themselves with a glut of inventory and capacity. Networking and telecom equipment makers were particularly hard hit; Cisco, more irrationally exuberant than most, was forced to write off a staggering $2.25 billion worth of gear. Throughout the first half of 2001, a procession of high-tech companies including such bellwethers as Nortel Networks, Lucent Technologies, Corning, and JDS Uniphase announced huge write-downs of unsalable inventory.

Today, high-tech companies are still loaded with rapidly depreciating goods. At one end of the food chain, the cyclical semiconductor industry is suffering through its deepest trough in demand since 1998, the year of the Asian crisis. In the middle, electronics contract manufacturers and their suppliers, customers,

and distributors are trying to figure out who owns which surplus components. At the other end of the chain, PC makers are waging price wars, and the gray market in networking equipment is thriving.

Flood of the century or not, tech companies are taking steps to limit their exposure to the next traumatic event. Some are revising their inventory models; others are implementing supply chain software and setting up Web supplier hubs. Everyone wants tighter collaboration with suppliers and timelier information from customers. Tech companies are trying, in short, to make their supply chains shorter, transparent, and as flexible as possible.

NEW LOGIC

Check out the recent earnings releases of semiconductor makers (not the pro forma kind) and you'll find a litany of inventory write-downs: Agere Systems, $270 million; Micron Technology, $260 million; Vitesse Semiconductor, $50.6 million; Alliance Semiconductor, $50 million; Xilinx, $32 million. Worldwide, chip sales in June were down 30.7 percent from a year ago, according to the Semiconductor Industry Association, and analysts predict a decline in 2001 revenues of more than 20 percent—the steepest ever.

Source: Edward Teach, *CFO Magazine*, September 1, 2001.

"I've been in the chip industry for 20 years," says Nathan Sarkisian, "and I've never seen anything like it." Sarkisian is senior vice president and CFO of Altera Corp., a San Jose, California–based chipmaker with 2000 revenues of $1.4 billion. "We grew roughly 65 percent last year with less than four months' supply of inventory throughout most of the year," he recalls. "That's pretty good when you think about semiconductor product cycles."

But in the fatal fourth quarter, units shipped to distributors fell 25 percent short of expectations. The slide continued into 2001, thanks to declining demand from Altera's major customers, communications companies. For Q2 2001, revenues were down 25 percent sequentially and 37 percent from Q2 2000. Altera was eventually forced to write down a whopping $115 million worth of inventory.

Going forward, Altera wants to ensure that future market dips won't savage the bottom line, and to that end it's revising its inventory model, for starters.

Altera designs programmable logic devices (PLDs). It's a "fabless" chipmaker, outsourcing manufacturing to giant foundry Taiwan Semiconductor Manufacturing Corp. Previously, it would build its mainstream PLDs through to finished goods, stockpiling them in Asian facilities in anticipation of customer demand. "We own the inventory as soon as it leaves the fab," notes Sarkisian. Also, it would essentially build new products on spec, producing quantities well beyond what the customer needed for prototyping. The virtues of this model are highlighted in Altera's annual report: "We, our distributors, and subcontract manufacturers—not our customers—hold stocks of inventory, thereby enhancing the cost advantage of PLDs for our customers."

Now, Altera will continue to build its mainstream products to stock, but only in die banks (stores of chips before packaging and testing). "By building die, we have taken out the biggest portion of the manufacturing lead time, but the inventory is in its most flexible form, with a minimum of value added," says Sarkisian. Only when orders are confirmed will Altera's subcontractors package, test, and ship the PLDs.

The lead time for these products will be measured in weeks. For Altera's mature products, "we will be strictly build-to-order," says Sarkisian, and the lead time for those will be measured in months. Finally, new products will no longer be built on spec; a customer order will be required.

VISIBLE IMPROVEMENTS

Chipmakers are at the mercy of the laws of physics. It takes anywhere from three to seven weeks to turn a raw silicon disk into a wafer with hundreds of chips, depending on the complexity of the chip and how much a customer is willing to pay, says Jim Kupec, president of United Microelectronics Corp. USA, a division of Taiwan-based foundry UMC. Additional time is required to separate, package, and test the chips. And in the real world, "things get spoiled in the fab," says Arnold Maltz, associate professor of supply chain management at Arizona State University College of Business. "Every now and then, somebody brings the wrong batch. Capacity isn't always available. Then you have the mismatch of supply and demand." In a 1999 study of major U.S. chipmakers, Maltz and his fellow researchers found that the average cycle time for semiconductors, from the fab to the customer, was 117 days—plenty of time for demand to change direction.

To reduce its exposure, a chip company can postpone adding value to die bank inventory. It also can seek better information from its customers, as Altera is now doing. "We're asking customers to give us more visibility in their inventories and build plans," says Sarkisian. That may seem like an obvious solution, but it isn't always available, says Maltz, because "there's some concern on the customer side that you're giving away strategic information." Nevertheless, Altera recently took two big steps toward greater visibility, announcing joint ventures with Nortel and Motorola to collaborate on product development.

Chipmakers also can shrink cycle times around wafer fabrication using supply chain management (SCM) software. Altera's i2 Technologies system, which is linked to its fabs, suppliers, and distributors, has cut weekly planning cycle time from 10 days to 1 day and reduced the long-term planning cycle time from four weeks to one week. About 85 percent of production is automatically scheduled by the system. "i2 runs our foundries," says Tom Murchie, vice president of operations. "It starts wafers by technology process, by fab, and by the strategic inventory targets we've chosen."

UMC's customers can forecast collaboratively with the foundry via its MyUMC Web portal, using i2 augmented by an available-to-promise order system. "What [MyUMC] does is automatically take a request for a customer's order, then almost instantaneously find the best manufacturing slot," explains Kupec.

FREAK SHOW

Other kinds of tech companies are using SCM planning tools, from such vendors as i2, Manugistics Group, and SAP. Cisco, for instance, uses Manugistics to run its Web supplier hub. At server maker Sun Microsystems, a combination of i2 and Rapt Inc. software enables "short, predictable lead times with the lowest possible costs," says Helen Yang, vice president of supply management.

But if SCM software is so great, why didn't it prevent the inventory glut? One reason is that not everyone uses it: Only about 20 percent of companies with more than $500 million in annual revenues have installed SCM tools, according to AMR Research.

A more compelling reason, however, is that software can't eliminate the problem of garbage in, garbage out. Supply chain planning tools rely on algorithms to crunch a mix of historical data, production numbers, and "guesswork," says Kevin O'Marah, service director for supply chain strategies at AMR. "How good is your guess? You're speculating on trends going forward."

This is feasible in mature industries, says O'Marah, but high tech, with its volatile swings in demand, is a very different story. In semiconductors, long cycle times mean that companies are always making a bet on an uncertain future. And at Cisco, "growth changed from 40 percent to negative 10 percent. That's a real freak show!" exclaims O'Marah. "Can you imagine a forecasting system even encompassing this scenario?"

"We recognize that forecasts will not be accurate," says Yang. "The game is how fast we can respond to changes."

O'Marah blames habit, in part, for the inventory overhang. Component shortages have plagued electronics manufacturing for the past decade, he points out, "and the habit of market leaders is to lock up allocations available for components. It's a reasonable way to think."

"When a new technology comes along—a faster chip, a new bus—there are constraints in supply," says Karen Peterson, research director at Gartner. "A lot of the [original equipment manufacturers] or contract manufacturers will lie about what they need. If I'm an OEM, I may say I need 200 percent more than I think I need. It's going to put my priority higher [with the supplier]."

Double ordering of chips, capacitors, and resistors from manufacturers and distributors also contributed to the glut, adds Pamela Gordon, president of Technology Forecasters, an Alameda, California–based consulting firm for the electronics manufacturing services (EMS) industries. Those parts were in particularly short supply in 2000, she says. As for other kinds of high-tech equipment, such as networking and telecom gear, Gordon faults manufacturers for not doing sufficient due diligence on shaky customers, dot-com or otherwise.

DON'T KNOW MUCH ABOUT HISTORY

"The telecom guys thought, 'We can do no wrong,'" says Dan Pleshko, vice president of global procurement and strategic supply-chain management at Flextronics International Corp. "They forgot to look at history, at business cycles. The PC guys had been through a couple of cycles. They had been through pain."

Flextronics, one of the world's largest EMS companies, with $12 billion in revenues, had an unusually good vantage point of the inventory glut. The Singapore-based company makes everything from printed circuit boards to cell phones for a variety of high-tech clients, including Cisco, Lucent, Nortel, and Ericsson. In 2000, the company's inventories ballooned from $470 million at the beginning of the year to $1.7 billion at year's end.

As orders poured in, Flextronics and other EMS companies could see the magnitude of the aggregated supply they were producing. Couldn't they have warned their clients? "In general, I don't think any of [the EMS companies] did that before," says Pleshko. "I think that will happen going forward."

Pleshko says Flextronics wants to obtain a better understanding with customers of consumer demand and product life cycles. Also, "we're moving very aggressively to a supplier-managed inventory environment," he says. The company wants to establish material hubs, where suppliers' facilities are located close to Flextronics's factories. "Compaq, Dell, and IBM have done this already," says Pleshko. "The EMS guys are just coming up to speed."

Meanwhile, there have been some disputes over the ownership of inventory in the EMS world. Some distributors have complained, for example, that they were being stuck with surplus parts. But that's a reversal of the situation in 2000, when "everyone was looking under every rock to find parts," says Pleshko. "When times were good, distributors were making a lot of money. They forgot."

THE CRYSTAL BALL

Times are bad, and tech companies are still working down inventories. They await an upturn of the business cycle, a new thing that will drive computer sales—Microsoft's Windows XP operating system, for instance, or an unforeseen killer app—and the start in 2002 of an especially robust three-year PC replacement cycle (companies stocked up because of the year 2000 problem).

Meanwhile, two computer companies are better positioned than most to weather the downturn, thanks to superior supply chain management. One is Dell Computer. With its build-to-order business model, Dell is the lowest-cost PC maker; it never has more than a few days' inventory on hand.

The other company is IBM. True, a third of Big Blue's revenues come from annuity-like businesses such as services and software. And even with its diversified risk, IBM isn't immune to the downturn. Sales were relatively flat in the second quarter ($21.6 billion), and IBM has warned that its chip sales will fall in the second half of the year. But IBM's inventories also have remained flat. Overall, they are at their lowest level since 1988, according to Steve Ward, general manager for IBM's Global Industrial Sector. That may owe something to old-fashioned vertical integration. Still, AMR's O'Marah and others regard IBM's supply chain management as among the best in the business.

Lean inventories are "absolutely critical," says Ward. "In parts of our business, the value of components drops about 1.5 percent per month."

IBM does build some items to order, but mostly it builds fast, on a pull or just-in-time basis. "Our suppliers have visibility to how much inventory we have," says Ward.

An SAP system provides crucial automation, but other practices also promote smaller inventories. For example, IBM has reduced the number of different parts by emphasizing commonality across platforms and products. Thus, for example, the flat screens used on ThinkPads and the flat-panel monitors sold for PCs are the same.

The number of suppliers is kept small, too. Purchasing is structured by commodities, with a market expert assigned full-time to each commodity. IBM buys all of its production parts electronically, via the Internet and EDI. "That means we can have much faster transactions, moving to much faster collaboration with suppliers," says Ward.

How far into the future does IBM peer? Ward says the company maintains a "very detailed" forecast for the next 90 days out, updated weekly and rolled out through all suppliers; a "fairly detailed" forecast for 90 days to a year; and a "strategic" forecast for longer periods. "I can't tell you right now what kind of hard file [disk] we're going to put in our ThinkPads two years from now," says Ward, "but I know how many we'll need."

The principal sources of inputs for those predictions are, of course, IBM's salespeople. They may not have quite the sobriety of their white-shirt-and-black-tie forebears, but they know their customers' businesses inside out, boasts Ward. Managers meet frequently to discuss and anticipate demand ("is this a conceptual need, or has it been confirmed by the customer?").

A rationally exuberant sales force—these days, that's about as close to a crystal ball as a high-tech company can get.

DISCUSSION QUESTIONS

1. How has Altera modified its strategy? Why?
2. Do you think Altera's new strategy will be successful? What are some advantages and disadvantages of the new strategy?
3. How do you anticipate Altera's customers will react to this new strategy? What are advantages and disadvantages for Altera's customers?
4. What information does Flextronics have that its clients do not? Why? How can Flextronics leverage this information?
5. How does IBM manage its suppliers in order to make its pull strategy more effective?

CHAPTER 6

Strategic Alliances

C A S E

How Kimberly-Clark Keeps Client Costco in Diapers

One morning, a Costco store in Los Angeles began running a little low on size-one and size-two Huggies. Crisis loomed.

So what did Costco managers do? Nothing. They didn't have to, thanks to a special arrangement with Kimberly-Clark Corp., the company that makes the diapers.

Under this deal, responsibility for replenishing stock falls on the manufacturer, not Costco. In return, the big retailer shares detailed information about individual stores' sales. So, long before babies in Los Angeles would ever notice it, diaper dearth was averted by a Kimberly-Clark data analyst working at a computer hundreds of miles away in Neenah, Wis.

"When they were doing their own ordering, they didn't have as good a grasp" of inventory, says the Kimberly-Clark data analyst, Michael Fafnis. Now, a special computer link with Costco allows Mr. Fafnis to make snap decisions about where to ship more Huggies and other Kimberly-Clark products.

Just a few years ago, the sharing of such data between a major retailer and a key supplier would have been unthinkable. But the arrangement between Costco Wholesale Corp. and Kimberly-Clark underscores a sweeping change in American retailing. Across the country, powerful retailers from Wal-Mart Stores Inc. to Target Corp. to J.C. Penney Co. are pressuring their suppliers to take a more active role in shepherding products from the factory to store shelves.

CHANGING SIZES

In some cases, that means requiring suppliers to shoulder the costs of warehousing excess merchandise. In others, it means pushing suppliers to change product or package sizes. In the case of Costco and Kimberly-Clark, whose coordinated plan is officially called "vendor-managed inventory," Kimberly-Clark oversees and pays for everything involved with managing Costco's inventory except the actual shelf-stockers in store aisles.

Whatever the arrangement and the terminology, the major focus for these big retailers is the same: Cutting costs along the so-called supply chain, which comprises every step from lumber mill to store shelf. The assumption is that suppliers themselves are in the best position to spot inefficiencies and fix them.

For consumers, it all translates to lower prices at the cash register. Indeed, big companies' increasing focus on the supply chain is one reason U.S. prices for general merchandise—goods from laundry detergent to wool sweaters—fell 1.5 percent in 1998 and again last year and are falling at the same rate this year, according to Richard Berner, chief U.S. economist at Morgan Stanley Dean Witter. "Supply-chain management has had a major impact," says Mr. Berner, who compiled his analysis from government data.

Source: Emily Nelson and Ann Zimmerman, *The Wall Street Journal* (interactive edition), September 7, 2000. Copied with permission.

RETURN TO UNISEX

There is also a potential downside for consumers: Fewer choices in brands and types of packages. For example, two years ago, Kimberly-Clark stopped making separate diapers for boys and girls and reverted to unisex-only. Less variety makes for easier inventory-tracking in its factories and trucks, the Dallas-based company says.

To a great extent, better cooperation between retailers and suppliers has been made possible by improved technology—such as the computer link Kimberly-Clark uses. It's also a consequence of the greater strength of major retailers as they consolidate and expand globally. Many economists say that closer retailer–supplier coordination on the supply chain is the model of the future and will ultimately determine which companies succeed in the new millennium.

"A shopper buys a roll of Bounty paper towel, and that would trigger someone cutting a tree in Georgia," says Steve David, who heads supply-chain work for Procter & Gamble Co., the Cincinnati consumer-products giant. "That's the holy grail."

These days, P&G stations about 250 people in Fayetteville, Ark., minutes from Wal-Mart's headquarters in Bentonville, solely to promote its products to the discount chain and ensure they move as quickly as possible to store shelves. The two giants share some inventory data.

The price of inefficiencies on the supply chain is high. Revlon Inc. this year slowed its product shipments because store shelves were backed up with older inventory. Kmart Corp.'s new chief executive, Charles Conaway, has publicly blamed the retailer's sagging profits in part on a weak supply-chain infrastructure. Last month, he said he expects to spend $1.4 billion over the next two years to update Kmart's technology, including systems for coordinating with suppliers. And earlier this year, Estee Lauder Cos. hired away Compaq Computer Corp.'s executive in charge of supply chain to bolster that operation at the cosmetics concern.

By several accounts, the close collaboration between Costco and Kimberly-Clark serves as a model for other merchandisers, and also helps explain strong recent sales gains by the two companies. In the past two years, Kimberly-Clark gradually expanded the program and now manages inventory for some 44 retailers of its products. The consumer-products company says it wrung $200 million in costs from its supply chain during that period, and it vows to squeeze out another $75 million this year.

"This is what the information age has brought to this industry," says Wayne Sanders, chairman and chief executive officer of Kimberly-Clark. "It gives us a competitive advantage." In fact, Kimberly-Clark says the cost savings it achieves on its supply chain are one reason its Huggies—and not rival P&G's Pampers—are sold at Costco stores in most areas of the country.

"If a company finds a way to lower its costs, it gets those deals," says Richard Dicerchio, Costco's chief operating officer. A spokeswoman for P&G says its supply chain is very efficient, and Costco carries many of its other products.

To oversee ordering for the retailers whose inventory it manages, Kimberly-Clark employs a staff of 24 people, including Mr. Fafnis. A Kimberly-Clark spokeswoman says the benefits of the program "more than offset" additional labor costs. Last year, Kimberly-Clark posted a 51 percent rise in net income to $1.67 billion on $13 billion in sales, capping three years of improving results.

For Costco, the benefits of such close cooperation with a major supplier are equally clear: Costco saves money not only on staffing in its inventory department, but also on storage. Before Kimberly-Clark began managing Costco's inventory, in late 1997, the retailer would keep an average of a month's supply of Kimberly-Clark products in its warehouses. Now, because Kimberly-Clark has proven it can replenish supplies more efficiently, Costco needs to keep only a two-week supply.

What's more, Costco says its shelves are less likely to go empty under the new system. That's important for both retailer and supplier, because consumer studies indicate that a majority of customers will walk out of a store empty-handed if they can't find a particular item they need. P&G, for example, estimates that an average retailer's loss from out-of-stocks runs about 11 percent of annual sales.

For Costco, which keeps its costs down by typically offering just one brand-name product and its own private-label Kirkland Signature product in each category, maintaining supplies on shelves is crucial. "If we're out of stock, it means we're out of a category, so the chance of a loss of a sale is greater," Mr. Dicerchio says.

Susanne Shallon of Redondo Beach, Calif., says she always buys size-four Huggies for her

22-month-old daughter, Beth, and Pull-Ups for her five-year-old son, Emil, at a nearby Costco because the store is well-stocked. "It's good to have the confidence that when I go into the store, the product will be on hand," she says.

A "Pull" Product

For now, Kimberly-Clark manages inventory in Costco stores everywhere but the Northeast. Kimberly-Clark recently sent analysts to Costco headquarters in Issaquah, Wash., to push for a possible next stage: expanding to the Northeast and collaborating on forecasts, not just recorded sales.

James Sinegal, CEO of Costco, says the chain has always managed its inventory well, but "we want to take things to a higher level." Costco has been a star performer among U.S. retailers, posting double-digit sales growth every year since 1996. Its sales rose 13 percent to $26.98 billion in the fiscal year ended Aug. 29, 1999.

At Costco, diapers are known as a "pull" product—meaning that shoppers make a trip to the store specifically to buy them. Parents are also particularly price-conscious, so the pressure is on for the retailer to keep diapers in stock and to make it as cheap as possible to do so.

For Mr. Fafnis, the 34-year-old Kimberly-Clark data analyst responsible for overseeing stock at 155 Costco stores across the Western U.S., that means arriving at his cubicle at 7:30 each morning to a stack of spreadsheets that show exactly how many boxes of Huggies, Kleenex tissues, and Scott paper towels sit on the shelves. He's privy to more sales and inventory detail than many Costco executives can see.

His mission: to keep each store's inventory as low as possible without risking empty shelves. That allows him very little margin for error, as it takes an average of a week from the time he types an order into his computer until a truck pulls up to a Costco store.

Scanning the spreadsheets one morning a few months ago, Mr. Fafnis, who studies baseball statistics as a hobby, quickly spots the potential problem in Los Angeles. The store's supply of size-one and size-two Huggies is down to 188 packages; in the past week, 74 were sold. That means the store could drop below its safety stock—typically, two weeks' worth of inventory—within days. The computer spits out a suggested order, but Mr. Fafnis cuts it by a few packages. As the father of a two-year-old Huggies wearer, he has a certain instinct for the market. "When the

next truck pulls in, you want to be right at your safety stock. That's the ideal situation," Mr. Fafnis says.

Mr. Fafnis, who has never been inside a Costco (there aren't any in Wisconsin), tries to tailor orders to shoppers' whims and the needs of particular neighborhoods. On a bulletin board in his cubicle, he posts a list of special requests heavily marked with orange highlighter. For example, a store in Reno, Nev., can receive deliveries only early Monday mornings to get around city noise ordinances.

After Mr. Fafnis enters orders in his computer, a Kimberly-Clark transportation analyst at the company's logistics center in Knoxville, Tenn., calls up the same computer file and assigns the order to a trucking company.

A CANCELED ORDER

Complaints are handled by Kimberly-Clark customer-service analyst Rachel Pope, who sits a few cubicles away from Mr. Fafnis. One afternoon, a Costco merchandise manager calls to say that a store in Spokane, Wash., is under construction and doesn't want its delivery. Ms. Pope phones the logistics center in Knoxville, which tells her the truck destined for Spokane is already at a loading dock in Ogden, Utah. She reaches the driver, via conference call, just before he begins filling the truck. "This was close," she says.

The drive for efficiency creates new problems. Last year, Costco store managers complained that some deliveries were incomplete. Kimberly-Clark managers visited 13 Costco stores and spotted some drivers accidentally unloading items intended for a later stop. Now, Kimberly-Clark uses a simple cardboard divider to separate each store's order.

Scouting store shelves for out-of-stocks is Donna Imes, Kimberly-Clark's saleswoman for Costco. Ms. Imes, who lives near Costco's headquarters, typically logs in to her home computer at 4:30 every morning, scanning reports from Mr. Fafnis. She walks every aisle of at least five Costco stores a week, taking notes in a spiral-ring pad about displays and competitors' prices and chatting up store managers and customers.

Recently, when Ms. Imes saw shoppers stowing diapers on the bottom rung of their carts, she called Huggies brand managers to caution them not to make the packages wider. Noticing that a particular store often ran low on Depend incontinence underwear at the beginning of the month, a Costco manager told

Ms. Imes that residents of a retirement center next door always shopped then. So she alerted Mr. Fafnis, who programmed his computer accordingly.

The importance of supply chain hasn't been lost on Kimberly-Clark itself, which is trying to apply the same principles to its own suppliers. These days, it keeps less than a month's supply of diapers in its own warehouses, down nearly 50 percent over the past two years.

For now, raw-material shipments remain the weak link. Advances are small, focusing on such details as how the company stocks Velcro tabs for its diapers. Two years ago, Kimberly-Clark began sharing its production plans with Velcro USA Inc. via weekly e-mails. That cut Velcro inventory 60 percent, saving several million dollars.

Kimberly-Clark says it's trying to cut costs further. Jim Steffen, the company's president of U.S. consumer sales, regularly reminds his staff that the retailer is the customer. "The last time I looked," he says, "we didn't own any stores."

By the end of this chapter, you should be able to answer the following questions:

- Why are major retailers moving toward relationships in which the supplier manages inventory levels at the retailer?
- When should a company handle its logistics needs in-house, and when should external sources be used?
- What other types of business partnerships can be used to improve supply chain performance?
- Can pressures such as the ones described in this case be used to a company's advantage?

6.1 INTRODUCTION

One of the paradoxes of business today is that at the same time that complex business practices (such as the ones we have discussed in the preceding chapters) are becoming essential for firms to survive and thrive, the necessary financial and managerial resources to implement these practices are becoming increasingly scarce. This is one reason why it may not always be effective to perform all of these key business functions in-house. Frequently, a company may find it effective to use other firms with special resources and technical knowledge to perform these functions.

Even if a firm has the available resources to perform a particular task, another firm in the supply chain may sometimes be better suited to perform that task simply because its relative location in the supply chain better positions it to do so. Often a combination of position in the supply chain, resources, and expertise determines the most appropriate firm in the supply chain to perform a particular function. Of course, it is not enough to *know* who in the supply chain should perform a particular function—steps must be taken so that the function is actually performed by the appropriate firm.

As with any business function, there are four basic ways for a firm to ensure that a logistics-related business function is completed [96]:

1. **Internal activities.** A firm can perform the activity using internal resources and expertise, if they are available. As we will discuss more completely in the next section, if this activity is one of the *core strengths* of the firm, this may be the best way to perform the activity.
2. **Acquisitions.** If a firm doesn't have the expertise or specialized resources internally, it can acquire another firm that does. This certainly gives the acquiring firm full control over the way the particular business function is performed, but it has several possible drawbacks. For one thing, acquiring a successful company can be difficult

and expensive. The culture of the acquired company may clash with that of the acquiring company, and the effectiveness of the acquired company could be lost in the assimilation process. The acquired company may have previously dealt with the acquiring company's competitors, and it could lose this business. This may hurt its overall effectiveness. For these reasons, as well as many others, an acquisition may not be appropriate.

3. **Arm's-length transactions.** Most business transactions are of this type. A firm needs a specific item or service, such as the delivery of a load of items, the maintenance of a vehicle, or the design and installation of logistics management software, and purchases or leases the item or service. Many times, an arm's-length transaction is the most effective and appropriate arrangement. Of course, the goals and strategies of the supplier might not match those of the buyer. In general, this kind of short-term arrangement fulfills a particular business need but doesn't lead to long-term strategic advantages.

4. **Strategic alliances.** These are typically multifaceted, goal-oriented, long-term partnerships between two companies in which both risks and rewards are shared. In many cases, the problems of outright acquisition can be avoided while at the same time mutual goals can lead to the commitment of many more resources than in the case of arm's-length transactions. Strategic alliances typically lead to long-term strategic benefits for both partners.

This chapter focuses on *strategic alliances* related to supply chain management. In the next section, we introduce a framework for analyzing the advantages and disadvantages of strategic alliances. In Sections 6.3, 6.4, and 6.5, the three most important types of supply chain–related strategic alliances are discussed in greater detail: third-party logistics (3PL), retailer–supplier partnerships (RSP), and distributor integration (DI).

6.2 A FRAMEWORK FOR STRATEGIC ALLIANCES

There are many difficult strategic issues that play a part in the selection of appropriate *strategic alliances*. In his classic book, *Partnerships for Profit*, Jordan Lewis [96] introduces an effective general framework for analyzing strategic alliances. This framework, which we briefly introduce in this section, is very helpful for considering the kinds of supply chain–related strategic alliances that we address in the rest of this chapter.

To determine whether a particular strategic alliance is appropriate for your firm, consider how the alliance will help address the following issues:

Adding value to products. A partnership with the appropriate firm can help add value to existing products. For example, partnerships that improve time to market, distribution times, or repair times help to increase the perceived value of a particular firm. Similarly, partnerships between companies with complementary product lines can add value to both companies' products.

Improving market access. Partnerships that lead to better advertising or increased access to new market channels can be beneficial. For example, complementary consumer product manufacturers can cooperate to address the needs of major retailers, increasing sales for everyone.

Strengthening operations. Alliances between appropriate firms can help to improve operations by lowering system costs and cycle times. Facilities and resources can be used more efficiently and effectively. For example, companies with complementary seasonal products can effectively use warehouses and trucks year-round.

Adding technological strength. Partnerships in which technology is shared can help add to the skills base of both partners. Also, the difficult transitions between old and new technologies can be facilitated by the expertise of one of the partners. For example, a supplier may need a particular enhanced information system to work with a certain customer. Partnering with a firm that already has expertise in this system makes it easier to address difficult technological issues.

Enhancing strategic growth. Many new opportunities have high entry barriers. Partnerships might enable firms to pool expertise and resources to overcome these barriers and explore new opportunities.

Enhancing organizational skills. Alliances provide a tremendous opportunity for organizational learning. In addition to learning from one another, partners are forced to learn more about themselves and to become more flexible so that these alliances work.

Building financial strength. In addition to addressing these competitive issues, alliances can help to build financial strength. Income can be increased and administrative costs can be shared between partners or even reduced owing to the expertise of one or both of the partners. Of course, alliances also limit investment exposure by sharing risk.

Strategic alliances have their downsides. The list above is useful for determining these. Each company has its *core strengths* or competencies—specific talents that differentiate the company from its competitors and give it an advantage in the eyes of its customers. These core strengths must not be weakened by the alliance, which can happen if resources are diverted from these strengths or if technological or strategic strengths are compromised to make the partnership successful. Similarly, key differences with competitors must not be diminished. This is possible if key technology is shared or if entry barriers are reduced for the competition.

Determining these core strengths is clearly very important; unfortunately, it is also very difficult; what they are depends on the nature of the business and of the firm. Core strengths don't necessarily correspond to a large investment of resources, and they may be intangible items such as management skills or brand image. To determine a firm's core strengths, consider how the firm's internal capabilities contribute to differentiating it from its competition in each of the seven key items listed above. Now, how will *strategic alliances* help or hurt in each of these areas? See more on this topic in Chapter 7 where we discuss outsourcing decisions.

The following example illustrates the advantages and disadvantages of strategic alliances. Consider how IBM, Intel, and Microsoft benefited and were hurt by the relationships described in this example.

EXAMPLE 6-1

Although not specifically related to logistics, the example of the IBM personal computer (PC) highlights the advantages and the disadvantages of outsourcing key business functions. When IBM decided to enter the PC market in late 1981, the company did not have the infrastructure in place to design and build a personal computer. Rather than take the time to develop these capabilities, IBM outsourced almost all the major components of the PC. For example, the microprocessor was designed and built by Intel and the operating system was provided by a small company in Seattle called Microsoft. IBM was able to release this computer to market within 15 months of beginning its design by tapping the expertise and resources of other companies. Furthermore, within three years IBM replaced Apple Computer as the number one supplier of personal computers. By 1985 IBM's market share was more than 40 percent. However, the downside to IBM's strategy soon became clear, as competitors such as Compaq were able to enter the market by utilizing the same suppliers

Example 6-1 *Continued*

as IBM. Furthermore, when IBM tried to regain control of the market by introducing its PS/2 line of computers, featuring a new, proprietary design and an operating system called OS/2, other companies did not follow IBM's lead, and the original architecture remained dominant in the market. By the end of 1995, IBM's market share had fallen to less than 8 percent, behind market leader Compaq's 10 percent [31].

Although strategic alliances are becoming increasingly prevalent in all walks of business, three types are particularly significant in supply chain management. Third-party logistics (3PL), retailer–supplier partnerships (RSP), and distributor integration (DI) are discussed in detail in the next three sections. As you read about these issues, try to place them in the framework described above.

6.3 THIRD-PARTY LOGISTICS

The use of third-party logistics (3PL) providers to take over some or all of a company's logistics responsibilities is becoming more prevalent. Indeed, the third-party logistics industry, which essentially began in the 1980s, was a $45.48 billion industry in 1999, and grew by 24 percent to $56.4 billion in 2000, and by 7.4 percent to $60.6 billion in 2001 ("State of Logistics Report," published by Roslyn Wilson and Robert V. Delaney).

6.3.1 What Is 3PL?

Third-party logistics is simply the use of an outside company to perform all or part of the firm's materials management and product distribution functions. 3PL relationships are typically more complex than traditional logistics supplier relationships: they are true strategic alliances.

Although companies have used outside firms to provide particular services, such as trucking and warehousing, for many years, these relationships had two typical characteristics: they were *transaction based* and the companies hired were often *single-function* specific. Modern 3PL arrangements involve long-term commitments and often multiple functions or process management. For example, Ryder Dedicated Logistics has a five-year agreement to design, manage, and operate all of Whirlpool Corporation's inbound logistics [88].

3PL providers come in all sizes and shapes, from small companies with a few million dollars in revenues to huge companies with revenues in the billions. Most of these companies can manage many stages of the supply chain.

Surprisingly, the use of third-party logistics is most prevalent among large companies. Firms such as Minnesota Mining & Manufacturing Co. (3M), Eastman Kodak, Dow Chemical, Time Warner, and Sears Roebuck are turning over large portions of their logistics operations to outside suppliers. Third-party logistics providers are finding it hard to persuade small companies to employ their services, although this may change as the use of 3PL becomes more prevalent and as 3PL providers make a larger effort to develop relationships with smaller companies [17].

6.3.2 Advantages and Disadvantages of 3PL

Most of the general advantages and disadvantages of strategic alliances described in Section 6.2 apply here.

Focus on Core Strengths The most frequently cited benefit of using 3PL providers is that it allows a company to focus on its core competencies. With corporate resources becoming increasingly limited, it is often difficult to be an expert in every facet of the business. Logistics outsourcers provide a company with the opportunity to focus on that company's particular area of expertise, leaving the logistics expertise to the logistics companies. (Of course, if logistics is one of the company's areas of expertise, then outsourcing may not make sense.)

EXAMPLE 6·2

The partnership between Ryder Dedicated Logistics and General Motors' Saturn division is a good example of these benefits. Saturn focuses on automobile manufacturing and Ryder manages most of Saturn's other logistics considerations. Ryder deals with vendors; delivers parts to the Saturn factory in Spring Hill, Tennessee; and delivers finished vehicles to the dealers. Saturn orders parts using electronic data interchange (EDI) and sends the same information to Ryder. Ryder makes all the necessary pickups from 300 different suppliers in the United States, Canada, and Mexico, using special *decision-support software* to effectively plan routes to minimize transportation costs [40].

EXAMPLE 6·3

British Petroleum (BP) and Chevron Corp. also wished to stick to their core competencies. To do this, they formed Atlas Supply, a partnership of about 80 suppliers, to deliver items such as spark plugs, tires, window-washing fluid, belts, and antifreeze to their 6,500 service stations. Rather than use the distribution networks of either BP or Chevron or create a new one, Atlas outsourced all logistics to GATX, which is responsible for running five distribution centers and maintaining inventory of 6,500 SKUs at each service station. Each service station orders supplies through its oil company, which forwards the order to Atlas and then to GATX. Each station has a preassigned ordering day to avoid system bottlenecks. GATX systems determine appropriate routes and configurations and transmit orders to the DC. The next day, the DC selects and packs the orders, and trucks are loaded in the appropriate order based on the delivery schedule. As deliveries are made, returns and deliveries from Atlas suppliers are picked up. GATX electronically informs Atlas, Chevron, and BP of the status of all deliveries. The companies save enough on transportation costs alone to justify this partnership, and the two oil companies have managed to reduce the number of DCs from 13 to 5 and significantly improve service levels [2].

Provides Technological Flexibility The ever-increasing need for technological flexibility is another important advantage of the use of 3PL providers. As requirements change and technology advances, the better 3PL providers constantly update their information technology and equipment. Often individual companies do not have the time, resources, or expertise to constantly update their technology. Different retailers may have different, and changing, delivery and information technology requirements, and meeting these requirements may be essential to a company's survival. Third-party logistics providers can often meet these requirements in a quicker, more cost-effective way [66]. Also, third-party providers already may have the capability to meet the needs of a firm's potential customers, allowing the firm access to certain retailers that might not otherwise be possible or cost-effective.

Provides Other Flexibilities Third parties also may provide greater flexibility to a company. One example is flexibility in geographic locations. Increasingly, suppliers are requiring rapid replenishment, which in turn may require regional warehousing. By utilizing third-party providers for this warehousing, a company can meet customer requirements without committing capital and limiting flexibility by constructing a new facility or committing to a long-term lease. Also, flexibility in service offerings may be achieved through the use of third parties, which may be equipped to offer retail customers a much larger variety of services than the hiring firm. In some cases, the volume of customers demanding these services may be low to the firm, but higher to the 3PL provider, who may be working for several different firms across different industries [152]. In addition, flexibility in resource and workforce size can be achieved through outsourcing. Managers can change what would be fixed costs into variable costs, in order to react more quickly to changing business conditions.

EXAMPLE 6-4

Working with the Simmons Company, a mattress manufacturer, Ryder Dedicated Logistics provided new technology that allowed Simmons to completely change the way it does business. Before its involvement with Ryder, Simmons warehoused between 20,000 and 50,000 mattresses at each of its manufacturing facilities to meet customer demand in a timely fashion. Now, Ryder maintains an on-site logistics manager at Simmons' manufacturing plant. When orders arrive, the logistics manager uses special software to design an optimal sequence and route to deliver the mattresses to customers. This logistics plan is then transmitted to the factory floor, where the mattresses are manufactured, in the exact quantity, style, and sequence required—all in time for the shipment. This logistics partnership has virtually eliminated the need for Simmons to hold inventory at all [40].

EXAMPLE 6-5

SonicAir, a division of UPS, provides an even more sophisticated third-party service. This company serves specialized customers who supply equipment for which every hour of downtime is very expensive; SonicAir rapidly delivers service parts where they are needed. SonicAir maintains 67 warehouses and uses specialized software to determine the appropriate inventory level for each part at each warehouse. When an order is placed, the system determines the best way to deliver the part and sends it out, usually on the next flight, where it is delivered by one of the company's ground couriers. This service enables customers to store fewer parts at each field service bureau than would otherwise be necesssary—and still provide the same level of service. With some parts valued at hundreds of thousands of dollars, this is clearly a cost savings to the customer. At the same time, this business is very profitable for SonicAir because customers are willing to pay well for this level of service [40].

Important Disadvantages of 3PL   The most obvious disadvantage of the use of 3PL providers is the *loss of control* inherent in outsourcing a particular function. This is especially true for outbound logistics where 3PL company employees themselves might interact with a firm's customers. Many third-party logistics firms work very hard to address these concerns. Efforts include painting company logos on the sides of trucks, dressing 3PL employees in the uniforms of the hiring company, and providing extensive reporting on each customer interaction.

Also, if logistics is one of the core competencies of a firm, it makes no sense to outsource these activities to a supplier who may not be as capable as the firm's in-house expertise. For example, Wal-Mart built and manages its own distribution centers and Caterpillar runs its parts supply operations. These are competitive advantages and core competencies of these firms, so outsourcing is unnecessary. In particular, if certain logistics activities are within the core competencies of the firm and others are not, it might be wise to employ 3PL providers for only those areas that outside providers can handle better than the hiring firm. For example, if VMI replenishment strategies and materials handling are core competencies of a company but transportation is not, a 3PL firm could be contacted to handle shipments from the dock to the customer exclusively. Similarly, pharmaceutical companies build and own DCs for controlled drugs, but often use public warehouses located closer to the customer for items that are less expensive and easier to control [6].

6.3.3 3PL Issues and Requirements

A third-party logistics contract is typically a major and complex business decision. Other than the pros and cons listed above, there are many considerations that are critical in deciding whether an agreement should be entered into with a particular 3PL provider.

1. **Know your own costs.** Among the most basic issues to consider in selecting a 3PL provider is to know your own costs so they can be compared with the cost of using an outsourcing firm. Often it is necessary to use activity-based costing techniques, which involve tracing overhead and direct costs back to specific products and services [66].

2. **Customer orientation of the 3PL.** Of course, it is not enough to select a provider based on cost alone. Many of the advantages listed above involve intangibles such as flexibility. Therefore, the strategic logistics plan of the company and how a 3PL provider would fit into this plan must be considered carefully. A 1995 survey of 3PL providers [88] identified the following characteristics as most critical to the success of a 3PL agreement. The most important was the customer orientation of the provider; that is, the value of a 3PL relationship is directly related to the ability of the provider to understand the needs of the hiring firm and to adapt its services to the special requirements of that firm. The second most important factor was reliability. The flexibility of the provider, or its ability to react to the changing needs of the hiring firm and the needs of that firm's customers, was third. Significantly further down the list were cost savings.

3. **Specialization of the 3PL.** When choosing a potential 3PL provider, some experts suggest that companies should consider firms whose roots lie in the particular area of logistics that is most relevant to the logistics requirements in question. For example, Roadway Logistics, Menlo Logistics, and Yellow Logistics evolved from major LTL carriers; Exel Logistics, GATX, and USCO started as warehouse managers; and UPS and Federal Express have expertise in the timely handling of small packages. Some firms have even more specialized requirements, and these should be considered carefully when choosing a 3PL partner [6]. Sometimes, a firm can use one of its trusted core carriers as its third-party logistics provider. For example, Schneider National, a firm that already worked closely with Baxter Healthcare Corp., recently agreed to take over Baxter's dedicated fleet routes [100].

4. **Asset-owning versus non-asset-owning 3PL.** There are also advantages and disadvantages to utilizing an asset-owning versus a non-asset-owning 3PL company. Asset-owning companies have significant size, access to human resources, a large customer base, economies of scope and scale, and systems in place, but they may tend to favor their own divisions in awarding work, to be bureaucratic, and to have a long decision-making cycle. Non-asset-owning companies may be more flexible and able to tailor services and have the freedom to mix and match providers. They also may have low overhead costs and specialized industry expertise at the same time, but limited resources and lower bargaining power [6].

6.3.4 3PL Implementation Issues

Once a potential partner has been selected, the process has only begun. Agreements need to be reached and appropriate efforts must be made by both companies to initiate the relationship effectively. Experts point to one lesson in particular that has come from failed 3PL agreements: Devote enough time to start-up considerations; that is, starting the relationship effectively during the first six months to a year is both the most difficult and the most critical part of any 3PL alliance. The company purchasing the services must identify exactly what it needs for the relationship to be successful, and be able to provide specific performance measures and requirements to the 3PL firm. The logistics provider, in turn, must consider and discuss these requirements honestly and completely, including their realism and relevance [17]. Both parties must be committed to devoting the time and effort needed to making a success of the relationship. It is critical that both parties remember that this is a mutually beneficial third-party alliance, with shared risk and reward. The parties are partners—neither party can take a "transaction pricing" mentality [5].

In general, *effective communication* is essential for any outsourcing project to succeed. First, within the hiring company, managers must communicate to each other and to their employees exactly why they are outsourcing and what they expect from the outsourcing process, so that all relevant departments are on the "same page" and can become appropriately involved. Obviously, communication between the firm and the 3PL provider is also critical. It is easy to speak in generalities, but specific communication is essential if both companies are to benefit from the outsourcing arrangement [17]. On a technological level, it is usually necessary to enable communications between the 3PL supplier's systems and those of the hiring customer. Along the same line, a firm should avoid 3PL providers who utilize proprietary information systems, because these are much more difficult to integrate with other systems.

Other important issues to discuss with potential 3PL providers include the following:

- The third party and its service providers must respect the confidentiality of the data that you provide them.
- Specific performance measures must be agreed upon.
- Specific criteria regarding subcontractors should be discussed.
- Arbitration issues should be considered before entering into a contract.
- Escape clauses should be negotiated into the contract.
- Methods of ensuring that performance goals are being met should be discussed [5].

6.4 RETAILER–SUPPLIER PARTNERSHIPS

The formation of strategic alliances between retailers and their suppliers is becoming ubiquitous in many industries. We saw in Chapter 4 that variations in demand to suppliers from retailers in traditional retailer–supplier relationships is far greater than the variation in demand seen by retailers. In addition, suppliers have far better knowledge of their lead times and production capacities than retailers do. Thus, as margins get tighter and customer satisfaction becomes even more important, it makes sense to create cooperative efforts between suppliers and retailers in order to leverage the knowledge of both parties.

6.4.1 Types of RSP

The types of retailer–supplier partnerships can be viewed on a continuum. At one end is information sharing, which helps the vendor plan more efficiently, and at the other is a consignment scheme, where the vendor completely manages and owns the inventory until the retailer sells it.

In a basic *quick response* strategy, suppliers receive POS data from retailers and use this information to synchronize their production and inventory activities with actual sales at the retailer. In this strategy, the retailer still prepares individual orders, but the POS data are used by the supplier to improve forecasting and scheduling and to reduce lead time.

EXAMPLE 6-6

Among the first companies to utilize this scheme was Milliken and Company, a textile and chemicals company. Milliken worked with several clothing suppliers and major department stores, all of which agreed to use POS data from the department stores to "synchronize" their ordering and manufacturing plans. The lead time from order receipt at Milliken's textile plants to final clothing receipt at the department stores was reduced from 18 weeks to 3 weeks [136].

In a *continuous replenishment* strategy, sometimes called *rapid replenishment,* vendors receive POS data and use these data to prepare shipments at previously agreed-upon intervals to maintain specific levels of inventory. In an advanced form of continuous replenishment, suppliers may gradually decrease inventory levels at the retail store or distribution center as long as service levels are met. Thus, in a structured way, inventory levels are continuously improved. In addition, the inventory levels need not be simple levels, but could be based on sophisticated models that change the appropriate level based on seasonal demand, promotions, and changing consumer demand [151].

In a *vendor-managed inventory (VMI)* system, sometimes called a *vendor-managed replenishment (VMR)* system, the supplier decides on the appropriate inventory levels of each of the products (within previously agreed-upon bounds) and the appropriate inventory policies to maintain these levels. In the initial stages, vendor suggestions must be approved by the retailer, but eventually the goal of many VMI programs is to eliminate retailer oversight on specific orders. This type of relationship is perhaps most famously exemplified by Wal-Mart and Procter & Gamble, whose partnership, begun in 1985, has dramatically improved P&G's on-time deliveries to Wal-Mart while increasing inventory turns [20]. Other discount stores followed suit, including Kmart, which by 1992 had developed over 200 VMI partners [136]. These VMI projects have in general been successful: projects at Dillard Department Stores, JCPenney, and Wal-Mart have shown sales increases of 20 to 25 percent, and 30 percent inventory turnover improvements [20].

EXAMPLE 6-7

First Brands, Inc., the maker of such products as Glad sandwich bags, has successfully partnered with Kmart. In 1991, the company entered Kmart's Partners in Merchandise Flow program, in which vendors are responsible for ensuring appropriate inventory levels to Kmart at all times, at Kmart's insistence. Initially, Kmart provided a three-year sales history, followed later by daily POS data to First Brands, which uses special software to convert these data into a production and delivery plan to each of Kmart's 13 distribution centers [39].

The main characteristics of RSP are summarized in Table 6-1.

6.4.2 Requirements for RSP

The most important requirement for an effective retailer–supplier partnership, especially one toward the VMI end of the partnership spectrum, is *advanced information systems*, on both the supplier and retailer sides of the supply chain. Electronic data interchange, EDI, or Internet-based private exchanges—to relay POS information to the supplier and delivery information to the retailer—are essential to cut down on data

TABLE 6-1

MAIN CHARACTERISTICS OF RSP

Criteria→ Type↓	Decision maker	Inventory ownership	New skills employed by vendors
Quick response	Retailer	Retailer	Forecasting skills
Continuous replnishment	Contractually agreed-to levels	Either party	Forecasting and inventory control
Advanced continuous replenishment	Contractually agreed to and continuously improved levels	Either party	Forecasting and inventory control
VMI	Vendor	Either party	Retail management

transfer time and entry mistakes. Bar coding and scanning are essential to maintain data accuracy. And inventory, production control, and planning systems must be on-line, accurate, and integrated to take advantage of the additional information available.

As in all initiatives that can radically change the way a company operates, top management commitment is required for the project to succeed. This is especially true because information that has been kept confidential up to this point will now have to be shared with suppliers and customers, and cost allocation issues will have to be considered at a very high level (this is covered in more detail below). It is also true because such a partnership may shift power within the organization from one group to another. For instance, when implementing a VMI partnership, the day-to-day contacts with retailers shift from sales and marketing personnel to logistics personnel. This implies that incentives for and compensation of the sales force have to be modified since retailer's inventory levels are driven by supply chain needs, not by pricing and discount strategies. This change in power may require significant involvement of top management.

Finally, RSP requires the partners to develop a certain level of trust without which the alliance is going to fail. In VMI, for example, suppliers need to demonstrate that they can manage the entire supply chain; that is, they can manage not only their own inventory but also that of the retailer. Similarly, in quick response, confidential information is provided to the supplier, which typically serves many competing retailers. In addition, strategic partnering in many cases results in significant reduction in inventory at the retailer outlet. The supplier needs to make sure that the additional available space is not used to benefit the supplier's competitors. Furthermore, the top management at the supplier must understand that the immediate effect of decreased inventory at the retailer will be a *one-time loss in sales revenue*.

6.4.3 Inventory Ownership in RSP

Several important issues must be considered when entering into a retailer–supplier partnership. One major issue is the decision concerning who makes the replenishment decisions. This places the partnership on the continuum of strategic partnership possibilities described above. This can be done in stages, first with information and, later, decision making, which is shared between the partners.

Inventory ownership issues are critical to the success of this kind of strategic alliance effort, especially one involving vendor-managed inventory. Originally, ownership of goods transferred to the retailer when goods were received. Now, some VMI partnerships are moving to a consignment relationship in which the supplier owns the goods until they are sold. The benefit of this kind of relationship to the retailer is obvious: lower inventory costs. Furthermore, since the supplier owns the inventory, it will be more concerned with managing it as effectively as possible. One possible criticism of the original VMI scheme is that the vendor has an incentive to move to the retailer as much inventory as the contract allows. If this is a fast-moving item and the partners had agreed upon two weeks of inventory, this may be exactly what the retailer wants to see in stock. If, however, this is a more complex problem of inventory management, the vendor needs to have an incentive to keep inventories as low as possible, subject to some agreed-upon service level. For example, Wal-Mart no longer owns the stock for many of the items it carries, including most of its grocery purchases. It only owns them briefly as they are being passed through the checkout scanner [33].

It is less clear, however, why this consignment arrangement is beneficial to the supplier since the supplier owns inventory for a longer period of time. Many times, as in the case of Wal-Mart, the supplier has no choice because the market dictates this kind of arrangement. Even if this is not the case, such an arrangement is beneficial to the supplier because it allows the supplier to coordinate distribution and production, thus reducing total cost. To better understand this issue, recall from Chapter 4 the discussion of the difference between *global optimization* and *local optimization*. In the traditional supply chain, each facility does what is best for that facility; that is, the retailer manages its own inventory without regard to the impact on the supplier. The supplier in turn identifies a policy that will optimize its own cost subject to satisfaction of the retailer demand. In VMI, one tries to optimize the entire system by coordinating production and distribution. In addition, the supplier can further decrease total cost by coordinating production and distribution for several retailers. This is precisely why global optimization allows for significant reductions in total system costs.

Sometimes, depending on the relative power of the supplier and the retailer, the supply contract must be negotiated so that the supplier and the retailer share *overall system savings*. Retailers must also take this into account when comparing the cost of competing vendors: Different logistics schemes have different costs.

EXAMPLE 6-8

Ace Hardware, a retail hardware dealer co-op, has successfully implemented a consignment VMI scheme for lumber and building materials. In this program, Ace maintains financial ownership of these goods at the retailer, but the retailer has custodial ownership that makes it responsible if the product is damaged or destroyed [3]. The program is considered extremely successful, with service levels increasing from 92 to 96 percent on VMI items. Ace would eventually like to expand it to other product lines [4].

In addition to inventory and ownership issues, advanced strategic alliances can cover many different areas. Issues such as joint forecasting, meshed planning cycles, and even joint product development are sometimes considered [126].

6.4.4 Issues in RSP Implementation

For any agreement to be a success, performance measurement criteria must also be agreed to. These criteria should include nonfinancial measures as well as the traditional financial measures. For example, nonfinancial measures could include point-of-sale (POS) accuracy, inventory accuracy, shipment and delivery accuracy, lead times, and customer fill rates.

When information is being shared between retailers and suppliers, *confidentiality* becomes an issue. Specifically, a retailer who deals with several suppliers within the same product category may find that category information is important to the supplier in making accurate forecasts and stocking decisions. Similarly, there may be a relationship between stocking decisions made by several suppliers. How can these potential conflicts be managed, with the retailer maintaining the confidentiality of each partner?

When entering any kind of strategic alliance, it is important for both parties to realize that there will initially be problems that can only be worked out through *communication* and *cooperation*. For example, when First Brands started partnering with Kmart, Kmart often claimed that its supplier was not living up to its agreement to keep two weeks of inventory on hand at all times. It turned out that the problem arose from different forecasting methods employed by the two companies. This problem was eventually solved by direct communication between Kmart's forecasting experts and those from First Brands—this type of communication would have occurred through salespeople before the VMI partnership began [39].

In many cases, the supplier in a partnership commits to fast response to emergencies and situational changes at the retailer. If the manufacturing technology or capacity do not currently exist at the supplier, they may need to be added. For example, VF Mills, the maker of Wrangler jeans and a pioneer of quick response methods in the clothing industry, had to completely reengineer its production processes, including retraining and additional capital investment [20].

6.4.5 Steps in RSP Implementation

The important points listed above can be summarized in the following steps in VMI implementation [73]:

1. Initially, the contractual terms of the agreement must be negotiated. These include decisions concerning ownership and when it is to be transferred, credit terms, ordering responsibilities, and performance measures such as service or inventory levels, when appropriate.
2. Next, the following three tasks must be executed:

   - If they do not exist, integrated information systems must be developed for both supplier and retailer. These information systems must provide easy access to both parties.
   - Effective forecasting techniques to be used by the vendor and the retailer must be developed.
   - A tactical decision support tool to assist in *coordinating* inventory management and transportation policies must be developed. The systems developed, of course, will depend on the particular nature of the partnership.

6.4.6 Advantages and Disadvantages of RSP

One advantage of VMI relationships is nicely illustrated by the following example.

EXAMPLE 6-9

Whitehall Robbins (WR), which makes over-the-counter drugs such as Advil, has an RSP relationship with Kmart. Like First Brands, WR initially disagreed with Kmart about forecasts. In this case, it turned out that WR forecasts were more accurate because the company has a much more extensive knowledge of its products than Kmart does. For example, Kmart's Chap Stick forecasts did not take the seasonality of the product into account. In addition, WR planners can take production issues, such as planned downtime, into account when planning shipments.

Also, WR benefits in another way. In the past Kmart would order large quantities of seasonal items at the beginning of the season, often linked to a promotion. This practice often led to returns

Example 6-9 *Continued*

because it was difficult for Kmart to accurately forecast the amount it would sell. Now WR supplies weekly demand at an "everyday low cost," so large orders and preseason promotions have been eliminated, which in turn has greatly reduced returns. Inventory turns for seasonal items have gone from 3 to more than 10, and for nonseasonal items from 12–15 to 17–20 [39].

Thus, in general, a huge advantage of RSPs is the knowledge the supplier has about order quantities, implying an ability to control the bullwhip effect (see Chapter 4). This of course varies from one type of partnership to another. In quick response, for instance, this knowledge is achieved through transfer of customer demand information that allows the supplier to reduce lead time, while in VMI the retailer provides demand information and the supplier makes ordering decisions, thus completely controlling the variability in order quantities. Of course, this knowledge can be leveraged to reduce overall system costs and improve overall system service levels. The benefits to the supplier in terms of better service levels, decreased managerial expenses, and decreased inventory costs are obvious. The vendor should be able to reduce forecast uncertainties and thus better coordinate production and distribution. To be more specific, reduced forecast uncertainties lead to reduced safety stocks, reduced storage and delivery costs, and increased service levels [73], as we noted in our discussion of the bullwhip effect in Chapter 4, Section 4.2.

In addition to the important benefits listed above, implementing a strategic partnership provides a variety of side benefits. It provides a good opportunity for the reengineering of the retailer–supplier relationship. For example, redundant order entries can be eliminated, manual tasks can be automated, tasks such as ticketing merchandise and designing displays can be reassigned for systemwide efficiency, and unnecessary control steps can be eliminated from the process [20]. Many of these advantages stem from the same changes and technology needed to implement partnerships in the first place.

Many of the problems with retailer–supplier partnerships have been discussed above and are summarized here.

- It is necessary to employ advanced technology, which is often expensive.
- It is essential to develop trust in what once may have been an adversarial supplier–retailer relationship.
- In a strategic partnership, the supplier often has much more responsibility than formerly. This may force the supplier to add personnel to meet this responsibility.
- Finally, and perhaps most critically, expenses at the supplier often increase as managerial responsibilities increase. Also, inventory may initially be shifted back to the supplier; if a consignment arrangement is used, inventory costs in general may increase for the supplier. Thus, it may be necessary to work out a contractual relationship in which the retailer shares decreased system inventory costs with the supplier.

Float is another issue with any EDI implementation, and it needs to be carefully considered when committing to a VMI partnership. Retailers who have become accustomed to waiting 30 to 90 days to pay for goods may now have to pay upon delivery. Even if they pay only when their goods are sold, this could be much sooner than their usual period of float [58].

6.4.7 Successes and Failures

We have cited several examples of RSP in the sections above. We include several other examples of successes—and one example of a failure—next.

EXAMPLE 6-10

Western Publishing is using VMI for its Golden Books line of children's books at several retailers, including more than 2,000 Wal-Mart locations. In this program, POS data automatically trigger reorders when inventory falls below a reorder point. This inventory is delivered either to a distribution center or, in many cases, directly to a store. In this case, ownership of the books shifts to the retailer once deliveries have been made. In the case of Toys "R" Us, Western Publishing has even managed the entire book section for the retailer, including inventory from suppliers other than Western Publishing. The company has generated significant additional sales in both cases, although the program has increased costs significantly: These are costs related to the additional inventory management duties, as well as the extra freight costs incurred by shipping directly to stores. Nonetheless, management believes that VMI has provided a net benefit for the company [3].

EXAMPLE 6-11

After Wal-Mart included supplier Mead-Johnson in its VMI program, the results were dramatic. Mead-Johnson has complete POS information to which it reacts instead of orders. Since this program was implemented, inventory turns at Wal-Mart have gone from under 10 to more than 100, and at Mead-Johnson from 12 to 52. Similarly, Scott Paper Company has been managing inventory in 25 of its customer distribution centers. In this effort, inventory turns at the customers have increased from about 19 to somewhere between 35 and 55, inventory levels have been reduced, and service levels have improved. One caveat can be drawn from the experiences of Schering-Plough Healthcare Products (SPHP) with Kmart's Partners in the Merchandise Flow Program. In the first year of implementation, SPHP did see decreased stockouts at Kmart, but not substantially improved sales or profits. By patiently continuing with the program, however, SPHP eventually did realize substantial benefits in these areas [153].

EXAMPLE 6-12

VF Corporation's Market Response System provides another success story of VMI. The company, which has many well-known brand names (e.g., Wrangler, Lee, and Girbaud), began its program in 1989. Currently, about 40 percent of its production is handled through some type of automatic replenishment scheme. This is particularly notable because the program encompasses 350 different retailers, 40,000 store locations, and more than 15 million levels of replenishment. Each division uses automatic software to manage the huge influx of data, and special techniques developed at VF to cluster the data so that they are more manageable. VF's program is considered one of the most successful in the apparel industry [133].

EXAMPLE 6-13

Spartan Stores, a grocery chain, shut down its VMI effort about one year after its inception. In examining the reasons for the failure of the program, some important ingredients for a successful VMI program became clear. One problem was that buyers were not spending any less time on reorders than they had before because they didn't trust the suppliers enough to stop their careful monitoring of the inventories and deliveries of the VMI items. Buyers intervened at the slightest hint of trouble. Further, the suppliers didn't do much to allay these fears. The problems were not with the suppliers' forecasts; instead they were due to the suppliers' inability to deal with product promotions, which are a key part of the grocery business. Because suppliers were unable to account for promotions appropriately, delivery levels were often unacceptably low during these periods of peak demand. In addition, Spartan executives felt that the inventory levels achieved by the VMI program were no lower than the levels the company could have achieved with a well-managed

---

Example 6-13 *Continued*

traditional supplier program. It should be noted that Spartan considered the VMI program successful with some suppliers. These were the suppliers with better forecasting skills. In addition, Spartan intends to maintain the continuous replenishment programs, in which inventory levels automatically trigger fixed delivery quantities with some of its suppliers [104].

6.5 DISTRIBUTOR INTEGRATION

For years business experts have advised manufacturers, particularly industrial manufacturers, to treat their distributors like partners [114]. Typically, this meant appreciating the value of the distributors and their relationship with the end users, and providing them with the necessary support to be successful. Distributors have a wealth of information about customer needs and wants, and successful manufacturers use this information when developing new products and product lines. Similarly, distributors typically rely on manufacturers to supply the necessary parts and expertise.

EXAMPLE 6-14

The chairman and CEO of Caterpillar Corporation, Donald Fites, credits Caterpillar dealers with much of his company's recent success. Fites points out that dealers are much closer to customers than to the corporation, and can respond more rapidly to customer needs. They arrange financing when the product is purchased and carefully monitor, repair, and service the product. Fites says that "the dealer creates the image of a company that doesn't just stand behind its products but with its products anywhere in the world." Caterpillar believes that its dealer network gives the company a tremendous advantage over its competition, especially the big Japanese construction and mining equipment manufacturers such as Komatsu and Hitachi [55].

This view of distributors is changing, however, as customer service needs present new challenges, and information technology rises to meet these challenges. Even a strong and effective distributor network can't always meet the needs of customers. A rush order might be impossible to meet from inventory or the customer might require some specialized technical expertise that the distributor does not have.

In the past, these issues were addressed by adding inventory and personnel, either to each distributor or to the manufacturer. Modern information technology leads to a third solution, in which distributors are integrated so that the expertise and inventory located at one distributor is available to the others.

6.5.1 Types of Distributor Integration

Distributor integration (DI) can be used to address both inventory-related and service-related issues. In terms of inventory, DI can be used to create a large pool of inventory across the entire distributor network, lowering total inventory costs while raising service levels. Similarly, DI can be used to meet a customer's specialized technical service requests by steering these requests to the distributors best suited to address them.

As we have pointed out in previous chapters, increased inventory is traditionally used to meet unusual rush orders and to provide spare parts quickly to facilitate repairs. In more sophisticated companies, risk-pooling concepts might be used to keep inventory earlier in the supply chain, where it can be distributed as needed. In a DI arrangement, each distributor can check the inventories of other distributors to locate a needed product or part. Dealers are contractually bound to exchange the part under certain conditions and for agreed-upon remuneration. This type of arrangement improves service levels at each of the distributors and lowers the total system inventory required. Of course, this type of arrangement is possible only because sophisticated information systems allow distributors to review each others' inventory and integrated logistics systems allow parts to be delivered cheaply and efficiently.

EXAMPLE 6-15

Machine tool builder Okuma America Corporation has implemented a DI system. Okuma carries many expensive machine tools and repair parts, but the high cost of carrying the full line makes it impossible for Okuma's 46 distributors in North and South America to do so. Instead Okuma requires each of its dealers to carry a minimum number of machine tools and parts. The company manages the entire system so that each tool and part is in stock somewhere in the system, either in one of the company's two warehouses or at one of the distributors. A system called Okumalink allows each of the distributors to check the warehouse inventories and to communicate with other distributors in finding a required part. Once a part is found, the company ensures that it is delivered quickly to the requesting dealer. There are plans to upgrade the system so that each distributor has full knowledge of the inventory held by all distributors. Since the system's implementation, inventory costs throughout the system have been reduced, the chance that a distributor will lose a sale because of inventory shortages has decreased, and customer satisfaction has increased [115].

Similarly, DI can be used to improve each distributor's perceived technical ability and ability to respond to unusual customer requests. In this kind of alliance, different distributors build expertise in different areas. A customer's specific request is routed to the distributor with the most expertise. For example, Otra, a large Dutch holding company with about 70 electrical wholesale subsidiaries, has designated some of them as *centers of excellence* in particular areas, such as warehouse layouts or point-of-sale materials. The other subsidiaries, as well as customers, are directed to these centers of excellence to meet particular requests [115].

6.5.2 Issues in Distributor Integration

There are two major issues involved in implementing a DI alliance. First, distributors may be skeptical of the rewards of participating in such a system. There is the chance that they will feel they are providing some of their expertise in inventory control to less skilled partners, especially when some of the distributors are larger and have bigger inventories than others. In addition, participating distributors will be forced to rely upon other distributors, some of whom they may not know, to help them provide good customer service.

This new kind of relationship also tends to take certain responsibilities and areas of expertise away from certain distributors, and concentrate them on a few distributors. It is not surprising that distributors might be nervous about losing these skills and abilities.

This explains why establishing a DI relationship requires a large commitment of resources and effort on the part of the manufacturing company. Distributors must feel sure that this is a long-term alliance. Organizers must work hard to build trust among the participants. Finally, the manufacturer may have to provide pledges and guarantees to ensure distributor commitment.

EXAMPLE 6-16

Dunlop-Enerka is a Dutch company that supplies conveyer belts to mining and manufacturing companies worldwide. Traditionally, the company met maintenance and repair requirements by storing vast quantities of inventory at distributors throughout Europe. To reduce inventories, the company installed a computer-based information system, Dunlocomm, to monitor inventory at the warehouses of each of its distributors. When a part is needed, a distributor uses the system to order the part and arrange for its delivery. To ensure distributor participation, Dunlop-Enerka guaranteed

Example 6-16 *Continued*

24-hour delivery of each part to each distributor—if a part wasn't in stock, Dunlop-Enerka custom-manufactured and shipped it within the available time window. This guarantee reassured distributors enough so they committed to the system and, over time, inventory throughout the system dropped by 20 percent [115].

SUMMARY

In this chapter, we examined various types of partnerships that can be used to manage the supply chain more effectively. We started off by discussing the different paths a firm can take to ensure that particular supply chain–related issues are addressed, including performing them internally or outsourcing them completely. Obviously, many different strategic and tactical issues play a part in the selection of the most appropriate strategy. We discussed a framework that can help in selecting the most appropriate way to address a particular logistics issue.

Increasingly, third-party logistics providers are taking over some of a firm's logistics responsibilities. There are both advantages and disadvantages to outsourcing the logistics function, as well as many important issues to consider once the decision has been made and a 3PL agreement is being implemented.

Retailer–supplier partnerships, in which the supplier manages a portion of the retailer's business—typically retail inventories—are also becoming common. There is a spectrum of possible types of retailer–supplier partnerships, ranging from agreements that cover only information sharing, to agreements in which the supplier has complete control over the retailer's inventory policy. We considered various issues and concerns relating to the implementation of these types of arrangement.

Finally, we discussed a class of alliances, called distributor integration, in which manufacturers coordinate the efforts of their (potentially competing) distributors to create risk-pooling opportunities across the various distributors and to enable different distributors to develop different areas of expertise.

DISCUSSION QUESTIONS

1. Consider a manager developing a logistics strategy. Discuss specific situations for which the best approach would be to
   a. Employ internal logistics expertise.
   b. Acquire a company with this expertise.
   c. Develop a strategy, and then employ specific suppliers to carry out well-defined portions of the strategy.
   d. Develop the strategy with a third-party logistics provider.
2. Why is the third-party logistics industry growing so rapidly?
3. In this chapter, we discuss three types of retailer supplier partnerships: *quick response, continuous replenishment,* and *vendor-managed inventory (VMI).* For each type, discuss situations where that type would be preferred over the other two. For instance, compare quick response to continuous replenishment: under what conditions is one preferred over the other?
4. Consider the quick response partnership. Suppose the retailer places an order at the beginning of each month but transfers POS data to the supplier every week. What is the impact of the manufacturer's weekly production capacity on the benefit from information sharing? That is, under what situations is information sharing

most beneficial: high weekly production capacity or low capacity? How should the supplier use the weekly demand data received from the retailer?

5. Discuss the various possibilities for inventory ownership policies in a VMI arrangement. What are the advantages and disadvantages of each of these policies?

6. Recall Example 6-13, the story of Spartan Stores' failed VMI effort. Discuss how Spartan might have done things differently in order to help the program succeed.

Audio Duplication Services, Inc. (ADS)

Audio Duplication Services is a compact disk and cassette duplication and distribution company. Its major customers, the big record companies, use ADS to duplicate and distribute CDs and cassettes. ADS stores the master tapes and, when a customer requests it, makes a certain number of copies and delivers them to its customers' customers, music stores and other points of sale such as department stores Wal-Mart and Kmart and electronics stores such as Circuit City and Best Buy. ADS is one of six big players in the audio duplication market. ADS has about 20 percent of the $5 billion market, while its two biggest competitors share another 40 percent.

Managers at ADS are currently trying to understand and react to some difficult supply chain–related issues.

- Some of the big national retailers are putting pressure on ADS's customers, the record companies, to manage inventory in the following way, known as a vendor-managed inventory, or VMI, agreement. The record companies will be put in charge of deciding how much of each album, CD, and cassette title is delivered to each store and when each delivery is made. To help with these decisions, the record companies will be provided with continuously updated point-of-sale (POS) data from each of the stores. Also, the record companies will own the inventory until it is sold, at which point payment will be transferred from the retailers to the record

companies. Since ADS provides the record companies with duplication and distribution services, the record companies have asked ADS to help with the logistics of the VMI agreement.

- In the past, ADS has shipped to the distribution centers of large national retailers, and the retailers have arranged for distribution to the individual stores. Now, the retailers are providing strong incentives to ship directly to individual stores. Of course, this means higher expenses for ADS.

- In general, ADS's shipping costs are increasing. Currently, ADS has a shipping manager who arranges with different shippers to make deliveries on a shipment-by-shipment basis. Perhaps there is a better way to manage these deliveries, either by purchasing a fleet of trucks and doing the shipping in house or by outsourcing the entire shipping function to a third party. Maybe something between these two extremes will be best.

Of course, ADS is facing even bigger issues, such as the future of the audio duplication industry as on-line audio distribution technologies become more prevalent. In any event, each record company periodically reviews its contract with its audio duplication service, so management must address each of the above issues effectively for the company to remain successful.

CASE DISCUSSION QUESTIONS

1. Why are ADS's customers' customers moving towards VMI arrangements?
2. How will this impact ADS's business? How can ADS management take advantage of this situation?
3. How should ADS manage logistics?
4. Why are the large national retailers moving toward a direct shipment model?

Source: ADS is a fictional company. The material in this case is loosely based on the authors' experience with several companies.

CHAPTER 7

Procurement and Outsourcing Strategies

FreeMarkets OnLine, Inc.

As Glen Meakem and Sam Kinney, the two cofounders of FreeMarkets OnLine, Inc., grabbed their sandwiches on the way to the conference room, their thoughts focused on how to position their company, both with clients and the capital markets. Finally, by January 1998, nearly three years after starting their business, they had something that was working—their company's monthly revenues were sufficient to cover its $300,000 monthly burn rate. The company had achieved 1997 revenues of almost $1.8 million and was aiming for over 200 percent growth in 1998 to $6 million. The two founders were already looking beyond that to when the company's revenues and valuation would allow them to raise a large amount of growth capital and provide investor liquidity through an IPO. But before that might happen, they knew they needed to lay out a clear and compelling strategy that would create the most value.

FOUNDING

FreeMarkets OnLine was founded in Pittsburgh in 1995 by three entrepreneurs. The founders chose Pittsburgh to take advantage of the city's unique blend of industrial and high-technology infrastructure. Important were its location close to major manufacturing centers, a hub airport, and a strong local skill base in both software and manufacturing. Having purchased the interests of the third founder, for all practical purposes Glen Meakem and Sam Kinney constituted the firm's founding team: their equity, combined with other equity investments, launched the company's technology and business development efforts.

By the end of 1993, it had been clear to Meakem that he had stumbled on a very big opportunity. Having worked on purchasing studies for clients while a member of McKinsey's Houston office, he knew that industrial buyers faced tough challenges sorting through the variety of suppliers available for any given purchase. His impression was that the average skill level of buyers in a wide range of manufacturing companies was low and the information available to help them make decisions was very limited. For a wide range of industrial input components and materials, identifying truly high-quality suppliers while also establishing fair market prices (including total acquisition costs) was extremely difficult. Because of these challenges, industrial buyers were unaware of the savings opportunities still lurking beneath their decisions, Meakem had concluded. So it was only natural

Source: Copyright © 1998 by the President and Fellows of Harvard College. This case was written by V. Kasturi Fangan of Harvard Business School.

that when he left McKinsey to join a Fortune 50 company's corporate business development group, he began working on purchasing improvement projects.

Even before Meakem arrived at the company, it was experiencing success by conducting supplier negotiations as "silent auctions." A group of suppliers would be assembled in a hotel ballroom surrounded by flip charts. On each flip chart was the most recent price bid by a supplier on a component such as a casting or a machined part. Over the course of the day, prices dropped as suppliers participated in this open-price discovery process. But the logistical difficulties of bringing together all of the suppliers made these events difficult to replicate.

Network technology could change all this, thought Meakem, who remembered an article he had read in the May–June 1989 issue of *Harvard Business Review*, "The Logic of Electronic Markets," by Thomas Malone, Joanne Yates, and Robert Benjamin:

> That's where electronic markets come in. Electronic markets offer cross-company electronic connections, just as single-source sales channels do, and therefore give customers the same convenience. But they include offerings from competing suppliers. Not only do customers have electronic connections to their suppliers but they can also choose which suppliers they want to use. From the customers' perspective, then, electronic markets are more desirable than single-source sales channels. If the technology exists to create electronic markets and customers want them, it is just a matter of time until services arise to meet that need. Making an unbiased electronic market is a potentially profitable business in its own right.

Working with another manager in this Fortune 50 company, Meakem led the development of a rudimentary interactive bidding system. They fielded this version in September 1994. And it worked—interactive bidding among competing suppliers generated price savings.

All the while, however, it became clear to Meakem that in order for such a bidding system to work, some important groundwork had to be put in place. First, the bidding was only as good as the product specifications. The suppliers needed a precise understanding of the components or materials on which they were bidding, including related services such as delivery and inventory management. Second, results depended upon having the right suppliers involved. When these "lower-tech" issues were not addressed, electronic markets failed. When he approached the company about backing a full-service approach, he found that managers were focused on the technology itself. Meakem concluded that he would have to make this happen on his own. Consulting legal counsel, he was advised that he needed to make an absolutely clean break, take nothing—no presentation documents, no supplier names, no software or documentation.

Meakem set up shop in his basement with his vision of what network technology would do to industrial markets. According to Meakem:

> It's an interesting challenge, starting a business in an industry that has yet to be created. I like to use the term "going to the basement" to describe early entrepreneurial ventures like ours. You start with very little—no team, no cash, no market, no technology, no product, no customers, and no business model. Fortunately, I did have four critical assets: an idea, experience, my Rolodex of contacts from my previous experiences, and about $75,000 of savings. I also had my wife Diane. Despite the fact that we had two children under three years of age, she was very supportive.

Sam Kinney, like Glen Meakem, had several years of experience under his belt, including five years of consulting at Booz-Allen and then McKinsey, and two years as a budget director at Lucas Aerospace. Sam Kinney described the genesis of the firm:

> Glen and I had been colleagues at McKinsey after he graduated from the Harvard Business School and I from Tuck (Dartmouth). After two years, Glen left McKinsey and I, too, was itching to leave to start a company. When Glen came up with the electronic bidding idea, I jumped at it, because it was a very good fit. We knew each other and liked working together and had similar entrepreneurial aspirations.

Meakem explained how they arrived at the name:

> You have to balance multiple objectives. The name must evoke in potential clients and investors a sense of what the business does. But to be acceptable as a trademark, you typically have to invent new words or new uses of words because you cannot trademark obviously descriptive names. We also felt that with the pace of Internet start-ups, there would be a land grab for good names in this field.

They settled on FreeMarkets OnLine to satisfy a number of objectives. First, it seemed to portray the essence of what the business would do: create a fair and open exchange. Second, it appeared to be available for trademark registration. Third, it would signal to investors through "OnLine" that this was a business that could partake in the venture capital and IPO boom emerging around the Internet.

SOFTWARE DEVELOPMENT

Creating the software necessary for bidding became the most time-consuming early challenge. By mid-1995, when FreeMarkets™ had to commit to technical design decisions, the Internet was just beginning to be recognized as a powerful new medium. Netscape's IPO, one of the milestone events in publicizing the Internet, was still three months away. Internet service providers were in the throes of upgrading to 28.8 modem speed and meeting demand—few were able to offer any technical assistance.

FreeMarkets wanted the system to be fast, allowing real-time interaction. Although a few relatively static bid boards for industrial components existed, most stayed open for days before closing. The company wanted to create a truly interactive market to close not after days, but in only a few hours. That presented some technical challenges. According to Vincent Rago, vice president of Information Technology:

> Our needs have always been one step ahead of the development tools. As a result, we have had to solve problems before ready-made solutions have been available. People speak about the costs of being on the "bleeding" edge of technology. While we haven't cut any arteries, we've clearly had to absorb some nicks and bruises.

Despite the lack of tools, FreeMarkets tested its BidWare® and BidServer® software by October 1995. On its maiden voyage in November 1995, the software conducted a live bid for about $3.2 million worth of injection-molded plastic appliance parts.

> "It was a thrilling feeling," recalled Meakem.
>
> At the end of that first Competitive Bidding Event™ (CBE), Sam, our whole team, and I were screaming and cheering as though we had just put a man on the moon. Seeing real suppliers bid across a network for real business using our BidWare® technology was electrifying. It was a resounding validation of our concept.

Below is a brief description of an on-line Competitive Bidding Event:

> It's 1:00 P.M. EST. The purchasing team from one of the world's largest manufacturers of air-conditioning equipment has gathered in a headquarters conference room to watch as 12 companies from across the United States and Canada engage in a live Internet bidding event in competition for new business.
>
> The stakes are high: nearly $2.5 million worth of precision-machined parts in eight categories, or "lots," will be awarded as a result of this bidding event. During

the preceding weeks, both the manufacturer's purchasing staff and prospective suppliers have been preparing for this moment with the help of FreeMarkets OnLine, the leading provider of on-line industrial market-making services. Now all sides are ready. The buyer and 12 suppliers log in to a secure private network with FreeMarkets OnLine's BidWare® software, and the bidding begins.

> Within minutes, the buyer has saved thousands of dollars from its historic spending level. New bids come in every couple of minutes, driving the unit price lower and lower. By 1:45, the buyer has saved tens of thousands of dollars below its historic costs—and there are still more than two hours remaining before the bidding concludes.
>
> Excitement in the room continues to build, as expectations for significant savings increase. By 3:45, the bidding intensifies as time begins to run out. The total savings now stand at more than $300,000, and bids are becoming even more frequent.
>
> Shortly after 4:00 P.M., the bidding ends. More than 250 interactive bids were received. All told, this air-conditioning equipment manufacturer saved more than $400,000—a 16 percent savings below its historic spending level of $2.5 million—thanks to FreeMarkets OnLine's innovative approach to on-line industrial market making.

The first CBE was also a resounding confirmation of the company's ability to design, build, and ship user-friendly commercial software. According to Meakem:

> I am passionate about the need for software to be self-trainable and easy to use for "normal" people. I am very much a follower of Scott Cook at Intuit in this regard. From the early versions of BidWare® right through to the present, we have proven that we can understand a market need, then design, build, and test complex, wide-area-networked, client–server applications. In what has been a capital-constrained environment, our software development team has not wasted any money.

Addressing the issue of how to successfully build software, Vincent Rago, vice president of Information Technology, offered this perspective:

> Money is not the key issue in software development. Yes, if you can't pay really talented software designers and engineers, you don't have a development effort. But the bigger issue is focus—focus by the development team on a real set of customer needs, including high-level market or business needs, detailed functionality, and usability. You can spend $50 million and completely fail in a software development effort. You can also spend $500,000 and create great software. Small teams fueled by intense senior management focus build great software. Large teams without focus fail.

In addition to proving out new software, early pilot CBEs thrust FreeMarkets into the operational elements of building requests for quotation (RFQs), identifying and recruiting potential suppliers, and supporting the bidding as suppliers participated from their place of business. "This was the moment of truth," declared Meakem, "where we had to put into practice the full-service vision. In addition to achieving excellence in operational tasks, we needed to become at least as knowledgeable as our clients about the industries in which we made markets, and we needed to get there fast."

According to Kinney:

> At that point, we thought of ourselves as being in the competitive bidding business—selling Competitive Bidding Events to buyers and running our technology in ways they never could. We were successful at developing reasonable expertise and market knowledge, and what became apparent was just how much of this was "art" rather than "science." The dynamics of each CBE—who was hungry, how hard the parts were to make, what was happening to material prices—made each CBE a very unique experience. That's when we began to see ourselves in broader terms—as "market makers" in industrial products.

The imagery of "market making" stuck, and became a powerful influence on the development of the company. Project managers are known in FreeMarkets as industrial market makers. Their job is to lead the art and science of making markets for custom products, where each buyer in the market has his own set of objectives and issues.

THE MARKET

"Unglamorous as it may sound, industrial purchasing is big, big businesses," wrote *Investor Relations* magazine (May 1997, pp. 75–77):

> In the U.S. alone, some $600 billion worth of industrial intermediate components are sold each year. The average U.S. manufacturer spends some 55 percent of sales on direct material purchases. And with labor downsized to the bone, but Wall Street still clamoring for ever higher margins and continual earnings growth, purchasing would seem to be a logical place to look for efficiencies.

According to Kinney there were many reasons why buyers should find value in a service that helps assemble suppliers into electronic bidding sessions:

> First of all, many supply industries are very fragmented. For example, in the $20 billion U.S. market for injection molded plastic parts, there are 3,000 suppliers. Second, in some of these industries the productivity variance between suppliers in the top quartile and the bottom quartile is simply enormous. In industries like plastic materials and metal stampings, the top quartile is 80–100 percent more productive than the bottom quartile. Some suppliers are really that much better. Third, in the face of this fragmentation and variation, buyers are left with an information problem: too many potential alternatives and no good way to sort them out. Buyers have had to rely on supplier sales representatives, themselves not disinterested parties, to educate them about the markets.

Meakem and Kinney knew that some degree of focus was necessary to ensure early success and prevent diluting the effort across too many fronts. They knew that in the industrial markets, some products were truly so sophisticated or rare as to require tight partnerships between buyers and suppliers. Other products had already become commodities—where market prices were reasonably easy to discover using published sources or quick telephone solicitations. The team decided to concentrate in the middle—those components that were not commodities, but for which competitive supply markets existed. According to Meakem, "The technique is most successful when the product is specifiable, when competition among suppliers is sufficient, and when the buyer's purchase is large enough to stimulate that competition." Table 7-1 describes the types of components that made up the target market. Using a couple of different estimating techniques, FreeMarkets concluded that this market was still huge—over $300 billion in the United States alone.

The target market decisions would emerge as an early source of differentiation for FreeMarkets. "What many observers of electronic commerce fail to realize," offered Kinney, "is that industrial purchasing is dominated by 'custom' products—those made by a supplier to the buyer's blueprint. Most electronic commerce applications are for standard products like light bulbs and gloves." This distinction was made clear in an *InformationWeek* article (November 13, 1997):

> Catalogs, which involve one buyer and one seller at a time, is [sic] the largest [market] segment, accounting for 60 percent of the $8 billion market [for business-to-business electronic commerce]. Noted examples include companies such as AMP, Cisco Systems, Dell Computer, and National Semiconductor selling to corporate buyers, resellers, and

TABLE 7-1		
THE TARGET MARKET		
No-tooling custom components	**Low-tooling custom components**	**Transferable-tooling custom components**
Fasteners	Machined parts	Stampings
Service center metals	Metal fabrications	Castings
Specialty chemicals	Corrugated packaging	Plastic moldings
Electronic components	Printed circuit boards	

distributors via the Web. Intermediaries such as GE TPN that post sellers' catalogs also fit into this category.

The [upward price] "auction" model also involves an on-line bidding event, but buyers compete for a successful bid from a single seller. Web start-ups such as FairMarket in Boston and FastParts in Chicago are testing this model, which has seen success in the business-to-consumer market through OnSale Inc. and more recently Internet Shopping Network's FirstAuction site.

The [downward price] "bid" model, which involves real-time bidding [by] multiple suppliers [to sell to a buyer], is the only one of the models that will increase its market share [of business-to-business electronic commerce] in the next five years, according to Forrester [Research].

But all three approaches ["catalog," "auction," and "bid"] will grow dramatically as the overall business-to-business e-commerce market more than doubles annually to reach $327 billion by 2002.

THE ORGANIZATION

Figure 7-1 shows the company's organization structure. According to Meakem:

Our business requires an eclectic blend of skills. We have a very-high-speed software development team, a network operations group, senior-level client sales, a laser-targeted consulting ability, an information agency, and a back office all in one company. We have grown up this way from the beginning so we do not have the organizational integration problems characteristic of so many information, software, and consulting companies. We work in cross-functional teams both to make markets and to develop and build software and information products.

The fact is we are in the business of selling and delivering a complex conceptual service. This service is made possible by people, process, software products, and unique

FIGURE 7-1 Organizational structure.

information. The fact that our service is difficult to deliver, requiring a blend of organizational skills, is our second most important competitive advantage. Our most important competitive advantage is the fact that we serve our clients very well, and they trust us in return.

THE SALES MODEL

Another important decision with long-term ramifications was how the company would sell its services. Convinced from the start that the message needed to reach senior executives and purchasing decision makers, it began to build a direct sales model. This direct model consisted of high bandwidth "client developers" networking into and establishing relationships with senior level purchasing, operations, and finance executives at large targeted corporations.

By January 1998, the Company had two full-time senior "client developers." Everyone else on the eight-member senior leadership team also had a direct role in client development. In particular, Meakem and Executive Vice President and COO David Becker spent significant amounts of their time pursuing client development activities. According to Meakem, "Old fashioned senior level sales will always be the life blood of our business. No one ever tells you this in business school, but without people who can sell a concept, ask for money, and close deals, you are dead."

Shunning the popular practice among Internet startups of "press-release markcting," FreeMarkets operated under a media silence policy from its founding until January 1997, fully 21 months into its existence. It put up a single-page website with the company's address and phone number. Kinney explained:

> We were trying to find multimillion-dollar negotiation projects for purchase of mission-critical parts. We were doing this by convincing senior-level executives to take a chance with us on millions of dollars of their purchasing spend. We didn't then believe, nor do we now, that this true industrial-strength commerce will happen as a result of a passive Web presence. Further, so much of the value of market making is off-line that it really would have confused matters to have solicited business directly via the Web.
>
> Too many people give away too much competitive intelligence through the press and on their websites. We didn't want to open ourselves up to copying before we had established our presence. Now, however, as recruiting has become a bigger part of our challenge, we've sought publicity and built a real website (http://www.freemarkets.com).

At this point, the risks of silence far outweigh the risks of publicity.

The client development effort was aimed at finding those opportunities where the buyer would be likely to engage FreeMarkets to use its technique in sourcing a basket of products. Typical situations were supplier consolidations or annual negotiations, or when corporatewide purchasing savings projects were underway.

THE MARKET-MAKING PROCESS

The company's core service was to provide on-line industrial market-making services that culminated in real-time competitive bidding events, also known as CBEs. In these events, a single industrial buyer used the FreeMarkets BidWare® software and a secure, private network to allow a number of potential suppliers to simultaneously submit price bids against one another, as they attempted to win a buyer's purchase order. The on-line auction process used by the company created a level of competitive intensity among suppliers that was more intense than sealed bidding or face-to-face negotiations.

The key enabling technology was FreeMarkets's proprietary BidWare® software for buyers and suppliers and the company's proprietary BidServer® software that ran CBEs from its server in Pittsburgh. On either end of the network were user-friendly software applications that ran in the Microsoft Windows 95 and 98 environments. BidWare® for Suppliers contained the functionality that allowed suppliers to monitor "market" prices, submit bids, and print valuable market benchmarking reports. BidWare® for Buyers contained the functionality to monitor the bidding and print detailed results reports.

The five steps in the FreeMarkets OnLine industrial market-making process are described below:

Phase 1: Identify savings opportunities. FreeMarkets worked directly with buyers, analyzing spending and applying FreeMarkets's market-making experience to help buying organizations identify potential savings.

Phase 2: Prepare total-cost RFQ. Since a detailed understanding of all requirements including logistics and quality levels was required by all competing suppliers, RFQ preparation involved much more than just providing drawings and volume forecasts. Working with client buyers and engineers, the FreeMarkets industrial market-making team created a comprehensive RFQ that defined all elements of total cost.

Phase 3: Identify, screen, and support suppliers. The FreeMarkets supply markets team took the lead in identifying and contacting suppliers. Throughout this process, the market-making team, along with the buyers they serviced, screened potential suppliers, narrowing the field to those whose capabilities best matched the buying organization's needs. FreeMarkets also provided extensive RFQ support to suppliers, answering questions and gathering feedback.

Phase 4: Conduct on-line competitive bidding events. Those suppliers selected by the buyer prepared their quotes with the support of the FreeMarkets team. All suppliers participated in training sessions to learn every aspect of BidWare, FreeMarkets's proprietary software used by suppliers, to submit real-time bids. On the bidding day, suppliers dialed into a secure global network. Buyers, meanwhile, watched the on-line bidding event from their facility.

Phase 5: Provide post-bid analysis and award support. FreeMarkets followed up CBEs by collecting cost breakdowns from suppliers to validate quotes. FreeMarkets also supported final supplier analysis and qualifications to achieve optimal award decisions.

As indicated in the above description, the on-line industrial market-making process was characterized by several stages. It usually started with interviews with the buyer and appropriate manufacturing and quality personnel, during which all the specifications—technical, commercial, logistical, and quality—were spelled out. FreeMarkets's industry experts assisted, drawing on their knowledge of the relevant manufacturers' processes and supply market conditions. This initial step was laborious and detailed, but was absolutely necessary in developing the requests for quote required for dissemination to the various potential suppliers.

According to Executive Vice President and Chief Operating Officer David Becker (a business school classmate of Meakem's):

> Our market-making staff works as a cross-functional team. In addition to the industrial market maker who leads the team, we engage an associate market maker who handles

much of the supplier screening and a market-making engineer who performs detailed part and drawing analyses to ensure drawings are correct and suppliers obtain complete, consistent technical information. The team is supported by our supplier support group that handles RFQ questions and BidWare® training. For this particular event, team members spend a number of days at the buyer's site, collecting the RFQ information, developing the lot-setting strategy, and selecting suppliers.

> The buyer also provides the technical documents and other requirements that become part of a solid RFQ. However, we try to take as much of the preparation workload off the buyer as possible. The time spent in preparing a great RFQ pays off on the back end, both in the quality of the bids and also because buyers can really implement the savings we obtain in the on-line marketplace. Suppliers understand exactly what they are bidding on, so the bids are real.

The next step consisted of grouping the various components (or part numbers) into several independent "all-or-nothing" lots. According to FreeMarkets OnLine's Jason Reneau:

> While a number of factors are important, it comes down to solid judgment and experience. First, the lots must make sense from the suppliers' point of view; that means, to the greatest extent possible, grouping parts with similar process requirements, sizes, volumes, materials, or tooling. It also means understanding differences in the buyer's quality, delivery, and technical support requirements. When the lots are properly set, we typically achieve a solid competitive outcome.

Simultaneously, FreeMarkets worked with the buyer to determine which suppliers to include for the bid, invariably introducing the buyer to several new suppliers who were capable of manufacturing the requested components. This was possible because of the up-front research done by them to unearth a larger pool of suppliers than traditionally used by the buyer. FreeMarkets prescreened every potential supplier. A detailed 10- to 15-page questionnaire was completed by each supplier. In addition to seeking general company information, the survey sought information on the supplier's marketing and sales, manufacturing, logistics, quality, and administrative systems. The most detailed part of the questionnaire was reserved for the targeted parts.

According to Glen Meakem:

> Buyers choose which suppliers they want to bid on their business. Incumbent suppliers are included if they're not already on the list, of course. And we've found that we introduce buyers to aggressive, world-class suppliers that they

may not have known about before. So without incurring the cost of identifying and qualifying these new suppliers, buyers can allow them to bid on their business.

Finally, FreeMarkets uses its proprietary Bidware® software and a global private network to hold an on-line competitive bidding event (CBE) at a previously chosen time. According to Meakem:

> We help buyers create fair, open, and aggressive competition—that's what results in large purchasing cost savings. On average, we save our buyer clients 15 percent. The CBE enables the right pool of high-quality suppliers to take part in an on-line, interactive competition for business.

CBEs took place in real time, over a 90-minute to two-hour time period. Suppliers submitted electronic bids on various lots of goods using their BidWare software. Suppliers watched the other bids come in— and counterbid—but they didn't know the identity of their competitors. The buyer saw both the bids' dollar value and which suppliers were submitting the bids.

Figure 7-2 shows two buyer side screens during different auctions in process. Benchmarks to evaluate the bidding were built in. One tracked the savings compared to "historic" costs and the other tracked savings compared to the buyer's goal, called "reserve." An automatic "overtime" functionality meant that "lots" of business only closed when new low bids on each lot were no longer submitted by suppliers. Even after the close of the bidding event, winners were not necessarily the lowest bidder. The buyer considered factors such as the results of final quality audits in making the awards, and multiple awards were not uncommon. The key ground rules were that the "lots" were the absolute lowest unit of award, the buyer had to award the business only to suppliers who participated in the on-line market, and no follow-on negotiations were permitted. Approximately 50 percent of awards had gone to low-bidding suppliers and approximately 35 percent had gone to second-place bidders.

THE REVENUE MODEL

"The revenue-generation model is at the heart of our new business development process," stated Kinney. He explained:

> We had a range of options available to us and only a few examples to follow. In 1995, all Internet businesses seemed to be built around a model of advertising revenue and site traffic. Popular focus was to build "content" and drive traffic to the site by registering with search engines. This type

of model just wouldn't work for us—we add much of our value "off-line."

Meakem and Kinney knew from their consulting days that corporations to some degree would pay fees for the kind of value-added big savings that the electronic bidding technique could bring. Cash flow could be attractive using a consulting model, and that would make it much easier to build the business on a pay-as-you-go basis. But such a model could not deliver the equity upside that seemed possible in the Internet IPO market, an upside necessary to attract risk capital and risk-takers as employees.

A higher aspiration, they thought, would be to turn the electronic bidding technique into a completely new channel in the industrial markets. Creating a new channel brought with it a number of challenges, not the least of which was the articulation of the value model. But the channel idea had strong appeal. Kinney explained:

> We had always been intrigued by the transformation of consumer markets by the likes of Wal-Mart, Sam's Club, and category killers like Best Buy. The quality of products sold by traditional consumer brand marketers like P&G and Magnavox had never been higher, but the pricing pressure brought down upon them by powerful channel intermediaries was intense. No comparable channel intermediaries existed for many industrial products.

The obvious direct channel comparison in industrial markets was the manufacturer's representative. Many of the suppliers ultimately targeted for CBEs were accustomed to paying commissions to these representatives. But in the case of manufacturers' reps, each representative was tied to one particular supplier's offerings—there was no channel that stimulated a direct price comparison between two or more independent offerings. In essence, there was no channel designed from the buyer's perspective, only channels designed around the needs of suppliers.

In the end, the company chose a pricing model that was a hybrid of service fees and sales commissions. To make a competitive market for a basket of purchased components, FreeMarkets charged buyers a monthly service fee based on the size of the market-making team dedicated to the event. Typically, that fee was a fraction of the fee that a major consulting firm would charge. A typical project with a fair complement of engineering work would cost the buyer $75,000 per month for two to three months. Expenses such as

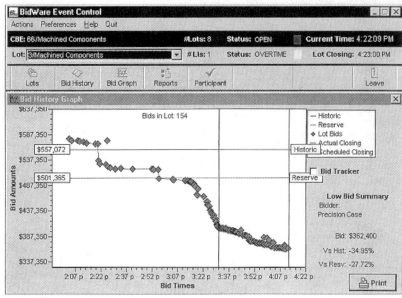

FIGURE 7-2 Buyer side screens.

travel and lodging were extra charges. In addition to the fee, buyers agreed that the winning supplier would pay sales commissions to FreeMarkets in lieu of the commission they might pay to a manufacturer's representative. The sales commission varied by supply industry. In general, though, FreeMarkets set the commission level at about one-half of the prevailing rate in order to provide the buyers a built-in level of savings off the current channel cost embedded in prices. For the industrial intermediate supply industries the company currently served, these commissions were generally 2.5 percent of purchase price. Commissions were paid in installments as suppliers shipped products to buyers. Most contracts the company placed were annual contracts that could be renewed; therefore, commissions resulting from any particular competitive bidding event could flow for two or three years.

Under normal circumstances, suppliers would have paid manufacturers' representatives a 4 to 7 percent commission for effecting the sale of their products to the buyers. Manufacturers' representatives usually carried many lines of complementary but noncompeting products. That is, they represented many suppliers across a wide range of markets. FreeMarkets OnLine effectively disintermediated the manufacturers' reps by "repping" all of the competing suppliers in a given bid at once.

The fee-plus-commission pricing model had its benefits and challenges. According to Meakem:

> Industrial buyers do not really understand channels that well. To them, the channel is the sales rep—the same channel that prevailed in Henry Ford's day. Channel evolution has been so glacial in industrial markets that we are forced to sell a very new concept. At times, buyers have a hard time understanding why the commission is a fair compensation model for us. But we persevere in making this sell, because we are confident in the value we add. Our sales commission, and the industrial purchasing channel we represent, is the right answer for buyers, suppliers, and our investors. In the end, the commission cost is typically trivial compared to the savings we generate for buyers.
>
> In addition to the selling challenges, the commission presents cash flow hurdles for us. A typical bid is for the annual quantity of products a buyer will purchase. The commission is only due from suppliers after the product ships, so the revenue stream from commissions amounts to a small monthly payment that does not begin until months after the bulk of the service costs have been incurred. We also face the administrative costs of tracking commissions and the chances for yield loss. On the benefit side, commissions usually last well beyond the first year. Currently, we have a little less than two years experience collecting these commissions, but we believe our average commission stream will run for over two years.

A SUCCESSFUL START

From the time of its founding in 1995 until the end of 1997, the company had handled 38 different CBEs for 15 buying clients, resulting in purchase awards totaling approximately $70 million over 40 different suppliers. The savings over historical costs to the buyers ranged from 1 to 43 percent, with the weighted average being 15 percent. Four of the company's 15 buying clients were repeat customers, and the company believed it would serve

TABLE 7-2			
PERFORMANCE OVERVIEW			
$000s	1995 (9 months)	1996	1997
New annual purchase awards	$249	$23,424	$46,831
Revenues	16	23,409	$1,783
Profits (losses)	($922)	($1,431)	($1,016)

virtually all of its buying clients again. Table 7-2 provides a brief overview of the company's performance through 1997, and Tables 7-3 and 7-4 provide detailed financial statements.

On the buyer side, the company's client base consisted of 15 Fortune 500 companies who had engaged FreeMarkets to make one or more industrial markets. Four of these companies had emerged as stable ongoing users of the service. On the supplier side, over 300 companies ranging from Fortune 50 conglomerates to small manufacturing houses had signed the company's Supplier Representation Agreement and participated in on-line bidding. Overall, its clients represented a wide cross-section of industries. Buyers were from both North America and Europe, while suppliers were from across the globe. See Table 7-5 for a summary of actual on-line market results through January 1998.

Importantly, of the company's 1997 revenues of $1.8 million, over $350,000 was from supplier sales commissions. The company's plans were for achieving $6.0 million in 1998 revenue, with over $200 million of new business being awarded to suppliers.

"By the year 2000, suppliers will win over $500 million per year worth of purchase contracts through our on-line market channel," predicted Meakem.

The company had just shipped out its second-generation proprietary global bidding system, BidWare® 2 and BidServer® 2, but it would need to constantly keep at the cutting edge of software development. Depending on the technical development agenda the company chose to pursue, at least $5 to $10 million would be needed over the next five years to develop new, improved, and expanded software products for the industrial marketplace. As the company expanded, its current staff of 43 people would also need to grow, especially because of the heavy upfront customization work needed in the early stages of the bidding process. The current market-making team

TABLE 7-3

STATEMENT OF OPERATIONS

	Actual FY 1995	Actual FY 1996	Actual FY 1997
Revenues			
Buyer fees	$10,000	$270,500	$1,425,000
Supplier commissions	6,512	138,320	358,179
Total revenues	16,512	408,820	1,783,179
Cost of Service—Market Making			
Payroll	11,372	327,108	801,601
Payroll taxes	1,105	28,727	60,583
Health benefits	278	18,163	36,645
BidWare cost and amortization	4,010	31,083	42,894
Other direct costs and office allocations	7,331	100,610	166,906
Total cost of services	24,095	505,691	1,108,629
Gross profit	(7,583)	(96,871)	674,550
Operating Expenses			
Technical Operations			
Payroll	40,837	59,408	97,019
Payroll taxes	3,520	5,226	8,045
Health benefits	1,074	3,234	5,186
Network expense	—	70,772	60,890
Other direct costs and office allocations	29,187	4,851	49,363
Total technical operations	84,618	143,491	220,503
Technical Development			
Payroll	178,610	253,704	208,663
payroll taxes	15,911	19,793	15,74
Health benefits	4,515	8,714	7,597
Other direct costs and office allocations	133,814	112,055	63,849
Total technical development	332,850	394,266	295,883
Client Development and Marketing			
Payroll	25,164	198,042	325,200
Payroll taxes	2,070	1,134	18,290
Health benefits	697	3,003	6,618
Travel and meals	—	53,252	91,143
Marketing and printing	—	43,349	62,057
Other direct costs and office allocations	31,455	17,155	42,066
Total client development and marketing	59,385	320,935	545,374
General and Administrative			
Payroll	152,383	207,030	275,173
Health benefits	4,173	10,425	14,889
Payroll taxes	12,598	23,110	20,310
Professional fees	69,713	81,239	160,034
Other direct costs and office allocations	198,499	153,821	158,467
Total general and administrative	437,366	475,625	628,882
Total Operating Expenses	914,219	1,334,317	1,690,642
Net income/(loss)	$(921,802)	$(1,431,188)	$(1,016,092)

Source: FreeMarkets OnLine.

consisting of 23 people was capable of handling about four CBEs per month. Recruiting and training additional market-making and software development staff would be of utmost priority, especially at a time when the company was attempting to rapidly ramp up to scale.

GOING FORWARD TO SCALE

As Meakem and Kinney entered 1998, the fundamental question of how to position the company with buyers, suppliers, and investors was as important as ever. What kind of company should FreeMarkets make

TABLE 7-4

BALANCE SHEET

	December 1995 actual	December 1996 actual	December 1997 actual
Assets			
Current Assets			
Cash and cash equivalent	$106,496	$557,648	$1,925,008
Accounts receivable	7,579	148,787	1,052,337
Other current assets	7,125	5,550	8,001
Total current assets	$121,200	$711,985	$2,985,346
Office Furniture and Equipment			
Office furniture and equipment	94,930	172,151	263,850
Accumulated depreciation	(11,680)	(36,861)	(74,384)
Net furniture and equipment	83,250	135,572	91,149
Other Assets	101,825	137,572	91,149
Total Assets	$306,275	$984,847	$3,265,961
Liabilities and Stockholders' Equity			
Current Liabilities			
Accounts payable	$185,112	$118,650	$88,360
Accrued liabilities	17,539	39,348	83,540
Current portion of debt	—	14,000	—
Total current liabilities	202,651	171,998	171,900
Long-Term Liabilities			
Long-term debt	—	21,000	58,332
Stockholders' Equity			
Preferred stock	—	85	187
Common stock	171	175	184
Additional paid in capital	1,025,255	3,144,580	6,404,441
Retained earnings (deficit)	—	(921,802)	(2,352,991)
Current year loss	(921,802)	(1,431,189)	(1,016,092)
Total stockholders' equity	103,624	791,849	3,035,729
Total Liabilities and Equity	$306,275	$985,847	$3,265,961

itself into in order to maximize its return to shareholders and make a lasting impact on industrial market making? This question was complicated enough but making it even more difficult to tackle was the range of options that were now available to the company as it molded a business strategy going forward.

During their offsite meeting in early January, the eight-member senior team had debated three critical strategic opportunities, but had failed to come to any solid conclusions.

1. **Horizontal market expansion or vertical market dominance?** Impressed by the savings that FreeMarkets had generated for its buying clients, both existing and potential buyers had suggested new supply markets. Some of these new supply markets were near commodities such as chemicals, pulp, coal, freight, and reinsurance. But even as these opportunities were coming in, there was internal momentum toward seeking vertical

market dominance in selected supply industries. It was argued by the supporters of this strategy that only through dedicated marketing efforts, including brand identity creation and tailored sales and pricing approaches, could FreeMarkets truly differentiate itself and showcase the huge value it brought to its clients. But this would involve a focused industry domination strategy that increased risk in the minds of some team members. "Given our current success," said Meakem, "there is no doubt that the path of least resistance is to follow the purchasing needs of our clients and not to focus too narrowly." But even as the team debated, new opportunities for horizontal market expansion were pouring in.

2. **Technology and user support subscription licensing?** Some buyers and third parties had requested that FreeMarkets license the bidding technology for their own use. Some had counterproposed with buyer fees only—no commission.

TABLE 7-5

FREEMARKETS ONLINE MARKETPLACE HISTORY (U.S. $000s—UNLESS OTHERWISE NOTED)

CBE number	CBE date	Buying client number	Supply industry	Historic cost	New market cost	Potential savings Actual	Potential savings Percent	Actual commissioned awards to suppliers
1.	November-95	1	Plastic molded parts	$3,542	$2,837	$705	20%	$249
2.	November-95	1	Plastic molded parts	844	802	43	5	0
3.	January-96	2	Plastic molded parts	1,494	1,359	134	9	1,655
4.	April-96	1	Plastic molded parts	706	475	231	33	446
5.	April-96	1	Plastic molded parts	1,836	1,421	414	23	1,192
6.	April-96	3	Metal stampings	700	608	92	13	608
7.	May-96	2	Plastic molded parts	1,387	1,073	314	23	105
8.	May-96	2	Metal stampings	3,629	3,178	451	12	3,035
9.	Jun-96	4	Plastic molded parts	2,667	2,159	507	19	2,170
10.	June-96	4	Plastic molded parts	5,725	4,913	812	14	5,611
11.	August-96	5	Plastic molded parts	3,348	2,967	382	11	266
12.	August-96	1	Plastic molded parts	633	486	147	23	505
13.	August-96	1	Plastic molded parts	1,278	996	282	22	0
14.	September-96	1	Plastic molded parts	1,245	1,200	45	4	0
15.	October-96	2	Metal stampings	1,062	1,049	13	1	802
16.	October-96	6	Metal castings	1,055	923	132	12	0
17.	November-96	6	Metal machinings	4,014	2,862	1,151	29	2,798
18.	December-96	7	Chemicals	4,941	4,311	629	13	4,090
19.	December-96	8	Plastic molded parts	2,131	1,822	308	14	141
20.	April-97	6	Plastic molded parts	3,631	3,187	444	12	3,187
21.	April-97	6	Service center metals	19,048	18,859	188	1	6,290
22.	May-97	9	Plastic molded parts	7,878	7,684	194	2	0
23.	June-97	10	Metal machinings	2,743	2,590	153	6	1,202
24.	August-97	11	Metal fabrication	723	632	92	13	580
25.	August-97	1	Plastic molded parts	2,197	1,712	485	22	1,900
26.	September-97	6	Plastic molded parts	9,691	7,649	2,043	21	5,500
27.	September-97	6	Plastic molded parts	7,200	6,300	1,000	14	500
28.	September-97	12	Metal fabrication	5,653	3,261	2,391	42	2,772
29.	October-97	13	Pole line hardware	1,169	1,095	74	6	570
30.	October-97	13	Pole line hardware	1,625	1,607	18	1	800
31.	October-97	12	Metal machinings	6,102	3,473	2,629	43	3,600
32.	October-97	12	Specialty metals	3,375	3,010	365	11	3,100
33.	November-97	12	Service center metals	11,048	9,740	1,308	12	9,800
34.	November-97	12	Metal machinings	1,681	1,180	501	30	1,200
35.	December-97	14	Metal fabrication	4,213	3,920	292	7	NA
36.	December-97	15	Metal machinings	1,017	913	104	/0	800
37.	December-97	15	Metal machinings	593	374	219	37	350
38.	December-97	6	Commercial valves	10,564	8,353	2,212	21	NA
39.	January-98	14	Metal fasteners	535	399	136	25	NA
40.	January-98	16	Corn sweetener	31,200	30,000	1,200	4	30,500
41.	January-98	6	Printed circuit boards	24,500	14,000	10,500	43	16,000
42.	January-98	12	Metal machinings and fabrication	11,000	9,130	1,870	17	9,300
Totals				$209,620	$174,407	$35,213	17%	$126,304

Based on direct customer requests, Meakem knew that there was a market for industrial bidding software similar to the BidWare®/BidServer® system exclusive of full-service on-line industrial market making. But because the very nature of the technology and the benefits it provided required best-practice purchasing skills and execution, there were strong feelings in the group that buyers who tried to use the bidding technology without high-quality, front-end market making would tarnish the whole concept of on-line, real-time, industrial market making. This group felt that poorly executed markets would not yield real (and ethical) business results for buyers or suppliers. There was strong anecdotal evidence of this from suppliers who had dealt with Meakem's old employer. This group argued passionately that if FreeMarkets did license the technology, it should ensure that any resulting "marketspace" and support services (telephone training, etc.) be branded separately from FreeMarkets OnLine®. "Pursuing this strategy will compromise our core business," Kinney had warned. But supporters had argued, "By having a strong position in the software and related services portion of the industrial on-line bidding space, the company could enhance its core full-service, on-line, industrial market-making business."

3. **Networked purchasing information systems?** In the course of working with its buying clients, the company had realized that buyers within large industrial companies had limited access to information about certain purchases. This lack of information extended within their companies as well as to the external market environment.

Meakem wondered if it was possible to develop a World Wide Web–based information system and service that met both the internal communications needs and the external information needs of buyers. A colleague had argued that FreeMarkets might be better off simply selling the information to information management companies. For example, the supplier survey done in support of various market-making events would be very valuable to many clients he had suggested. It was clear that any major business and technology development effort in support of these ideas would require major incremental external investment in the company.

WHAT NEXT?

The senior team at FreeMarkets was convinced they had identified a set of real market needs and were at the leading edge of an important set of business applications and services to meet these needs. Recruiting at a furious pace to keep up with core market-making growth, they debated the direction and pace they should be taking to maximize the opportunity. "Euphoria is one thing, but it has to be based on sound business strategy," said Kinney. "So let's figure it out," urged Meakem.

B y the end of this chapter, you should be able to answer the following questions:

- What are the roles that outsourcing and procurement play in the supply chain? What are the risk and benefits associated with outsourcing many of the firm's activities?
- What are the key issues involved in deciding what to make (internally) and what to buy from outside suppliers? What are the make/buy policies that are available for a particular company?
- When you outsource, how do you ensure timely supply of components?
- What is the impact of the Internet on the procurement process?
- Should a company use a public e-market or a consortium-based e-market or focus on developing its own e-marketplace?
- What procurement strategy should a company use for individual products? Is there a framework that identifies the procurement strategy that the firm needs to consider for each product? What are the issues that should be considered when making these decisions?

7.1 INTRODUCTION

In the 90s, outsourcing was the focus of many industrial manufacturers; firms considered outsourcing everything from the procurement function to production and manufacturing. Executives were focused on stock value, and huge pressure was placed on the organization to increase profits. Of course, one "easy" way to increase profit is by reducing costs through outsourcing. Indeed, in the mid 90s there was a significant increase in purchasing volume as a percentage of the firm's total sales. More recently, between 1998 and 2000, outsourcing in the electronic industry has increased from 15 percent of all components to 40 percent [137].

Consider, for instance, the athletic shoe industry, a fashion industry with products that require significant investment in technology [127]. No company in this industry has been as successful as Nike, a company that outsources almost all of its manufacturing activities. As observed by Quinn and Hilmer, Nike, the largest supplier of athletic shoes in the world, focuses mainly on research and development on the one hand, and marketing, sales, and distribution on the other. Indeed, this strategy allowed Nike to grow in the 90s at an annual rate of about 20 percent [127].

Cisco's success story is even more striking. According to Peter Solvik, CIO of Cisco, "Cisco's Internet-based business model has been instrumental in its ability to quadruple in size from 1994 to 1998 ($1.3 billion to over $8 billion), hire approximately 1,000 new employees per quarter while increasing their productivity, and save $560M annually in business expenses." Specializing in enterprise network solutions, Cisco used, according to John Chambers, Cisco CEO, a "global virtual manufacturing strategy." As he explains, "First, we have established manufacturing plants all over the world. We have also developed close arrangements with major suppliers. So when we work together with our suppliers, and if we do our job right, the customer cannot tell the difference between my own plants and my suppliers in Taiwan and elsewhere" [86]. This approach was enabled by Cisco's single-enterprise system, which provides the backbone for all activities in the company, and connects not only customers and employees, but also chip manufacturers, component distributors, contract manufacturers, logistics companies, and systems integrators. These participants can perform like one company because they all rely on the same Web-based data sources. All its suppliers see the same demand and do not rely on their own forecasts based on information flowing from multiple points in the supply chain. Cisco also built a dynamic replenishment system to help reduce supplier inventory. Cisco's average turns in 1999 were 10 compared with an average of 4 for competitors. Inventory turns for commodity items are even more impressive; they reach 25–35 turns a year.

Apple Computers also outsources most of its manufacturing activities; in fact, the company outsources 70 percent of its components including major products such as printers. As Quinn and Hilmer point out, "Apple focused its internal resources on its own disk operating system and the supporting macro software to give Apple products their unique look and feel" [127].

Unfortunately, the landscape has changed for Nike, Cisco, Apple, and other companies who rely heavily on outsourcing, particularly for manufacturing.

- In 2001, Nike reported an unexpected profit shortfall due to inventory buildup in some products, shortages for others as well as late deliveries [144]. The company blamed both the weak U.S. economy as well as complications with the implementation of a supply planning system.
- In 1999, Apple's ability to satisfy customer demand was significantly reduced due to shortages in the G4 chip supplied by Motorola [86].
- In 2000, Cisco was forced to announce a $2.25 billion write-down for obsolete inventory. This was the result of a significant reduction in demand for telecommunication infrastructure to which Cisco was not able to respond effectively.

What went wrong? Are these problems merely a reflection of supply chain strategies that need fine-tuning or a need for more effective information technology? Perhaps these problems uncover fundamental difficulties with outsourcing. Clearly, Nike, Apple, and Cisco represent industries with short life-cycle products, where technologies change rapidly and uncertainty in customer demand is enormous. Can these characteristics explain the problems that these companies are facing, or are there more fundamental principles that need to be considered?

To answer these questions, we first discuss the buy/make decision process. We identify the advantages and the risks associated with outsourcing and present a framework for optimizing buy/make decisions.

After presenting this framework, we discuss the procurement process, which can be a very expensive process for many buyers. Since 1995, when the first on-line marketplace was established, the procurement landscape has changed considerably with the introduction of independent (also referred to as public), private, and consortium-based e-marketplaces. These developments increase both the opportunities and challenges faced by many buyers. Specifically, executives are faced with an important question: Should the firm invest in a costly private marketplace, use a public marketplace that provides data standards and spreads cost investment among many buyers, or perhaps use a hybrid approach in which certain types of goods are purchased in a public marketplace while others are purchased in a private marketplace? To answer this question, we develop a framework for selecting the correct procurement strategy. As we shall see, this framework implies that the procurement strategy is tightly linked to the firm's outsourcing strategy.

7.2 OUTSOURCING BENEFITS AND RISKS

Throughout the 90s, strategic outsourcing, that is, outsourcing the manufacturing of key components, was used as a tool to rapidly cut costs. In their recent study, Lakenan, Boyd, and Frey [86] reviewed eight major contract equipment manufacturers (CEMs)—Solectron, Flextronics, SCI Systems, Jabil Circuit, Celestica, ACT Manufacturing, Plexus, and Sanmina—which were the main suppliers to companies such as Dell, Marconi, NEC Computers, Nortel, and Silcon Graphics. The aggregated revenue for the eight CEMs quadrupled between 1996 and 2000 while their capital expenditure grew 11-fold [86].

Some of the motivations for outsourcing are [86, 127]

Economies of scale. An important objective in outsourcing is to reduce manufacturing costs through the aggregation of orders from many different buyers. Indeed, the aggregation allows suppliers to take advantage of economies of scale, both in purchasing and in manufacturing.

Risk pooling. Outsourcing allows buyers to transfer demand uncertainty to the CEM. One advantage that the CEMs have is that they aggregate demand from many buying companies and thus reduce uncertainty through the risk-pooling effect. The CEMs can thus reduce component inventory levels while maintaining or even increasing service level.

Reduce capital investment. Another important objective in outsourcing is to transfer not only demand uncertainty to the CEM but also capital investment. Of course, the CEM can make this investment because it is implicitly shared between many of the CEM's customers.

Focus on core competency. By carefully choosing what to outsource, the buyer is able to focus on its core strength, that is, the specific talent, skills, and knowledge sets that differentiate the company from its competitors and give it an advantage in the eye of the customers. For instance, Nike focuses on innovation, marketing, distribution, and sales, not on manufacturing [127].

Increased flexibility. Here we refer to three issues: (i) The ability to better react to changes in customer demand, (ii) the ability to use the supplier's technical knowledge to accelerate product development cycle time, and (iii) the ability to gain access to new technologies and innovation. These are critical issues in industries where technologies change very frequently, for example, high-tech, or when products have a short life cycle, for example, fashion products.

These benefits come with new and considerable risks. Consider how IBM benefited and was hurt by outsourcing.

EXAMPLE 7-1

When IBM decided to enter the PC market, in late 1981, the company did not have the infrastructure in place to design and build a personal computer. Rather than take the time to develop these capabilities, IBM outsourced almost all of the major components of the PC. For example, the microprocessor was designed and built by Intel and the operating system was provided by a small company in Seattle called Microsoft. IBM was able to get this computer to market within 15 months of starting the design by tapping into the expertise and resources of these companies. Furthermore, within three years, IBM replaced Apple as the number-one supplier of personal computers, and by 1985, IBM had over 40 percent of market share. However, the downside to IBM's strategy soon became clear, as competitors such as Compaq were able to enter the market *by utilizing the same suppliers as IBM*. Furthermore, when IBM tried to regain control of the market by introducing its PS/2 line of computers, featuring a new, proprietary design and an operating system called OS/2, other companies did not follow IBM's lead, and the original architecture remained dominant in the market. By the end of 1995, IBM's market share had fallen to less than 8 percent, behind market leader Compaq's 10 percent [31].

The IBM personal computer example and the more recent Cisco example reveal two substantial risks associated with outsourcing. These include [51, 86, 127]

Loss of competitive knowledge. Outsourcing critical components to suppliers may open up opportunities for competitors (as in the IBM PC example). Similarly, outsourcing implies that companies lose their ability to introduce new designs based on their own agenda rather than the supplier's agenda [127]. Finally, outsourcing the manufacturing of various components to different suppliers may prevent the development of new insights, innovations, and solutions that typically require cross-functional teamwork [127].

Conflicting objectives. Suppliers and buyers typically have different and conflicting objectives. For instance, increased flexibility is a key objective when buyers outsource the manufacturing of various components. This implies an ability to better match supply and demand by adjusting production rates as needed. Unfortunately, this objective is in direct conflict with the suppliers' objectives of long-term, firm, and stable commitment from the buyer. Indeed, this is an important issue for suppliers since unlike the buyers, their profit margins are relatively small and hence they have to focus on cost reduction, rather than flexibility. In good times, when demand is high, this conflict can be addressed by buyers who are willing to make long-term commitments to purchase minimum quantities specified by a contract. However, in a slow economy, when there is a significant decline in demand, these long-term commitments entail huge financial risks for the buyers [86]. Similarly, product design issues are affected by the conflicting objectives of suppliers and buyers. Again, buyers, insisting on flexibility, would like to solve design problems as fast as possible, while suppliers focus on cost reduction that typically implies slow responsiveness to design changes.

7.3 A FRAMEWORK FOR BUY/MAKE DECISIONS

How can the firm decide on which component to manufacture and which to outsource? Consultants and supply chain pundits typically suggest to focus on core competencies, but how can the firm identify what is in the core, and hence should be made internally, and what is outside the core, and hence should be purchased from outside suppliers?

Below we introduce a framework developed by Fine and Whitney [51]. To introduce the framework, they classify the reasons for outsourcing into two major categories:

Dependency on capacity. In this case, the firm has the knowledge and the skills required to produce the component but for various reasons decides to outsource.

Dependency on knowledge. In this type of dependency, the company does not have the people, skills, and knowledge required to produce the component and outsources in order to have access to these capabilities. Of course, the company has to have the knowledge and skills to evaluate customer needs and convert these into key requirements and characteristics that the component should have.

To illustrate these two concepts, Fine and Whitney consider outsourcing decisions at Toyota. As a successful Japanese car manufacturer, the company designs and makes about 30 percent of its car components. The details are quite revealing:

- Toyota has both the knowledge and the capacity to produce its engines and indeed 100 percent of the engines are produced internally.
- For transmissions, the company has the knowledge and indeed designs all the components but depends on its suppliers' capacities, since 70 percent of the components are outsourced.
- Vehicle electronic systems are designed and produced by Toyota's suppliers. Thus, in this case the firm has a dependency on both capacity and knowledge.

Fine and Whitney observe that "Toyota seems to vary its outsourcing practice depending on the strategic role of the components and subsystems." The more strategically important the component is, the smaller the dependency on knowledge or capacity. This suggests the need for a better understanding of product architecture when considering what to outsource.

For this purpose, and following Ulrich [154] and Swaminathan [149], we distinguish between integral and modular products. A modular product can be made by combining different components. A personal computer is an excellent example of a modular product in which the customers specify memory and hard-drive sizes, monitor, software, and so forth. Other examples that are frequently cited include home stereo equipment and high-end bicycles. The definition of modular products implies [50]

- Components are independent of each other.
- Components are interchangeable.
- Standard interfaces are used.
- A component can be designed or upgraded with little or no regard to other components.
- Customer preference determines the product configuration.

An integral product, on the other hand, is a product made up from components whose functionalities are tightly related. Thus,

- Integral products are not made from off-the-shelf components.
- Integral products are designed as a system by taking a top-down design approach.
- Integral products are evaluated based on system performance, not based on component performance.
- Components in integral products perform multiple functions.

Of course, in real life, very few products are either modular or integral. Indeed, the degree of modularity or integrality may vary with personal computers being on one end of the spectrum, that is, highly modular products, and airplanes being on the other end of the spectrum, that is, highly integral products. For instance, a car is a product that includes many modular components, for example, the stereo system or other electronic systems, and many integral components, for example, the engine.

Table 7-6 presents a simple framework for make/buy decisions, developed in Fine [50] and Fine and Whitney [51].

This framework considers both modular and integral products, and the firm's dependency on knowledge and capacity. For modular products, capturing knowledge is important, whereas having the production capacity in-house is less critical. For example, for a PC manufacturer, capturing knowledge may refer to the design of the various components. Thus, if the firm has the knowledge, outsourcing the manufacturing process provides an opportunity to reduce cost. On the other hand, if the firm has neither knowledge nor capacity, outsourcing may be a risky strategy as the knowledge developed by the supplier may be transferred to a competitor's products. For integral products, capturing both knowledge and capacity is important as long as it is possible to have both. This implies that if the firm has both the knowledge and the capacity, then in-house production is appropriate. On the other hand, if the firm does not have both, perhaps it is in the wrong business.

7.4 E-PROCUREMENT

In the mid to late 90s, business-to-business automation was considered a trend that would have a profound impact on supply chain performance. Between 1998 and 2000, hundreds of e-markets were established in dozens of industries, from chemicals and steel to utilities and human resources. These marketplaces promised, among other things, increased market reach for both buyers and suppliers, reduced procurement costs, and paperless transactions. Indeed, companies such as Ariba and CommerceOne were founded on the premise that e-procurement software that automates the requisitioning process will be able to reduce processing cost per order from as high as $150 per order to as low as $5 per order [141].

TABLE 7-6

A FRAMEWORK FOR MAKE/BUY DECISIONS

Product	Dependency on knowledge and capacity	Independent for knowledge, dependency for capacity	Independent for knowledge and capacity
Modular	Outsourcing is risky	Outsourcing is an Opportunity	Opportunity to reduce cost through outsourcing
Integral	Outsourcing is very risky	Outsourcing is an option	Keep production internal

To better understand the huge expectations from e-procurement as well as the need for a new business model that will allow manufacturers and suppliers to improve supply chain performance, consider the business environment in the mid 90s. At that time, many manufacturers were desperately looking to outsource their procurement functions. These companies recognized that the procurement process is highly complex, requires significant expertise, and is very costly. Indeed, business-to-business transactions represent an enormous portion of the economy (much larger than business-to-consumer transactions), and the business-to-business marketplace is frequently highly fragmented, with a large number of suppliers competing in the same marketplace and offering similar products.

Of course, a fragmented marketplace provides both opportunities and challenges. Indeed, buyers recognize that by forcing many suppliers that offer similar products to compete against each other, procurement costs can be significantly reduced. Unfortunately, to achieve these lower costs, buyers need significant expertise in the procurement process, which many of them did not have.

It is this environment that led to the initial offering of independent e-marketplaces with either a vertical-industry focus or a horizontal-business-process or functional focus. Companies such as FreeMarkets or VerticalNet offered both expertise in the procurement process and the ability to force competition between a large number of suppliers. In particular, the value proposition offered to buyers by many of the start-up e-markets included

- Serving as an intermediary between buyers and suppliers.
- Identifying saving opportunities.
- Increasing the number of suppliers involved in the bidding event.
- Identifying, qualifying, and supporting suppliers.
- Conducting the bidding event.

Thus, between 1996 and 1999, the focus was on reducing procurement cost. Indeed, depending on the industry, e-markets were reported to reduce procurement cost by a few percentage points to as much as 40 percent and, on average, about 15 percent. Clearly, this business model is appropriate when buyers are focused on the spot market and long-term relationships with suppliers are not important. Indeed, if long-term relationships are important, selecting a supplier based on an on-line bidding event may be a risky proposition.

The problem, of course, was that the value proposition for the suppliers was not as clear. Evidently, e-markets allow relatively small suppliers to expand their market horizon and reach buyers that they could not have reached otherwise. E-markets allow suppliers, particularly in fragmented industries, to access spot markets where buyers are looking not for long-term relationships but rather for a great price at an acceptable quality. Equally important, these markets allow suppliers to reduce marketing and sales costs and thus increase their ability to compete on price. Finally, e-markets allow suppliers to better utilize their available capacities and inventories. The natural question to ask is whether these benefits compensate for a reduction in revenue by on average 15 percent, and sometimes as high as 40 percent. At the same time, it is not clear that many suppliers feel comfortable competing on price alone. Thus, suppliers, especially those with brand-name recognition, may resist selling their services through e-markets.

What about the e-markets themselves? How do they generate revenue? Initially, many of the markets charged a *transaction fee* paid by either the buyer, the suppliers, or both. This fee was typically a percentage of the price paid by the buyer and varied from

1 to 5 percent [81]. As pointed out in [81], transaction fees pose serious challenges to the market maker because

1. Sellers resist paying a fee to the company whose main objective is to reduce the purchase price.
2. The revenue model needs to be flexible enough so that transaction fees are charged to the party that is more motivated to secure the engagement. For instance, if demand is much larger than supply, buyers are more motivated than sellers and hence the transaction fee should be paid by the buyers.
3. Buyers also resist paying a fee in addition to the purchase price.

Finally, low barriers to entry created a fragmented industry flooded with participants. For instance, just in the chemical industry there were about 30 e-markets, including CheMatch, e-Chemicals, ChemB2B.com, ChemCross, OneChem, Chemi-calDesk, ChemRound, and Chemdex [36]. Low margins and inability to build scale resulted in a major shake-up of this industry.

These challenges have motivated a continuous evolution of the e-markets' business model. To start, many exchanges have changed the way they charge their clients. Indeed, two other types of charge mechanisms have been used by some e-markets. These include a *licensing fee* and a *subscription fee*. In the former case, the market maker licenses its software so that the company can automate the access to the marketplace. In the latter case, the marketplace charges a membership fee that depends on the size of the company, the number of employees who use the system, and the number of purchase orders [81].

At the same time, many e-markets have completely modified their value proposition. Initially, the focus of the value proposition was on market reach for buyers and sellers as well as lower purchase cost. The landscape has completely changed in the last few years with the introduction of four types of markets:

Value-added independent (public) e-markets. Independent e-markets have expanded their value proposition by offering additional services such as inventory management, supply chain planning, and financial services [76]. For instance, Instill.com focuses on the food service industry and provides an infrastructure that links together operators, that is, restaurants, distributors, and manufacturers. This e-marketplace provides value to its customers by offering not only procurement services but also forecasting, collaboration, and replenishment tools.

Private e-markets. Private e-markets have been established by Dell Computers, Sun Microsystems, Wal-Mart, and IBM, among others. These companies are not using the e-market to force suppliers to compete on price. Rather, they see the e-market as a way to improve supply chain collaboration by providing demand information and production data to their suppliers. Other companies use their private e-market to consolidate their purchasing power across the entire corporation. For instance, the Subway restaurant franchise with 16,000 members in over 70 countries has a private e-market that allows the different restaurants to purchase from over 100 suppliers.

Consortia-based e-markets. These e-markets are very similar to the public e-markets except that they are established by a number of companies within the same industry. Examples include Covisint in the automotive industry, Exostar in the aerospace industry, Trade-Ranger in the oil industry, and Converge and E2Open in the electronic industry. The objective of these consortia-based e-markets is not only to aggregate activities and use the buying power of consortia members but, more importantly, to provide suppliers with a standard system that supports all the consortia's buyers and hence allows suppliers to reduce cost and become more efficient.

Content-based e-markets. These include two types of markets. The first focuses on maintenance, repair, and operations (MRO) goods while the second focuses on industry-specific products. As its name suggests, the focus of the e-marketplace is on content, which is achieved by integrating catalogs from many industrial suppliers. To achieve scale and increase efficiencies, content-based e-markets unify suppliers' catalogs and provide effective tools for searching and comparing suppliers' products. For example, Aspect Development offers electronics parts catalogs that integrate with CAD systems.

To emphasize the difference between private and consortia-based e-markets, consider the automotive industry.

EXAMPLE 7-2

Covisint was established in early 2000 by Detroit's big-three automakers. In April 2000, Renault and Nissan joined the marketplace. More recently, Mitsubishi and Peugeot have signed on. Interestingly, not all automakers have joined. For example, focusing on its own suppliers and processes, Volkswagen established its own private e-market, VWgroupsupply.com. Volkswagen's e-market provides not only similar capabilities to that of Covisint's, but also provides suppliers with real-time information on production plans so that suppliers can better utilize their production capacities and other resources. In both cases, the e-marketplaces do not focus on reducing purchase costs but rather on improving supply chain processes and thus supply chain efficiencies. For instance, both are integrating design activities within the marketplace so that if an automaker's engineer changes the design of a component, the relevant suppliers are involved in the process and can respond quickly, cutting cycle time and, effectively, reducing cost, to the design change. Of course, one important challenge faced by Covisint is whether competing automakers will be willing to risk their most sensitive procurement standards and processes by using the consortia [65].

These issues are not unique to the automotive industry, as is illustrated by the following example from the electronic industry.

EXAMPLE 7-3

Celestica and Solectron are competitors with similar products and customers but different procurement strategies. In 1999 Celestica established a private e-marketplace for its 10,000 suppliers. The company uses its private marketplace to provide its suppliers with production data. Demand forecast data received by Celestica from its customers are transferred to its suppliers through the private portal so that suppliers can coordinate the back end of Celestica's supply chain, that is, the suppliers' production activities, with the front end of Celestica's supply chain, that is, its customer-demand forecast. Unlike Celestica, Solectron is using a public e-marketplace. According to Bud Mathaisel, CIO of Solectron, it could cost more than $80 million to build and support an integrated private marketplace for its 8,000 suppliers. By focusing on a public marketplace, Solectron can take advantage of standard data and standard business processes provided by the exchange and thus reduce cost [155].

Table 7-7 compares public/consortia and private e-marketplace; see [150] for a similar comparison.

Finally, it is appropriate to point out that the boundaries between the different types of e-markets are blurred. Indeed, many consortia-based e-markets provide content-based services. For instance, the Covisint custom catalog provides detailed MRO information

TABLE 7-7

PRIVATE AND PUBLIC MARKETPLACES

	Private marketplace	Public/consortia marketplace
Owner	A single buyer	Independent owner or a group of companies from the same industry
Objectives	1. Share proprietary data including product design, demand forecast, and production plans 2. Allow for logistics and supply chain collaboration	1. Buying and selling commodities by focusing on price 2. Finding new suppliers 3. Buying and selling excess inventory and capacity
Participants	Selected group of suppliers	Open market
Buyer cost	Building and maintaining the site	1. Subscription fee 2. Licensing fee 3. Transaction fee
Supplier cost	No fee	1. Transaction fee 2. Subscription fee
Main problems	1. Initial investment 2. Data normalization and uploading	1. Recent collapse of many marketplaces 2. Objections by referred suppliers because of price focus 3. Sharing of proprietary information 4. Data normalization and uploading

to buyers. In addition, Covisint recognizes the potential of the exchange in improving communication between trading partners and hence provides collaborative tools used by buyers and suppliers in a secure environment. Thus, this consortia-based marketplace provides services similar to those provided by private exchanges.

7.5 A FRAMEWORK FOR E-PROCUREMENT

The changes in the business-to-business marketplace described in the previous section provide both opportunities and challenges. E-markets allow buyers to increase market reach, better collaborate with suppliers, and remove inefficiencies from their supply chains. However, with the introduction of different types of e-marketplaces, it is unclear whether the firm should build a private marketplace, use independent markets, or perhaps participate in a consortia-based market. Below, we provide a framework that allows executives and managers to better match procurement strategies with products.

For this purpose, we distinguish between the different types of goods purchased by the firm [8]:

Strategic components. These are components that are part of the finished goods and are not only industry specific but also company specific. These are typically integral products, such as a PC motherboard and chassis that are specific for every computer.

Commodity products. These are products that can be purchased from a variety of vendors and whose price is determined by market forces. These are typically the modular components that go directly into the finished product, such as the memory unit in a PC. Also inclued here are commodities that do not go directly into the finished product, that is, electricity.

Indirect materials. Indirect materials are often referred to as maintenance, repair, and operations (MRO) and include components that are not part of the finished product or the manufacturing process but are essential for the business. Examples include lighting, janitorial supplies, office supplies, fasteners, and generators.

The appropriate procurement strategy clearly depends on the **type of product** the firm is purchasing as well as the **level of risk** the firm is willing to take. This risk is associated with [13]

- **Uncertain demand**, implying inventory risk.
- **Volatile market price**, implying price risk.
- **Component availability**, implying a shortage risk with an impact on the firm's ability to satisfy customer demand.

To illustrate the various types of risks, consider the purchase of commodity products, that is, components that go directly into the finished good. By their nature, these can be purchased either in the open market through on-line auctions or through the use of long-term contracts. Long-term contracts guarantee a certain level of supply, but may be risky for the buyer if realized demand is either lower or higher than the demand forecast. In the former case, the buyer faces huge inventory holding costs; in the latter case, the buyer faces either shortage risk or price risk. This price risk is associated with the need to purchase additional components in the open market at a time of shortage, which typically implies higher prices. It is also completely possible that components are not available in the open market, thus the shortage risk.

Consider the following framework:

Indirect material. The risk associated with indirect material is typically low and hence the focus is on using **content**-based hubs. Specifically, here the firm should use MRO hubs that specialize in unifying catalogs from many suppliers.

Strategic components. These are high-risk components that can be purchased from a small number of suppliers. Thus, our analysis suggests that a private or consortia-based e-marketplace is appropriate. In this case the focus of the organization is on a marketplace that allows for better **collaboration** with the suppliers. That is, the focus is on using the marketplace to provide suppliers with real-time demand information as well as the buyer's production plans, so that suppliers can better use their capacities and resources. Of course, the decision whether to establish a private marketplace or to use a consortia-based e-market depends on

- Transaction volume.
- Number of suppliers.
- Cost to build and maintain a private site.
- The importance of protecting proprietry business practices.
- Technology and product life cycles.

The last item needs some explanation: clearly, the shorter the technology and product life cycles, the closer the required collaboration with key suppliers. With current exchange technology, a private exchange, controlled by the buyer, better facilitates this type of relationship, which allows buyers and suppliers to cut design cost and development cycle time using the features of this private exchange.

Commodity products. This is the most challenging product category, since on the one hand, many of these products go directly into finished goods, so the risk is quite high, while on the other hand, the firm has a variety of potential options to choose from. These include selecting from many potential suppliers offering long-term, sometimes flexible contracts, and/or using the spot market for short-term purchasing. The high risk and the available options suggest that in this case the focus should be both on price and risk management. This is achieved by using a **portfolio approach** focused on the appropriate trade-offs between risk and cost [13]. To implement a portfolio approach, the firm should use a combination of

1. Long-term contracts where the buyer and supplier commit to a certain volume and the supplier guarantees a level of supply for a committed price; we refer to the committed level of supply as the **base commitment** level.
2. Flexible, or option, contracts, in which the buyer prepays a relatively small fraction of the product price up front, in return for a commitment from the supplier to satisfy demand up to a certain level. We refer to that level as the **option** level. If the buyer does not exercise the option, the initial payment is lost. The buyer can purchase any amount up to the option level, by paying an additional price (agreed to at the time the contract is signed) for each unit purchased. Of course, the total price (prepayment plus the exercise price) paid by the buyer for each purchased unit is higher than the unit price in a long-term contract.
3. Spot purchasing, in which buyers look for additional supply in the open market. In this case, the firm should use an independent e-marketplace to select a supplier. The focus at this stage is on using the marketplace to find new suppliers and on forcing **competition** between suppliers to reduce product price.

How does this portfolio approach address risk? Observe that if demand is much higher than anticipated and the base commitment level plus the option level do not provide enough protection, the firm must use the spot market for additional supply. Unfortunately, this is typically the worst time to buy in the spot market, since prices are high due to shortages. Thus, the buyer can select a trade-off level between price risk, shortage risk, and inventory risk by carefully selecting the level of long-term commitment and the option level. For instance, for the same option level, the higher the initial contract commitment, the smaller the price risk but the higher the inventory risk taken by the buyer. On the other hand, the smaller the level of the base commitment, the higher the price and shortage risks due to the likelihood of using the spot market. Similarly, for the same level of base commitment, the higher the option level, the higher the risk assumed by the supplier since the buyer may exercise only a small fraction of the option level. These trade-offs are summarized in Table 7-8 where in parentheses we identify the party that takes on most of the risk.

TABLE 7-8

RISK TRADE-OFF IN PORTFOLIO CONTRACTS

Option level		Base commitment level	
		Low	High
	High	Inventory risk (supplier)	N/A*
	Low	Price and shortage risks (buyer)	Inventory risk (buyer)

*For a given situation, either the option level or the base commitment level may be high, but not both.

SUMMARY

In this chapter, we examined outsourcing and procurement strategies. Outsourcing has both benefits and risks, and we considered a framework for making buy/make decisions. These decisions should depend on whether a particular component is modular or integral, and whether or not a firm has the expertise and capacity to manufacture a particular component or product.

We also considered the growth of e-markets and their impact on business strategies. A variety of e-markets have appeared, and each of these types addresses a different business need. Depending on the type of component being procured, a different type of e-market is appropriate. For commodity products, a portfolio of procurement strategies may be most appropriate.

DISCUSSION QUESTIONS

1. Discuss the impact of product life cycle on the buy/make framework developed in Section 7.3.
2. In a typical product, different components are viewed differently by the customers. That is, customers consider some features and components to be critical when they buy a product, while other features and components have very little impact on a customer's decision. Discuss the impact of the importance of a component in the eyes of the end consumer on the buy/make framework developed in Section 7.3.
3. In the portfolio approach described in Section 7.5 the supplier takes on all the risk when the option level is high and the base commitment level is low. Why would suppliers agree to take on that risk?
4. According to Bill Paulk, IBM's vice president of e-marketplaces, "IBM has saved about $1.7 billion since 1993 by being able to divulge sensitive price and inventory information over a private exchange built for 25,000 suppliers and customers." As the host of the exchange, the company helped defray the cost of connecting suppliers. The payoff: On-time delivery to customers soared from about 50 percent to close to 90 percent, "which helped justify the cost," Paulk says. In 1999, IBM invested in E2open, a consortia-based e-marketplace for the electronics industry. Why do you think IBM needs both a private exchange and a consortia based e-marketplace?

CHAPTER 8

International Issues in Supply Chain Management

C A S E

Wal-Mart Changes Tactics to Meet International Tastes

São Bernardo, Brazil. Wal-Mart Stores Inc. is finding out that what plays in Peoria isn't necessarily a hit in suburban São Paulo.

Tanks of live trout are out; sushi is in. American footballs have been replaced by soccer balls. The fixings for *feijoada*, a medley of beef and pork in black bean stew, are now displayed on the deli counter. American-style jeans priced at $19.99 have been dropped in favor of $9.99 knock-offs.

But adapting to local tastes may have been the easy part. Three years after embarking on a blitz to bring "everyday low prices" to the emerging markets of Brazil and Argentina, Wal-Mart is finding the going tougher than expected.

Brutal competition, markets that don't play to Wal-Mart's ability to achieve efficiency through economies of scale, and some of its own mistakes have produced red ink. Moreover, the company's insistence on doing things "the Wal-Mart way" has apparently alienated some local suppliers and employees.

DEEP POCKETS

No one is counting Wal-Mart out, of course. With sales of nearly $105 billion last year and profits of $3.1 billion, the Bentonville, Arkansas, behemoth has deep pockets. And it has revised its merchandising in Brazil and Argentina and made other changes. Its four newest stores are smaller than the initial outlets in São Paulo and Buenos Aires and are in mid-size cities where competition isn't so fierce.

Bob L. Martin, Wal-Mart's head of international operations, is confident that the company will eventually become the dominant retailer in South America. "There is low-hanging fruit all over the place," he says. "The market is ripe and wide open for us." He adds that Wal-Mart plans to add eight stores in both Argentina and Brazil next year, doubling the number now in each country.

A lot is riding on Wal-Mart's global expansion drive, which is targeting not only South America but also China and Indonesia, two other markets full of promise and pitfalls. With opportunities for growth

Source: Jonathan Friedland and Louise Lee, *The Wall Street Journal* (interactive edition), October 8, 1997. Copied with permission.

dwindling at home, the company is opening fewer than 100 domestic stores a year, down from as many as 150 in the early 1990s. The current rate of openings can't generate the profit gains that Wal-Mart wants, and its main hopes lie overseas.

"If we're good enough in international, we can duplicate Wal-Mart," chief executive David D. Glass said in an interview in June. "We have very high expectations."

A SMALL OPERATION SO FAR

So far, though, the six-year-old international operation is relatively tiny; it accounted for only 4.8 percent of Wal-Mart's 1996 sales. Most of the company's international revenue comes from Canada, where Wal-Mart purchased 120 stores from Woolworth Corp. in 1994, and from Mexico, where earlier this year it bought a controlling stake in Cifra, SA, its partner, and now has about 390 stores. Last year, the international unit had an operating profit of $24 million, its first, compared with a $16 million loss in 1995. Mr. Martin says he expects further improvement this year.

Mr. Glass said he expects international growth to account for a third of Wal-Mart's annual increase in sales and profits within three to five years.

The performance of Wal-Mart's 16 South American stores may well indicate the future outlook. In Canada and Mexico, many customers were familiar with the company from cross-border shopping trips, and by acquiring local retailers, Wal-Mart quickly reached the size necessary to hold down costs. In South America and Asia, by contrast, Wal-Mart is building from scratch in markets already dominated by savvy local and foreign competitors such as Grupo Pão de Acucar SA of Brazil and Carrefour SA of France.

LOSSES FORECAST

Wal-Mart doesn't break out financial data on its South American Operations. However, retail analysts, citing the accounts of Wal-Mart's Brazilian partner, Lojas Americanas SA, expect Wal-Mart to lose $20 million to $30 million in Brazil this year, on top of an estimated $48 million in losses since starting up in South America in 1995. In Argentina, where the company doesn't have a partner, Wal-Mart executives concede that it is losing money but say its performance meets expectations. The company expects operations in both countries to be profitable by early 1999.

"What counts is that we are finding great customer acceptance," Mr. Martin says. Wal-Mart says its supercenter in Osasco, Brazil, was the top-grossing store in the entire company last year. And at a recent supercenter opening in the mid-size Brazilian city of Ribeirão Prêto, shoppers practically beat down the doors to scoop up bargain-priced microwave ovens and television sets.

But such enthusiasm is hard to sustain. At an older supercenter in Avellaneda, a suburb of Buenos Aires, a few shoppers are in the store during peak hours one Sunday. Hugo and Mariana Faojo help explain why. Browsing in the shoe section, the young couple say they see little difference between the goods at Wal-Mart and those at nearby Carrefour. For groceries, they prefer Supermercados Jumbo SA, a Chilean-owned chain, where they say they find high-quality products and fresh meats. Clothes and household goods, Wal-Mart's mainstays, are similar in quality and price to those at Carrefour, says Mr. Faojo, a government surveyor.

Not only did Carrefour arrive first—it now has a total of about 60 stores in Argentina and Brazil—but it is maneuvering with prices and promotions to keep Wal-Mart off balance. When Thomas Gallegos, who manages Wal-Mart's new store here, prints up fliers advertising bargains, the nearby Carrefour responds in just a few hours by offering the same product for a few cents less—and its fliers are handed out at the entrance to the Wal-Mart parking lot. "Gccz, the competition is aggressive," says Mr. Gallegos, who previously ran a Wal-Mart in Harlingen, Texas.

Carrefour, which, like Wal-Mart in the United States, drives hard bargains with its suppliers, can afford to play low-ball because it has the critical mass that Wal-Mart lacks here. And it holds down its overhead by stocking a far-narrower selection of merchandise; for example, the Carrefour in La Plata, Argentina, stocks 22,000 items, while the Wal-Mart next door carries 58,000.

Mr. Martin contends that Carrefour's advantage is ephemeral and that customers value Wal-Mart's broader choice. "It's costing them something to fight us," he adds. Carrefour didn't respond to requests for an interview.

DISTRIBUTION PROBLEMS

Right now, however, Wal-Mart's effort to stock such a wide variety of merchandise is hurting it. Squeezing out costs in the supply chain is crucial to its "every-day low pricing" formula. In the United States, the company runs like a well-oiled machine, maintaining a highly sophisticated inventory-management system and its own network of distribution centers.

But timely delivery of merchandise is a relative concept in the bumper-to-bumper traffic of São Paulo, where Wal-Mart depends on suppliers or contract truckers to deliver most of its goods directly to stores. Because it doesn't own its distribution system, it can't control deliveries nearly as well as it does in the United States, vendors say. Stores here sometimes process 300 deliveries daily, compared with seven a day at U.S. locations, and some shipments have mysteriously disappeared somewhere between the port and the store.

"The biggest issue Wal-Mart has is shipping product on time and getting on the shelf," says Jim Russel, a national account manager for Colgate-Palmolive Co. in Bentonville. Wal-Mart recently built a warehouse in Argentina and one in Brazil that it says will eventually reduce its distribution problems.

But logistics aren't the only issue. Some local suppliers have difficulty meeting Wal-Mart's specifications for easy-to-handle packaging and quality control, forcing the retailer to rely so heavily on imported goods that it could have problems if Brazil's economic stabilization policies falter. Eleven South American suppliers have taken umbrage at Wal-Mart's aggressive pricing policies and for a time refused to sell goods to the chain.

Wal-Mart also has sought to drive hard bargains with divisions of its major suppliers back in the United States. The pitch hasn't been altogether successful. Wal-Mart doesn't get special deals just because it's a big U.S. customer, some large domestic suppliers say.

VARIOUS MISTAKES

Wal-Mart's troubles in South America stem partly from its own mistakes. Analysts say it failed to do its homework before plunging in. In addition to the live trout and American footballs, the company initially imported items such as cordless tools, which few South Americans use, and leaf blowers, which are useless in a concrete jungle such as São Paulo.

And merchandise flubs weren't the only mistakes. In Brazil, Wal-Mart brought in stock-handling equipment that didn't work with standardized local pallets. It also installed a computerized bookkeeping

system that failed to take into account Brazil's wildly complicated tax system. Vincente Trius, who heads Wal-Mart's Brazilian operations, says, however, that the company hasn't lost money as a result of tax miscalculations.

Wal-Mart has also been slow to adapt to Brazil's fast-changing credit culture. Not until last February did the company start accepting postdated checks, which have become the most common form of credit since Brazil stabilized its currency in 1995. Pão de Acucar, whose Extra hypermarkets compete with Wal-Mart, has been taking postdated checks since they first became popular and has installed a sophisticated credit-checking system at its registers. Wal-Mart is hurrying to do so, too.

The six South American Sam's Club locations, the members-only warehouse stores that sell merchandise in bulk, got off to a slow start largely because shoppers weren't used to paying a membership fee and don't have enough room at home to store bulk purchases. In Argentina the clubs have faced another barrier: Small-business customers are reluctant to sign up for fear Wal-Mart could provide tax information to the authorities on their purchases.

Wal-Mart won't disclose Sam's Club membership data in South America. But it now offers shoppers free one-day memberships tied to specific purchases. Mr. Martin says that Wal-Mart is "disappointed" in the club's performance in Argentina but that it is improving in Brazil. The company says it plans more Sam's outlets in South America but hasn't disclosed details.

PROBLEMS CALLED TEMPORARY

Wal-Mart's Mr. Glass characterized the missteps as temporary problems and inevitable in entering a new market. "It's a lengthy process to go to South America, recruit good managers, bring them to Wal-Mart, and train them and indoctrinate them and teach them what you want to teach them," he said in June. "It's slow going early on, and you spend a lot of money. You pay a lot of tuition to learn what you need to learn."

Wal-Mart says that it is developing a strong group of young executives and hasn't suffered high turnover. But Francisco de Narvaez, the owner of Argentine supermarket chain Casa Tia SA, says some managers have left because Wal-Mart "didn't listen to their senior-level local employees." In the past six months, Wal-Mart has hired two managers who had worked at its Mexican operations to take over two São Paulo locations.

Mr. Trius, a Spanish-born executive who earlier turned around Dairy Farm Ltd.'s Spanish supermarket chain, says he believes the criticisms of Wal-Mart's South American operations go too far. "If Joe Blow was to open in Brazil with the same concept and within two years had everything in place, people would say, 'What an incredible job,' "he says. "People expected us to snap our fingers and be Wal-Mart in the United States overnight. To me, the criticisms are more related to expectations than to reality."

By the end of this chapter, you should be able to answer the following questions:

- Other than a need to expand, what other reasons would Wal-Mart have for opening stores globally?
- Why would it be beneficial for Wal-Mart to have suppliers in different countries?
- Why would Wal-Mart want strong centralized control of its stores? Why would Wal-Mart want strong local control of stores?
- What pitfalls and opportunities other than those mentioned in *The Wall Street Journal* article would Wal-Mart face over the next few years?

8.1 INTRODUCTION

It is readily apparent that global operations and supply chains are becoming increasingly significant. Dornier et al. [43] collected the following statistics, which help to indicate the magnitude of this trend:

- About one-fifth of the output of U.S. firms is produced overseas.
- One-quarter of U.S. imports are between foreign affiliates and U.S. parent companies.
- Since the late 1980s, over half of U.S. companies increased the number of countries in which they operate.

In many ways, international supply chain management is the same as domestic supply chain management spread over a larger geographic area. However, as we will discuss in the remainder of this chapter, international supply chain networks can provide a wealth of additional opportunities if they are managed effectively. At the same time, there are many additional potential problems and pitfalls to be aware of.

International supply chains can run the gamut from a primarily domestic business with some international suppliers to a truly integrated global supply chain. Some of the advantages and disadvantages that we will discuss apply equally to all of the systems in the following list, while others apply only to the most complex integrated systems.

International distribution systems. In this type of system, manufacturing still occurs domestically, but distribution and typically some marketing take place overseas.

International suppliers. In this system, raw materials and components are furnished by foreign suppliers, but final assembly is performed domestically. In some cases, the final product is then shipped to foreign markets.

Offshore manufacturing. In this type of system, the product is typically sourced and manufactured in a single foreign location, and then shipped back to domestic warehouses for sale and distribution.

Fully integrated global supply chain. Here products are supplied, manufactured, and distributed from various facilities located throughout the world. In a truly global supply chain, it may appear that the supply chain was designed without regard to national boundaries. Of course, this is far from the truth! As we shall see, the true value of a global supply chain is realized by taking advantage of these national boundaries.

Clearly, a supply chain can fit more than one of these categories. Throughout the following discussion, consider how each of the issues discussed applies differently to firms, depending on their position in this global supply chain spectrum.

In any event, many firms cannot help but become involved in global supply chain issues. Dornier et al. [43] identified the following forces that collectively drive the trend toward globalization:

- Global market forces.
- Technological forces.
- Global cost forces.
- Political and economic forces.

8.1.1 Global Market Forces

Global market forces involve the pressures created by foreign competitors, as well as the opportunities created by foreign customers. Even if companies don't do business overseas, the presence of foreign competitors in home markets can affect their business significantly. To defend domestic markets successfully, companies may find it necessary to move into foreign markets. Sometimes the threat of a presence is sufficient, as in the dry breakfast cereal business, dominated by Kellogg Co. in the United States and Nestlé in Europe. Apparently, failed attempts in the past to penetrate each other's home markets, combined with the threat of retaliation, are enough to maintain the status quo.

In addition, much of the demand growth available to companies is in foreign and emerging markets. Recently, companies have made great sacrifices (particularly in terms of proprietary technology) and taken on considerable business risk to become involved in ventures in mainland China. Indeed, the United States is accounting for less and less of the total consumption of goods in the world.

One cause of this increasing demand for products throughout the world is the global proliferation of information. Television introduces products to Europeans. Japanese vacation abroad. Businesses send overnight mail between continents. Most recently, the Internet provides instant international exposure, as well as the ability to purchase goods in one country that will be delivered in another without leaving home or office.

EXAMPLE 8-1

In Brazil thousands of people move from preindustrial villages to rapidly growing cities. Once there, their first goal is to install television sets, even as they continue to "make sacrificial offerings of fruit and fresh-killed chickens to Macumban spirits by the candlelight" [95].

As Kenichi Ohmae, head of management consulting firm McKinsey's Japanese office, points out, people have "all become global citizens, and so must the companies that want to sell us things" [117]. Products are universally desired, and many companies are willing to sell them globally. This is clearly a self-amplifying trend for an industry, because, as companies become global, their competitors must also become global in order to compete. Thus, many companies are becoming global citizens with universal products and the opportunity to hire talented employees worldwide.

Along similar lines, particular markets often serve to drive technological advances in some areas. By participating in these competitive markets, companies are forced to develop and enhance leading-edge technologies and products. These products can then be used to increase or maintain market position in other areas or regions where the markets are not as competitive. To be a leader in software, for example, you have to compete in the U.S. market. Similarly, the German machine tools market and the Japanese consumer electronics market are hotly contested.

8.1.2 Technological Forces

Technological forces are related to the products themselves. Various subcomponents and technologies are available in different regions and locations around the world, and many successful firms need to have the ability to use these resources quickly and effectively. To achieve this, it may be necessary for firms to locate research, design, and production facilities close to these regions. This is often particularly useful if suppliers are involved in the design process, as discussed in Chapter 9. The same logic applies to collaborations and interfirm development projects. To gain access to markets or technology, companies in different regions frequently collaborate, resulting in the location of joint facilities close to one of the partners.

Along similar lines, global location of research-and-development facilities is becoming more common, primarily for two reasons. First, as product cycles become shorter and time more important, companies have discovered how useful it is to locate research facilities close to manufacturing facilities. This helps transfer technology from research facilities to manufacturing facilities, and speeds up the resolution of problems that inevitably arise during this transfer. In addition, specific technical expertise may be available in certain areas or regions. For example, Microsoft recently opened a research lab in Cambridge, England, to take advantage of the expertise available in Europe.

8.1.3 Global Cost Forces

Cost forces often dictate global location decisions. In the past the low cost of unskilled labor was a decisive factor in determining factory location. Recently, studies have found that in many cases, the costs of cheaper unskilled labor were more than offset by the increase in other costs associated with operating facilities in remote locations. In some cases, of course, cheaper labor is sufficient justification for overseas manufacturing. More recently, however, other global cost forces have become more significant.

For example, cheaper *skilled labor* is drawing an increasing number of companies overseas. Many of the analyses and programs that U.S. consulting firms undertook to address the Year 2000 problem (in which computer programs might fail when the year changed from 1999 to 2000) were done in India, where programming skills are much cheaper.

We have discussed how a supplier and the customer supply chain must often be tightly integrated to deliver certain products effectively. Often this can be accomplished most cost-effectively if the various participants are located close together. This may necessitate establishing integrated supply chains in different markets.

Finally, the capital costs of building a new facility often dominate labor costs. Many governments are willing to provide tax breaks or cost-sharing arrangements to lower the cost of the new facility. In addition, supplier price breaks and cost-sharing joint ventures may dictate these types of decisions.

8.1.4 Political and Economic Forces

Political and economic forces may greatly affect the drive toward globalization. In Section 8.2.1, we will discuss exchange rate fluctuation and the operational approaches to dealing with this issue. There are also several other political and economic factors. For example, regional trade agreements may drive companies to expand into one of the countries in the regional group. It may be to a company's advantage to obtain raw materials from or to manufacture within European, Pacific Rim, or North American trading blocks. In some cases, production processes may even be redesigned to avoid tariffs; for example, almost-finished goods may be shipped into a trading block to avoid tariffs on "finished goods."

Similarly, various trade protection mechanisms can affect international supply chain decisions. Tariffs and quotas affect what can be imported, and may lead a company to decide to manufacture within the market country or region. More subtle regulations, including local content requirements, affect supply chains. To address local content requirements, for example, TI and Intel, both U.S. firms, make microprocessors in Europe, and various Japanese automakers produce cars in Europe. Even voluntary export restrictions can affect the supply chain: Japanese manufacturers began to manufacture more expensive cars after agreeing voluntarily to limit exports to the United States. Recall that this is why brands such as Infiniti and Lexus came into existence. Government procurement policies can affect the ability of international companies to be successful in various markets. In the United States, for example, the Department of Defense gives as much as a 50 percent advantage to U.S. companies in the bidding on contracts.

8.2 RISKS AND ADVANTAGES OF INTERNATIONAL SUPPLY CHAINS

We have looked at the various forces that drive companies to develop international supply chains. In this section, we take a slightly different perspective by examining the various advantages and risks inherent in different types of international supply chains. Certain advantages of sourcing, manufacturing, and selling globally are immediately obvious.

Clearly, the world is converging in many instances toward standardized products. This means that more and more, vast markets have opened up for products—far greater than anything managers in the past could have imagined. By taking advantage of this trend, companies can realize vast economies of scale in terms of production, management, distribution, marketing, and so forth [95].

Indeed, as we discussed in the previous section, costs can be lowered with greater potential raw material, labor, and outsourcing sources and a greater number of potential manufacturing sites. At the same time, the increase in potential markets allows for an increase in sales and profits. These advantages are due to the increase in the size and scope of the supply chain—they are independent of the specific characteristics of the global supply chain.

To utilize these advantages, it is essential that management understand the different *demand characteristics* and *cost advantages* of different regions. We will discuss this issue in more depth in the next section. This discussion is greatly influenced by Kogut [84].

Most important, the global supply chain can provide a firm with the *flexibility* to address the uncertainty in international markets. In particular, this flexibility can be used to counteract the inherent risks from various factors that are particularly relevant to global companies.

8.2.1 Risks

So what are these risks? First, fluctuating exchange rates change the relative value of production and the relative profit of selling a product in a particular country. Relative costs change so that manufacturing, storing, distributing, or selling in a particular region at a particular price can change from being extremely profitable to a total loss.

The same is true domestically. In many cases, certain regions within the same country may be less expensive for storage or manufacturing than others. However, the cost differences between domestic regions are not typically as dramatic as those across countries and, more importantly, they don't change as frequently.

It should be stressed that although managers typically think of exchange rates as affecting the dollar value of assets and liabilities denominated in foreign currencies, it is the *operating exposure* described in the previous paragraphs that can have the most dramatic effect on annual operating profit. This operating exposure reflects the fact that in the short run, changes in currency exchange rates do not necessarily reflect changes in relative inflation rates between countries. Thus, over the short term, regional operations can become relatively more or less expensive in terms of dollars. Note that this operating exposure is not only a function of a firm's global supply chain, but also its competition's global supply chain. If a competitor's relative costs decrease more, a firm can be underpriced in the market [94].

Indeed, Dornier et al. [43] identified several factors that affect the impact of operating exposure on a firm. *Customer reactions* influence how a firm adjusts prices in various markets in response to changes in operating expenses. As discussed above, *competitor reactions* also influence how a firm can react to changes in the relative cost of doing business. Competitors can react to price increases by raising their own prices to increase profitability or gain market share. As we discuss in the next section, *supplier reaction*—the ability of suppliers to respond with flexibility to varying demands—is a strong factor in the effectiveness of certain strategies that help firms address the risk of operating exposure. Finally, *government reactions* play a large role on the global stage. Governments can intervene to stabilize currencies or even directly support endangered firms by providing subsidies or tariffs. In addition, other political instabilities can also affect multinational companies. Tax situations can change rapidly because political factors dictate different treatment of corporations, particularly foreign corporations, in various regions.

Likewise, foreign companies can enter domestic markets. These companies may even use domestic profits to subsidize low-priced goods in foreign markets. This could even affect companies that have decided not to compete on the global stage.

8.2.2 Addressing Global Risks

Bruce Kogut [84] identified three ways a global supply chain can be employed to address global risks: speculative, hedge, and flexible strategies.

Speculative Strategies   Using *speculative strategies*, a company bets on a single scenario, with often spectacular results if the scenario is realized, and dismal ones if it is not. For example, in the late 1970s and early 1980s, Japanese automakers bet that if they did all of their manufacturing in Japan, rising labor costs would be more than offset by exchange rate benefits, rising productivity, and increased levels of investment and productivity. For a while these bets paid off, but then rising labor costs and unfavorable exchange rates began to hurt manufacturers, and it became necessary to build plants overseas. Of course, if it had remained favorable to do all the manufacturing in Japan, the Japanese manufacturers would have "won the bet" because building new facilities is time-consuming and expensive.

Hedge Strategies   Using *hedge strategies*, a company designs the supply chain in such a way that any losses in part of the supply chain will be offset by gains in another part. For example, Volkswagen operates plants in the United States, Brazil, Mexico, and

Germany, all of which are important markets for Volkswagen products. Depending on macroeconomic conditions, certain plants may be more profitable at various times than others. Hedge strategies, *by design*, are simultaneously successful in some locations and unsuccessful in others.

Flexible Strategies   When properly employed, *flexible strategies* enable a company to take advantage of different scenarios. Typically, flexible supply chains are designed with multiple suppliers and excess manufacturing capacity in different countries. In addition, factories are designed to be flexible, so that products can be moved at minimal cost from region to region as economic conditions demand.

When considering the implementation of a flexible strategy, managers have to answer several questions:

1. Is there enough variability in the system to justify the use of flexible strategies? Clearly, the more variability in international conditions, the more a company can benefit from utilizing flexible strategies.
2. Do the benefits of spreading production over various facilities justify the costs, which may include loss of economies of scale in terms of manufacturing and supply?
3. Does the company have the appropriate coordination and management mechanisms in place to take rapid advantage of flexible strategies?

If the supply chain is appropriately designed, several approaches can be utilized to implement flexible strategies effectively:

Production shifting.   Flexible factories and excess capacity and suppliers can be used to shift production from region to region to take advantage of current circumstances. As exchange rates, labor cost, and so on change, manufacturing can be relocated.

Information sharing.   Having an increased presence in many regions and markets often will increase the availability of information, which can be used to anticipate market changes and find new opportunities.

Global coordination.   Having multiple facilities worldwide provides a firm with a certain amount of market leverage that it might otherwise lack. If a foreign competitor attacks one of your main markets, you can attack back. Of course, various international laws and political pressures place limits on this type of retaliation.

EXAMPLE 8-2

When Michelin began to target North American markets aggressively, Goodyear was able to drop its tire prices in Europe. This forced Michelin to slow its overseas investment program.

Political leverage.   The opportunity to move operations rapidly gives firms a measure of political leverage in overseas operations. For example, if governments are lax in enforcing contracts or international law, or present expensive tax alternatives, firms can move their operations. In many cases, the implicit threat of movement is sufficient to prevent local politicians from taking unfavorable actions.

8.2.3 Requirements for Global Strategy Implementation

Any company, even a huge global company, is not immediately ready for integrated global supply chain management on this scale. Michael McGrath and Richard Hoole [105] discuss important developments that are necessary to set the stage for this kind of massive global integration. These developments are outlined below for each of the **five basic functions of firms:** product development, purchasing, production, demand management, and order fulfillment.

1. **Product development.** It is important to design products that can be modified easily for major markets, and which can be manufactured in various facilities. As we discuss in the next section, this is not always possible, but it is certainly helpful in those cases where it is achievable. While it is dangerous to design a product to be the "average" of what several markets require, it may be possible to design a base product or products that can be more easily adapted to several different markets. An international design team may be helpful in this regard.

2. **Purchasing.** A company will find it useful to have management teams responsible for the purchase of important materials from many vendors around the world. In this way, it is much easier to ensure that the quality and delivery options from various suppliers are compatible, and that a qualified team is present to compare the pricing of various suppliers. Also, these teams can work to guarantee that sufficient suppliers in different regions are at hand to ensure the flexibility necessary to take full advantage of the global supply chain.

3. **Production.** As we discussed above, excess capacity and plants in several regions are essential if firms are to take full advantage of the global supply chain by shifting production as conditions warrant. To utilize this kind of strategy, however, effective communications systems must be in place so that this global supply chain can be managed effectively. Centralized management is thus essential to this system, which implies that centralized information must be available. Indeed, knowledge of the current status of factories, supplies, and inventory is essential when making the types of decisions described above. In addition, since factories are typically supplying each other in a complex supply chain, it is important that interfactory communication is solid and that centralized management makes each factory aware of the system status.

4. **Demand management.** Often demand management, which involves setting marketing and sales plans based on projected demand and available product, is carried out on a regional basis. For the supply chain to be managed in an integrated way, demand management clearly has to have at least some centralized component. On the other hand, much of this sensitive, market-based information is best supplied by analysts located in each region. Thus, once again communication is a critical component of the success of global supply chain management.

5. **Order fulfillment.** To successfully implement a truly flexible supply chain management system, a centralized system must be in place so that regional customers can receive deliveries from the global supply chain with the same efficiency as they do from local or regionally based supply chains. All the flexibility in the world is of little use if it makes the system so cumbersome and unpleasant that customers turn elsewhere. We discuss the kinds of advanced information systems that this centralized order fulfillment requires in Chapter 11.

Only when a company is sufficiently prepared to implement flexible strategies can it take advantage of all that the global supply chain has to offer.

8.3 ISSUES IN INTERNATIONAL SUPPLY CHAIN MANAGEMENT

In this section, we will discuss other important issues of international supply chains that were not appropriate for the previous sections.

8.3.1 International versus Regional Products

The preceding discussion suggests that the ideal company builds "universal products" that can be sold in many markets. In many cases, however, this is not that simple. Ohmae [117] pointed out that there are several categories of products, each of which has different "international requirements."

Region-specific products. Some products have to be designed and manufactured specifically for certain regions. For example, automobile designs are often region specific. The 1998 Honda Accord has two basic body styles: a smaller body style tailored to European and Japanese tastes and a larger body style catering to American tastes. Of course, even if regional designs are different, effective supply chain management can take advantage of common components or subassemblies within the different designs. We discuss this issue in detail in Chapter 9.

EXAMPLE 8-3

Nissan designates "lead-country" status to each of its car models. For example, the Maxima and Pathfinder are designed for American tastes, often by American design studios. Similar designs are developed primarily for Japanese and European markets. Once regional product managers ensure that vehicles meet lead-country requirements, other regional product managers suggest slight changes that might promote local sales. But the focus is on developing cars for regions. Otherwise, Nissan fears "the trap of pleasing no one well by pleasing everyone half way." There is no effective way to average size, color, and other aesthetic and substantive differences in cars across regions without ending up with a model that no customers in that region particularly like. Of course, if models can be modified slightly to increase sales in other regions, it helps, but that isn't the primary focus [117].

True global products. These products are truly global, in the sense that no modification is necessary for global sales. For example, Coca-Cola is essentially the same throughout the world, as are Levi's jeans and McDonald's burgers. Similarly, luxury brands such as Coach and Gucci are essentially the same worldwide. It should be noted, however, that some of these brands and products, such as Coke and McDonald's, depend on very specific regional manufacturing and bottling facilities and distribution networks, while others are essentially distributed and sold in the same way throughout the world [95].

The difference between region-specific products and global products does not imply that one is inherently better than the other. However, it is important to consider carefully which of the two product types is more appropriate for a particular situation because employing strategies for regional products that are designed for global products, or vice versa, can lead to disastrous results.

8.3.2 Local Autonomy versus Central Control

Centralized control can be important in taking advantage of some of the strategies we have discussed, but in many cases it makes sense to allow local autonomy in the supply chain. Sometimes, after independent regional operations have proven to be successful, headquarters can't resist the temptation to tamper with the system, and performance suffers.

In addition, it is important to temper expectations for regional business depending on the characteristics of the region involved. For example, companies typically experience, in the short term, relatively low returns in Japan, medium returns in Germany, and higher returns in the United States. Indeed, those companies that are successful in Japan had often settled initially for low returns [117].

However, managers may be tempted to follow local conventional wisdom, and thus miss some of the opportunities derived from the knowledge acquired in the operation of a global supply chain.

EXAMPLE 8-4

When it first introduced the decongestant Contac 600 to Japanese markets, SmithKline Corporation was advised to use the traditional approach, involving more than 1,000 distributors with which the firm would have little contact. Rather than accept this advice, SmithKline used 35 wholesalers, with whom it remained in close contact. SmithKline had used this approach successfully elsewhere. Despite the naysayers, the introduction was highly successful [95].

8.3.3 Miscellaneous Dangers

To be sure, there are many potential dangers that firms must face as they expand their supply chains globally. Exchange rate fluctuations, discussed earlier as an opportunity, can just as easily be a risk if not properly managed. It may be harder to administer offshore facilities, especially in less-developed countries. Similarly, the promise of cheap labor may mask the threat of reduced productivity [103]. Expensive training may be required, but even then productivity may not reach domestic levels.

Often local collaboration occurs in the global supply chain. In this case, collaborators can ultimately become competitors.

EXAMPLE 8-5

- Hitachi, which used to manufacture under license from Motorola, now makes its own microprocessors.
- Toshiba, which manufactured copiers for 3M, is now a major supplier of copiers under the Toshiba brand name.
- Sunrise Plywood and Furniture, of Taiwan, was for many years a partner of Mission Furniture in California. Now it is one of Mission's major competitors [103].

Similar dangers exist with foreign governments. To deal with China and gain access to that country's huge markets, many companies are handing over critical manufacturing and engineering expertise to the Chinese government or to Chinese partners. It is only a matter of time until these Chinese companies, or other companies selected by the government, begin to compete under favorable terms with their original partners. The only question is whether the overseas firms that gave away their technology will still be able to compete successfully in the Chinese market, or if they will lose this opportunity even as Chinese companies begin to compete on the world stage.

Indeed, this serves to highlight only one of the dangers that foreign governments pose to the international supply chain. Although world markets are becoming more open all the time, the world is far from becoming a giant free trade zone. At any time the threat of *protectionism* might appear, and if the global supply chain is not set up with some kind of counter to this threat, companies will not be able to do much about it. Sometimes the threat comes not from the foreign government, but from the domestic government, dealing with the concerns of smaller local firms.

EXAMPLE 8-6

In 1986 Taiwan had a $15.7 billion trade surplus with the United States, heightening domestic pressure on the U.S. government to impose trade restrictions on Taiwanese products. This occurred despite the fact that the vast majority of Taiwanese imports were parts to supply American companies, such as GE, IBM, Hewlett-Packard, and Mattel, which had moved manufacturing offshore to take advantage of lower costs. In response, Taiwan was forced to increase the value of its currency relative to the U.S. dollar, thus effectively removing much of the cost advantage of manufacturing to Taiwan [103].

8.4 REGIONAL DIFFERENCES IN LOGISTICS

In the previous sections, we discussed the general advantages, disadvantages, and strategies for utilizing global supply chains effectively. Of course, it is important to be aware of the cultural, infrastructural, and economic differences between regions when decisions are made about particular foreign links in the global supply chain. Wood et al. [157] identified several categories of differences that managers must consider when designing international supply chains. In particular, major differences can be highlighted between the so-called *triad*, or First World, nations, Japan, the United States, and the nations of western Europe; *emerging nations* such as Thailand, Taiwan, China, Brazil, Argentina, and the countries of eastern Europe; and the *Third World* nations. These differences are summarized in Table 8-1 and analyzed below.

8.4.1 Cultural Differences

Cultural differences can critically affect the way international subsidiaries interpret the goals and pronouncements of management. Wood et al. [157] highlighted beliefs and values, customs, and language, all of which play a big role in global business and can strongly affect negotiation and communication.

Language consists not only of words but also of expressions, gestures, and context. Many times, the words appear to be translated correctly, but the meaning is not. We've all heard stories of American businesspeople using the wrong gestures in Asia, leading to disastrous consequences. It is important to utilize appropriate resources to make sure that communication is effective.

Beliefs, or specific values about something, can differ widely from culture to culture. The belief that effective communication is important, for instance, can vary from culture to culture. Similarly, values, or more general conceptions, can vary. For example, American manufacturers value "efficiency" in ways that some other cultures do

TABLE 8-1

MAJOR DIFFERENCES BETWEEN DIFFERENT REGIONS

	First World	Emerging	Third World
Infrastructure	Highly developed	Under development	Insufficient to support advanced logistics
Supplier operating standards	High	Variable	Typically not considered
Information system availability	Generally available	Support system not available	Not available
Human resources	Available	Available with some searching	Often difficult to find

not [157]. Also, some cultures may value time more than others, so that late delivery may be viewed in some places as a serious problem, while in others it is not particularly important.

Customs, of course, vary greatly from country to country. In many cases, it is important for the businessperson to adhere to local customs to avoid offending anyone. For example, the practice of gift giving varies greatly from country to country.

8.4.2 Infrastructure

In First World countries, the manufacturing and logistics infrastructure is highly developed. Highway systems, ports, communication and information systems, and advanced manufacturing techniques allow the development of advanced supply chains. Regional differences do exist, primarily for geographical, political, or historical reasons. For example, road widths, bridge heights, and communications protocols may differ from region to region, but, in general, techniques have been developed to overcome these differences.

Regardless of the infrastructure, geography also affects supply chain decisions, even within First World countries. In the United States, for example, where large distances often exist between major cities, more inventory might be held than in countries such as Belgium, where the distance between cities is small.

Similarly, relative economic conditions have affected the mix of logistics and supply chain components in many First World countries. For example, countries with relatively cheap land and cheap labor, such as France, have built many large, "low-tech" warehouses, while the Scandinavian countries have developed warehouse automation because labor in those countries is so expensive [48].

In the emerging nations, the supply chain infrastructure is usually not fully in place. Most domestic companies in emerging nations see logistics as a necessary expense and not a strategic advantage, so they limit investments in logistics infrastructure. In many cases, gross national income in an emerging nation may not yet be sufficient to fully implement an advanced logistics infrastructure. In addition, the focus of infrastructure development may have been on exports instead of building a system appropriate for imports and exports. This is true in China [157]. Nonetheless, these nations are "emerging" because they have begun to address these issues. For example, many countries have national transportation policies in place, and are beginning or continuing to implement them.

In the Third World, the infrastructure is generally insufficient to support advanced logistics operations. Roads are often in poor shape. Warehousing facilities are frequently unavailable. Distribution systems may be nonexistent. In general, specific supply chain decisions have to be considered carefully, because many of the things taken for granted in the triad or emerging nations may not exist here.

8.4.3 Performance Expectation and Evaluation

Although regional differences remain among First World nations, operating standards are generally uniform and high. For example, overnight carriers are expected to make deliveries overnight. Contracts are legally binding documents. Environmental regulations and constraints are typically present, and companies are expected to obey them.

However, the approaches to developing and enforcing relationships do differ from region to region. For example, European and American companies use formal partnership contracts more frequently than Japanese firms, which tend to favor informal partnership agreements built over time [21].

In emerging nations, operating standards typically vary greatly. Some firms may have—and meet—high expectations, and place great value on contracts and agreements. Others, however, might not be so scrupulous. Research and negotiation are essential to successful deal making in the emerging nations. In addition, the government typically plays a large role in business, so foreign partners and corporations often must be ready to respond to the government's changing whims.

In the Third World, traditional performance measures have no meaning. Shortages are common and customer service measures that are used in the West (e.g., stock availability, speed of service, and service consistency) are irrelevant; given this situation, a firm has little control of the timing and availability of inventory [157].

8.4.4 Information System Availability

Within the triad nations, computer technology has increased at more or less the same rate across different nations. In most cases, POS data, automation tools, personal computers, and other information system tools are just as available in Spain as in California.

Of course, there may be incompatibilities in various systems. For example, European EDI standards may vary from country to country and industry to industry. In addition, legal standards relating to data protection and document authentication vary from country to country. Nevertheless, efforts are underway to overcome these hurdles, and technology exists to overcome the technical incompatibilities [109].

Support systems in the emerging nations may not be in place to implement efficient information systems. Communications networks may be incomplete and not reliable enough to support the traffic. Technical support expertise may not be available to utilize and maintain the equipment. However, governments in these nations typically have plans or programs in place to address these issues.

Advanced information technology is simply not available in Third World countries. Systems such as EDI and bar coding cannot be supported in this type of environment. Even the value of a personal computer is limited because of inefficient communications systems. In addition, data on the economy and population typically are unavailable.

8.4.5 Human Resources

Within most First World countries, technically and managerially competent workers are available. As Wood et al. [157] pointed out, "Cultural differences aside, a logistics manager from Japan would be functionally at home in a counterpart's position in America." Unskilled labor, however, is relatively expensive in these regions.

While it may be true that skilled managerial and technical personnel are frequently not available in emerging nations, sometimes this is not the case. It might take some searching, but employees with the appropriate skills can often be found. In particular, the eastern European countries have generally well-educated populations [64]. In addition, the wages of skilled workers in emerging nations are generally competitive on the world market. On the other hand, many Chinese managers have been selected for political reasons, rather than technical or managerial expertise, so experience in this case may not be an appropriate indicator of ability [64].

Although it may be possible to find employees that are appropriate to the available technology level, it is often difficult to find trained logistics professionals and managers familiar with modern management techniques in Third World countries. Thus, training becomes especially important in this type of environment.

SUMMARY

In this chapter, we examined issues specific to *global* supply chain management. First, we discussed various types of international supply chains, covering the spectrum from primarily domestic supply chains with some international product distribution all the way to fully integrated global supply chains. We then examined the various forces compelling companies to develop international supply chains. Both advantages and risks are inherent in global supply chains. Besides the obvious cost advantages, we discussed the advantages of having a truly flexible global supply chain to address the inherent risks in operating a global company. However, even with a flexible supply chain, the strategies and approaches used to address these risks will work only if the appropriate infrastructure is in place.

We next surveyed some of the many issues in global supply chain management, including the concepts of international and regional products, and the issue of centralized versus decentralized control in an international context. We concluded with a discussion of regional logistics differences that influence the design of effective supply chains in different parts of the world.

DISCUSSION QUESTIONS

1. Discuss situations in which each of these supply chains might be the appropriate choice for a firm:
   a. International distribution systems.
   b. International suppliers.
   c. Offshore manufacturing.
   d. Fully integrated global supply chain.
2. You are the CEO of a small electronics manufacturing firm that is about to develop a global strategy. Would you prefer a speculative strategy, a hedge strategy, or a flexible strategy? Would your answer to this question change if you were the CEO of a large electronics firm?
3. Discuss some examples of regional products and of true global products. What is it about the products that makes them better suited to being regional or global products?
4. You are the manager of a regional bakery. Contrast the issues you would face if your firm is located in each of the following countries:
   a. Belgium
   b. Russia
   c. Singapore
   d. Canada
   e. Argentina
   f. Nigeria
5. Answer these questions about the article at the beginning of this chapter:
   a. Other than a need to expand, what other reasons would Wal-Mart have for opening stores globally?
   b. Why would it be beneficial for Wal-Mart to have suppliers in different countries?
   c. Why would Wal-Mart want strong centralized control of its stores? Why would Wal-Mart want strong local control of stores?
   d. What pitfalls and opportunities, other than those mentioned in this article, will Wal-Mart face over the next few years?

CHAPTER 9

Coordinated Product and Supply Chain Design

CASE

Hewlett-Packard: DeskJet Printer Supply Chain

Brent Cartier, manager for special projects in the Materials Department of Hewlett-Packard (HP) Company's Vancouver Division, clicked off another mile. It had been a long week and it looked like it would be a long weekend as well, based on the preparation that needed to be done for Monday's meeting with group management on worldwide inventory levels for the DeskJet Printer product line. Even when he was busy, he always took time for the 25-mile bike ride to work—it helped reduce stress in times like this.

The DeskJet printer was introduced in 1988 and had become one of HP's most successful products. Sales had grown steadily, reaching a level of over 600,000 units in 1990 ($400 million). Unfortunately, inventory growth had tracked sales growth closely. Already, HP's distribution centers had been filled with pallets of the DeskJet printer. Worse yet, the organization in Europe was claiming that inventory levels there needed to be raised even further to maintain satisfactory product availability.

Each quarter, representatives from the production, materials, and distribution organizations in Europe, Asia-Pacific, and North America met to discuss "the I-word"—as they referred to it—but their conflicting goals prevented them from reaching consensus on the issues. Each organization had a different approach to the problem. Production had not wanted to get involved, claiming it was "just a materials issue," but had taken the time to rant about the continued proliferation of models and options. The distribution organization's pet peeve was forecast accuracy. They didn't feel that the distribution organization should have to track and store warehouses of inventory, just because the Vancouver Division couldn't build the right products in the right quantities. The European distribution organization had even gone so far as to suggest that they charge the cost of the extra warehouse space that they were renting back to the Vancouver Division directly, instead of allocating it among all the products that they shipped. Finally, Brent's boss, David Arkadia, the materials manager at the Vancouver Division, had summarized the perspective of group management at the last meeting when he said, "The word is coming down from corporate: We can't run our business with this level of unproductive assets. We're just going to have to meet customer needs with less inventory."

As Brent saw it, there were two main issues. The first issue was to find the best way to satisfy customer needs in terms of product availability while

---

Source: Copyright © 1993 by the Board of Trustees of the Leland Stanford Junior University. All rights reserved. This case was written by Laura Kopczak and Professor Hau Lee of the Department of Industrial Engineering and Engineering Management at Stanford University.

minimizing inventory. The second and stickier issue involved how to get agreement among the various parties that they had the right level of inventory. They needed to develop a consistent method for setting and implementing inventory goals and get everyone to sign off on it and use it. It was not going to be easy. The situation was especially urgent in Europe. His mind was still filled with the faxed picture that he had received the previous day, showing the dip in product availability levels for some versions of the product at the European Distribution Center (DC), yet he was sure that loads and loads of DeskJets had been shipped to Europe in the past months. His voice mail had been filled with angry messages from the sales offices, and yet the European DC was telling Vancouver that it had run out of space to store Vancouver's products.

Brent parked his bike and headed for the company showers. His morning shower was another ritual—this was the time he had to review his plans for the day and play out different scenarios. Perhaps a solution would come to him...

BACKGROUND

Hewlett-Packard Company was founded in 1939 by William Hewlett and David Packard, with headquarters in Palo Alto, California. It grew steadily over the next 50 years, diversifying from its base in electronic test and measurement equipment into computers and peripherals products, which now dominated its sales. In 1990 HP had over 50 operations worldwide, with revenues of $13.2 billion and net income of $739 million.

HP was organized partially by product group and partially by function. The Peripherals Group was the second largest of HP's six product groups, with 1990 revenues of $4.1 billion. Each of the group's divisions acted as a strategic business unit for a specific set of products. Products included printers, plotters, magnetic disk and tape drives, terminals, and network products.

The Peripherals Group had set technological standards with many of its products, with innovations such as the disposable print head used in its ink-jet printers and moving-paper plotters. While these innovations contributed to its success, the Peripherals Group was also recognized for its ability to identify and profitably exploit market opportunities, as in the case of its most successful product, the LaserJet printer.

THE RETAIL PRINTER MARKET

Worldwide sales of small workgroup/personal printers in 1990 were about 17 million units, amounting to $10 billion. The market tracked personal computer sales closely; the market was mature in the United States and western Europe but was still developing in eastern Europe and in the Asia-Pacific region. Small workgroup/personal printers were sold almost exclusively through resellers. The reseller channels were changing rapidly, particularly in the United States. Traditionally, printers had been sold through computer dealers, but as personal computers became commodity products, more and more sales were flowing through superstores and consumer mass merchandisers such as Kmart and Price Club.

The retail printer market was composed of three technology segments: impact/dot matrix (40 percent), ink-jet (20 percent), and laser (40 percent). Dot matrix was the oldest technology and was viewed as noisy and of lower print quality compared to the other two types. The dot-matrix printer market share was expected to fall to 10 percent during the next few years as the technology was replaced by either ink-jet or laser printers in all applications except multipart forms and wide-carriage printing. Prior to 1989 most customers were not aware of ink-jet technology. However, customers were discovering that ink-jet print quality was almost as good as laser print quality—and at a much more affordable price. Sales had increased dramatically. In the monochrome market, it remained to be seen which technology would eventually dominate at the low end. Much would depend on the pace at which technology developed in both areas and on the relative costs.

HP and Canon pioneered ink-jet technology separately at their respective corporate laboratories during the early 1980s. The key technological breakthroughs had been ink formulation and the disposable printhead. HP had introduced its first disposable head model, the ThinkJet printer, in the late 1980s, while Canon had just introduced one in 1990.

HP led the ink-jet market in the United States, while Canon led the market in Japan. European competitors included Epson, Mannesmann-Tally, Siemens, and Olivetti, though only Olivetti had introduced a printer with a disposable printhead by 1991. Some dot-matrix printer companies were also starting to offer ink-jet printer products.

Ink-jet printers were rapidly becoming commodity products. The end customer, choosing between two ink-jet printers of equal speed and print quality, increasingly used general business criteria such as cost, reliability, quality, and availability to decide. Product loyalty continued to decrease.

THE VANCOUVER DIVISION AND ITS QUEST FOR ZERO INVENTORY

In 1990 the Vancouver Division's mission statement read: "Our Mission Is to Become the Recognized World Leader in Low-Cost Premium-Quality Printers for Printed Communications by Business Personal Computer Users in Offices and Homes."

The Vancouver Division, located in Vancouver, Washington, was established in 1979. HP saw an opportunity to provide personal printers for the relatively new, fast-growing personal computer market. HP consolidated personal printer activities from four divisions (Fort Collins, Colorado; Boise, Idaho; Sunnyvale, California; and Corvallis, Oregon) to the Vancouver site. The new division became part of HP's Peripherals Group and was chartered with the design and manufacturing of ink-jet printers.

As Bob Foucoult, the production manager and one of Vancouver's first employees, recalled, "Management was pulled from all over HP and plopped down in Vancouver. There was no cohesive staff and no cohesive set of business practices—perhaps that's why we were so open to new ideas."

The manufacturing organization realized early on that a fast, high-volume manufacturing process would be required for success in the printer market. With the current (1979) 8- to 12-week manufacturing cycle time and 3.5 months of inventory, the Vancouver Division would be doomed to fail. They looked within HP for knowledge of high-volume processes, but found none. HP, being an instrument company, only had experience building low-volume, highly customized products using batch processes.

One day in mid-1981 two Vancouver managers happened to take seats on a plane next to two professors: Richard Schoenberger (Nebraska University) and Robert Hall (Indiana University). Schoenberger had just written a rough draft for a paper called "Driving the Productivity Machine" about a manufacturing process being used in Japan: *kanban*. Vancouver's management recognized the promise of this "new" manufacturing concept and Robert Hall recognized an opportunity to have his ideas tested in the United States. They decided to work together.

Within a year Vancouver had converted the factory to stockless production just-in-time (JIT) and had reduced inventory from 3.5 months to 0.9 month, with a drastic reduction in cycle time. Vancouver became a showcase factory for the *kanban* process; between 1982 and 1985 more than 2,000 executives from within and outside HP toured the process. Vancouver impressed visitors by having them sign a raw printed circuit board as they arrived, then presenting them with a finished printer, made with that PC board using the standard process, an hour and a half later.

There was one key element missing, however. As Bob Foucoult puts it, "We were all dressed up but had no one to take us to the dance." Vancouver had not yet introduced a successful, high-volume product that would take full advantage of the advanced production line. Vancouver had introduced products based on HP's latest ink-jet technology but, as with any new technology, they had to gain experience to work the bugs out. The early models had poor resolution and required special paper for printing, resulting in limited success in the marketplace. In 1988 things started to change. Vancouver introduced the DeskJet printer, a new model with near-letter-quality resolution that used standard paper. The introduction was a wild success. Since the manufacturing process had been in place and had been thoroughly exercised, all that was needed was to "flip the switch." HP's knowledge and implementation of the ink-jet technology, combined with its streamlined manufacturing process, gave it the edge needed to become the market leader in the ink-jet printer market.

THE DESKJET SUPPLY CHAIN

The network of suppliers, manufacturing sites, distribution centers (DCs), dealers, and customers for the DeskJet product comprised the DeskJet supply chain (Figure 9-1). Manufacturing was done by HP in Vancouver. There were two key stages in the manufacturing process: (1) printed circuit board assembly and test (PCAT) and (2) final assembly and test (FAT). PCAT involved the assembly and testing of electronic components such as ASICs (application-specific integrated circuits), ROM (read-only memory), and raw printed circuit boards to make logic boards and printhead driver boards for the printers. FAT involved the assembly of other subassemblies such as motors,

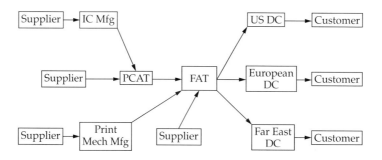

Key: IC Mfg = Integrated circuit manufacturing
PCAT = Printed circuit assembly and test
FAT = Final assembly and test
Print Mech Mfg = Print mechanism manufacturing

FIGURE 9-1 The Vancouver supply chain.

cables, keypads, plastic chassis and "skins," gears, and the printed circuit assemblies from PCAT to produce a working printer, as well as the final testing of the printer. The components needed for PCAT and FAT were sourced from other HP divisions as well as from external suppliers worldwide.

Selling the DeskJet in Europe required customizing the printer to meet the language and power supply requirements of the local countries, a process known as "localization." Specifically, the localization of the DeskJet for different countries involved assembling the appropriate power supply module, which reflected the correct voltage requirements (110 or 220) and power cord terminator (plug), and packaging it with the working printer and a manual written in the appropriate language. The design of the product was such that the assembly of the power supply module had to be done as part of the final assembly and test process, and therefore the localization of the printer was performed at the factory. Hence, the finished products of the factory consisted of printers destined for all of the different countries. These products were then sorted into three groups destined for the three distribution centers: North America, Europe, and Asia-Pacific. Figure 9-2 details the bill of materials and the various options available.

Outgoing products were shipped to the three distribution centers by ocean. In Vancouver, inventories of the components and raw materials were maintained to meet production requirements, but otherwise, no significant buffer inventories between the PCAT and FAT stages were kept. Management had continued to prefer to maintain no finished goods inventory at the factory,

a tradition that was started in 1985 as described in the previous section.

The total factory cycle time through the PCAT and FAT stages was about a week. The transportation time from Vancouver to the U.S. DC, located in San Jose, California, was about a day, whereas it took four to five weeks to ship the printers to Europe and Asia. The long shipment time to the DCs in Europe and Asia was due to ocean transit and the time to clear customs and duties at ports of entry.

The printer industry was highly competitive. Customers of HP's computer products (resellers) wanted to carry as little inventory as possible, yet maintaining a high level of availability to end users (consumers) was critical to them. Consequently there had been increasing pressure for HP as a manufacturer to provide high levels of availability at the DCs for the resellers. In response, management had decided to operate the DCs in a make-to-stock mode in order to provide very high levels of availability to the dealers. Target inventory levels, equal to the forecasted sales plus some safety stock level, were set at the three DCs.

As mentioned earlier, Vancouver prided itself as an almost "stockless" factory. Hence, in contrast to distribution, manufacturing of the DeskJet printer operated in a pull mode. Production plans were set weekly to replenish the DCs "just in time" to maintain the target inventory levels. To ensure material availability, safety stocks were also set up for incoming materials at the factory.

There were three major sources of uncertainty that could affect the supply chain: (1) delivery of incoming

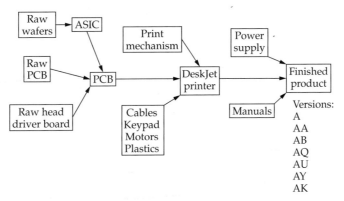

FIGURE 9-2 Bill of material in the Vancouver supply chain.

materials (late shipments, wrong parts, etc.), (2) internal process (process yields and machine downtimes), and (3) demand. The first two sources of uncertainties resulted in delays in the manufacturing lead time to replenish the stocks at the DCs. Demand uncertainties could lead to inventory buildup or back orders at the DCs. Since finished printers were shipped from Vancouver by ocean, the consequence of the long lead time for the European and Asian DCs was that the DC's ability to respond to fluctuations in the demand for the different versions of the product was limited. In order to assure high availability to customers, the European and Asian DCs had to maintain high levels of safety stocks. For the North American DC the situation was simpler; since an overwhelming majority of demand was for the U.S. version of the DeskJet printer, there was little localization-mix fluctuation.

THE DISTRIBUTION PROCESS

At HP, while a typical DC shipped hundreds of different peripheral and computer products, a small number of products accounted for a large share of the unit volume. The DeskJet printer was one of these high-volume products.

The Operations Manager of each regional DC reported to a Worldwide Distribution Manager, who reported directly to HP's Vice President of Marketing, and by dotted line to the Peripherals Group Manager (peripherals made up the bulk of shipments through distribution centers). Each Operations Manager had a staff of six functional managers, representing Finance, MIS, Quality, Marketing, Physical Distribution, and Distribution Services. The first

three functions were similar to their respective functions in a manufacturing organization. Marketing was responsible for interactions with customers. Physical Distribution was responsible for the "physical process," that is, from receiving through shipping. Distribution Services was responsible for planning and procurement.

The major performance measures for a typical DC included line item fill rate (LIFR) and order fill rate (OFR). LIFR was calculated as the total number of customer order line items filled on time divided by the total number of customer line items attempted. (Each time HP tried to pull material for a line item, it was counted as an attempt.) OFR was a similar measure, but was based on orders completed, where an order contains multiple line items. Secondary performance measures included inventory levels and distribution cost per gross shipment dollar. The two major costs were outbound freight and salaries. Freight was charged back to the product lines based on the actual number of pounds of product shipped. In addition, the DC estimated the "percentage of effort" required to support a particular product line and charged that percentage of nonfreight costs back to that product line. The system was somewhat informal, and major negotiations took place between the DCs and the major product lines during the budget-setting process to determine the percentage allocation that was appropriate for each product line.

The DCs had traditionally envisioned their process as a simple, straight-line, standardized process. There were four process steps:

1. Receive (complete) products from various suppliers and stock them.

2. Pick the various products needed to fill a customer order.
3. Shrink-wrap the complete order and label it.
4. Ship the order by the appropriate carrier.

The DeskJet printer fit well into the standard process. In contrast, other products, such as personal computers and monitors, required special processing, called "integration," which included addition of the appropriate keyboard and manual for the destination country. Although this extra processing didn't require much additional labor, it was difficult to accommodate in the standard process and disrupted the material flow. Furthermore, the DCs' materials management systems supported distribution (pass-through processing of "end-items" in the form of individual models and options) and did not support manufacturing (assembly of components into a final product). There were no MRP (material resource planning) nor BOM (bill of materials) explosion systems, and the DCs did not have adequate people trained in component procurement.

There was considerable frustration within the distribution organization regarding the support of assembly processes. In general, top management stressed the DC's role as a warehouse and the need to continue to "do what they were best at—distribution." Tom Beal, the U.S. DC materials manager, expressed the general concern when he said, "We have to decide what our core competency is and what value we add. We need to decide whether we are in the business of warehousing or integration, then adopt strategies to support our business. If we want to take on manufacturing processes (here), we have to put processes in place to support them."

THE INVENTORY AND SERVICE CRISIS

To limit the amount of inventory throughout the DeskJet supply chain and at the same time provide the high level of service needed had been quite a challenge to Vancouver's management. The manufacturing group in Vancouver had worked hard on supplier management to reduce the uncertainties caused by delivery variabilities of incoming materials, on improving process yields, and on reducing downtimes at the plant. The progress made had been admirable. However, improvement of forecast accuracy remained a formidable task.

The magnitude of forecast errors were especially alarming in Europe. It was becoming quite common to have product shortages for model demands from some countries, while inventory of some other models kept piling up. In the past, the target inventory levels at the DCs were based on safety stocks that were a result of some judgmental rule of thumb. It seemed like the increasing difficulty of getting accurate forecasts meant that the safety stock rules would have to be revisited.

David Arkadia had solicited the help of a young inventory expert from corporate HP, Dr. Billy Corrington, to help him put in place a scientifically based safety stock system that would be responsive to forecast errors and replenishment lead times. Billy had formed a team consisting of Laura Rock, an industrial engineer, Jim Bailey, the planning supervisor, and José Fernandez, the purchasing supervisor from Vancouver, to overhaul the safety stock management system. They were to recommend a method for calculating appropriate safety stock levels for the various models and options at the three DCs. Gathering appropriate data turned out to be a task that the team spent a lot of time at. They now felt that they had a good sample of demand data (see Table 9-1) and were developing the safety stock methodology. Brent was hoping that this new methodology would solve the inventory and service problem. It would be nice if he could tell his management that all this inventory and service mess was due to their lack of a sound safety stock methodology, and Billy's expertise would then be their savior.

One issue that continually came up was the choice of inventory carrying cost to be used in safety stock analyses. Estimates within the company ranged from 12 percent (HP's cost of debt plus some warehousing expenses) to 60 percent (based on the return on investment [ROI] expected of new product development projects). Another issue was the choice of target line item fill rate to be used. The company target was 98 percent, a number that had been "developed" by marketing.

As faxes and phone calls about the worsening situation at the European DC kept pouring in, Brent also began receiving other suggestions from his colleagues that were more aggressive in nature. Talks about Vancouver's setting up a sister plant in Europe had surfaced. Would the volume in Europe be large enough to justify such a site? Where should it be located? Brent knew that the European sales and

TABLE 9-1

SOME SAMPLE DESKJET DEMAND DATA: EUROPE

Option	Nov.	Dec.	Jan.	Feb.	Mar.	Apr.	May	June	July	Aug.	Sept.	Oct.
A	80	0	60	90	21	48	0	9	20	54	84	42
AA	400	255	408	645	210	87	432	816	430	630	456	273
AB	20,572	20,895	19,252	11,052	19,864	20,316	13,336	10,578	6,096	14,496	23,712	9,792
AQ	4,008	2,196	4,761	1,953	1,008	2,358	1,676	540	2,310	2,046	1,797	2,961
AU	4,564	3,207	7,485	4,908	5,295	90	0	5,004	4,385	5,103	4,302	6,153
AY	248	450	378	306	219	204	248	484	164	384	384	234
Total	29,872	27,003	32,344	18,954	26,617	23,103	15,692	17,431	13,405	22,692	30,735	19,455

marketing folks would like such an idea. He also liked the idea of having a European plant to take care of the inventory and service problem in Europe. Maybe that would put a halt to his recent loss of sleep.

There was certainly a group that advocated more and more inventory. It was simple logic, according to them. "When it comes down to real dollars, inventory costs do not enter into the P&L statements, but lost sales hurt our revenues. Don't talk to us about inventory–service trade-offs. Period."

Kay Johnson, the Traffic Department supervisor, had long suggested the use of air shipment to transport the printers to Europe. "Shortening the lead time means faster reaction time to unexpected changes in product mix. That should mean lower inventory and higher product availability. I tell you, air freight is expensive, but it is worth it."

Brent recalled his conversation at lunch with a summer intern from Stanford University. The enthusiastic student was lecturing Brent that he should always try to tackle the "root of the problem." Going to the root of the problem, according to the intern, is what the professors taught at school, and was also what a number of quality gurus preached. "The root of the problem is that you have a horrible forecasting system. There is no easy way out. You've got to invest in getting the system fixed. Now, I know this marketing professor at Stanford who could help you. Have you ever heard of the Box-Jenkins method?" Brent also remembered how he lost his appetite at that lunch, as he was listening to the student who was so eager to volunteer his advice.

WHAT NEXT?

Brent reviewed his schedule for the day. At 11:00 he planned to meet with Billy, Laura, Jim, and José to review the recommended inventory levels they had calculated using the safety stock model. He was somewhat concerned about what level of change the model would recommend. If it suggested small changes, management might not feel the model was useful, but if it suggested large changes, they might not accept it either.

After lunch he would meet briefly with the materials and manufacturing managers to review the results and sketch out their recommendations. At 2:00 he would talk with the U.S. DC materials manager by phone. That night he could reach Singapore and Saturday morning he could reach Germany. Hopefully he could get buyoff from everyone.

He wondered, too, if there wasn't some other approach that he should be considering. He knew that whatever numbers he came up with would be too high.

By the end of this chapter, you should be able to answer the following questions:

- How can design for logistics concepts be used to control logistics costs and make the supply chain more efficient?
- What is delayed differentiation and how can Hewlett-Packard use delayed differentiation to address the problems described in the case above? How can the advantages of delayed differentiation be quantified?

- When should suppliers be involved in the new product development process?
- What is mass customization? Does supply chain management play a role in the development of an effective mass customization strategy?

For many years manufacturing engineering was the last stop in the product engineering process. The researchers and design engineers worked on developing a product that worked, and perhaps one that used materials as inexpensively as possible. Then manufacturing engineers were charged with determining how to make this design efficiently. In the 1980s this paradigm began to change. Management began to realize that product and process design were key product cost drivers, and that taking the manufacturing process into account early in the design process was the only way to make the manufacturing process efficient. Thus, the concept of design for manufacturing (DFM) was born.

Recently, a similar transformation has begun in the area of supply chain management. We have discussed appropriate strategies for supply chain design and operation, assuming that *product design decisions were already made* by the time the supply chain is designed. Designing the supply chain, we have assumed, involves determining the best way to supply existing products using existing manufacturing processes. In the last few years, however, managers have started to realize that by taking supply chain concerns into account in the product and process design phase, it becomes possible to operate a much more efficient supply chain. Obviously, this is analogous to the design for manufacturing (DFM) practice of taking manufacturing into account during the product design phase. In the following sections, we discuss various approaches that leverage product design in order to manage the supply chain more effectively.

In the next section, we discuss a series of concepts introduced by Professor Hau Lee [92] and known collectively as design for logistics (DFL). These concepts suggest product and process design approaches that help to control logistics costs and increase customer service levels.

Following that, we discuss the advantages of including suppliers in the product design process. This discussion is based on an extensive report issued by The Global Procurement and Supply Chain Benchmarking Initiative at Michigan State University, which is titled *Executive Summary: Supplier Integration into New Product Development: A Strategy for Competitive Advantage.*

Finally, we discuss the concept of mass customization, developed by Joseph Pine II with several coauthors. In particular, we focus on the ways in which advanced logistics and supply chain practices help to enable this exciting new business model.

9.1 DESIGN FOR LOGISTICS

9.1.1 Overview

Transportation and inventory costs, as we have seen, are often critical supply chain cost drivers, particularly when inventory levels must be kept fairly high to ensure high service levels. These are exactly the issues that DFL addresses, using the following three key components [92]:

- Economic packaging and transportation.
- Concurrent and parallel processing.
- Standardization.

Each of these components addresses the issue of inventory or transportation costs and service levels in complementary ways. They are discussed in detail in the following subsections.

9.1.2 Economic Packaging and Transportation

Of the various DFL concepts, perhaps the most obvious involves designing products so that they can be efficiently packed and stored. Products that can be packed more compactly are cheaper to transport, particularly if delivery trucks "cube out" before they "weigh out." In other words, if the space taken up by a product and not its weight constrains how much can fit in a delivery vehicle, products that can be stored more compactly can be transported less expensively.

EXAMPLE 9-1

Swedish furniture retailer Ikea, with $9.6 billion in sales, is the world's largest furniture retailer. Started in Sweden by Ingvar Kamprad, Ikea currently has 143 stores in 35 countries [77]. It has grown so dramatically by "reinventing the furniture business" [101]. Traditionally, furniture sales were split between department stores and small, locally owned shops. Typically, customers would place an order, and delivery could take place up to two months after the order was placed.

Ikea changed that formula by displaying all of its 10,000 products in large warehouselike spaces in out-of-town stores and keeping all of these items in the warehouse. This was accomplished by designing products so that they can be packed compactly and efficiently in kits, which customers take from the stores and assemble at home. These kits are easy and cheap to transport, so products can be manufactured efficiently in a small number of factories and then shipped relatively cheaply to stores all over the world. Since Ikea has so many stores, each of which is very large, the company is able to take advantage of vast economies of scale. This has enabled the firm to sell good-quality furniture at prices lower than that of its competitors [101].

Ikea continues to work toward improved design and packaging to continue its dramatic growth—"recently the company figured out how to shave one-third off the width of bookcase packing boxes by making the back panels a separate assembly piece" [121].

There are other reasons to design products to pack compactly. For example, many major retailers favor products that take up less storage space and stack easily. Efficient storage reduces certain components of inventory cost because handling costs typically decrease, space per product (and thus rent per product) decreases, and revenue per square foot can increase. For example, many of the large plastic items available in discount stores, such as garbage pails, are designed to stack, so that they take up less shelf (or floor) space in the store. Thus, while it might not be enough to design packaging efficiently after the product design is completed, it may be valuable to redesign the product itself in order to take these issues into account.

EXAMPLE 9-2

Recently Rubbermaid won several design awards from *Business Week* magazine. When describing why the Clear Classics food storage containers won an award, the writers mention that "Wal-Mart loves products designed to fit 14-by-14-inch shelves," which is one of the reasons these products were so successful. In addition, when describing the children's Icy Rider sled designed by Rubbermaid (which also won the award), the writers state, "Of course, not all products sold in Wal-Mart can fit into 14-by-14 shelving. But if designers create them to stack and save space, they have a shot of selling to Wal-Mart . . . After researching Wal-Mart's needs, Rubbermaid made the Icy Rider thin and stackable" [116].

Similarly, it is often possible to ship goods in bulk and only complete final packaging at the warehouse or even at the retailer. This may save on transportation costs because bulk goods tend to be shipped more efficiently.

EXAMPLE 9-3

The Hawaiian sugar industry switched over to bulk transportation after World War II, when costs began to increase. They estimate that the cost of transporting a bulk ton of sugar is about $0.77 today, whereas the cost of transporting the same quantity of sugar in bags would be about $20.00 [38].

In some cases, final packaging can even be delayed until the goods are actually sold. For example, many grocery stores now sell flour, cereal, and many other goods in bulk, allowing consumers to package as much as they want.

Recall that cross-docking (see Chapter 3) involves moving goods from one truck (e.g., from the supplier) to another set of trucks (e.g., perhaps going to individual retail stores). In some cases, boxes or pallets are taken off an incoming truck and moved directly to an outgoing one. However, it is often necessary to repackage some of the products. In many cases, bulk pallets of single items come in from suppliers, but mixed pallets with many different items have to go out to individual retailers. In this case, goods must be repacked at the cross-dock point, so more identification or labeling also might be needed if packages are broken up [138]. In general, packaging and products that are designed to facilitate this type of cross-docking operation by making repacking easier will clearly help to lower logistics costs.

9.1.3 Concurrent and Parallel Processing

In the previous section, we focused on simple ways that redesign of the product and packaging could help control logistics costs. In this subsection, we will focus on modifying the manufacturing *process*—which may also require modification of the product design.

We have seen that many difficulties in operating supply chains are due to long manufacturing lead times. Most manufacturing processes consist of manufacturing steps performed in sequence. The requirements of short start-up times and ever-shorter product life cycles often dictate that certain manufacturing steps be performed in different locations to take advantage of existing equipment or expertise. *Concurrent and parallel processing* involves modifying the manufacturing process so that steps that were previously performed in a sequence can be completed at the same time. This obviously helps reduce manufacturing lead time, lower inventory costs through improved forecasting, and reduce safety stock requirements, among other benefits.

A key to keeping the manufacturing process parallel is the concept of decoupling. If many of the components of the product can be decoupled, or physically separated, during manufacturing, it is possible that these components can be manufactured in parallel. If manufacturing each of the individual components takes the same amount of time in the newly decoupled design, but the manufacturing steps are performed in parallel, lead time will decrease. Even if some of these modular components take slightly more time to manufacture, the overall lead time may still decrease since various components are being manufactured in parallel. An added advantage of this manufacturing strategy of decoupling is that it may be possible to design different inventory strategies for the various decoupled components. If the supply of raw materials or manufacturing yield is uncertain for a particular component, a higher inventory level can be held of that single component, rather than for the entire end product.

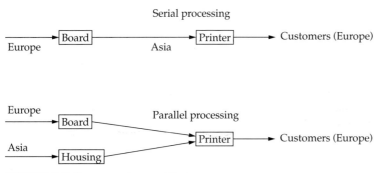

FIGURE 9-3 Concurrent processing.

A European manufacturer produces network printers for the European market in alliance with a manufacturer in the Far East. The main printer PC board is designed and assembled in Europe. It is then shipped to Asia, where it is integrated with the main printer housing in a process that involves building the printer, including the motor, printhead, housing, and so forth, around the board. The finished product is then shipped to Europe. The manufacturer is concerned with the long production and transportation lead times, which make it essential to maintain a large safety stock in Europe. However, much of the long manufacturing lead time is due to the sequential manufacturing process.

Redesigning the printer manufacturing process and product so that the board can be integrated with the rest of the printer at the end of the manufacturing process will decrease lead times by allowing parallel manufacturing in Europe and the Far East. In addition, moving final assembly to Europe can serve to further increase responsiveness and decrease lead times. The two manufacturing processes are diagrammed in Figure 9-3 [92].

9.1.4 Standardization

As we have discussed above, it is possible in some cases to shorten lead times (e.g., by taking advantage of parallel processing) in order to reduce inventory levels and increase forecast accuracy. Sometimes, however, it is impossible to reduce the lead time beyond a certain point. In these cases, it may be possible to achieve the same objectives by taking advantage of standardization.

Recall the third principle of forecasting described in Chapter 3: aggregate demand information is always more accurate than disaggregate data. Thus, we can better forecast demand for a continent than a country or for a product family (e.g., ski jackets) than a specific product (or style). Unfortunately, in a traditional manufacturing environment, aggregate forecasts are not of much use—the manufacturing manager has to know exactly what needs to be made before starting the process. However, by effectively using standardization, it may be possible to make effective use of the information in aggregate forecasts. Specifically, approaches based on product and process commonality make it possible to delay decisions about which specific product will be manufactured until after some of the manufacturing or purchasing decisions have been made. Thus, these decisions can be made on an aggregate level, using the more accurate aggregate forecasts.

Professor Jayashankar Swaminathan has developed a wide-ranging framework for effective implementation of standardization through the use of the correct operational strategy [149]. Swaminathan suggests that product modularity and process modularity are the key drivers that enable a standardization strategy that lowers inventory costs and increases forecast accuracy.

Following Swaminathan, we define the following concepts:

A modular product is a product assembled from a variety of modules such that for each module there are a number of options. The classic example of a modular product is the personal computer, which can be customized by combining different video cards, hard drives, memory chips, and so forth. Recall that this concept of modularity is also important for the implementation of *concurrent and parallel processing*, which was described in the previous subsection.

A modular process is a manufacturing process consisting of discrete operations, so that inventory can be stored in partially manufactured form between operations. Products are differentiated by completing a different subset of operations during the manufacturing process. Observe that modular products are not necessarily made of modular processes, as it may not be possible to store intermediate, or semifinished, inventories.

Swaminathan identifies four different approaches to standardization:

- Part standardization
- Process standardization
- Product standardization
- Procurement standardization

In **part standardization**, common parts are used across many products. Common parts reduce required part inventories due to risk pooling and reduce part costs due to economies of scale. Of course, excessive part commonality can reduce product differentiation, so that less expensive customization options might cannibalize sales of more expensive parts. Sometimes, it is necessary to redesign product lines or families to achieve commonality.

Process standardization involves standardizing as much of the process as possible for different products, and then customizing the products as late as possible. In this case, products and manufacturing processes are designed so that decisions about which specific product is manufactured—differentiation—can be delayed until after manufacturing is under way. The manufacturing process starts by making a *generic* or *family* product that is later differentiated into a specific end-product. For this reason, this approach is also known as *postponement* or *delayed product differentiation* [92]. By delaying differentiation, production starts can be based on aggregate forecasts. Thus, design for delayed product differentiation can be effectively used to address the uncertainty in final demand even if forecasts cannot be improved.

It is usually necessary to redesign products specifically for delayed differentiation. For example, it may be necessary to resequence the manufacturing process to take advantage of process standardization. *Resequencing* refers to modifying the order of product manufacturing steps so that those operations that result in the differentiation of specific items or products are postponed as much as possible. One famous and dramatic example of a firm utilizing resequencing to improve its supply chain operation is Benetton Corporation.

EXAMPLE 9-5

Benetton is a major supplier of knitwear, at one point (in 1982) the largest consumer of wool in the world, supplying hundreds of shops. The nature of the fashion industry is that consumer preferences change rapidly. However, because of the long manufacturing lead time, store owners frequently had to place orders for wool sweaters up to seven months in advance before the sweaters would appear in

---

Example 9-5 *Continued*

their stores. The wool sweater manufacturing process typically consists of acquiring yarn, dyeing it, finishing it, manufacturing the garment parts, and then joining those parts into a completed sweater. Unfortunately, this left little flexibility to respond to the changing tastes of consumers.

To address this issue, Benetton revised the manufacturing process, postponing the dyeing of the garments until *after* the sweater was completely assembled. Thus, color choices could be delayed until after more forecasting and sales information were received. Hence, because of the postponement of the dyeing process, yarn purchasing and manufacturing plans could be based on aggregate forecasts for product families, rather than forecasts for specific sweater/color combinations. This revised process made sweater manufacturing about 10 percent more expensive and required the purchasing of new equipment and the retraining of employees. However, Benetton was more than adequately compensated by improved forecasts, lower surplus inventories, and, in many cases, higher sales [142].

A U.S. disk drive manufacturer provides another notable example. Notice in this example that although lower levels of inventory need to be held to achieve specific service levels, the per unit inventory cost tends to be more expensive.

EXAMPLE 9-6

A major U.S. manufacturer of mass storage devices makes different unique hard-drive products for each of a variety of customers. Orders are placed to be delivered by a certain time and, since lead times are very long, the manufacturer has to keep a variety of products in process in order to meet promised delivery dates. Since variability of demand is high and each product is unique, the manufacturer has to maintain high levels of in-process inventory to meet demand reliably.

The manufacturing process involves a brief generic segment, through which products intended for all customers must go, and then an extensive customization portion. Clearly, the ideal point to hold inventory is before customization begins. Unfortunately, however, the majority of manufacturing time, due particularly to time-consuming testing, occurs after differentiation has started. This testing has to take place after differentiation starts because a particular circuit board has to be added to the assembly for the testing to take place, and this circuit board is different for each customer.

In order to delay differentiation, it is possible to insert a generic circuit board into the assembly, complete much of the testing, remove the generic circuit board, and add the customer-specific boards later. In this way, disk drive differentiation can be delayed until more order information is available. Clearly, this will decrease the level of required in-process inventory needed to meet demand reliably. However, this will add some additional manufacturing steps. In particular, the generic board has to be added and removed. Thus, it is necessary to compare the manufacturing inefficiencies caused by adding and removing this circuit board with the gains in inventory savings. The manufacturing processes are illustrated in Figure 9-4 [92].

FIGURE 9-4 Delaying differentiation.

Part and process standardization are frequently connected. Sometimes part standardization is necessary for implementing process standardization.

A major printer manufacturer was preparing to introduce a new color printer into the market. Demand for the new printer and an existing printer was expected to be highly variable and negatively correlated. The manufacturing processes for the two products were similar, except that different circuit boards and printhead assemblies were used. Differences in head assemblies and circuit boards led to very different manufacturing processes. To implement process standardization, that is, delayed differentiation, it is necessary to ensure that the manufacturing processes are similar until the final step. To do this, the printers have been redesigned so that both products share a common circuit board and printhead. This ensures that differentiation can be delayed as much as possible. Thus, part standardization enables process standardization in this case [92].

In some cases, the concepts of resequencing and commonality allow the final manufacturing steps to be completed at distribution centers (DCs) or warehouses instead of at the factory. One of the advantages of this approach is that if DCs are much closer to the demand than the factories, products can be differentiated closer to the demand, thus increasing the firm's ability to respond to rapidly changing markets. This is one of the approaches we will discuss in more detail in Section 9.1.8, when we analyze the case from the beginning of this chapter.

Sometimes, processes can be redesigned so that the differentiating steps don't have to be performed in a manufacturing facility or distribution center at all, but can take place in the retailer after the sale is made. Often this is accomplished by focusing on modularity during the design phase, placing functionality in *modules* that can be easily added to a product. For example, some printers are sold in generic Macintosh/PC versions. Along with the printer, each retail store stocks separately packaged modules that differentiate the product for the Mac or PC. Obviously, this can greatly lower required inventory since only modules have to be stocked in Mac and PC versions, instead of entire printers. Similarly, many color ink-jet printers are black-and-white printers with added "color kits."

In **product standardization**, a large variety of products may be offered, but only a few kept in inventory. When a product not kept in stock is ordered, the order may be filled by a product that offers a superset of the features required by a customer. This process, known as *downward substitution*, is common in many industries. For example, in the semiconductor industry, it is quite common to sell a higher-speed or a higher-functionality chip as a lower-speed/functionality chip when the low-end chip is out of stock. Similarly, car rental agencies and hotels frequently fill reservations with higher-end vehicles or rooms when the lower-end vehicles or rooms are not available.

Sometimes, it may be possible to redesign products so that one product can be adjusted to meet several end-customer requirements. For example, as we have seen previously, many products are similar, except that power supplies have to be different for different markets. Instead of manufacturing two versions of a product, however, manufacturers can utilize a standardized product, with a switchable power supply. We discuss this issue further in the case at the end of this chapter.

Finally, **procurement standardization** involves standardizing processing equipment and approaches, even when the product itself is not standardized. This is particularly valuable when processing equipment is very expensive. In the production of application specific integrated circuits (ASICs), for example, very expensive equipment is required. Although end-products are highly customized and demand is

TABLE 9-2

OPERATIONAL STRATEGIES FOR STANDARDIZATION

		Process	
		Nonmodular	Modular
Product	Modular	Part standardization	Process standardization
	Nonmodular	Product standardization	Procurement standardization

unpredictable, the same equipment is used to produce each of the possible end-products. Thus, equipment procurement can be managed independent of the final demand.

9.1.5 Selecting a Standardization Strategy

To help with the selection of the appropriate standardization strategy, Swaminathan [149] proposed a framework based on the observation that the firm's choice of standardization strategy is a function of the firm's ability to modularize its products and processes. Table 9-2 illustrates the proposed strategic choices under different conditions.

- If process and product are modular, process standardization will help to maximize effective forecast accuracy and minimize inventory costs.
- If the product is modular, but the process is not, it is not possible to delay differentiation. However, part standardization is likely to be effective.
- If the process is modular but the product is not, procurement standardization may decrease equipment expenses.
- If neither the process nor the product is modular, some benefits may still result from focusing on product standardization.

9.1.6 Important Considerations

The various strategies described above are designed to deal with inaccurate forecasts and product variety; frequently, it may not be possible or cost-effective to implement these strategies in the context of a particular product or a specific supply chain. Even if implementing a particular strategy is theoretically possible, in many cases the expenses resulting from product and packaging redesign will exceed the savings under the new system. In addition, capital expenditures are likely to be required to retool assembly lines. Sometimes, as we discussed above, it may even be necessary to add manufacturing capability at distribution centers. Typically, the value of these types of changes is higher at the start of the product life cycle, when expenditures can be amortized over the entire life of the product. It is possible that DFL initiatives that make a great deal of sense at the start of the product life cycle don't pay for themselves when implemented later [92].

It may also be more expensive to manufacture a product with a new process. In many of the examples mentioned above, the products and manufacturing processes became more expensive. It is therefore necessary to estimate the savings produced by a more effectively designed product or process, and compare these savings to the increased cost of manufacturing. Many of the benefits of implementing such a system are very difficult to quantify; increased flexibility, more efficient customer service, and decreased market response times may be hard to place a value on, which only serves to make the analysis more difficult. To add to the difficulty, engineers are often forced to take a broader perspective than they have been trained to take when they are making these kinds of decisions.

To add to these complications, process modifications such as resequencing will cause the level of inventory in many cases to go down, but the per unit value of inventory being held will be higher. In the sweater example, it may be possible to hold less wool in inventory because it doesn't have to be dyed before it is assembled. However, much of this wool will be held in the form of sweaters, which have a higher value than dyed wool.

Of course, if manufacturing or customizing steps are postponed, the generic products may have a lower value than customized products, so value is added later in the supply chain than it would be otherwise.

Finally, in some cases tariffs and duties are lower for semifinished or nonconfigured goods than for final products [92]. Thus, implementing a strategy of completing the manufacturing process in a local distribution center may help to lower costs associated with tariffs and duties.

All of these issues have to be taken into consideration when implementing a specific design for logistics strategy. Nevertheless, it is clear that in many cases, DFL can help to improve customer service and greatly reduce the costs of operating the supply chain.

9.1.7 The Push–Pull Boundary

Recall our discussion of the push–pull boundary in Chapter 5. In push-based systems, production decisions are based on long-term forecasts, while in pull-based supply chains, production is demand driven. We listed many advantages of pull-based systems and concluded that compared to push-based systems, pull-based systems typically lead to a reduction in supply chain lead times, inventory levels, and system costs, while simultaneously making it easier to manage system resources.

Unfortunately, it is not always practical to implement a pull-based system throughout the entire supply chain. Lead times may be too long, or it may be necessary to take advantage of economies of scale in production or transportation. The standardization strategies we have been discussing in this section can be viewed as a method to combine push and pull systems within a single supply chain into what we called, in Chapter 5, a push–pull system. Indeed, that portion of the supply chain prior to product differentiation is typically a push-based supply chain. That is, the undifferentiated product is built and transported based on long-term forecasts. In contrast, differentiation occurs as a response to market demand. Thus, the portion of the supply chain starting from the time of differentiation is a pull-based supply chain.

For instance, in the Benetton example, Example 9-5, uncolored sweaters are made to forecast, but dyeing takes place as a reaction to customer demand. We call the point of differentiation the **push–pull boundary**, since this is the point where the system changes from a push-based system to a pull-based system.

One way to view the push–pull boundary concept is through the third rule of inventory management discussed in Chapter 3. Since aggregate demand information is more accurate than disaggregate data, the push portion of the supply chain includes only activities and decisions made prior to product differentiation. These activities and decisions are based on aggregate demand data.

Clearly, then, an additional advantage of postponement is that it allows firms to realize many of the advantages of pull-based systems, while at the same time allowing for the economies of scale inherent in push-based systems. Often, when implementing a standardization strategy, if there is more than one possible differentiation point, it may be useful to think in terms of locating the push–pull boundary in order to achieve a balance between the advantages of the push- and the pull-based systems.

9.1.8 Case Analysis

Consider the Hewlett-Packard case that you read at the beginning of this chapter. Although several problems and issues are outlined in the case, we will focus on analyzing the inventory problems in the European distribution center. In particular, HP faces long delivery lead times of about four to five weeks from its production facility in Vancouver, Washington, to Europe. The Vancouver plant is a high-speed, high-volume facility where manufacturing takes about a week.

In particular, HP is concerned with high inventory levels and inventory imbalance in Europe. One of the characteristics of the DeskJet product line is that it is customized for local markets, a process called *localization*. This involves adding labeling and documentation in the correct language and customizing the power supply for the correct voltage level and plug. Customization is done in Vancouver many weeks before the products arrive in Europe. Furthermore, once the printers arrive in Europe, inventory imbalance might occur in the following sense: The European DC often finds itself with too much inventory of printers customized for certain markets, and not enough inventory of printers customized for others.

What are the causes of these problems? Based on the case and material we have discussed in previous chapters, the following issues are clear:

- There is significant uncertainty about how to set the correct inventory level.
- The many different localization options make inventory difficult to manage.
- Long lead times lead to difficulty in forecasting and high safety stocks.
- Uncertainty in the many local markets makes forecasting difficult.
- Maintaining cooperation between the various HP divisions is challenging.

In the short term, the first issue can be addressed by rationalizing safety stock utilizing the methods we discussed in Chapter 3. To address these problems in the longer term, the following solutions have been proposed:

- Switch to air shipments of printers from Vancouver.
- Build a European factory.
- Hold more inventory at the European DC.
- Improve forecasting practices.

Unfortunately, there are significant problems with each of these suggestions. Air shipments are prohibitively expensive in this competitive, low-margin business. European volumes are not sufficient to justify building a new factory. Inventory is already a problem; more would simply magnify the problem. Finally, it is unclear how to improve forecasts.

Thus, HP management is motivated to consider another option: process standardization or *postponement*. Specifically, this option involves shipping "unlocalized" printers to the European DC and localizing them after observing local demand. The question is, what are the inventory savings of such a strategy? To address this issue, we utilize the inventory management policies detailed in Chapter 3.

Recall that we can calculate required safety stock for each of the customized products by noting that safety stock must equal $z \times STD \times \sqrt{L}$, where z is selected to maintain the required service level (see Table 3-2). In the analysis below, we assume that lead time is five weeks, and we require a 98 percent service level. By dividing this quantity by average demand, we determine the number of weeks of safety stock required. Thus, the first six rows of Table 9-3 contain the results of these calculations for each of the customization options specified in Table 9-1. The second-to-last row totals all of

TABLE 9-3

INVENTORY ANALYSIS

Parameter	Average monthly demand	Standard deviation of monthly demand	Average weekly demand	Standard deviation of weekly demand	Safety stock	Weeks of safety stock
A	42.3	32.4	9.8	15.6	71.5	7.4
AA	420.2	203.9	97.7	98.3	450.6	4.6
AB	15,830.1	5,624.6	3,681.4	2,712.4	12,433.5	3.4
AQ	2,301.2	1,168.5	535.1	563.5	2,583.0	4.8
AU	4,208.0	2,204.6	978.6	1,063.2	4,873.6	5.0
AY	306.8	103.1	71.3	49.7	227.8	3.2
Total	23,108.6		5,373.9		20,640.0	3.8
Generic	23,108.6	6,244	5,373.9	3,011.1	13,802.6	2.6

the required safety stock. We see that by utilizing effective inventory management strategies and the current distribution system, HP needs over three-and-a-half weeks of safety stock on hand to meet the 98 percent service level requirement.

The table also shows the effect of postponing localization until after demand is observed. In this case, the DC keeps safety stock of only the generic printer, customizing the printers as demand is realized. This allows the DC to focus on aggregate demand levels and, therefore, as we saw in the section on risk pooling in Chapter 3, aggregate demand has a much smaller standard deviation than individual demand. The standard deviation of the aggregate demand is calculated in the last row of the table. This new standard deviation is used to determine safety stock for the generic model. Observe that this new system, in which localization is postponed, requires less safety stock than the currently existing system.

The dollar savings in inventory carrying cost obviously depend on the rate of carrying cost used. For example, if carrying cost is taken to be 30 percent and a product value of $400 is assumed, annual savings are about $800,000. In addition, there are other benefits to implementing a postponement strategy. These include

- The value of inventory in transit, and thus insurance costs, goes down.
- It may be possible to reduce freight handling costs.
- Some of the localization materials can be locally sourced, reducing costs and meeting "local content" requirements.

On the other hand, there are costs associated with implementing this process standardization strategy. First, the product and packaging have to be redesigned so that localization can be delayed. This entails expense and requires research-and-development work on a product that is already working well. Also, the European distribution center has to be modified to facilitate localization there. Recall that in addition to capital investments, the mind-set of the distribution operation—"Distribution, not manufacturing, is our core competency"—has to be changed.

Hewlett-Packard did indeed implement such a strategy, with great success. Inventory declined while service levels rose, leading to significant cost savings and increased profitability. To achieve these results, the printer was redesigned for localization and the distribution center took on more work and responsibilities.

9.2 SUPPLIER INTEGRATION INTO NEW PRODUCT DEVELOPMENT

Another key supply chain issue involves the selection of appropriate suppliers for components of the new product. Traditionally, this has been done after design and manufacturing engineers have determined the final design for a product. Recently, a study in *The Global Procurement and Supply Chain Benchmarking Initiative*, Michigan State University [111], found that firms often realize tremendous benefits from involving suppliers in the design process. Benefits include a decline in purchased material costs, an increase in purchased material quality, a decline in development time and cost and in manufacturing cost, and an increase in final product technology levels.

In addition to the competitive forces that drive managers to seek out all types of supply chain efficiencies, several competitive forces are specifically encouraging managers to find opportunities to work with suppliers during the product design process. These forces include the continuing focus on strategies that encourage companies to focus on their core competencies and outsource other business capabilities, and to continually reduce the length of product life cycles. Both of these forces encourage companies to develop processes that make the design process more efficient. Taking advantage of supplier competencies is certainly one way to do this.

9.2.1 The Spectrum of Supplier Integration

The supplier integration study [111] notes that there is no single "appropriate level" of supplier integration. Instead, they develop the notion of a *spectrum of supplier integration*. In particular, they identify a series of steps from least to most supplier responsibility as follows:

None. The supplier is not involved in design. Materials and subassemblies are supplied according to customer specifications and design.

White box. This level of integration is informal. The buyer "consults" with the supplier informally when designing products and specifications, although there is no formal collaboration.

Grey box. This represents formal supplier integration. Collaborative teams are formed between the buyer's and the supplier's engineers, and joint development occurs.

Black box. The buyer gives the supplier a set of interface requirements and the supplier independently designs and develops the required component.

Of course, just because the black-box approach is at one end of the continuum doesn't mean that it is the best approach in all cases. Instead, firms must develop a strategy that helps them determine the appropriate level of supplier integration for different situations.

The Global Procurement and Supply Chain Benchmarking Initiative has developed a strategic planning process to help firms make this determination [111]. The first several steps of the process are summarized below:

- Determine internal core competencies.
- Determine current and future new product developments.
- Identify external development and manufacturing needs.

These three steps help management determine what is going to be procured from suppliers and what level of supplier expertise is appropriate. If future products have components that require expertise that the firm does not possess, and development of these components can be separated from other phases of product development, then taking a black-box approach makes sense. If this separation is not possible, then it makes more sense to use the grey-box development. If the buyer has some design expertise but wants to ensure that the supplier can adequately manufacture the component, perhaps a white-box approach is appropriate.

9.2.2 Keys to Effective Supplier Integration

Simply selecting an appropriate level of supplier integration is not sufficient. Much work goes into ensuring that the relationship is a success. The next steps of the strategic planning process [111] help to ensure this success:

- Select suppliers and build relationships with them.
- Align objectives with selected suppliers.

Selecting suppliers in general involves various considerations, such as manufacturing capacity and response time. Since supplier integration partners typically supply components (in addition to cooperating in their design), all of the traditional considerations still apply. In addition, the special nature of supplier integration presents an additional set of supplier requirements.

The same study identifies many of these, including

- The capability to participate in the design process.
- The willingness to participate in the design process, including the ability to reach agreements on intellectual property and confidentiality issues.
- The ability to commit sufficient personnel and time to the process. This may include colocating personnel if appropriate.
- Sufficient resources to commit to the supplier integration process.

Of course, the relative importance of these requirements depends on the particular project and type of integration. Once suppliers are identified, it is critical to work on building relationships with them. For example, firms have found it useful to involve suppliers early in the design process. Companies that do so report greater gains than those that involve suppliers only after design concepts have been generated.

Sharing future plans and technologies with suppliers helps to build this relationship, as does a joint continuous improvement goal. Separate organizational groups dedicated to managing the relationship are also useful. In all of these cases, the goals of the purchasing firm revolve around building long-term, effective relationships with trusted suppliers. These will naturally lead to the alignment of buyer and supplier objectives, which will result in more effective integration.

9.2.3 A "Bookshelf" of Technologies and Suppliers

The Michigan State group also developed the idea of a "bookshelf" of technologies and suppliers within the context of supplier integration. This involves monitoring the development of relevant new technologies and following the suppliers that have demonstrated expertise in these technologies. Then, when appropriate, a buyer firm can quickly introduce these technologies into new products by integrating the supplier design team with its own. This enables a firm to balance the advantages and disadvantages of being on the cutting edge of new technology. On one hand, there is no need to use the technology immediately in order to gain experience with it: suppliers are developing this knowledge with other customers. On the other hand, the danger of being slow to introduce cutting-edge technology and concepts is lessened. The bookshelf concept is a dramatic example of the power of supplier integration.

9.3 MASS CUSTOMIZATION

9.3.1 What Is Mass Customization?

In his book *Mass Customization* [124], Joseph Pine II introduced a concept that is becoming important to more and more businesses: *mass customization*. In this section, we will first review the concept and then discuss how logistics and supply chain networks play an important role in the implementation of related ideas.

Mass customization has evolved from the two prevailing manufacturing paradigms of the 20th century: craft production and mass production. Mass production involves the efficient production of a large quantity of a small variety of goods. Spurred by the Industrial Revolution, so-called *mechanistic firms* developed in which management put a high priority on automating and measuring tasks. A very bureaucratic management structure, with rigid, functionally defined groups and tasks, and tightly supervised employees, is common. This kind of organization enables tight control and predictability, which tends to lead to high degrees of efficiency. The quality of a small number of items can be quite high and prices can be kept relatively low. This is particularly critical for commodity products, where firms have typically competed on price and, more recently, on quality.

Craft production, on the other hand, involves highly skilled and flexible workers, often craftsmen in the manufacturing setting, who are governed by personal or professional standards, and motivated by the desire to create unique and interesting products or services. These workers, found in so-called *organic organizations*, are typically trained through apprenticeships and experience; the organization is flexible and continually changing. This type of organization is able to produce highly differentiated and specialized goods, but it is very difficult to regulate and control. As a consequence, the quality and production rates of these goods are hard to measure and reproduce, and they are typically much more expensive to manufacture [125].

In the past managers often had to make a decision between these two types of organizations with their inherent trade-offs. For some products, a low-cost, low-variety strategy was appropriate while for others, a higher-cost, higher-variety, more adaptable strategy was more effective. The development of mass customization demonstrates that it is not always necessary to make this trade-off.

Mass customization involves the delivery of a wide variety of customized goods or services quickly and efficiently at low cost. Thus, it captures many of the advantages of both the mass production and craft production systems described above. Although not appropriate for all products (e.g., commodity products may not benefit from differentiation), mass customization gives firms important competitive advantages and helps to drive new business models.

9.3.2 Making Mass Customization Work

Pine points out [125] that the key to making mass customization work is highly skilled and autonomous workers, processes, and modular units, so that managers can coordinate and reconfigure these modules to meet specific customer requests and demands. Each module continually strives to upgrade its capabilities; a module's success depends on how effectively, quickly, and efficiently it completes its task, and how good it is at expanding its capabilities. Managers are charged with determining how these capabilities "fit together" efficiently. Thus, management's success depends on how effectively it can develop, maintain, and creatively combine the links between modules in different ways to meet different customer requests, and on the creation of a work environment that encourages the development of a variety of different modules.

Since each unit has highly specialized skills, workers can develop expertise and efficiency in the manner of mass production. Since these units or modules can be assembled in many ways, the differentiation of craft production is achievable. Pine calls this type of organization a *dynamic network*.

There are several key attributes that a company, or more specifically, the *systems within a company that link different modules*, must possess to implement mass customization successfully [125]. They are

Instantaneousness.   Modules and processes must be linked together very quickly. This allows rapid response to various customer demands.

Costless.   The linkages must add little if any cost to the processes. This attribute allows mass customization to be a low-cost alternative.

Seamless.   The linkages and individual modules should be invisible to the customer, so customer service doesn't suffer.

Frictionless.   Networks or collections of modules must be formed with little overhead. Communication must work instantly, without taking time for the team building this is necessary in so many other types of environments.

With these attributes in place, it becomes possible to design and implement a dynamic, flexible firm that can respond to varying customer needs quickly and efficiently.

EXAMPLE 9-8

National Bicycle is a subsidiary of Matsushita that sells bicycles under the Panasonic and National brand names in Japan. Several years ago management found that sales were not at acceptable levels, primarily because the company was unable to predict and satisfy varying customer demand. In the year before beginning the mass customization efforts, 20 percent of bicycles from the previous year remained in inventory. Rather than market to a particular niche or try to improve forecasts, National became a mass customizer.

The company developed a highly flexible bicycle frame manufacturing facility, noting that painting and the installation and tuning of components were separate functions that could be performed by other "modules" in its manufacturing facility. Next, they installed a sophisticated custom-order system called the Panasonic Order System at retailers. This system includes a unique machine that measures customer weight and size, and the appropriate dimensions of the frame, position of the seat, and extension of the bar stem. The customers can also select model type, color patterns, and various components. Information from the dealer is instantaneously transmitted to the factory, where a computer-aided design (CAD) system produces technical details in three minutes. The information is transmitted automatically to the appropriate modules, where manufacturing is completed. The bike is then delivered to consumers two weeks later.

Thus, by noting that the production process could be separated into independent production modules in a seamless and essentially costless manner, and by installing sophisticated information systems, National Bicycle was able to increase sales and customer satisfaction without significantly increasing manufacturing costs [52].

9.3.3 Mass Customization and Supply Chain Management

Clearly, many of the advanced supply chain management approaches and techniques that we have discussed in this and earlier chapters are essential if mass customization is to be successfully implemented. This is particularly true if the components in the network stretch across several companies.

The same information technology that is so critical for effective supply chain management is also critical for coordinating the different modules in the dynamic network and ensuring that together they meet customer requirements. The required system attributes listed above make effective information systems mandatory.

Similarly, in many cases the modules in the dynamic network exist across different firms. This makes concepts such as strategic partnerships and supplier integration essential for the success of mass customization. Finally, as many of the printer-related examples indicate, postponement can play a key role in implementing mass customization. For instance, postponing regional differentiation until products have reached regional distribution centers facilitates regional customization. As the following example illustrates, postponing differentiation until orders have been received allows customer-specific customization.

EXAMPLE 9-9

Dell Computer has become one of the dominant players in the PC industry—in 1998 it was the second largest manufacturer of PCs for business—by adopting a unique strategy based on mass customization. Dell never builds a PC for a customer until the customer's order has been placed. This allows the customer to specify unique requirements, and Dell builds the computer to these requirements. A growing majority of orders come in over the Internet. The order-taking system interfaces with Dell's own supply chain control system, which ensures that inventory is where it needs to be for the computer to be quickly manufactured. In addition, Dell stores very little inventory. Instead, Dell's suppliers have built warehouses close to Dell's facilities, and Dell orders parts on a just-in-time basis. By implementing these strategies, Dell has been able to provide customers with exactly what they want very quickly. In addition, inventory costs are low and Dell minimizes the danger of parts obsolescence in the rapidly changing computer industry. In this way, Dell has become one of the dominant players in the desktop PC market, and is well on its way to doing so in the laptop and server markets.

Dell has utilized many of the important concepts we have discussed to achieve its goals. The company is driven by advanced information systems that do everything from taking many of the orders (over the Web) to managing inventory in the supply chain. Strategic partnerships have been established with many of Dell's suppliers. Dell is even establishing supplier integration partnerships with some of its key suppliers (e.g., 3Com, the network equipment supplier) to ensure that new computers and networking devices are compatible. Finally, Dell has utilized the concept of postponement, deferring final assembly of computers until orders have been received, to achieve mass customization [107].

SUMMARY

In this chapter, we focused on various ways that product design interacts with supply chain management. First, we considered various design for logistics concepts, in which product design is used to lower the costs of logistics. Products designed for efficient packaging and storage obviously cost less to transport and store. Designing products so that certain manufacturing steps can be completed in parallel can cut down on manufacturing lead time, leading to a reduction in safety stocks and increased responsiveness to market changes. Finally, standardization enables risk pooling across products, leading to lower inventories, and allows firms to use the information contained in aggregate forecasts more effectively.

Another critical design/supply chain interaction involves integrating suppliers into the product design and development process. We discussed different ways that suppliers can be integrated into the development process and considered guidelines for managing this integration effectively.

Finally, advanced supply chain management helps to facilitate mass customization. Mass customization involves the delivery of a wide variety of customized goods or services quickly and efficiently at low cost. Obviously, this approach helps to provide firms with important competitive advantages and, just as obviously, effective supply chain management is critical if mass customization is to be successful.

DISCUSSION QUESTIONS

1. Discuss some examples of products that are designed to lower shipping and storage costs.
2. How does the proliferation of products, models, and options make the supply chain more difficult to manage?
3. What are the advantages of downward substitution? What are the disadvantages?
4. What are some products or industries that have been damaged by excessive part standardization?
5. Discuss some examples of modular and nonmodular products and processes.
6. How do standardization strategies help managers deal with demand variability and the difficulty of making accurate forecasts?
7. What are the advantages and disadvantages of integrating suppliers into the product development process?
8. You are the CEO of a medium-sized apparel manufacturer, and you are considering a mass customization strategy for some of your products. How will you decide which, if any, of your products are appropriate candidates for mass customization?

CASE

Hewlett-Packard Company: Network Printer Design for Universality

INTRODUCTION

Sarah Donohoe, manufacturing engineering manager of the network laser printer division at Hewlett-Packard Company (HP), listened intently to her colleagues at the project review meeting for the development of their latest new product. With Sarah at the meeting were Jane Schushinski, marketing manager; Leo Linbeck, head of product design; and David Hooper, the controller of the division.

The main topic for this meeting was the decision of whether or not to use a universal power supply for the next generation of network laser printer, code-named Rainbow. Previously, printers in the North American and the European market have distinct power supplies and the associated fusers in the main engine of the printer. For North American printers, a 110-volt power supply was installed. For European printers, a 220-volt power supply was added. This printer engine was built by HP's manufacturing partner in Japan. Due to the long lead time for engine manufacturing, HP had to specify the requirements of the two types of printers at least 14 weeks ahead. The time that it takes the Japanese partner to commit the printers for shipment, the transportation times, and customs clearance totals about four weeks. Hence, if a universal power supply is used, then HP would have the flexibility of postponing the specification of the printer engine by at least two months in the planning process. Consequently, the production team believed that a universal power supply can enable HP to better respond to the

Source: Copyright © 1993 by the Board of Trustees of the Leland Stanford Junior University. All rights reserved. This case was written by Professor Hau L. Lee, based on an original case written by Steven Plous and Toni Cupal. It is intended as the basis for class discussion rather than to illustrate either effective or ineffective handling of an administrative situation. The product and individuals' names have been disguised.

changing demand in the individual markets and reduce its inventory costs.

Linbeck had begun the meeting by reviewing a fax he had received from the Japanese partner. "We have been asking our partner for a universal power supply and fuser for a long time, and now, when we are about to finalize our design of the next generation network printer, they are telling us that designing the new power supply is finally feasible and can be completed within the time constraints we have set for delivering the product to market on time. However, we must make the decision within the next two weeks so our Japanese partner can line up its design engineers to work on the project." Hooper summed up finance's position as follows, "I do not know what other costs or benefits to the supply chain will be derived from this new change, but what I do know is that our Japanese partner quoted that universal power supply would increase costs by $30 per unit."

As the conversation progressed around the room, Hooper's words became more and more indicative of the group's feelings as a whole. The only hard number available for analyzing the costs and benefits of the change was the $30 increase as quoted by the Japanese partner. If the team was to implement the change, they would have to convince management that the benefits outweighed the costs. Unfortunately, as the meeting went on, quantifying the advantages and disadvantages appeared more and more difficult.

THE HEWLETT-PACKARD COMPANY

Hewlett Packard was one of Silicon Valley's legends. Established by two Stanford University graduates, William Hewlett and David Packard, in 1939, the company initially prided itself on supplying superior engineering tools, designed for engineers by engineers. As the company grew and diversified, the strong belief in technological innovation as the key to competitive advantage persisted.

Innovation was the key to HP's strategy. In 1957, Packard expressed his belief in the importance of this capability:

> Improvement is accomplished by better methods, better techniques, better machinery and equipment and by people continually finding better ways to do their jobs and to work together as a team. I will never see the day when there is not yet room for improvement.

Through time, HP's focus on innovation had brought the world products such as the hand-held calculator and the ink-jet printer. In 1992, the company continued to invest heavily in technology, spending $1.6 billion, or 10 percent of revenue, on research and development. The high levels of investment have paid off: For three straight years, over half of HP's orders had been for products introduced within the last two years.

CHANGING MARKET CONDITIONS

In the early 1990s, while technological innovation continued to drive the company's success, many business units were being forced to compete on other dimensions. In consumer product lines, low prices, broad availability, and ease of use had become competitive requirements. Lew Platt, HP's current president and chief executive officer, once acknowledged the importance of improving customer service and responsiveness:

> We're not doing as good a job in order fulfillment as we need to. In fact it's where we get our lowest marks from customers. We have to be a lot easier to do business with. Improvement in order fulfillment will strengthen HP's competitiveness, increase customer satisfaction, and reduce expenses, so this is an area of great urgency. Along with improving profitability, it's our top priority.

In addition, product life cycles were continually shrinking, making time to market the difference between maximizing market opportunities and missing them. Nowhere were these demands more important than in the laser printer division. HP held a dominant 57 percent of the worldwide laser printer market, but several formidable competitors, including Apple, Fuji-Xerox, Kyocera, Oki, and Compaq, had recently entered the market; life cycles had fallen to under three years; and the quality of competitive products made consumers willing to switch brands if HP's price was too far above the market average or if the product was not easily available.

To meet these challenges, HP had aggressively worked to improve its product development process. Cross-functional teams that brought specialists from all functional areas together to create a new product were becoming standard. The primary benefit of such teams was their ability to identify and eliminate potential problems early in the design cycle while the financial and time-to-market costs of changing the product design were low. As intended, the different perspectives of the team members often gave rise to heated debates over design decisions.

THE NETWORK PRINTER DIVISION SUPPLY CHAIN

The laser products as a group constitute a major and rapidly rising portion of HP's revenue. In 1992 the revenue of laser products was $3 billion, but was projected to reach close to $8 billion by 1998. The network printer is a high-end laser printer that has networking capabilities and special functionalities. Rainbow, the network printer under development, is a product with much more configurable options and features for the printer, such as memory, stapling ability, firmware, system software, fax modems, paper handling, linkage to print server, scanner, and printer stand. It will be priced between $5,000 to $6,000.

The network printer division at HP currently outsources the procurement and assembly of the product's main engine to a Japanese partner. The components, including the power supply and fuser unit, were fully integrated with a printed circuit board from HP's Boise factory into the printer engine at the partner's factory. Monopoly control of one of the key components allowed this partner to require a 14-week lead time from HP.

The design team of Rainbow recognized that the multiple thousands of configurable options for the new product would be a nightmare for forecasting and production planning. Consequently, special efforts were spent in the design of the products so that most of the customization of the products, like the installation of paper input units, cabinet stands, fax modems, paper output units, stapler upgrade package, memory, and print server linkage, can all be carried out at the distribution centers (DCs). Hence, all these options can be installed as accessories at the DCs. In addition, the localization of the product through the inclusion of driver software disks, manuals, power cords, and front panels (with the correct mix of languages) are also done at the DCs.

Hence, the supply chain process involves the transportation of the base printer, almost exclusively by boat, from the partner's facility to HP's DCs in either North America or Europe. The shipment process lasted one month. The demand for a network printer in Asia and Latin America was still minimal compared with the demand in North America or Europe.

Similarly, all necessary accessories and localization materials are also shipped to the DCs from the respective suppliers. Both the printers and other materials are stocked at the DCs. When customer orders from resellers arrive, the printers are customized and localized, followed by appropriate labeling and packaging. Final transportation time, typically via truck, to the resellers in each region, the United States or Europe, ranges from a few days to approximately a week.

THE UNIVERSAL POWER SUPPLY DECISION

The Marketing Perspective

Jane Schushinski, marketing manager:

> I think changing to a universal power supply is a fantastic idea if it does not add cost to the product. Customers will not pay for features that they don't need, and universal power supply is irrelevant to them—the network printer is not like a portable hair dryer that they would carry with them to travel around the world.
>
> The biggest difficulty we have in marketing is not will there be demand for our product, but how much and where. HP makes great printers. We have always been the leader in innovation, reliability, and service. Rainbow is just the first of our series of new network printer line, and we expect to sell 25,000 per month of the product worldwide, with North America having about 60 percent of the market.
>
> What hurts us is our inability to accurately forecast the mix of demands in geographical regions. We may think that Europe will need 10,000 units and North America 2,000 when the numbers may turn out to be 15 and 15,000 respectively. The problem lies in market conditions where increased competition and constantly changing technical innovations can drastically change the demand for a product in a few weeks. In addition, there are a lot of firms trying to compete on price. This too changes demand. Predicting these changes is quite difficult.
>
> Finally, the long lead time from Japan causes my marketing staff to pull their hair out. We have to specify the market for the printer four and a half months ahead of delivery. We estimate that the entire life cycle of the product is at most 18 months. Four-and-a-half-months lead time in an 18-month market—it's ridiculous! The last thing that we want is a repeat of the VIPER debacle. That episode has my hair turning prematurely gray. We had so much of that product laying around we started calling our factory the "snake pit!"
>
> It is easy to see why we love the universal power supply. With the universal power supply, we only need to estimate worldwide product demand four months ahead of time

instead of numbers for each market. We can make the determination of individual market demands much later, and this postponement will help us create more accurate forecasts and help prevent expensive localization errors.

The VIPER was an earlier-generation HP laser printer. While the printer itself was very successful, the VIPER's story illustrates the difficulties with demand uncertainties. The VIPER was developed in the same manner as the new printer being considered. The main components of the VIPER were sourced from Japan and resulted in the same three-and-a-half-month lead time to the factories. The product required a dedicated power supply and fuser, 110V or 220V, and these were not interchangeable. Specification of the dedicated power supply, at the beginning of the three and a half months, committed the product either to the North American or the European market.

HP had not forecasted the correct mix of European and North American VIPER demand. The printer was sold out in Europe while demand in the United States was less than anticipated—HP filled a warehouse with unwanted North American printers that could not be used to satisfy demands for the European market without incurring heavy costs of disassembling the printer and reconfiguring the power supply and fuser in the engine. Eventually, heavy discounting, or "fire sales," was needed to rid the excess inventory, incurring very high cost. Buyers in the North American market now expected HP to reduce printer prices over time. Inadvertently, HP had undercut its ability to command premium prices in the market.

The Product Development Perspective

The product life cycle of printers can be divided into three stages: ramp-up, maturity, and end of life. The ramp-up period is the time from the initial introduction of the product until HP's production volume levels off. During this stage the product is usually the only printer on the market providing its distinctive features. The maturity stage reflects a period of increasing competition. Comparable printers will be introduced and price will become a more influential aspect of the product market. In the last stage, end of life, there is fierce competition on all fronts. Retail profits at this stage reach their lowest point as margins are squeezed. It is here that HP aims to introduce its next generation product.

When there is an imbalance of demand in North America and Europe, the division can live with the consequence of having excess inventory in one continent and shortages in another, or ship the excess from one continent to another (an operation known as "transshipment"), where the printer is reconfigured and sold.

In the end-of-life stage, in addition to transshipping the products across the continent to correct for some of the imbalances, the division can also discount the product to create demand, dismantle the product and sell the parts to HP's service division in Roseville, or just write the product off.

Leo Linbeck's office was stacked high with what must have represented every available trade journal related to printing technology. From behind his HP workstation, he explained his point of view regarding the universal power supply:

While Jane gains "responsiveness," I'm staring at a $30-per-unit cost increase. With the pressure to lower material costs, the design team would find it hard to justify this seemingly unnecessary increase in material cost. Although the printer engine costs about $1,000 each, so that $30 may not seem that much, every single dollar increase in material cost is a decrease of a dollar in our profit. That is why our design group is getting so much heat to get the material cost down. My concern is that we have no way to reliably predict how much value the so-called benefits of universal power supply truly represent.

Now, I'm the first to admit that I'm no marketing expert, but it's pretty clear to me that if we could just learn to forecast demand better, this universal supply would literally be a worthless idea. Maybe pumping $30 per unit into improving the forecasting process makes more sense than sending it out the door in a cardboard box. At least in the first case we have some hope of recovering it again.

I do agree with Jane's point regarding the benefits late in the product life cycle. Currently, reconfiguring the product with a different power supply is a real pain. We have to purchase new power supplies rated at the correct voltage, ship the printers across the Atlantic from the undersold region, swap the power supply, change the fuser electronic circuit and the fuser bulb, and, finally, distribute the product to retailers. The old power supplies have to be disposed of. To make matters worse, there are all kinds of regulatory issues that surface. A universal power supply eliminates all rework that is now required, but whether the gains it provides outweigh the increase in materials cost remains unclear.

Whichever way we end up going, one thing is certain. We cannot delay our development schedule in order to make this decision. We need to decide on a strategy quickly and GO!

As early as 1991, in order to improve their cost position and speed up time to market, the printer divisions in Boise had implemented two new product development metrics. First, they had instituted cost reduction goals for each new generation of printer. The costs captured in this measure included labor, material, and manufacturing overhead. The second metric, called break-even time (BET), had been mandated by upper management. It measured the time from project initiation to break even, defined as the point where total discounted cash outflow equaled total discounted cash inflow.

The Finance Perspective

Neatly arranged on David Hooper's desk were the latest sets of pro-forma income statements and balance sheets for the new project. Pointing out the effect of the universal power supply on income, he noted,

> If we incorporate the universal power supply and sell 450,000 units of Rainbow, it will cost us approximately $13.5 million in additional material costs. If we are not able to pass this increase along to the customer, or at least our retailers, that comes straight out of our bottom line.
>
> I sure agree that there will be benefits from universal power supply. Maybe we should take a hard look at the costs of stockouts and inventory.
>
> Demand fluctuates during each of the three life-cycle periods and so do the costs of making or missing a sale. We typically estimate that for each lost sale we actually forgo multiple times our profit margin. The reason for this is that if a customer buys a competitive brand due to our inability to keep the resellers on stock, there is a chance that he will stay with that brand when he purchases a printer in the future. This effect might cover three or four generations of printers. Moreover, we may lose the profits from the sales of consumables such as toner cartridges and perhaps even other HP peripheral products.
>
> The cost of stockouts when the product is first introduced into the market is even higher, as the potential word-of-mouth and publicity effects can damage the future sales and ultimate success of the product. On the other hand, the cost of stockouts at the end-of-life stage is probably considerably lower, as there is less fear of adverse effect on future sales, and the resellers might in some cases steer the customer to wait for the new, incoming, replacement product.
>
> Although the cost of stockouts in the ramp-up stage is the highest, it is also this stage when we know the least about the market response to our new product, and our forecast errors are usually much greater. I understand that Sara's material planning people had done some homework and found that the standard deviation of our monthly forecast error (a new measure of forecast accuracy that the group has started to measure) was close to 40 percent of the average monthly demand in both markets in the mature and end-of-life stages. Their perception is that the corresponding percentage is 80–90 percent in the ramp-up stage.
>
> The other major cost that I have to monitor is inventory. My financial analysts have estimated that our annual holding cost rate is approximately 30 percent, which covers warehousing, insurance, cost of capital, and shrinkage.

The Manufacturing Perspective

Sara Donohoe, manufacturing engineering manager, commented,

> I think the universal power supply is a great idea. This innovation will improve our flexibility to respond to orders in two key ways. The first is the obvious gain of delaying the regional allocation decision by two and a half months. I'm sure marketing has expounded on this ad infinitum. The second gain is more subtle. You see, while transshipment has always been possible in theory, we have avoided it whenever possible. Let me explain.
>
> At the ramp-up stage, we always try to stockpile our DC's with loads of printers so that we don't ever run out of stock, and, given the high cost of shortage at this stage, this seems reasonable. There is not much of a need for transshipment. In the mature phase, if we keep doing what everyone at HP does and keep enough safety stock to meet the standard service target of around 98 percent then again, the chance of our needing transshipment is still small. However, I am not sure if we want to keep having 98 percent service goals at the end-of-life stage, and indeed that is when transshipments will be most needed.
>
> The whole idea behind transshipment is to adjust inventories in response to market demand. To do this effectively, you need to move the product quickly. Unfortunately, to send a printer by air across the Atlantic costs us $75. Sea shipment reduces costs significantly to approximately $15/unit, but a month out on the ocean does not do much for responsiveness, which is exactly what you're trying to achieve! In addition to the transportation cost, we know how tedious and complex it is to reconfigure the power supply and fuser. I would put my conservative estimate of the activity-based cost for reconfiguration to be at least $250 per printer.
>
> As you might imagine, the quality people go nuts when they find out we're doing this. How can you establish a controlled process if you only do something once a year? Even worse, since the rework involves electrical components, safety standards require the reconfiguration process to be certified by Underwriter's Laboratory. If you've ever dealt with UL, you'll realize how much trouble you'd have getting a process like this approved.

The universal power supply would allow us to avoid this mess, making transshipment a distinct possibility. The cost of reconfiguration is almost zero. It is at least a possibility, although I'm not sure who would coordinate it or decide when to ship . . . our friends in distribution, I guess.

My only real concern with developing the universal supply is the potential power play that could emerge at the time of allocation of the production build to the two regions. Again, I would like some visibility and control over how many units I can count on receiving.

The Distribution Perspective

Rob Seigel runs the North America distribution center. Rob worked in a variety of positions before he moved to management and his present position.

Given a universal product, transshipment won't present a big problem for the DC; it's just another shipment to us and we can easily "localize" the product by adding manuals and plug adapters at the DC. Personally, however, I feel like it's a great way to chew up company profits. I can just see us sending 1,000 units to Germany in February only to have them ship another 1,000 back to me in March. Both actions may seem to make sense at the time the decision was made, but in the end the company's out hundreds of thousands dollars!

Who is going to make the decision to shift inventory from DC to DC? I can see a real firefight if one DC wants more but the other is unwilling to give up its excess. We all have pressures for high customer service and even if I have some excesses now, that does not mean that I may not need it next month. Sending the product to Europe helps their performance, but what about mine? I hope I do not have to do it! One thing I don't have time for is spending half of my day on the phone to Germany trying to negotiate a transfer.

I guess, though, if we can avoid what happened with the VIPER we have got to be better off. That was an interesting time. See that warehouse, pretty big. It was so full we stopped leaving the aisles clear and just stacked printers solid, from floor to ceiling, all the way from front to back. I would pay money to prevent that from happening again. All other work grinds to a halt when a crisis like that emerges.

THE DECISION

The team had decision-making authority, but they would have to defend their decision to upper management. From past experience, they knew that if they decided to adopt the universal power supply, management would want to ensure they had performed adequate analyses of all the costs and benefits of such a decision, as well as some estimate of the risks involved. In addition, some consideration of how the decision would impact future generations of products will have to be made.

CASE DISCUSSION QUESTIONS

1. In what way is a universal power supply a postponement strategy?
2. What are the costs and benefits of a universal power supply (feel free to make assumptions)?
3. How would such costs and benefits be different over the product life cycle?
4. Besides deciding on a universal power supply, what other operational improvements can you suggest to HP Boise?
5. What would be your recommendations about the adoption of a universal power supply?

CHAPTER 10

Customer Value and Supply Chain Management

Dell's Direct Business Model

Michael Dell started a computer business in his dormitory room in 1984 with this simple insight: He could bypass the dealer channel through which personal computers were being sold and instead sell directly to customers and build their personal computers (PCs) to order. This idea, now called the *direct business model*, eliminated the cost of inventory and the reselling expenses. The model had other benefits that were not apparent when Dell founded his company, Dell Computer Corporation. "You actually get to have a relationship with the customer," Michael Dell explains, "and this creates valuable information which, in turn, allows us to leverage our relationships with both suppliers and customers. Couple that information with technology, and you have the infrastructure to revolutionize the fundamental business models of major global companies."

Dell Computer's model involves building computers based on components that are available in the market. The decision not to manufacture the computer components has relieved Dell of the burden of owning assets, research and development risks, and managing a large number of employees. Spreading the development and manufacturing risk among several suppliers allowed Dell to grow much faster than if these functions were performed inside the company.

Dell's use of technology and information to blur the traditional boundaries in the supply chain between suppliers, manufacturers, and end users has been named *virtual integration*. In a traditional computer company, such as Digital Computer, processes were *vertically integrated*, with all the research, development, manufacturing, and distribution capabilities in-house. This allowed for a high level of communication and ability to develop products based on the company's interaction with its clients. The disadvantage was the high risk and costs of development and the ownership of assets in a volatile industry. To achieve the advantages of an integrated company, Dell treats suppliers and service providers as if they were inside the company. Their systems are linked in real time to Dell's system and their employees participate in design teams and product launches. Technology enhances the economic incentives to collaborate because it makes it possible to share design databases and methodologies and speed the time to market.

Dell measures *inventory velocity*, the reciprocal of the average amount of time a product spends in inventory. For this purpose, each component is marked with a date stamp. Accumulating inventory in the fast-moving PC industry is a high-risk proposition since the components can become obsolete very quickly.

Source: The case above is based on [99].

In some cases, such as Sony monitors, Dell does not keep any inventory but has UPS or Airborne Express pick up the monitors from Sony's Mexican factory, the computer from Dell's Austin, Texas, facility, and then match and deliver them to the customers. Dell suppliers benefit from the real-time information about demand and a commitment from Dell for a certain level of purchases. The results are impressive. While Compaq, IBM, and Hewlett-Packard all announced plans in late 1998 to emulate portions of Dell's business model, with various build-to-order plans, all have had difficulty in making the transition. Most are moving to a target inventory level of four weeks, while Dell maintains just eight days of inventory, allowing it to turn over inventory 46 times a year.

On the customer side, Dell has segmented its customer base so that it can offer value-added services to different customers. Dell configures PCs and supports them for large customers. It will also load standard software and place asset stickers on the machines based on customer requests. For some clients, Dell has an on-site team that assists in PC purchasing and servicing. "The whole idea behind virtual integration is that it lets you meet customers' needs faster and more efficiently than any other model." Furthermore, it allows Dell to be efficient and responsive to change at the same time. By spending time with customers and following technological trends, Dell tries to be a few steps ahead of the change, and even create and shape it.

By the end of this chapter, you should be able to answer the following questions:

- What is customer value?
- How is customer value measured?
- How is information technology used to enhance customer value in the supply chain?
- How does supply chain management contribute to customer value?
- How does strategic pricing affect customer value?

10.1 INTRODUCTION

Not long ago this chapter would have been titled "Customer Service and Logistics." In today's customer-driven market, however, it is not the product or service itself that matters but the perceived value to the customer of the entire relationship with the company. The way companies measure the quality of their product and services has evolved from internal quality assurance to external customer satisfaction and from there to *customer value*. Internal quality measures, such as the number of defects, dominated company goals in the era of supply-driven manufacturing. Customer satisfaction concentrated on the company's current customers and their use of a company's product and impression of its service. This provided valuable information about current customers and generated ideas for areas of improvement and ways to compensate for performance in the company. The current emphasis on customer value goes a step further and tries to establish the reasons a customer chooses one company's product over another's, and looks at the entire range of product, services, and intangibles that constitute the company's product and image.

Thinking in terms of customer value promotes a broader look at a company's offerings and customers. It requires learning why customers purchase, continue to purchase, or defect from a company. What are their preferences and needs and how can they be satisfied? Which customers are profitable and have potential for revenue growth, and which customers may incur losses? Assumptions about customer value need to be examined carefully to make sure the trade-offs made are the correct ones. Some examples of these trade-offs include

- Does the customer value low prices more than superior customer support services?
- Does the customer prefer next day delivery or lower prices?

- Does the customer prefer to purchase the item in a store that specializes in this type of item or from a large megastore that allows one-stop shopping?

These are critical questions for any business, and should be the driving force behind business strategy and performance measures.

Indeed, *logistics*, previously considered a back-office function, has evolved into the highly visible discipline of supply chain management partly because of this change in perspective. Supply chain management is naturally an important component in fulfilling customer needs and providing value. Equally important, supply chain management determines the availability of products, how fast they will arrive in the market, and at what cost. Our definition of *supply chain management* (see Chapter 1) implies that the ability to respond to customer requirements is the most basic function of this discipline. This function includes not only the physical attributes of product distribution, but also the related status information and access to this information.

Supply chain management can also impact the important customer value of price by significantly reducing costs. Dell's strategy to reduce its supply chain costs by postponing the final product assembly until after the purchase (i.e., by building to order) has allowed Dell to underprice its competitors in the personal computer industry (see Chapter 9). Wal-Mart has been able to lower costs by introducing the cross-docking strategy (see Chapter 5) and by engaging in strategic partnering with its suppliers (see Chapter 6). Finally, the policy of everyday low prices, applied by Wal-Mart and other retailers, is also motivated in large part by supply chain efficiencies, as we have seen in Chapter 4.

EXAMPLE 10-1

The recent downfall of Kmart is attributed in part to its strategy of competing on price with Wal-Mart. As observed in Chapter 1, Wal-Mart's goal since the early 80s was to provide customers with access to goods when and where they want them, and to develop cost structures that enable competitive pricing. The key to achieving this goal was to make supply chain efficiencies the centerpiece of its strategy. On the other hand, Kmart's strong desire to keep up earnings discouraged investments in supply chain efficiencies and, in particular, in information technology. By the late 90s, it became clear that Kmart's supply chain was not as efficient as that of Wal-Mart [143].

The example suggests the importance of linking pricing strategies with supply chain efficiencies. We discuss this issue in section 10.3.

Customer value drives changes and improvements in the supply chain, some forced by customer and competitor activities and others undertaken to achieve competitive advantage. Furthermore, large manufacturers, distributors, or retailers place certain requirements on their suppliers that force suppliers to adopt supply chains that will make these requests possible. Specifically, Wal-Mart requires many of its suppliers to practice vendor-managed inventory (see Chapter 6). Large manufacturers such as Hewlett-Packard and Lucent Technologies require that their parts manufacturers have 100 percent availability of stock for the parts they use. In return, they are willing to commit to a single supplier for the product or service, or at least commit to a minimum volume of purchases from a primary supplier.

Finally, customer value is also important for determining the type of supply chain required to serve the customer and what services are required to retain customers. A company's supply chain strategy is determined by the type of products or services it offers and the value of various elements of this offering to the customer. For example, if customers value one-stop shopping, that would entail carrying a large number of products and options, even if that is costly in terms of inventory management. If customers value innovative products, then companies who produce them need to apply their supply chain to supply these products efficiently while demand lasts. If a company offers personal customization of its products, then its supply chain needs to be flexible enough to provide the infrastructure for this offering. Thus, the supply chain needs to be considered in any product and sales strategy and could, in itself, provide competitive advantages leading to increased customer value.

10.2 THE DIMENSIONS OF CUSTOMER VALUE

We have defined customer value as the way the customer perceives the entire company's offerings, including products, services, and other intangibles. The customer perception can be broken into several dimensions:

- Conformance to requirements.
- Product selection.
- Price and brand.
- Value-added services.
- Relationships and experiences.

The list of dimensions starts with the essentials—the first three items above—and goes on to more sophisticated types of features that may not always be critical. However, the less critical features can be mined for ideas to create a unique way to add value and differentiation to a company's offering. In this section, we suggest how each dimension is affected by supply chain management and how supply chain management needs to take into account the customer values inherent in each dimension.

10.2.1 Conformance to Requirements

The ability to offer what the customer wants and needs is a basic requirement to which supply chain management contributes by creating availability and selection. Marshall Fisher calls it the *market mediation* function of the supply chain [54]. This function is distinct from the supply chain physical function of converting raw materials into goods and shipping them through the chain to the customer. The costs associated with the market mediation function occur when there are differences between supply and demand. If the supply exceeds demand, there are inventory costs throughout the supply chain; if demand exceeds supply, there are lost sales and possibly market share.

If product demand is predictable, as in *functional items* such as diapers, soup, or milk, market mediation is not a major issue, but when dealing with fashion items or other high-variability items, the nature of demand can create large costs due to lost sales or excess inventory. Clearly, efficient supply chains for functional items can reduce costs by focusing on reducing inventory, transportation, and other costs. This is the strategy Campbell Soup and Procter & Gamble employ for their supply chains.

On the other hand, high-variability products require responsive supply chains, which stress short lead times, flexibility, and speed over cost efficiencies. When the supply chain strategy does not match the product characteristics, there are major implications in the ability to conform to the market, as illustrated in the following example.

EXAMPLE 10-2

Consider a Korean company that manufactures electronic relays. Since competition is intense in this industry, customers can pick and choose their supplier. Thus, if the manufacturer does not have

Example 10-2 *Continued*

the right products at the right time, it will lose customers to the competition. To make matters worse, forecasting customer demand is a challenge because variation in monthly demand is very high. To reduce cost, the manufacturer ships products from a number of manufacturing facilities in the Far East by sea. Unfortunately, by the time the product has arrived at the U.S. warehouse, the demand has changed and there is a shortage of one type of component and obsolete inventory of another. Therefore, the manufacturer is considering shipping the products by air, which would reduce lead times and hence inventory levels and costs, as well as improve customer sales and retention (see Chapter 3).

Conformance to requirements is also related to **customer access** which is the ability to easily find and purchase a product. For companies such as McDonald's, Starbucks, and Walgreens access involves prime real estate. Providing mail, phone, and web access in addition, or instead of stores, can enhance the customer's ability to purchase the product conveniently. Finally, **access** includes the perception of providing the consumers with a store or website layout that makes it easy to find and purchase the product they are seeking [37]. Grainger's success in integrating the web with its older business channels is a good example of the ability to provide customers with the access they need to a company's services.

EXAMPLE 10-3

The business that William W. Grainger founded in 1927 has been one of the success stories of the Internet. Grainger wanted to provide an efficient solution to the need for a speedy and consistent supply of electric motors. The MotorBook, as it was originally called, was the basis for today's Grainger® Catalog. The product line has since expanded to over 220,000 MRO supplies and parts. Grainger is the largest firm in the market for industrial products, with 1999 revenues of $4.5 billion. In 1995 Grainger started its Web initiative with a variety of goals:

- Provide customers with access to all the products Grainger makes available, over 220,000, and not just the 86,500 that could be presented in the paper catalog.
- Provide customers with much better tools for searching, locating, and selecting the product that best suits their needs.
- Deliver products the same day from the branch closest to the customer who placed the order, or ship them from one of Grainger's five regional distribution centers and have them delivered the next day.

  Grainger faces a variety of challenges:

- Grainger offers 65 million different price points so no "one price fits all" and the Internet needs to honor each business account's unique pricing structure.
- Servicing business accounts requires checking credit and establishing payment guidelines.
- Real-time inventory availability—many customers looking for parts cannot wait and need immediate service.
- Compensating the sales force—Grainger decided to pay commissions on Internet orders, thus getting a buy-in from their sales reps, who have relationships with the customers and can encourage customers to use the Web, which is more cost-effective than other channels.

  The initiative had a huge impact on Grainger. In 1999 Grainger spent $20 million for the development, marketing, and customer service of grainger.com, which led to $100 million worth of orders. In the first half of 2000, Grainger generated $120 million in revenue with the size of the average order on the website being $250, compared with $140 for branch and phone orders [139].

10.2.2 Product Selection

Many products come in a large variety of options, styles, colors, and shapes. For instance, a car may come in five styles, 10 different exterior colors, and 10 interior colors and with automatic or manual transmission—a total of 1,000 configurations. The difficulty is that distributors and retailers need to stock most of the various configurations and combinations of products. As explained in Chapter 3, this proliferation of options makes it difficult to predict customer demand for a specific model, thus forcing retailers and distributors to build large and diverse inventories.

The contribution of product proliferation to customer value is difficult to analyze and understand. Three successful business trends exist:

- Specializing in offering one type of product. Examples include companies such as Starbucks and Subway.
- Megastores that allow one-stop shopping for a large variety of products. Examples include Wal-Mart and Target.
- Megastores that specialize in one product area. Examples here include Home Depot, Office Max, and Sportmart.

These trends have also emerged on the Internet where some sites have been successful in offering a large variety of different products while others specialize in a single offering. For instance, www.BlueDenimShirts.com is touted as the "World's only factory outlet for Blue Denim Shirts. Whether you are shopping for 1 shirt for yourself or 1,000 shirts with your company's logo you can buy them here—directly from the factory. And, by the way, we guarantee The World's lowest prices." Along similar lines, consider BlackLeatherBags.com and WhiteTowels.com.

The PC industry has seen significant changes in the way products are sold. In the mid-1980s, PCs were sold through specialized stores such as Egghead. At the beginning of the 1990s PCs were sold in department stores such as Sears. More recently, however, the direct business model has caught on. Finally, Gateway, one of the leaders in the direct business model, has opened its own retail stores. This suggests that there may be a need for a company to sell its products through various outlets to reach the largest number of customers. In fact, companies such as Circuit City enable customers to shop on the Web and pick up at the store.

As observed earlier, the proliferation of products and the difficulty in predicting demand for a specific model force retailers and distributors to hold large inventories. We next discuss several ways to control the inventory problem of a large variety of configurations or products.

1. The approach pioneered by Dell is the **build-to-order model**, where the configuration is determined only when the order comes in. This is an effective way to implement the push–pull strategy discussed in Chapter 5 by employing the concept of postponement introduced and analyzed in Chapter 9. An interesting way to implement this strategy is described in the following example.

EXAMPLE 10-4

Amazon.com is the most famous and successful e-tailer. It started in 1995 by selling a huge variety of books and later added music and videos. More recently, Amazon started selling toys, electronics, and other merchandise. Amazon's fulfillment strategy has evolved over time (see Chapter 5). Initially, the company did not hold any inventory. When a customer ordered a book, Amazon would transfer the order to Ingram Books. Recently, however, Amazon established its own seven large warehouses (one warehouse was later closed) and started shipping directly to the customers. In 2001, Amazon.com shifted its focus to improving its distribution operations in a push towards profit. It has improved its

Example 10-4 *Continued*

fulfillment costs, which include costs associated with six warehouses, customer service, and credit card fees, to 9.8 percent in the fourth quarter of 2001, down from 13.5 percent of sales in the fourth quarter of 2000. Amazon did this by

- Improving sorting order and utilization of sophisticated packing machines, which allowed Amazon to ship 35 percent more units with the same number of workers as the previous year.
- Using software to forecast purchasing patterns, which allowed Amazon to slash inventory levels by 18 percent in the fourth quarter.
- Consolidated shipping of 40 percent of goods into full trucks driven directly into major cities, bypassing regional postal sorting facilities and cutting transportation costs significantly.
- Partnering to sell goods for other companies such as Toys 'R' Us and Target, who pay Amazon for handling distribution and customer service. These partnerships brought in $225 million in revenue with gross profit margins double Amazon's overall 25 percent margins.
- Allowing other sellers to offer used books, which increased sales during the holiday season by 38 percent. For these products, Amazon's gross margins were about 85 percent—a business model similar to that of eBay.

Amazon.com has also had challenges on the pricing front: Amazon discounts nearly all books over $20 by 30 percent. Amazon once offered discounts of as much as 50 percent on best sellers and 20 percent discounts on other books. Early in 2001, the company started to raise book prices—with 5 percent to 10 percent discounts more common—only to reverse the increases as sales fell. In the book business, few other retailers have offered discounts, other than for best sellers. There is good reason Amazon can afford to cut book prices: the average book may sit on the shelf of a store for six months or a year before it is bought. The cost of this inventory in a chain of hundreds of stores is huge. Amazon, on the other hand, can keep just one or two copies in its warehouse—and still make the title available to the whole country—and restock as quickly as customers buy books [70].

2. A different strategy, suitable for products with long manufacturing lead times, such as vehicles, is to keep **larger inventories at major distribution centers**. These distribution centers allow the manufacturer to reduce inventory levels by taking advantage of risk pooling (see Chapter 3) and delivering the vehicles quickly to customers. General Motors has initiated this approach with its Cadillac unit in Florida. Dealers can order cars that they do not have on their lot from a regional warehouse that can ship the car out in a day. Of course, two major issues need to be raised when considering this strategy:

- *Inventory costs of cars at the regional warehouse.* Is the manufacturer (i.e., General Motors) going to pay for the inventory at the regional warehouse? If it is, then there is an incentive for the dealers to reduce inventory in their lots and reduce their cost while increasing that of the manufacturer.
- *Equalizing small and large dealers.* If all dealers have access to the regional warehouse, then there is no difference between the different dealers. Thus, it is difficult to see why large dealers would be interested in participating in such an arrangement, especially if they are going to pay for inventory at the regional warehouse.

3. Another possibility is to offer **a fixed set of options that cover most customer requirements**. For instance, Honda offers a limited number of options on its cars. Dell offers few options for modems or software that can be installed on its machines, although the overall number of possible configurations remains quite high. Indeed, large product variety is not required in all cases. For example, a dysfunctional level of variety exists in many grocery products—28 varieties of toothpaste, to give one example [54]. It is not clear whether this variety actually adds any customer value.

10.2.3 Price and Brand

Price of products and the level of service are essential parts of customer value. Although the price may not be the only factor a customer considers, there may be a narrow price range that is acceptable for certain products. For instance, for commodity products (and even sophisticated items such as personal computers are commodities), there is very little flexibility in price. Therefore, companies achieve cost advantages through innovations in their supply chains. As we have seen in Dell's direct business model, allowing clients to configure their own systems and building a supporting supply chain not only improve customer value but also reduce costs.

Wal-Mart has been a supply chain innovator, which has enabled it to provide low-cost merchandise and undercut its competition (see Example 10-1). In addition, we have seen that the "everyday low pricing" policy applied by retailers such as Wal-Mart and manufacturers such as Procter & Gamble is an important tool in reducing the bullwhip effect (see Chapter 4). This policy appeals to customers who do not have to worry about buying at the wrong time, and to the retailer and manufacturer who do not need to plan for demand variations as a result of promotions.

An important factor affecting the product price is its brand. In today's market, there are fewer salespeople and more customers looking for supermarket-style shopping [130]. This is true across a wide variety of retail environments, from auto superstores to e-tailers.

EXAMPLE 10-5

Consider prices for books and CDs sold on the Internet. A recent study found "substantial and systematic differences in price across retailers on the Internet. Prices posted on the Internet differ by an average of 33 percent for books and 25 percent for CDs." More importantly, Internet retailers with the lowest price do not necessarily sell more. For instance, the research found that Books.com had a lower price than Amazon.com in 99 percent of the cases, yet Amazon had about 80 percent of the market at the time of the study, while Books.com had about 2 percent. One way to explain this behavior is through "trust consumers have for the various Internet retailers and the associated value of branding" [19].

Apparently, the Internet and its impact on consumer behavior have increased the importance of brand names, because a brand name is a guarantee of quality in the buyer's mind. Brand names such as Mercedes cars, Rolex watches, and Coach purses can be promoted for high quality and prestige and command much higher prices than products that lack this aura. Furthermore, the higher price in itself may be a large part of the prestige and perceived quality. The product's high margins will require a focus on service level, and hence the supply chain needs to be more responsive; the increase in supply chain cost will be offset by the higher margin.

EXAMPLE 10-6

One of the key elements in the rise of Federal Express as the most successful small package carrier is that it was the first carrier to narrow its focus to overnight delivery, thereby owning the word "overnight" in the market. Even though there are cheaper alternatives, customers are willing to pay a premium to ship by Federal Express because of the brand name and the perception of dependability it conveys [130].

In many industries "product" typically means both the "physical product" and associated "services." Typically, pricing the physical product is not as difficult as pricing services. At the same time, it is quite difficult to compare different services and as a result, variability in pricing increases. This suggests opportunities for companies that develop new offerings and services that are more difficult to turn into commodities. As we will see below, there is a challenge in turning these opportunities into offerings that customers are actually willing to pay for.

In Section 10.3, we examine strategic pricing, where companies can employ sophisticated analysis to align customer service preferences with supply chain costs.

10.2.4 Value-Added Services

Many companies cannot compete on product price alone in an economy that has an over-abundance of supply. Therefore, they need to consider other sources of income. This drives companies toward value-added offerings that differentiate them from competitors and provide them with more profitable pricing structures.

Value-added services, such as support and maintenance, can be a major factor in the purchase of some products, especially technical products. Indeed, many companies are now adding more services around their products [83]. This is due in part to

1. The commoditization of products, where only the price matters and all other features are identical, reducing profitability and competitive advantage from the sale of products alone.
2. The need to get closer to the customer.
3. The increase in information technology capabilities that make this offering possible.

A sophisticated service offering is illustrated in the following example.

EXAMPLE 10-7

Goodyear Tire & Rubber Co. provides truck manufacturer Navistar International Transportation Corp. with an automated supply chain service that includes delivering mounted tires sequenced for just-in-time use on automated assembly lines. Goodyear has a 13-person information technology group dedicated to the tire maker's materials management division. This division acts as systems integrator on supply chain projects it takes on with wheel manufacturer Accuride, Inc., in Henderson, Kentucky. Under a joint venture called AOT, Inc., Goodyear and Accuride furnish entire wheel assemblies, painted and ready for use, to Mitsubishi Motor Co. and Ford Motor Co. as well as Navistar. Those assemblies include Goodyear's or competitors' tires, depending on customer specifications [83].

A recent example of a market with a low entry barrier and many companies initially competing mostly on price is the business-to-business e-marketplace. It only took a few years for many of these market makers to realize that they need to extend their service offerings; they now provide a variety of additional services, including financial, logistics, and supply chain services (see Chapter 7 for more detail).

As observed in the previous section pricing services is not an easy task. For many years companies such as IBM did not charge for their services, although the company's slogan was "IBM Means Service." Today, service provides most of IBM's income. Companies that have not stressed customer support, such as Microsoft, are enhancing their capabilities in this area. In many cases, there is a charge associated with receiving support, such as a one-time call fee or a service agreement. As we saw in the Dell case, service and support not only can generate additional revenue, but, more importantly, they can bring the company closer to the customer and provide it with insight on how to improve its offering, tailor support, and find the next idea to add value to its products and services.

An important value-added service is information access. Allowing customers access to their own data—such as pending orders, payment history, and typical orders—enhances their experience with the company. For example, it is well known that customers value the ability to know the status of an order, sometimes even more than the actual turnaround time. This capability provides reliability and enables planning. FedEx pioneered the package tracking systems that are now standard in the package handling industry. As we will see below, this not only enhances service, but can result in large savings for the provider of the information by handing over to its customers some of the data entry and inquiry functions from its own employees.

The ability of customers to access information is becoming an essential requirement in supply chain management, as visibility of information is what an increasing number of customers expect. The Internet enables these capabilities and companies will need to invest in information systems that support it. In Chapter 11, we consider these issues in more detail.

10.2.5 Relationships and Experiences

The final level of customer value is an increased connection between the firm and its customers through development of a relationship. This makes it more difficult for customers to switch to another provider, since a relationship requires an investment of time from both the customer and the provider. For example, Dell configures PCs and supports them for large customers. When Dell manages the entire PC purchase for a large customer, including special custom features, it becomes more difficult for the customer to switch to another vendor.

The learning relationship, where companies build specific user profiles and utilize this information to enhance sales as well as retain customers [123], is another example of a relationship providing customer value. Companies such as Individual Inc., which builds tailored information services, and USAA, which uses its databases to offer customers other services and products, are examples of this kind of organization.

EXAMPLE 10-8

Founded in 1989 by brothers Andrew and Thomas Parkinson, Peapod has grown to be one of America's leading Internet grocers. Peapod is a wholly owned subsidiary of international food provider Royal Ahold and works in partnership with Ahold USA supermarket companies, including Stop & Shop and Giant Food. The company, which operates in Boston, southern Connecticut, Washington, Chicago, and Long Island, New York, serves over 103,000 members. Shoppers browse through Peapod's offerings on its Internet site through a personalized interface based on their location. Peapod's computers are linked directly to the databases of the supermarkets from which it purchases the groceries. The shoppers can create their own virtual supermarket by accessing the information according to category and creating customized shopping lists that can be saved for repeated use. At the end of each shopping session, Peapod has the opportunity to learn about its service by asking, "How did we do on the last order?" and using the relatively high response rate of its customers (35 percent) to institute requested changes to its services [123].

The approach used by Peapod Inc. is an example of the *one-to-one enterprise* concept suggested by Peppers and Rogers in [119]. In this concept, companies learn about each customer through databases and interactive communications, and sell to one customer as many products and services as possible throughout the lifetime of the customer's patronage. Indeed, Peapod is using its databases to suggest new offerings to customers, tracking the customer's preferences and needs, and further tailoring the company's offering to the customer.

The learning process can take time, but this will make it difficult for competitors to emulate the strategy. In addition, it typically ensures that a customer who considers switching to another provider will have to take into account the investment in time and money required to make the switch.

Indeed, some Internet sites, such as Amazon.com, are applying new modes of learning, with suggestions to customers based on their own previous purchases or those of customers who make similar purchases. Of course, one issue with an Internet service that provides customer reviews and suggestions is that a customer can distinguish between a website where they purchase the product and the website in which they receive information about the product. That is, it is not clear that a service offering in which a website provides suggestion tools and customer reviews may convince the consumer to purchase the product at that site. The consumer may receive information from one site and make the purchase on another [19].

A different approach, tailored towards large customers and designed to make it difficult to switch to another vendor, was introduced by Dell. Dell offers large corporations custom PC configurations loaded with specific software, tags, and other special requirements. Dell has also tailored its website so that different types of users can access it according to their needs. In many ways, this approach is a more extensive application of mass customization, which we discussed in Chapter 9.

Beyond relationships, some companies are also designing, promoting, and selling unique experiences to their customers, which, according to Pine and Gilmore [122], is the trend in the new economy. The authors define experience as an offering distinct from customer service:

> An experience occurs when a company intentionally uses services as the stage, and goods as props, to engage individual customers in a way that creates memorable events [122].

Some current examples include airline frequent flyer programs, theme parks, Saturn owner gatherings, and Lexus weekend brunch and car wash events.

EXAMPLE 10-9

Silicon Graphics opened the Visionarium Reality Center in June 1996. The Visionarium was a virtual reality center intended for use as a sales and marketing tool. The idea was that designers who develop products using Silicon Graphics technology can simulate the experience achieved with new products. The virtual reality center was used for the design of automobiles, airplanes, and architecture. It allowed the developers, or potential customers, to view, hear, touch, and even drive, walk, or fly various prototype product configurations. This enabled customers to know what their products will look, feel, and sound like before manufacturing [122].

The Internet provides other opportunities for creating experiences that have not yet been fully explored. One of the strengths of the Internet is the creation of collaborative communities that can be used to develop relationships between people with similar interests or desire to collaborate. One such technology is "eRoom," which is a virtual workspace in which multiple parties can view and work with almost any form of unstructured data, such as drawings and presentations that are far too big for e-mail. These can be placed in an eRoom and discussed and walked through with clients or prospects via teleconference and Web demo. In addition, participants can trade comments within eRoom with no phone contact at all. Since the room is always there, it works for everyone's schedule. Companies use the same technology to create "communities of interest," some of which involve only its own employees, others a mix of internal staff and outside partners [93].

As with the initial introduction of services, companies do not yet charge for experiences. Before a company can charge for this offering, experiences must be seen by the customer as worth the price. This requires a large investment in making the experience valuable in itself. Disney's theme parks are the prime example of a successful experience that many are willing to pay for. The parks can be viewed as a means of selling Disney's products—movies and various spin-off toys and accessories.

The ability to provide sophisticated customer interactions (e.g., relationships and experiences) is very different from the ability to manufacture and distribute products. This suggests the emergence of firms that specialize in providing the former.

According to Patricia Seybold [139], there are eight steps to delivering a great total customer experience:

1. Create a compelling brand personality—a distinct offering that customers can identify with.
2. Deliver a seamless experience across channels and touch points. In other words, make sure that customers' experience and information are the same no matter what access method they choose to use at a certain point.
3. Care about customers and their outcomes.
4. Measure what matters to customers: the quality of the customer's experience as opposed to internal company measures.
5. Hone operational excellence.
6. Value customers' time.
7. Place customer's information requirements and needs at the core. This requires the ability to be proactive; for instance, reminding customers of maintenance requirements and training opportunities.
8. Design to morph—the ability to change practices based on customer requirements.

10.3 STRATEGIC PRICING

No company underscores the impact of the Internet on product pricing strategies more than Dell Computers. The exact same product is sold at different prices on Dell's website depending on whether the purchase is made by a private consumer; a small, medium, or large business; the federal government; or an education or health care provider. A more careful review of Dell's strategy [1] suggests that even the price of the same product for the same industry is not fixed; it may change significantly over time.

Dell is not alone in its use of a sophisticated pricing strategy. Consider:

- IBM and Compaq say they have begun investigating software that will allow them to adjust their prices according to demand for certain machines [108].
- Nikon Coolpix Digital Camera is sold either on-line or in stores for about $600. The manufacturer provides a rebate of $100 independently of where the camera is purchased.
- Sharp VL-WD255U Digital Camcorder is sold for about $500 at retail or virtual stores. Sharp provides a rebate to the customer of $100 independently of where the product was purchased.
- Boise Cascade Office Products sells many products on-line. Boise Cascade states that prices for the 12,000 items ordered most frequently on-line might change as often as daily [79].

Thus, the question is what are these companies doing? Why does Dell charge a different price for different consumers? If Dell can do it, why not other companies?

What is the impact of the mail-in rebate? In fact, shouldn't Nikon and Sharp just reduce the wholesale price paid by the retailers instead of asking the consumer to mail in the coupon? More importantly, if rebates work, shouldn't the retailer give the rebate to the consumer? And, finally, what is wrong with a traditional fixed-price policy?

A careful review of these companies suggests that they have one thing in common: they are trying to boost profit by using revenue management techniques, techniques that have been applied very successfully in the airline, hotel, and rental car industries. In the airline industry, revenue management increased revenue significantly; American Airlines estimates that revenue management provides incremental revenue of $1 billion annually [34]. In fact, if it were not for the combined contributions of revenue management and airline schedule planning systems, American Airlines would have been profitable only one year in the last decade [35].

In the next subsection, we review the fundamentals of revenue management while in Subsection 10.3.2 we identify effective pricing strategies and their impact on supply chain performance.

10.3.1 Revenue Management

Revenue management techniques have received significant attention in recent years from companies trying to improve profitability. These methods, which integrate pricing and inventory strategies to influence market demand, provide controls for companies to improve the bottom line. Revenue management has been described as "selling the right inventory unit to the right type of customer, at the right time, and for the right price" [82].

As observed earlier, revenue management techniques have been traditionally applied in the airline, hotel, and rental car industries. A number of characteristics are common to all these applications. These include (see [82]) (i) the existence of perishable products, that is, products that expire or are irrelevant after a certain date, (ii) fixed capacity of the system; and (iii) segmentation of the market based, for instance, on sensitivity to price or service time.

To understand revenue management, we proceed with the following example.

Hotel Rooms

Consider an exclusive resort with 400 identical rooms. Management is focusing on pricing rooms for the next five-day holiday. The goal is to price rooms so as to maximize revenue. Based on past experience, management estimates the relationship between demand, D, and price, p, by the linear function

$$D = 1,000 - 0.5p$$

This implies that when the price is $1,600, there is demand for 200 rooms, while if the price is $1,200, there is demand for 400 rooms. Notice that revenue equals price times demand at that price. Thus, when rooms for the holiday season are priced at a level of $1,200, revenue equals

$$1,200 \times 400 = 480,000$$

Figure 10-1 depicts the demand–price curve, where the shaded area represents total revenue. Since supply is 400 rooms, at first glance it seems that this is the best pricing strategy. However, observe that, according to the demand–price curve, the resort charges many customers who are willing to pay a higher price only $1,200. In fact, there are about 200 customers among the 400 who are willing to pay $1,600 per room. Out of these 200 customers, there are about 100 who are willing to pay $1,800. All these customers are charged the same price, $1,200.

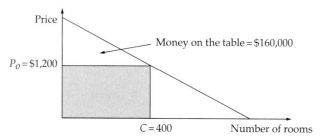

FIGURE 10-1 Revenue-sharing contract.

This simple analysis illustrates that by charging a single price, management is leaving a large amount of money on the table. In fact, the amount of money left on the table is represented by the upper triangle in Figure 10-1 and it is equal to (why?)

$$(2,000 - 1,200) \times 400/2$$

The question is thus, how can management increase revenue by taking advantage of the amount of money left on the table?

For this purpose, consider a more sophisticated pricing strategy in which the hotel introduces a *differential* or *customized* pricing strategy. In differential pricing, the firm tailors its pricing to different market segments: those who can pay the higher price and those who are willing to pay only the lower price. For instance, consider a two-price strategy in which the hotel introduces two fare classes, $1,600 and $1,200. Observe that at a price of $1,600, there is demand for 200 rooms, while at a price of $1,200, there is demand for 400 rooms, out of which 200 customers pay the higher price. Thus, total revenue in this case is

$$1,600 \times 200 + 1,200 \times (400 - 200) = 560,000$$

Hence, using this strategy, the hotel was able to increase its revenue by $80,000 by capturing 50 percent of the money left on the table.

Can the hotel increase revenue even more? Observe that a three-tier pricing strategy can do even better. Indeed, consider a strategy in which the hotel introduces three classes of fare: $1,800, $1,600, and $1,200. At a price of $1,800, there is demand for 100 rooms; at a price of $1,600, there is demand for 200 rooms, out of which 100 customers pay thc higher price. Finally, at a price of $1,200, there is demand for 400 rooms, out of which 200 customers pay higher prices. Thus, total revenue equals

$$1,800 \times 100 + 1,600 \times (200 - 100) + 1,200$$
$$\times (400 - 200) = 580,000$$

an increase of $20,000 relative to the two-tier strategy.

The example illustrates the opportunities and challenges of revenue management. By increasing the number of price fares, the firm can increase total revenue and, in fact, can capture the entire amount left on the table. Of course, the main challenge is ensuring that those who can pay the higher price do not pay a lower one. This is achieved by building fences between the various classes of customers, fences that make it difficult for customers in one class to switch and pay the lower price.

To illustrate this, consider the airline industry [44]. Airline passengers can be classified into two segments: leisure and business travelers. Leisure customers are highly sensitive to price but not that sensitive to the duration of the trip. On the other hand, business travelers are highly sensitive to the duration of the trip but not that sensitive to price. Similarly, business travelers need high flexibility so that they can adjust their travel plans as needed while typically leisure travelers do not need that level of flexibility. This suggests the framework developed by Duadel and Vialle [44], which we introduce in Table 10-1.

TABLE 10-1

MARKET SEGMENTATION IN THE AIRLINE INDUSTRY

		Sensitivity to price	
		Low	*High*
Sensitivity to duration;	*High*	Business travelers	No offer
need for flexibility	*Low*	No demand	Leisure travelers

Thus, the airlines build fences to prevent business travelers from moving from the top-left box to the bottom-right box. This is done by requiring weekend stays and early booking. Of course, the more fare classes, the more fences need to be built between the different market segments.

10.3.2 Smart Pricing

The pricing strategies applied by Dell, Nikon, Sharp, and Boise Cascade Office Products have one thing in common. These companies use price as a tool to influence customer demand and, hence, they apply the principles of revenue management techniques to their respective industries. Two different but complementing approaches are used.

Customized pricing.   In customized pricing, the objective is to distinguish between customers according to their price sensitivity. Dell does that by distinguishing between private consumers, small or large businesses, government agencies, and health care providers. Sharp and Nikon use mail-in rebates to differentiate between customers based on their sensitivity to price. This is done by adding a significant hurdle to the buying process; to receive the rebate, you have to complete and mail the coupon to the manufacturer. The assumption is that those customers willing to pay the higher price will not necessarily send the coupon. Of course, the problem with that assumption is that unlike traditional revenue management techniques, mail-in rebates do not incorporate fences that will prevent customers willing and able to pay the higher price from sending their coupon back and claiming the discount. Thus, mail-in rebates require a more detailed analysis.

- With no rebate, each retailer decides on the price and the amount to order from the manufacturer so as to maximize its profit. The retailer trade-offs are clear: the higher the price, the smaller the demand. Thus, the retailer needs to find a price and an order quantity so as to maximize its expected profit. The manufacturer, on the other hand, would like the retailer to order as much as possible. Its profit is proportional to the wholesale price, not to the price paid by the customers.

- With mail-in-rebates, the manufacturer influences customer demand and provides an upside incentive to the retailer to increase its order quantity. Indeed, by introducing the rebate, the effective price paid by (some of) the customers to the retailers is reduced and hence the retailer faces a higher demand level. Thus, the retailer's profit increases. Of course, the increase in demand forces the retailer to order more from the manufacturer. By selecting the rebate appropriately, this increase in order quantity more than compensates for the rebate and, hence, it implies an increase in the manufacturer's expected profit.

- From the manufacturer's point of view, the question, of course, is why not discount the wholesale price? Various answers may be given. First, the rebate strategy has the advantage that not every consumer will mail the coupon to the manufacturer. Second, if the manufacturer merely reduces the wholesale price, the retailer may keep the discount and not transfer it to the customers. Finally, and most importantly, even if the retailer uses the discounted wholesale price to optimize its pricing and ordering decisions, and even if every consumer mails back the rebate, the mail-in rebate strategy is a better strategy for the manufacturer. That is, it increases the manufacturer's profit more than a discounted wholesale price. To understand this issue, suppose the retailer orders the same amount in both strategies, that is, in the mail-in rebate strategy and the discounted wholesale price strategy. Consider two situations: one in which the order quantity is smaller than realized demand and another in which the order quantity is larger than realized demand. If the order quantity is smaller than realized demand, the two strategies provide the manufacturer with exactly the same profit (why?). On the other hand, if the order quantity is larger than demand, the manufacturer's profit with rebate is larger than its profit under discounted wholesale price (again, why?).

Dynamic pricing. Dynamic pricing, or changing prices over time without necessarily distinguishing between different types of customers, has been employed for ages, but has traditionally been used only for sales or promotions. For example, fashion clothing retailers may offer discounts later in the season to reduce inventory, and this discount is the same for all customers at a given time. The current wave of smart pricing applies this strategy to the manufacturing environment by using price as a tool to better match demand and supply. This, of course, requires executives in the front-end of the supply chain, that is, those who make pricing decisions, to have complete visibility into the back-end of the supply chain—to suppliers' inventory—as well as into their own production schedule.

The key challenge when considering dynamic pricing strategies is to identify conditions under which this strategy provides significant profit benefit over (the best) fixed-price strategy:

- **Available capacity:** Assuming everything else is equal, the smaller the production capacity relative to average demand, the larger the benefit from dynamic pricing [27].
- **Demand variability:** The benefit of dynamic pricing increases as the degree of demand uncertainty, measured by the coefficient of variation, increases [46].
- **Seasonality in demand pattern:** The benefit of dynamic pricing increases as the level of demand seasonality increases ([27], [46]).
- **Length of the planning horizon:** The longer the planning horizon, the smaller the benefit from dynamic pricing [46].

All in all, research [27, 46] indicates that, depending on the data and the model assumptions, dynamic pricing may increase profit by 2 to 6 percent. This increase in profit due to dynamic pricing is very significant for industries with low profit margins, for example, retail and computer industries.

The Internet has made these developments possible:

1. **Menu cost,** the cost that retailers incur when changing the posted price (see [19]) is much lower on the Internet than in the off-line world. This allows on-line sellers such as Dell and Boise Cascade Office Products to update their prices on a daily basis.

2. **Lower buyer search price,** which is the cost that buyers incur when looking for a product, forces competition between sellers ([19], [158]), and hence leads to a focus on smart pricing strategies.
3. **Visibility** to the back-end of the supply chain, such as that provided to Dell by its private e-marketplace (see Chapter 7), makes it possible to coordinate pricing, inventory, and production decisions.
4. **Customer segmentation** using buyers' historical data is possible on the Internet and very difficult in conventional stores [10].
5. **Testing** capability—because of its low menu cost, the Internet can be used to test pricing strategies in real time [10]. As suggested by Baker, Marn, and Zawada [10], an on-line seller may test a higher price on a small group of the site visitors and use those data to determine a pricing strategy.

A word of caution is in order. Recent experiments by a number of companies reveal that anyone who considers using smart pricing strategies must avoid the appearance of unfair treatment of their customers:

- Amazon.com experimented with a pricing strategy in which customers were paying different amounts for the same DVD based on demographics or even the browser they used. As reported in [148],

    "Amazon was trying to figure out how much their loyal customers would pay," said Barrett Ladd, a retail analyst with Gomez Advisors. "And the customers found out." A number of DVDTalk.com visitors were particularly distressed to find that prices seemed to be higher for the best customers. "They must figure that with repeat Amazon customers they have 'won' them over and they can charge them slightly higher prices since they are loyal and don't mind and/or don't notice that they are being charged 3 percent to 5 percent more for some items," wrote a user whose online handle is Deep Sleep.

    Customers responded negatively to the strategy, and Amazon.com stopped the pricing tests.
- Doug Ivester, the former chairman of Coca-Cola Co., had considered a dynamic pricing strategy in which price would vary by season. Rumors have it that Ivester left Coca-Cola in part due to customer dissatisfaction over the pricing strategy.
- On-line sites such as Priceline and San Francisco–based Hotwire.com provide an outlet for last-minute, unsold seats and hotel rooms through what are called opaque fares. That means travel providers can cut their losses by offering unsold tickets and rooms at deep discounts without identifying which airline or hotel, for example, is selling the ticket or room. That "protects" the published fares promoted by the airlines and hotels themselves. Opaque fares are like the store-brand merchandise in grocery stores that sells for much less than the same goods with a brand name attached. However, opaque fares are supposed to be ancillary sources of income, and finding the right balance can be tricky. In an unstable economy, when many published fares are about as good as the opaque fares, it is harder to attract customers to the Priceline and Hotwire sites [42].

10.4 CUSTOMER VALUE MEASURES

Because customer value is based on customer perceptions, it requires measures that start with the customer. Typical measures include service level and customer satisfaction. Our objective in this section is to introduce various measures of customer value as well as supply chain performance measures. The latter are important since supply chain performance is an important contributor to customer value.

1. **Service level.** Service level is the typical measure used to quantify a company's market conformance. In practice, the definition of service level can vary from company to company, but *service level* is usually related to the ability to satisfy a customer's delivery date, for instance, the percent of all orders sent on or before the promised delivery date. Many companies consider this measure so critical to their ability to succeed in today's markets that they invest heavily in decision-support systems that allow them to quote delivery dates accurately by analyzing information from the entire supply chain.

   There is a direct relationship between the ability to achieve a certain level of service and supply chain cost and performance. For instance, demand variability and manufacturing and information lead times determine the amount of inventory that needs to be kept in the supply chain (see Chapter 3). Clearly, when setting the level of service that should be used for a particular offering, it is important to understand customer value. For instance, customers may value low cost, information about the delivery date, and the ability to customize the product more than they value immediate delivery itself. This is definitely the case for PC buyers, where Dell's direct business model, with the additional time it takes to build and deliver the PC, seems to be winning over off-the-shelf store purchases.

2. **Customer satisfaction.** Customer satisfaction surveys are used to measure sales department and personnel performance as well as to provide feedback for necessary improvements in products and services. In addition, as in the Peapod example, there are other innovative ways to receive information about customer satisfaction. However, customer surveys may not be the best way to learn about customer value. As Reichheld [129] points out, relying on customer satisfaction surveys can often be misleading. These surveys are easy to manipulate and are typically measured at the selling point while nothing is said about retaining the customer.

   Indeed, more important than what customers say about their satisfaction is *customer loyalty*, which is easier to measure than customer satisfaction. This can be accomplished by analyzing customer repurchase patterns based on internal databases.

EXAMPLE 10-10

Lexus is a consistent winner of auto satisfaction awards, but it refuses to consider surveys as the best measure of satisfaction. To Lexus the only meaningful measure of satisfaction is repurchase loyalty. Lexus considers the repurchase activities of cars and services as the only measure for its dealers' success. Each Lexus dealership has a satellite dish that keeps information flowing back and forth to headquarters, where these measures are constantly tracked [129].

An additional option is to learn from customer defections. Unfortunately, identifying those customers is not an easy task because dissatisfied customers seldom cancel an account completely. Instead, they gradually shift their spending, making a partial defection. However, if this type of tracking is possible, it may provide the key to increasing customer value.

Another example is Charles Schwab (see [139]). The on-line broker tracks customer asset accumulation, customer satisfaction, customer retention, and employee retention. These are the measures on which managers and employees receive incentives.

TABLE 10-2		

SCOR LEVEL 1 METRICS

Perspectives	Metrics	Measure
Supply chain reliability	On-time delivery	Percentage
	Order fulfillment lead time	Days
	Fill rate	Percentage
	Perfect order fulfillment	Percentage
Flexibility and responsiveness	Supply chain response time	Days
	Upside production flexibility	Days
Expenses	Supply chain management cost	Percentage
	Warranty cost as percentage of revenue	Percentage
	Value added per employee	Dollars
Assets/utilization	Total inventory days of supply	Days
	Cash-to-cash cycle time	Days
	Net asset turns	Turns

3. **Supply chain performance measures.** As we have seen, supply chain performance affects the ability to provide customer value, especially in the most basic dimension of availability of products. Therefore, there is a need to develop independent criteria to measure supply chain performance. The need for well-defined measures in the supply chain stems from the presence of many partners in the process and the requirement of a common language. This is precisely the motivation behind standardization initiatives such as the SCOR model.

The Supply Chain Operations Reference Model (SCOR) uses a *process reference model* that includes analyzing the current state of a company's processes and its goals, and quantifying operational performance and comparing it to benchmark data. For this purpose, SCOR has developed a set of metrics for supply chain performance; its members are in the process of forming industry groups to collect best-practice information that companies can use to evaluate their supply chain performance. Table 10-2 lists examples of metrics used to evaluate supply chain performance in SCOR based on [106].

Once a specific company's metrics are calculated, they are compared to those of industry benchmarks such as average and best-in-class. This enables identifying the company's advantages as well as opportunities for supply chain improvement.

Examples of these metrics are reported in the "Overall Business Performance" survey conducted by PRTM [59]:

- **Total supply chain management costs:** This includes the total cost to manage order processing, acquire materials, manage inventory, and manage supply chain finance and information systems. The survey found that leading companies have total costs between 4 and 5 percent of sales. Median performers spend 5 to 6 percent more.
- **Cash-to-cash cycle time:** The number of days between paying for raw materials and getting paid for product, as calculated by inventory days of supply plus days of sales outstanding minus average payment period for material. The survey shows that best in class have less than 30-days' cycle time, while median performers can be up to 100 days.
- **Upside production flexibility:** The number of days required to achieve an unplanned, sustainable, 20 percent increase in production. This measure is now

under two weeks for best in class and even less than a week for some industries. The main constraint is material availability and not internal manufacturing or labor constraints.

- **Delivery performance to request:** The percentage of orders that are fulfilled on or before the customer's requested date. The survey indicated that best-of-class performance is at least 94 percent and in some industries approaches 100 percent. The median performance ranges from 69 percent to 81 percent.

The SCOR model is a good example of supply chain metrics, and is a way to compare performance to other companies in the same industry or in others. It has the additional advantage of possibly becoming an industry standard. However, as we saw in the Dell case, every company needs to understand its own unique environment and determine its measures based on that insight. For instance, Dell measures inventory velocity and not inventory turns, which is the standard measure of inventory management performance (see Chapter 3).

10.5 INFORMATION TECHNOLOGY AND CUSTOMER VALUE

Information technology has produced many valuable benefits for customers and businesses. We will briefly review three aspects below. The first is exchange of information between customers and businesses, the second is the use of information by companies to learn more about their customers so that they can better tailor their services, and the third is enhanced business-to-business capabilites. For more details on this subject, see Chapters 7 and 11.

1. **Customer benefits.** Customer service has changed for many reasons. One of the most dramatic is the opening of corporate, government, and educational databases to the customer. This started with kiosks and voice mail and has accelerated significantly with the uniform data access tools of the Internet. These innovations have had the effect of increasing customer value while reducing costs for the supplier of the information. Banks were the first to realize that by installing automated teller machines (ATMs), they could reduce their workforce. Voice mail was at first derided as dehumanizing, preventing interactions with a live person, but it actually allowed unmediated access to a user's accounts at any time of the day from almost anywhere. The Internet has expanded these capabilities and allows users to access their accounts and perform transactions from any location at any time. This opening of the information boundaries between customer and company is part of the new customer value equation, where the information is part of the product.
   The Internet has also had some less obvious effects [15]:

   - *Increased importance of intangibles.* Customers have become accustomed to ordering even high-priced products from unseen salespeople over the phone or Internet. This increases the importance of brand names and other intangibles, such as service capabilities or community experience in purchasing decisions.
   - *Increased ability to connect and disconnect.* The Internet makes it easier not only to identify business partners and connect to them but also to disconnect and find new partners. Increasing availability of information, including performance measures and data, reduces the need to develop long-term trust relationships. Companies can rely on accessible, published track records to make decisions on quality of service. This ability is mainly important when there is not a considerable

initial investment in setting up the partnership. If there is, then frequent changes of partners may have a major impact on cost and available resources.

- *Increased customer expectations.* The ability to compare and the ease of performing various transactions over the phone and the Internet have raised expectations of similar services from every type of business as well as for business-to-business interactions.
- *Tailored experience.* The ability to provide each customer an individual experience is an important part of the Internet. Amazon.com saves the customer's information and recommends books and other items based on previous purchases. Mass customization can allow users to store their individual preferences or sizes and order custom-fit clothes and shoes from various vendors without having to reenter the information.

2. **Business benefits.** One way to enhance customer value is to use the information captured in the supply chain to create new offerings for customers. The information now available allows companies to "sense and respond" to customers' desires rather than simply make and sell products and services. Indeed, as we have seen, learning about customers takes time, requires some of the customers' time, and eventually makes switching vendors more difficult. The learning process takes many forms from sophisticated data mining methods used to correlate purchasing patterns, to learning about each individual customer by keeping detailed data of preferences and purchases. The method applied depends on the industry and business model. Retailers would use the first method while service companies, as in the example below, would be more likely to track individual customer preferences and requirements.

EXAMPLE 10-11

In the 1930s it was difficult for military personnel to obtain reasonably priced insurance, so a group of officers formed United Services Automobile Association (USAA) to provide insurance for military officers. USAA still offers services only to active and former military officers and their families and handles all transactions by mail and phone. USAA has used its extensive databases to expand into financial and shopping services for its members. When a customer calls USAA, the information about him or her can be accessed and updated and the customer can be offered a variety of services to match his or her needs. For instance, if a customer owns a boat purchased or financed through USAA, he or she could receive an offer to acquire insurance [123].

---

3. **Business-to-business benefits.** The Dell Computer case introduced at the beginning of the chapter illustrates how information technology allows companies to improve the performance of their suppliers and service providers. More recently, with the establishment of its private e-marketplace (see Chapter 7), Dell is using the Internet to improve supply chain collaboration by providing demand information and production data to its suppliers. Thus, these developments make it possible to outsource important parts of a company's business, but still keep close control over what it produces or services. For instance, strategic partnering relies heavily on information sharing and enables the partners to achieve supply chain efficiencies (see Chapter 6).

Other examples of information sharing between businesses can be found in [115]. The authors describe various arrangements between manufacturers and distributors for sharing information on inventory that results in cost reduction. These arrangements, motivated by the risk-pooling concept introduced in Chapter 3, allow manufacturers and distributors to reduce overall inventory by sharing information about inventory in all locations and allowing any member of the channel to share the inventory.

SUMMARY

Creating customer value is the driving force behind a company's goals, and supply chain management is one of the means of achieving customer value.

Our analysis shows that companies need to select their customer value goals since the supply chain, market segmentation, and skill sets required to succeed depend on this choice. In the book *The Myth of Excellence* [37], the authors analyze many companies along the lines of how they rank on price, product, service, access, and relationship. Their conclusion is that companies cannot excel along all these dimensions (thus the name of the book). Their analysis shows that in order to succeed, a company needs to be dominating in one attribute, differentiate itself on another, and be adequate in all the rest, but not below that. Some of the examples:

1. Wal-Mart stands out on price, as in its motto "Always low prices, Always," and secondarily in large brand selection.
2. Target competes by emphasizing brand selection before price. Nike Stores emphasize experience first and product second.
3. McDonald's provides access first (they have stores almost everywhere) and service second.
4. American Express emphasizes service first and access as a second attribute.

As we have seen, the Dell Computer case illustrates many of the current and future trends in creating customer value, in general, and using supply chain management, in particular. Below we summarize the major issues covered in the chapter and how they are illustrated in the Dell case.

Supply chain management strategy affects customer value; its considerations affect every aspect of customer value and must be part of any strategy or plan, not an afterthought. It is important to choose the appropriate supply chain strategy to match customer value with the company's market. Excellence in supply chain management translates into customer value in many dimensions, from availability and selection to influencing the price at which a product can be sold.

The supply chain strategy in the Dell case was the business model, and it created the customer value of low prices.

Customer access to information about the availability of products and the status of orders and deliveries is becoming an essential capability. This also creates opportunities to learn about customers and their preferences, and to create new modes of interaction. Dell uses this information to enhance its services.

Adding services, relationships, and experiences is a way for companies to differentiate their offerings in the market and learn about their customers. It also makes it difficult for the customers to switch to another service provider. Dell has added excellent customer support to its capabilities. Larger companies find that it provides more extensive options, from custom preloaded PCs to in-house service and support.

Measuring customer value is at the heart of company goals and objectives, but identifying the appropriate measure is not an easy task. Dell measures inventory velocity, not the classical inventory turnovers.

The ability to provide sophisticated customer interactions (for example, relationships and experiences), is very different from the ability to manufacture and distribute products. Because a distinctive expertise is required for each function, companies will gain by specializing. This concept has been applied successfully by Dell through virtual integration. Dell has relationships with many of the suppliers that provide the components of its product.

We also observe this trend in consumer product industries, where firms such as Nike and Sara Lee lend their name to products produced by many manufacturing companies.

A virtually integrated company can lose some of its ability to innovate and collaborate if it does not pay close attention to its relationships with suppliers. This is also true for other third-party providers performing tasks for the company. Communication systems, methods of sharing information and resources, and proper incentives need to be in place to make these relationships work. Dell, a company built on outsourcing, has been working on this type of collaboration for many years. It has practices in place to make sure that the quality of work performed by its partners meets its own standards.

There is no real customer value without a close relationship with customers. Today this is possible not only through direct interaction, but also through information and communications technology. By allowing customers to state their preferences and learning from them—a true two-way interaction—a firm can develop the means to achieve greater customer value and therefore loyalty. Dell has inadvertently been able to achieve this because of its direct supply chain model. The company has taken full advantage of its close relationships with its customers to become the largest PC seller in the world.

DISCUSSION QUESTIONS

1. Discuss the trade-off between product quality and price in traditional and on-line retailing.
2. Consider dynamic pricing strategies and their impact on profit. Explain why dynamic pricing provides significant profit benefit over (the best) fixed-price strategy as
   a. Available capacity decreases.
   b. Demand uncertainty increases.
   c. Seasonality in demand pattern increases.
3. Discuss how supply chain management decisions impact the ability to excel in certain dimensions. Specifically, consider
   a. Conformance to requirements.
   b. Product selection.
   c. Price and brand.
   d. Value-added services.
   e. Relationships and experiences.
4. What is the dominant customer value the following companies bring?
   a. Starbucks
   b. The Gap
   c. Expedia.com
5. What additional experience opportunities does the Internet enable?
6. What measures would you use in a business like Amazon.com to evaluate the company's performance? The supply chain?

CHAPTER 11

Information Technology for Supply Chain Management

Backup in the Espresso Lane

You have to admire the enthusiasm of Starbucks Corp. employees. Store managers have been known to stuff sacks of coffee beans into their cars and race over to help out other stores running low on java. Exceptional customer service, but certainly no way to run a business—especially one that's growing as quickly as Starbucks.

"With 2,000 stores, you can't have 2,000 people with coffee in their trunks," says Tim Duffy, director of supply chain systems and support for Starbucks in Seattle. The specialty coffee supplier plans to have 2,000 retail locations up and running by the turn of the century, up from 1,400 today. To make sure none of those locations is beholden to a distribution system backed by a fleet of employee cars, Starbucks is in the midst of overhauling its supply chain management system.

Unfortunately, what was supposed to be a three-year project is now slated to be finished in five, primarily because Starbucks chose a best-of-breed approach over an integrated ERP (enterprise resource planning) solution. With supply chain software vendors such as Manugistics Inc. bragging about full implementations of their applications being completed in less than a year, it's fair to ask what's taking Starbucks so long.

The answer to that question provides lessons for any IT executive looking to revamp his or her company's supply chain operations with a best-of-breed system. This approach, where companies hand-pick the best software product for each piece of the supply chain process, comes with its share of headaches. Among them: an extended vendor evaluation period, complex software integration hurdles, and version control problems. These issues are all the more pertinent since supply chains are top-of-mind these days. Purchases of supply chain management software will shoot up 45 percent, from $419 million today to $2.7 billion in 2001, according to a new report by Advanced Manufacturing Research Inc., of Boston.

"For a fast-growing company, even putting a single ERP system in place in three years would have been a pretty average time," says John Bermudez, group director of supply chain research for AMR. "I don't know that Starbucks really planned this thing out."

RECIPE FOR GROWTH

To get a clear picture of Starbucks' situation, you have to fully appreciate its challenges. Although it's a 26-year-old company, the coffee powerhouse has been on its caffeine-jolted growth curve for only the

Source: Lawrence Aragon, *PC Week*, November 10, 1997. Copied with permission.

past five years. Since it went public in 1992, the company has opened 1,235 retail locations. Sales from those stores account for 86 percent of the company's annual revenue.

But Starbucks' expansive retail operation is just a piece of its supply chain. As part of its effort to establish itself as a major brand, Starbucks launched joint ventures with Dreyer's Grand Ice Cream Inc., Pepsi-Cola Co., and Redhook Ale Brewery to create products based on its coffee. It also hammered out a deal with Capital Records to produce jazz compact disks, began selling its products through grocery stores, and struck a deal for its coffee to be carried by Aramark Food & Services Inc. Then there are the partnerships to sell its brew through other venues, including bookstore chain Barnes & Noble Inc. and United Airlines.

Amazingly, Starbucks was able to handle the growth—from $103 million in annual sales when it went public to about $700 million in 1996—with its original supply chain management systems. Duffy says the fact that Starbucks continued to thrive, even though it didn't have formal supply chain processes in place, is a tribute to the company's "ambitious and impassioned" employees.

That isn't hyperbole. Consider that the only real technology Starbucks used was a merchandise management system called JDA software, running on an AS/400. The rest of the supply chain processes were done manually. "For a long time, we didn't do production planning at the SKU level," Duffy says. Instead, planning was based around the company's 30-odd flavors of coffee. Today, Starbucks manages about 3,000 SKUs with software from Manugistics.

Forecasting was another area limited by the manual approach. Prior to the overhaul, it was essentially done through messages swapped between business unit managers and production managers on voice mail and e-mail, Duffy says. Now, business units use Retek Information Systems Inc.'s SkuPlan forecasting software to create a rolling monthly forecast for sales and a rolling 24-month forecast for SKUs in general. That data feeds into Manugistics' software, which draws up an enterprise supply chain plan.

Starbucks even had problems with the fundamental BOM (bill of materials). "There were as many BOMs in the company as the people who needed them," Duffy says. And that meant higher costs because of redundancies and multiple and divergent forecasts. Today, BOMs are part of a comprehensive process

run by several applications, including Numetrix Laboratories Ltd.'s Schedule X software, which tells Starbucks the most efficient way to schedule its manufacturing resources.

Although it was getting by with its old system, Starbucks management knew it was spending more than it should to support its supply chain. "We had grown so much and had so much volume, what the employees had built up to that point wasn't good enough anymore," Duffy explains.

So, in early 1995, Starbucks resolved to revamp the technology behind the supply chain. The stated goal: to create a state-of-the art, integrated supply chain system that would reduce costs by an undisclosed amount, improve customer service, and maintain consistent quality.

Initially, Starbucks figured that an ERP package would be the best solution. With that in mind, the company's supply chain operations and IT groups defined the company's needs, in part by using Expert Buying Systems Inc.'s Choose Smart software to query more than 50 people inside and outside the company. The next step was to send out requests for information to top ERP vendors and consult with industry experts, such as Gartner Group Inc., AMR, and the American Production Inventory Control Society. Demos and customer visits followed for five ERP vendors—Baan Co., Datalogix International Inc. (now part of Oracle Corp.), Oracle, QAD Inc., and System Software Associates.

Some six months after the whole process began, however, Starbucks decided that none of these ERP packages could meet its needs. Instead, it opted for a best-of-breed approach, which meant pulling together nine separate components. (See Table 11-1.) "We're building this thing so that at any given point in time, if we need to upgrade any part of the supply chain, we can probably more readily pull and replace any one component than we could with an ERP system," Duffy says. "The overriding reason is functional flexibility—to be able to react to the dynamic needs of our business environment."

Although the project is taking longer than anticipated, Duffy hammers home the point that "we deliver something every six to nine months. We have an overall vision that has been sliced into phases."

So far, Starbucks has purchased five of the applications outlined in its nine-piece plan. Software from Manugistics and Numetrix has been in place for about a year. Retek's SkuPlan went live in September,

> **TABLE 11-1**

STARBUCKS' SUPPLY CHAIN MENU

Vendor	Product	Function
Retek Information Systems Inc. (subsidiary of HNC Software Inc.)	SkuPlan	Forecasting
Manugistics Inc.	Materials planning, deployment, constrained production planning Distribution planning Manufacturing planning	Supply chain planning
Numetrix Laboratories Ltd.	Schedule X	Finite capacity scheduling
Oracle Corp.	GEMMS	Production activity control
Industri-Matematik International Corp.	System ESS	Order processing
TBD*	TBD*	Data warehouse for sales and operations
TBD*	TBD*	Purchasing
TBD*	TBD*	Warehousing/distribution
TBD*	TBD*	Transportation planning

*TBD = To be determined.

and Oracle Corp.'s GEMMS (Global Enterprise Manufacturing Management System) was launched in October. IMI's order processing software is scheduled to be in place by the spring, while applications for transportation planning, purchasing, and warehousing/distribution are set to be purchased and installed between 1998 and 1999. The final piece will be a data warehouse for sales and operations planning—a project that Starbucks plans to do itself.

BEST-OF-BREED CHALLENGES

Counter to what Starbucks is doing, most users today typically take a hybrid approach to automating their supply chains, says Ann Grackin, a partner in charge of the supply chain practice for Benchmarking Partners Inc., of Cambridge, Massachusetts. Most users purchase an ERP system as a "vine," then buy the "best fruit" in supply chain management software to hang onto it, she says.

Given that customers are demanding a bit of both worlds, ERP vendors have purchased, partnered, or made their products work with the top supply chain management software packages. For example, Oracle bought Datalogix last year for GEMMS, the company's client/server process manufacturing software. It also partnered in February with supply chain software vendors Manugistics

and Industri-Matematik International Corp. to create Oracle CPG, an enterprisewide solution for the consumer packaged-goods industry.

While Starbucks' Duffy insists that an ERP package wasn't an option when Starbucks made its decision, he admits that the best-of-breed approach is the primary culprit for the extended supply chain overhaul. "We were able to deliver key functionality faster, but the overall length of the project is longer," he says.

In contrast, Green Mountain Coffee Roasters Inc., a $47-million specialty coffee roaster in Waterbury, Vermont, went with PeopleSoft Inc. to revamp its supply chain management system and expects the entire project to be finished in less than two years. (See related case, "ERP Brews Instant Success.")

One of the reasons the best-of-breed method takes longer is that companies spend more time selecting and integrating packages. "Vendor management is a lot of work," says Duffy. "When you get into a partnership with each niche player, you have to establish a good, solid working relationship. That doesn't happen overnight."

As Starbucks works through its implementation—which it is doing by itself with a little help from consultants—the company faces a series of challenges typical of best-of-breed projects. One is retaining talent. If a project stretches into five years, "it can become a demotivating process," AMR's Bermudez says. "And when you have a hotshot company like Starbucks that's working with top-end applications like IMI, people become prime recruiting targets."

Duffy says he doesn't expect much poaching because Starbucks has a distinctive culture that is promoted by CEO Howard Schultz. "People are committed and driven to be a part of a fun time in our history," he says. "I think that alone is a key factor to keeping turnover low."

If headhunters weren't enough of a headache, companies pursuing best-of-breed projects face the migraine-inducing process of juggling new versions of each of their applications. It can be a political nightmare because certain departments may need a new version of an application, while those that don't could resent having to go through the upgrade process, says Benchmarking's Grackin.

The best-of-breed method also creates extra work. You have to constantly build "bridges" between applications, says Jim Prevo, CIO of Green Mountain. "Doing that once is one thing, but when you're faced with revisions as the best-of-breed applications evolve, you have to make sure your bridges hold together," he says. "For example, if you have an order management application from Vendor A and a warehouse management application from Vendor B, you have to make sure the interface to Vendor B holds up after a revision to Vendor A."

That could pose problems for Starbucks. "In pockets of the company, they will have superior performance, with, say, Manugistics," Grackin says. "But where they might fall down is keeping different business functions communicating with each other seamlessly."

Duffy concedes that "the challenge is managing integration and staying current on versions." But he says: "We have enough bright people, and we're confident that we'll find an effective solution."

THE UPSIDE

The best-of-breed approach does have some advantages, according to Grackin, who specifically cites flexibility. But Starbucks might do well to look into making Oracle its framework and plugging in select best-of-breed applications, since it is already using some of the components of Oracle CPG, she says. "It really depends on how far along they are. Either it's too late or they should run to the telephone," she says.

In fact, Starbucks is showing interest in CPG and is keeping a close eye on how Oracle develops it.

For now, Duffy says Starbucks is happy with its best-of-breed approach. The company has seen reductions in its overall inventory, inventory obsolescence, overtime hours and emergency orders, as well as in other areas, he says. Duffy declines to give specific numbers, but says that his department is still committed to a 40 percent return on investment. "I fully expect to be able to go back to our chief financial officer and say, 'These are what these dollars bought you,'" he says.

Evidence that the best-of-breed approach is working, Duffy says, is the fact that top management is watching the process closely and has not called him on the carpet even though the project is taking longer than expected. "If they weren't seeing improvement, we'd be seeing second-guessing today," he says. "But this company is twice the size it was two years ago and we're delivering. We've met or exceeded expectations to date."

ERP Brews
Instant Success

Green Mountain Coffee Roasters Inc. won't be catching up to Starbucks Corp. anytime soon. But that doesn't mean the small coffee roaster doesn't have the same double cappuccino–size supply chain problems as its larger competitor.

The main difference is that the $47 million Green Mountain went with an ERP (enterprise resource planning) system and is on track to finish the project in less than two years. Meanwhile, $700 million Starbucks opted for a best-of-breed approach that's taking it about two years longer than expected to implement.

Starbucks' approach is not necessarily wrong. But for smaller companies, an ERP solution may be just the ticket to solve supply chain woes without getting into the timely—and costly—process of cobbling together best-of-breed projects.

NO MORE HOMEGROWN

Green Mountain had been using a homegrown system that integrated its financial, manufacturing, and distribution systems. It worked well for about 10 years, but "as we started growing, we hit the wall on scalability," says Jim Prevo, CIO of Green Mountain, in Waterbury, Vermont. "For example, when we tried to bring on our four regional operation centers, we couldn't perform transactions outside the Waterbury area without locking up the database."

Green Mountain couldn't dally. In addition to about a dozen retail stores, 5,000 wholesale outlets depend on the roaster for their coffee, as well as a mail-order catalog and business partners such as the Delta Shuttle and Amtrak.

Prevo figured he and his skilled crew of programmers could write a new application, but they found tools lacking for building a three-tier client/server system. They pulled the plug on the project after four months.

The next decision was relatively simple: Find a suitable ERP system. Prevo didn't even entertain the thought of buying best-of-breed applications and integrating them because he had seen the high maintenance associated with his own homegrown application. "What happens is you have a lot of redundant maintenance of tables, or you have to build bridges to feed changes back and forth between systems," he says.

To choose an ERP vendor, Prevo and his team put together a software selection document outlining their functional requirements and a demonstration script. They followed that with invitations to top ERP vendors to make a one-day pitch and a two-day demo. The short list included SAP AG, Baan Co., and QAD Inc. It wasn't until Prevo went to an American Production Inventory Control Society conference in October 1996 that he gave serious consideration to PeopleSoft Inc.

After less than three months of evaluations, Green Mountain chose Enterprise Solutions from dark horse PeopleSoft. Prevo was impressed by PeopleSoft's track record for quality products, its flexibility, and its tool set.

Green Mountain purchased 17 modules of the Enterprise Solutions in late January, and by early June it went live with seven of them: general ledger, accounts payable, purchasing, production management, bill of materials and routing, cost management, and inventory management. Prevo expects the entire project to be completed within the two-year projection or possibly six months earlier.

Green Mountain has not yet seen a return on its $2 million investment, but Prevo expects the system to start paying for itself soon after it's fully installed.

One of the reasons the implementation has been speedy, according to Prevo, is because Green Mountain hired some PeopleSoft contractors and an integrator, Strategic Information Group, of San Jose, California. "Because we had a rapid deployment schedule, we knew that we'd need rapid knowledge transfer, and it takes way too long to send people to training classes and develop that purely internally," Prevo says.

Green Mountain is running Enterprise Solutions on an Oracle Corp. database sitting on a Windows NT server running atop a Compaq Computer Corp. ProLiant 5000 equipped with two 200 MHz Pentium Pro processors, 640 MB of RAM and 28 GB of storage on a RAID 5 stack. "In general, the performance is adequate," Prevo says. He expects to see some improvements with the recent release of PeopleSoft 7 and the follow-on, PeopleSoft 7.5.

Prevo hopes to see further improvements as PeopleSoft continues to integrate planning software from Red Pepper Inc., a best-of-breed vendor PeopleSoft acquired last year. If all goes as planned, PeopleSoft will keep Green Mountain brewing for a while to come.

By the end of this chapter, you should be able to answer the following questions:

- What are the goals of software installations like the ones described at Starbucks and Green Mountain?
- Why have Starbucks and Green Mountain chosen such different approaches to the same problem?

- What is the relationship between ERP software and decision-support software used in the installations?
- How will current trends in the information technology area affect the companies' ERP implementations?
- How does the Internet affect supply chain management?

11.1 INTRODUCTION

Information technology (IT) is an important enabler of effective supply chain management. Much of the current interest in supply chain management is motivated by the possibilities that are introduced by the abundance of data and the savings inherent in sophisticated analysis of these data. The innovative opportunities coming to the fore with electronic commerce (e-commerce), especially through the Internet, have also increased the interest in IT.

Supply chain management spans the entire enterprise and beyond, encompassing suppliers on one end and customers on the other. Therefore, our discussion of IT for supply chains will include both systems that are internal to an individual company as well as external systems, which facilitate information transfer *between* various companies and individuals.

In addition, supply chain management typically spans many functional areas within a company and is affected by the way the various groups communicate and interact. Thus, in this chapter we will also discuss topics that relate to company IT infrastructure, supply chain applications, and intercompany communications.

For many firms, IT provides a competitive advantage. Though this has been true for some time in service industries such as banks, it is also becoming more relevant for firms such as large retailers, airlines, and manufacturers. Prominent examples include Wal-Mart with its satellite-connected Information Technology, American Airlines with its innovative Sabre reservation system, Federal Express with its superb tracking system, and Cisco with its "virtual manufacturing environment" (see Chapter 7).

Indeed, as we have observed in Chapters 3 and 4, when applying supply chain strategies that reduce cost and lead times and increase service level, the timeliness and availability of relevant information are critical. In addition, an increasing number of companies are providing value-added IT-based services to their customers as a way of differentiating themselves in the marketplace and developing strong long-term relationships with their customers. Of course, once these kinds of services are offered by even one company within an industry, they can very quickly become a basic requirement for all others.

In many cases, current IT that supports the components in the supply chain process is diverse and disconnected. It has typically evolved throughout the years based on various local and companywide requirements that were rarely integrated. This issue must be addressed if a company is to position itself to manage its supply chain effectively.

Various strategies are utilized by companies to overcome these problems and create systems that can use the multitude of data in the system effectively. In this chapter, we will explain how these systems are typically implemented in the supply chain management process, how different systems relate to each other, and how the systems and relationships are evolving.

As we will review in more detail in this chapter, information flow between suppliers, manufacturers, and customers is critical for effective supply chain management. This entails information flow between different companies, a relatively new concept that is already widely practiced to varying degrees (e.g., e-mail, EDI, exchanges). We will also discuss how developing standards for communications and user interfaces, particularly through the use of the Internet, are facilitating fairly inexpensive, simple-to-implement solutions to problems that previously would have required massive investments of time and money.

The implementation of advanced IT solutions typically requires changes in organizational structure, as well as in employee job descriptions and behavior. Although these issues are not the focus of this chapter, they need to be kept in mind; for a discussion of these issues, see [134].

Specifically, in this chapter we will discuss the following questions:

- What are the goals of IT from the perspective of supply chain management?
- What IT components are needed to achieve the goals of supply chain management?
- What are the supply chain component systems and how should they be approached?
- What are the trends in IT and how do they affect supply chain management?
- What are the stages in the development of enterprise IT?

11.2 GOALS OF SUPPLY CHAIN INFORMATION TECHNOLOGY

In this section, we consider some of the ultimate goals of IT as it relates to the supply chain. Some companies and industries are currently far from achieving these goals, while others are well on their way to accomplishing many of them.

To utilize information, we need to collect it, access it, analyze it, and have the ability to share it for collaboration purposes. Supply chain management system goals in these areas are

- Collect information on each product from production to delivery or purchase point, and provide complete visibility for all parties involved.
- Access any data in the system from a *single point of contact*.
- Analyze, plan activities, and make trade-offs based on information from the entire supply chain.
- Collaborate with supply chain partners. As we have seen in Chapters 1 and 6, collaboration allows companies to manage uncertainty, for example, through risk sharing or information sharing, and achieve global optimization.

The primary goal of IT in the supply chain is to link the point of production seamlessly with the point of delivery or purchase. The idea is to have an information trail that follows the product's physical trail. This allows planning, tracking, and estimating lead times based on real data. Any party that has an interest in the whereabouts of the product should be able to have access to this information. As we can see in Figure 11-1, information and products flow from the supplier to the manufacturer, internally through the manufacturer's distribution system, and then on to the retailers.

Below we discuss each goal:

- **Collect information:** Evidently, the retailer needs to know the status of its orders and the suppliers need to be able to anticipate an incoming order from the manufacturer. This entails access to data that reside in other companies' information systems as well as across functions and geographic locations inside a company. Furthermore, the participants need to see data in their own terms; that is, if suppliers of cotton are looking at the demand for Q-Tips, they need it translated into pounds of cotton consumed. Therefore, translation tables, such as bills of material, are required throughout the system.

FIGURE 11-1 Flow of information and goods in the supply chain.

The availability of information regarding the status of products and material is the basis on which intelligent supply chain decisions can be made. Furthermore, it is not sufficient to simply track products across the supply chain; there is also a need to alert diverse systems to the implications of this movement. If there is a delay in a delivery that will affect production schedules, the appropriate systems need to be notified so they can make the proper adjustments by either delaying the schedules or seeking alternative sources. This goal requires standardization of product identification (e.g., bar coding) across companies and industries. For example, Federal Express has implemented a tracking system that provides ongoing information on the whereabouts of any package handled by the company and makes this information available internally as well as to customers.

- **Access to data:** Here we introduce an important concept, the single-point-of-contact concept. The goal here is that all the available information, either information provided to a customer or required internally, can be accessed in one stop and be the same, regardless of the mode of inquiry used (e.g., phone, fax, Internet, kiosk) or who is making the inquiry. This requirement is complicated by the fact that to satisfy a customer's query, information may be required that resides in various locations within one company and, in some cases, across several companies.

  In many companies, information systems tend to be islands, depending on their functions within the company. Customer service will work with one system, accounting with another, and the manufacturing and distribution systems are completely separate (see Figure 11-2). Occasionally there may be a transfer of some crucial information that needs to be accessed across systems, but if the transfer is not done in real time, then the systems never have exactly the same data. The customer service representative receiving an order may not be able to provide shipping status information, and the plant may not be able to inquire about current outstanding orders. Ideally, everyone who needs to use certain data should have access to the same real-time data through any interface device (see Figure 11-3).

  Banking applications are advanced in this respect: you can access the same account information the bank tellers use, from almost anywhere over the telephone, computer, or ATM machine. Nevertheless, these systems may still be weak at linking all of a customer's accounts into a single point of inquiry—for example, accessing mortgage information at the same time as a bank account.

- **Analyze based on supply chain data:** The third goal is related to analyzing the data, especially in a way that takes into account the global supply chain picture. In addition, the information system must be utilized to find the most efficient ways to

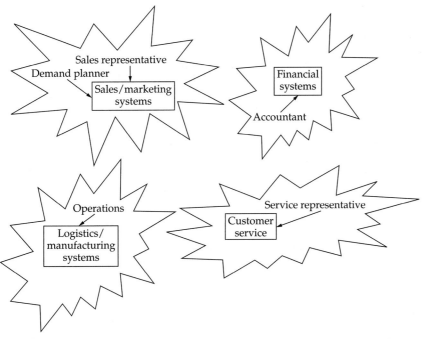

FIGURE 11-2 Current information systems.

produce, assemble, warehouse, and distribute products—in other words, the best way to operate the supply chain. As we have seen, this entails various levels of decision making: from operational decisions involving the way to fulfill a customer order, to tactical decisions related to which warehouse to stock with what product, or what the production plan for the next three months should be, to strategic decisions about where to locate warehouses, and what products to develop and produce. To facilitate this, systems need to be flexible enough to accommodate changes in supply chain strategies. To achieve this kind of flexibility, systems need to be highly configurable and new standards need to be developed. We will discuss these issues in detail below.

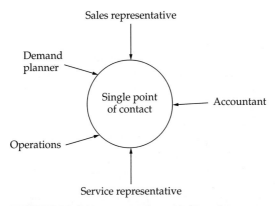

FIGURE 11-3 New generation of information systems.

- **Collaborate with supply chain partners:** The ability to collaborate with supply chain partners is essential to a company's success. Indeed, as observed in Chapter 1, an important objective in supply chain management is replacing sequential processes with global optimization. This requires not only sophisticated alignment of IT systems but also the integration of business processes. Depending on its supply chain role, a company may be required to either integrate with a customer's procurement system or require its own suppliers to link into its own systems or collaborative platforms, or both. The level and type of collaboration vary between industries. For instance, collaborative forecasting was initiated in the consumer packaged goods industry while supplier integration is more common in the hi-tech industry where outsourcing of critical components requires systems that support the product and logistics coordination.

  In recent years, collaboration has become the focus of supply chain systems. The ability to link and work effectively with suppliers has produced new systems called supplier relationship management (SRM). In addition, the various exchanges that were developed during the Internet boom of the late 90s are becoming collaboration platforms, whether private or public. On the other end of the supply chain, customer relationship management (CRM) systems are evolving to provide better contact and understanding of customer needs. For more on these systems, see Section 11.4.6.

As we will see, the four goals of supply chain management do not all have to be achieved at the same time, and are not necessarily dependent on each other. They can be targeted in parallel, with the order of importance depending on the industry, company size, internal priorities, and return on investment considerations. For instance, a bank could not survive without single-point-of-contact capability, a delivery company without a sophisticated tracking system, and a high-tech manufacturer without a production planning system.

To achieve these goals and to master the decisions and problems that arise when considering how to address them, it is helpful to understand many of the major issues in IT development, particularly as they relate to supply chain management. As we see in Figure 11-4, the following are the means toward achieving these goals.

- *Standardization*: IT standards are what allow systems to work together. They drive the cost and sometimes the feasibility of implementation.

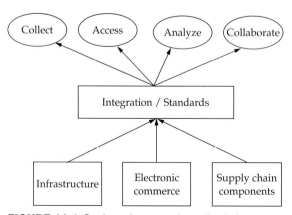

FIGURE 11-4 Goals and means of supply chain management.

- *IT infrastructure*: The IT infrastructure, whether internal or external to a company, is a basic component of system capabilities. Without the communications and database capabilities, some of the goals outlined cannot be achieved.
- *Electronic commerce*: Electronic commerce has been the most important emerging IT field in the last few years. It has enabled not only internal efficiencies but also the ability to collaborate with partners in the supply chain.
- *Supply chain system components*: These components comprise the various systems that are involved directly in supply chain planning. These are typically systems that combine short-term and long-term decision support system and intelligence elements.
- *Integration-related issues*: How should priorities be set in order to achieve the goals discussed above? What kind of investments should be made in the short term and in the long term?

11.3 STANDARDIZATION

Although it is hard to predict in an ever-changing field such as information technology (IT), some trends and practices are evident. Primary among these is the push toward IT standards. Although some issues are specific to logistics and supply chain management, most developments are occurring across industries and application areas. The IT field is evolving to a high level of standardization for the following reasons:

- *Market forces*: Corporate users need standards in order to reduce the cost of system development and maintenance.
- *Interconnectivity*: The need to connect different systems and work across networks has pushed the development of standards.
- *New software models*: The internet has produced the need for network software that has new purchase, development, and deployment characteristics.
- *Economies of scale*: Standards reduce the price of system components, development, integration, and maintenance.

The standardization of IT has gone through four major phases:

- **Proprietary:** The initial computer development until the early 80s involved proprietary systems, mostly mainframe computers that were accessed through key punches and later terminals with no processing capabilities (so-called dumb terminals). There was little communication between systems and that was performed through private networks or physical media.
- **Stand alone:** The IBM personal computer (PC) software and hardware, introduced in the early 80s, became the first standard platform. This eventually created a large user base and a large market for applications—called Wintel, the Microsoft Windows and Intel standard. Communication standards were also developed mostly for local networks—Ethernet and IBM token ring were the leading contenders. For business networks, some standards were developed, but mostly private networks were used for file transfers. Electronic data interchange (EDI), a common transaction format, was introduced at this time. It allowed companies to electronically transmit data that used to be handled in paper form and by data entry. We will expand on the topic of EDI in Section 11.4.5, "Electronic Commerce." A further development, client/server technology, integrated the PC capabilities and standards with business systems, applying the PC computing powers to create a more sophisticated client-controlled interface.

- **Communications:** The Internet provided the missing link in communications and display standards beyond the local network. Initially developed by the U.S. government and used primarily in research institutes, the development of the browser in the early 90s created a standard and accessible interface and caused the spread of use to individuals and later companies. Another benefit was that the Internet enabled forms of communication that heretofore existed internally in many companies to work across companies and to become as ubiquitous as phone calls. The most obvious example is electronic mail (e-mail), but this is by no means the only form. File and information transfer between individuals and companies was greatly simplified by the Internet. The Internet then spawned expanded electronic commerce from shopping, bidding, and exchanges to shipment tracking and collaboration between companies. In the meantime, due in large part to year 2000 fears, many companies replaced their legacy systems with client/server-based enterprise resource planning (ERP) systems, which have become the standard backbone of companys' IT. These systems typically covered manufacturing, finance, and human resource applications with some distribution functionality. Supply chain management systems have been more varied and less standard, although ERP vendors have added these capabilities to their offerings.
- **Collaboration:** The next phase of standards, which is currently largely under development, will address collaboration, a more sophisticated form of communication between companies. There are various efforts to address these issues—we will describe some of the most prominent ones, although only time will tell what will evolve to be the next standard. Indeed, it is worth pointing out that in the previous phases, successful developments came about quite unexpectedly and hence it is hard to predict which standard will succeed. The major issue is specifying a common language format that will enable diverse systems to understand each other. In addition, software vendors are introducing technology that will simplify integration and enable systems to access each other's information and processes in a standard way.

The new phase of collaboration has also increased the importance of ERP systems as well as the need for a new generation of systems that support internal and external integration. This is true, since the ability to expand processes and capabilities outside the company requires improved internal processes as well as new capabilities that the first-generation of ERP systems does not have. For this purpose, ERP systems are evolving into the so-called ERP II, a term introduced by the Gartner Group. ERP II is an application and deployment strategy that expands out from ERP functions in the following ways:

- *Role* has changed from enterprise optimization (in the first-generation ERP systems) to collaborative commerce and supply chain management (in ERP II).
- *Domain* has changed from a focus on manufacturing and distribution (in the first-generation ERP systems) to include supply chain, customer-facing, and supplier-facing systems (in ERP II).
- *Function* has changed from internal processes such as finance, manufacturing, and distribution (in the first-generation ERP systems) to addressing cross-industry and specific industry concepts (in ERP II).
- *Process* has changed from internal and hidden (in the first-generation ERP systems) to externally connected (in ERP II).
- *Architecture* is evolving from closed and monolithic (in the first-generation ERP systems) to a Web-based, open, and component-based environment (in ERP II).

- *Data* has changed from internally generated and consumed (in the first-generation ERP systems) to internally and externally published and subscribed (in ERP II).

One of the cornerstones of all new IT standards development is the eXtensible Markup Language (XML), which is a language description format that is fast becoming the standard for Internet transactions. XML was developed by the SGML Editorial Board formed under the auspices of the World Wide Web Consortium (W3C) beginning in 1996. Since gaining W3C recommendation status in February 1998, its text-based structure has proved easy to understand and use. In many instances, businesses can exchange information without intermediate format conversions, provided they use the same XML document formats. The design goals for XML were (see http://www.thesupplychain.com/eng/resources/glossary/xml.asp)

- XML shall be straightforwardly usable over the Internet.
- XML shall support a wide variety of applications.
- It shall be easy to write programs that process XML documents.
- The number of optional features in XML is to be kept to the absolute minimum, ideally zero.
- XML documents should be human-legible and reasonably clear.
- The XML design should be prepared quickly.
- The design of XML shall be formal and concise.
- XML documents shall be easy to create.

XML is a general standard that does not address the issue of terminology in a specific industry. This is being addressed in one case by a high-tech company industry consortium called RosettaNet (see *www.rosettanet.org*) that views itself as an e-business equivalent of the Rosetta stone, which carried the same message in three different languages, enabling translation from hieroglyphics. The RosettaNet-based initiative is aimed at producing a flexible standard governing on-line business collaboration between manufacturers and suppliers. RosettaNet defines dictionaries and Partner Interface Processes, which handle multiple data transactions among partners. It is being used by some high-tech vendors but has proven expensive to implement. This could change if the standard is adopted widely and vendors provide systems that support it.

Another important challenge in the development of standards is the issue of application-to-application interaction across companies, that is, the ability to allow the integration of various applications between different companies. Web services, touted by major vendors such as IBM, Microsoft, and Sun, are an emerging set of protocols and standards that reside on the Internet and allow applications to describe their function to each other so that they can integrate with no, or minimal, programming effort.

The Web services architecture is based on standards such as XML, UDDI (Universal Description, Discover and Integration), a directory service for applications, and communication protocols such as SOAP (Simple Object Access Protocol); see [63]. Web services will initially address mostly integration issues such as access to data in systems that are currently closed. Eventually, if security issues are addressed, Web services will provide self-defined stand-alone applications. In addition, the ramifications of Web services will be critical to the way software is developed, paid for, and deployed. Since Web services are offered as components, companies can purchase only the functionality they need, possibly in the form of services purchased over the Internet. Software updates will be automatic and payment will be on a per-use basis. Web service applications will make collaboration easier by deploying a loose-coupling approach to integration since the integration methods are part of the service and do not need to be tailored for each two applications that are being integrated.

For all the obvious advantages of standardization, we should mention a few of its drawbacks and challenges.

- **Availability:** Problems surround the cost of creating a standard and the power of those who hold standards, especially if these standards are proprietary. Proprietary standards are problematic because they may not necessarily be the "best" standards, just those belonging to the most powerful company. This happened in the video battle of Beta versus VHS and in the PC operating system battle of Apple versus Microsoft. Proprietary standards limit competition and therefore selection and advances in products beyond what the company owning the standard is willing to offer. Even Open Group standards, such as EDI, may sometimes limit growth because of (1) the difficulty of making changes acceptable to a committee and (2) producing timely improvements.
- **Security:** The easy access to the Internet exposes systems that are connected to attacks by hackers and conceivably industrial spies. In addition, there are inherent security issues that arise when everyone is running the same software: if someone finds a problem or takes advantage of a security flaw, he or she can access or bring down every system of the same type.
- **Scalability:** Standards that work in a certain context or size of problem may not be adequate for a different set of industries or for a large number of users. For example, RosettaNet, mentioned above, which is being developed by the high-tech industry, may not be appropriate for other types of industries because of its cost and complexity. This is an important challenge because of the enormous variety of supply chain applications that cut across industries, companies, and specialized supply chain functions.

11.4 INFORMATION TECHNOLOGY INFRASTRUCTURE

The information technology (IT) infrastructure is a critical factor in the success or failure of any system implementation. The infrastructure forms the base for data collection, transactions, system access, and communications.

IT infrastructure typically consists of the following components:

- Interface/presentation devices
- Communications
- Databases
- System architecture

11.4.1 Interface Devices

Personal computers, voice mail, terminals, Internet devices, bar-code scanners, and personal digital assistants (PDAs) are some of the interface devices most commonly utilized. A key trend in IT is toward uniform access capability anytime and anywhere, and interface devices clearly play a major role in this area. The Internet browser is fast becoming the interface of choice for information access, although it is still not as sophisticated as Windows in displaying forms and graphical data. In addition, other devices such as PDAs and phones are also competing as access devices to user systems.

Supply chain management requires a standard way to track products in order to provide participants with the information they need to perform efficiently. For instance, it is important to record point-of-sale information, especially if these data are accessible by the supplier, as in vendor-managed inventory systems.

The Uniform Code Council created the bar code system, Universal Product Code (UPC), in 1973, and it has been used extensively for scanning and recording information about products. Automatic data capture interfaces, such as bar-code readers and radio frequency (RF) tags, are standardized and commonly used. RF tags on products or packaging are used to locate items, particularly in large warehouses. The same technology, together with wireless communication devices and GPS capabilities, enables tracking of tagged cargo while in shipment.

A more recent development in this area is being introduced at the Auto-ID center (see www.autoidcenter.org), where many companies are collaborating with MIT researchers to develop Auto-ID technology. This technology will embed intelligence in physical objects that will allow them to communicate with each other and with businesses and consumers. A 96-bit code of numbers called an Electronic Product Code (ePC) will be embedded in a memory chip (smart tag) on individual products. Each smart tag will be scanned by a wireless radio frequency reader, which will transmit the product's embedded identity code to the Internet, where the detailed information on the product is kept. The necessary information about the product is then communicated back to the user.

The system also includes a Product Markup Language (PML) and an Object Naming Service (ONS). PML is a new standard language for describing physical objects to the Internet in the same way that HyperText Markup Language (HTML) is the common language for describing website information. The ONS tells computer systems where to find information about any object that carries an ePC code, or smart tag. ONS is based in part on the Internet's existing Domain Name System (DNS), which routes information to appropriate websites. The ONS will likely be many times larger than the DNS, serving as a lightening fast "post office" that locates data for every single one of trillions of objects carrying an ePC code.

When this new technology is operational, it will help businesses save billions of dollars in lost, stolen, or wasted products. Shoppers will be able to point their scanner-equipped cell phones at a product and learn about its features from the manufacturer's website while they are in the store. Items will be scanned and billed to the customer's personal account as they leave the store. In addition, another related technology called smart shelves will notify manufacturers when it is time to restock items. Finally, tracking products for supply chain purposes will be simplified, providing real-time information about inventory status.

To summarize, the impact of the Auto-ID technology on supply chain performance cannot be overstated. It includes

- Improved service level by reducing store/shelf stockout rate through an accurate inventory database that triggers an order when the inventory level is low.
- Reduction of the stockout level, especially for promotional and advertised items, can have a major impact on sales.
- Better utilization of store and warehouse space (why?).
- Significant increase in the ability to locate items at the store and in the backroom.

11.4.2 Communications

Interface devices are connected to either an internal system (e.g., LAN, mainframe, intranet) or an external network—either a private company network or the Internet. Sometimes direct links to another company's system are utilized for efficiency and security. There are two major trends in communications: the first is wireless communications, which is fast replacing the hard-wired computer and phone links most of us use today; the second is the single point of contact for communications.

Advanced communications capabilities enable many applications, including

Electronic mail (e-mail) can be internal to a company or external. The Internet provides for simple cross-company interaction that was unavailable until recently because every company had its own internal system. E-mail allows for communication across time zones and transfer of information and data.

Data exchange, the ability to electronically exchange transactions such as purchase orders and status between supplier and vendors, has been for many years supported by EDI. Recently, XML technology is enhancing and replacing EDI as well as supporting new Internet-based technology for information exchange.

Groupware enables group work by allowing shared access to information and specialized software so that knowledge can be shared throughout the company. There are also applications that allow sharing of electronic whiteboards and work on joint documents.

Transportation product tracking is the ability to locate a truck or cargo at any time during distribution. This technology requires a combination of the Global Positioning System (GPS) and wireless communications. As we have seen, the Auto-ID technology aims to address this area in a comprehensive way.

Supply Chain Event Management (SCEM) systems track predefined performance measures for inventory, transportation, or other events and alert users to problems in the supply chain such as stockouts or delays. The alerts can reach the user in any form he specifies, such as phone, e-mail, or pager. In addition, these systems can provide performance measures.

Exchange platforms are used to share information, track products, and trade with supply chain partners. The exchanges can be private or public and provide a means of communication between companies. They are typically Web-based and provide a means to share information and processes that is important for the development of collaboration and visibility in the supply chain. We expand on exchanges in Chapter 7.

11.4.3 Databases

Data need to be organized in some form of a database, including transaction information, status information, general information (prices and so on), forms, and group work. Organizing these data is an extremely challenging activity and may require specialized databases, depending on the type of data. Some types of databases are described below:

Legacy databases.   These systems are usually built around a hierarchical or network database. These databases can store large amounts of data, typically transaction data, and perform extensive processing. They typically have an on-line and batch component. Programs are written in COBOL (*co*mmon *b*usiness *o*riented *l*anguage) and reporting tools are somewhat cumbersome to use.

Relational databases.   These databases allow the storage of related data in such a way that standardized reporting and querying of related data are facilitated. For example, Structured Query Language (SQL) is designed only for relational databases. Relational databases may be centralized on a mainframe computer or server, or they may be distributed across a network of personal or minicomputers.

Object databases. These can hold not only numeric and character data but more sophisticated objects such as pictures and graphic structures. Object databases are used to store different kinds of information in a way that relates them to database operations. These databases already exist for some applications but are not yet standard and are costly to maintain. Storing graphic and other nonstandard data requires considerably more storage space than text/numeric data and is more complicated to manipulate.

Data warehouses. These databases combine data from other system databases to allow query by sophisticated analysis tools. Data warehouses usually involve enterprise data and hold extremely large amounts of data.

Datamarts. Datamarts are smaller versions of data warehouses and usually store a smaller set of data and are more departmental in scope.

Groupware databases. These are specialized databases designed to accommodate group functions, such as keeping track of updates, allowing multiple-user access, and so forth. Group databases are also important in the age of telecommuting and virtual companies, where keeping everyone up-to-date with relevant data is impossible without a shared database.

11.4.4 System Architecture

System architecture encompasses the way the components—databases, interface devices, and communications—are configured. We have added this topic to the section on information technology infrastructure because the design of the communications networks and choice of systems depend on the implementation of these systems.

Legacy systems evolved as departmental solutions using mainframe or minicomputers that were accessed through "dumb" terminals (see Figure 11-5). The PC was initially used apart from a company's main systems for special applications such as word processing or spreadsheets. Eventually the PCs in an office were connected by means of local area networks (LANs) so users could share files, e-mail, and other applications. These networks were then extended across companies with wide area networks (WANs) that connected the dispersed offices of a company. Finally, new systems were developed to take advantage of the PC's computing power and friendly graphic interface. In these systems, the PC is typically called the "client" and the main processor is the "server." *Client/server computing* is a form of distributed processing whereby some processes are performed centrally for many users while others are performed locally on a user's PC.

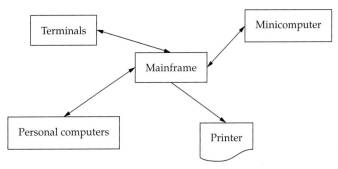

FIGURE 11-5 Legacy system architecture.

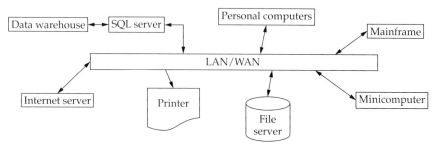

FIGURE 11-6 Client/server system architecture.

Most current system design involves client/server structure (see Figure 11-6), although the sophistication and price of the client, the number and type of servers, and various other design parameters vary greatly from system to system. Examples of servers include database servers that allow Structured Query Language (SQL) requests from users, transaction-processing monitors, directory/security servers, and communications servers. See [62] for an introduction to client/server concepts.

The Internet is a form of client/server where the local PC browser processes the HTML (hypertext markup language) pages and Java applets (i.e., small applications) that are retrieved from servers—in this case from all over the world. The client/server model is now evolving towards a Web-centric model where the client is a Web browser connected to a Web server.

The power of the client/server concept is in distributing functions among specialist servers that perform them efficiently; it is also easier to add new modules and functions. The disadvantage is the added complexity of navigating between servers and making sure that data are processed correctly and updated across the network. The implementation of client/server systems has also given impetus to the trend toward standardization because each server needs to be able to communicate tasks and processes across the network. This feature is called *interoperability*, which means two systems are capable of interacting in a sophisticated way that is a built-in feature of their design. Many interfaces between systems are created through file transfers or other temporary schemes, as we will see in the Aerostructures case in Chapter 12, because the systems use different file formats and communications schemes. When standards for intrasystem operation become common, tools will be available to perform these interfaces and provide full data and process-sharing interface mechanisms.

The applications that reside between the server and the client are collectively called *middleware*, literally the slash (/) in the term *client/server*. These are typically tools that facilitate communication between different system architectures, communication protocols, hardware architectures, and so forth. The parts of an application that reside on a server, client, or as middleware depend on specific implementations. This is the three-tiered architecture model now favored by many client/server designers.

Middleware can be important in the implementation of supply chain systems since, in many cases, the information for the planning tool exists in a number of locations and forms across the company. The appropriate middleware can be used to collect the data and format it in a way that can be used by various planning tools. That is how many supply chain applications are currently implemented. For instance, a telecommunications company may have billing information for the company's various services, such as long distance and wireless, stored on different systems. A customer service representative might have to search multiple locations for a customer's bills if the customer purchased more than one service. Middleware would perform the function of looking through the databases and combining the information.

When these types of processes are applied between companies over the Internet, they are called Enterprise Application Integration (EAI).

A more advanced generation of system infrastructure attempts to provide interconnectivity and collaboration platforms between companies. In Section 11.3 we reviewed the evolution from ERP to ERP II, which will provide extended support for these new infrastructure requirements. In Section 11.4.2 we mentioned exchanges, Web-based trading platforms, that currently provide the technology used for collaboration across enterprises. Finally, we described Web services in Section 11.3, a technology that has the potential to provide flexible links between systems. This can improve the interoperability of diverse systems and allow processes to more easily communicate.

11.4.5 Electronic Commerce[1]

Electronic commerce (e-commerce) refers to the replacement of physical processes with electronic ones and the creation of new models for collaboration with customers and suppliers. E-commerce can be used to facilitate the interaction between different companies as well as the interaction of individuals within companies. Examples include purchasing over the Internet, exchanges, order tracking, and e-mail.

E-commerce has been in existence for many years, using private networks for corporations (e.g., WANs) and public ones at universities and government agencies. The acceptance of Internet standards has accelerated the adoption of e-commerce, especially between individual buyers and companies but also between companies. The initial use of the Internet, showcasing marketing material, has expanded to allow user status and tracking inquiries as well as product purchases. Companies allow users to access their databases to troubleshoot product problems, thus saving the company money in support calls.

Companies use Internet standards internally—*intranets*—as well as externally—*extranets* and *exchanges*. The difference between Internets, intranets, and extranets is explained mostly by who is allowed access to the system. Intranets allow companies to implement internal applications without having to develop custom interfaces and avoid incompatible types of hardware and special dial-in procedures. Internet applications typically allow unlimited access but extranets allow limited access by restricting partners and customers from outside the company to certain applications and data. Internet standards have been used in recent years to create exchanges—private and public—that allow participants to trade or exchange information.

Another concept that has developed around internal company use of the Internet is the portal—a role-based entry into a company's systems. A portal aggregates all the applications and sources of information employees need in order to perform their job into a single desktop environment, typically through the Web browser. This capability not only empowers an employee to be productive individually, but also makes it simpler for employees to interact with others, whether within the company or outside. Portals require integration technology for structured and unstructured data sources, including databases, Java classes, Web services, and XML. As more organizations begin to deploy an enterprise portal framework, they are looking at ways to reduce the time and cost associated with building portals. The ability for end users to aggregate content and provide faster access to more information sources is critical to the success of building and maintaining portals.

---

[1] While there is a difference between the definition of a e-business and e-commerce in general (see Chapter 5), in practice these terms are used interchangeably.

████████ EXAMPLE 11-1 ████████

At office-furniture maker Herman Miller Inc., approximately 300 employees who spend most of their days in contact with suppliers use a customizable portal that gives them fast access to news and information. This allow the employees to deal with business partners more effectively, because they don't have to hunt for or combine various bits of data. The company was originally attracted to the technology from Top Tier Software (which was acquired by SAP in March 2001) because it provided a way for suppliers to interact with Herman Miller's enterprise resource planning system. Once the company saw how effective a portal interface could make employees, it began to roll it out for internal use as well. Today the company has several separate portals for various types of employees, but it is considering evolving its website into a sort of "superportal" that will then lead customers, suppliers, and employees to different subportals, depending on their needs. The benefits of collaboration are tremendous. For example, employees can decide what kind of alerts they want to have fed to their screens ("supplier X is three days late with a delivery") and then drill into data to identify the cause of the problem and the potential ramifications. The system has not been a panacea, however. While the technology is very good at sifting through structured data such as those contained in databases, it is far less effective in handling unstructured data, such as correspondence, computer-aided design drawings, and the like. SAP recently combined its portals division with another business unit that dealt with on-line marketplaces, where unstructured data predominate, so, over time, all that functionality can be brought to bear in a single product [93].

11.4.6 Electronic Commerce Levels

There are various levels of e-commerce depending on the sophistication of the transaction and the level of data interchange. Table 11-2 illustrates the four levels of e-commerce based on the type of exchange and data and process sharing.

Below, we describe the various levels in more detail and provide additional information about each example.

Level 1—One-way communication. This level has only one-way communication—the other party does not need to respond, as in the case of e-mail, file transfer, or Web browsing, or at least does not need to respond in real time. The browser or file data are usually for general use, through hypertext links, and cannot be accessed on the basis of any input data. This form of e-commerce has been around for more than 10 years, when Gopher and similar systems provided the browsing options before *World Wide Web* standards, developed at CERN,[2] became widely used.

Level 2—Database access. At this level the user of e-commerce is accessing a database for personal or tailored information by entering data through data-entry forms. In addition, the user can make personalized requests and orders, such as status inquiries and purchases over the Internet. The database access level also includes searches in company knowledge bases for obscure error messages and problem

████████ TABLE 11-2 ████████

SUMMARY OF ELECTRONIC COMMERCE LEVELS

Level number	Description	Example
1	One-way communication	E-mail, FTP, browsing
2	Database access	Inquiries, forms, purchases, tracking
3	Data exchange	EDI, clearinghouse
4	Sharing processes	CPFR, exchanges

[2]Conseil Européen pour la Recherche Nucleaire (the European Laboratory for Nuclear Research) in Geneva, Switzerland.

reports as well as use of vendor catalogs. Individual purchases can be made on the Internet using credit cards. This has raised some security issues, but it is no less safe than making a store purchase with a credit card. Business purchasing is typically more complex because there are restrictions concerning who can order and what configurations are acceptable. For that reason, Dell Computer created custom pages for businesses.

A more advanced application at this level is the creation of Internet sites that match buyers and sellers. These include electronic brokerages such as E*TRADE (www.etrade.com), transportation exchanges such as the National Transportation Exchange (www.nte.net), and auction and trading sites such as eBay (www.ebay.com) or ChemConnect (www.chemconnect.com).

These sites enable individuals and companies to either cut out the intermediary (in stock transactions), utilize available capacity more efficiently (as in the transportation exchange), or enlarge the market and force competition between suppliers (in public e-markets). See Chapter 7 for a detailed discussion.

Level 3—Data exchange. This level applies mainly to business-to-business transactions and requires computers on both ends to exchange information typically using *electronic data interchange (EDI)* and more recently XML-based processes. Another form of data exchange is the automated clearinghouse, which enables an industry to consolidate data and allows inquiries by all parties. This approach is used in the banking industry, for instance, to process student loans and in health care to process claims.

The data exchange level of application will soon be applied more extensively to individual transactions, for instance, filing Internal Revenue Service forms and receiving confirmation and corrections electronically. There are still many security issues, such as the use of digital signatures and authentication schemes, that need to be agreed upon to make this effective. Another development that will allow individuals to participate at this level is the application of electronic cash. This will allow charging small amounts for various electronic transactions and will make it easier to use networks for low-cost transactions such as phone calls, reading an article, software use, and many others. Finally, because of the global reach of the Internet, issues such as taxes, tariffs, and exchange rates need to be resolved before the full global potential is unleashed.

Level 4—Sharing processes. The final level occurs when different entities share processes, not just data, electronically. For this to happen, standards need to be agreed upon so that different applications can communicate with each other; see Section 11.3.

In recent years companies have started to invest in systems that allow for collaboration with supply chain partners. Two types of systems have been developed, supplier relationship management (SRM) applications and customer relationship management (CRM) applications. These applications can span a variety of forms, including access, data transfer, trading exchange, and collaborative ventures such as product design and planning.

SRM drives the optimization of production goods and materials for manufacturers. These systems include the following capabilities:

- **Strategic supply management** ensures that a company has the right set of suppliers, that they are performing, and that the company is paying the best possible pricing across the board.

- **Supply chain collaboration** allows a company to share information with its suppliers in real time, cutting materials costs, minimizing inventory, and reducing shortages and expediting.
- **Direct materials procurement execution** uses the Internet to automate the process of dealing with suppliers. Benefits include cutting cycle times, increasing inventory turns, and allowing purchasing people to eliminate low-value activities and focus on important issues.

CRM systems aim to drive and optimize the interaction with clients. Typical applications include

- **Sales-force automation** provides the ability to track interactions with customers and have a single point of contact for all types of activities and customer access.
- **Sales-pitch customization** enables cross-selling opportunities using analytical CRM software. It provides the ability to understand what customers are buying and offer them complementary products.
- **Managing and using customer information** analyzes how customers interact with the company and the ability to centralize and take advantage of customer activities.

Another example for sharing processes is collaborative planning, forecasting, and replenishment (CPFR), a Web-based standard that enhances vendor-managed inventory and continuous replenishment by incorporating joint forecasting. With CPFR, parties exchange electronically a series of written comments and supporting data that include past sales trends, scheduled promotions, and forecasts. This allows the participants to coordinate joint forecasts by concentrating on differences in forecast numbers. The parties try to find the cause of the differences and come up with joint and improved figures. As we emphasized in Chapter 4, the results of multiple forecasts can be very expensive across the supply chain. Indeed, sharing forecasts with distributors and other parties can result in a significant decrease in inventory levels since it tends to reduce the bullwhip effect (see Chapter 4). To do this, systems need to be designed to allow data verification and ensure standard practices of coordination.

Collaborative planning, forecasting, and replenishment was developed by the Voluntary Interindustry Commerce Standards Association (VICS) committee, made up of retailers, manufacturers, and solution providers. This group has developed a set of business processes that entities in a supply chain can use for collaborating along a number of buyer/seller functions, towards improving supply chain performance. According to the committee, its mission is to create collaborative relationships between buyers and sellers through co-managed processes and shared information. By integrating demand and supply-side processes, CPFR will improve efficiencies, increase sales, reduce fixed assets and working capital, and reduce inventory for the entire supply chain while satisfying consumer needs.

The VICS committee created the CPFR Voluntary Guidelines to explain the business processes, supporting technology, and change management issues associated with implementing CPFR. The CPFR Guidelines gained VICS board approval in June 1998. The committee published the CPFR Roadmap in November 1999, explaining how manufacturers and retailers can implement a CPFR partnership. This Roadmap, see www.cpfr.org, includes the following nine steps:

1. Develop guidelines for the relationships.
2. Develop a joint business plan.
3. Create a sales forecast.
4. Identify exceptions for the sales forecast.

5. Collaborate on exception items.

6. Create an order forecast.

7. Identify exceptions for the order forecast.

8. Resolve/collaborate on exception items.

9. Generate orders.

EXAMPLE 11-2

Henkel is a large German company with over 57,000 employees worldwide and over 11 billion euros in sales. Henkel manufactures over 10,000 products, including detergents, cosmetics, adhesives, and many others. Eroski is the leading food retailer in Spain, with over four billion euros in sales each year. Eroski is one of Henkel's largest Spanish customers. In December 1998, the two companies decided to undertake collaborative planning and forecasting (CPFR) in order to address customer service and stockout issues relating to Henkel products in Eroski stores. The effort initially focused on detergents, with a goal of improving customer service, reducing lost sales, and increasing the turnover rate. Using commercially available software, the two companies collaborated on business and promotional plans and sales forecasts. The process was started in December 1999, and the companies have seen dramatic improvement in the quality of forecasts. Before the process started, half of the sales forecasts had an average error of over 50 percent. Several months after the implementation, 75 percent of the forecasts show an error of less than 20 percent. Similar improvements were seen in stockout levels. One of the challenges of implementing CPFR between these two firms was involving business organizations in the forecasting process that had not been involved in the past. For example, Henkel customer service personnel had to develop close working relationships with Eroski sales forecasters. Once initial reluctance was overcome, the benefits of this process were quickly realized. Forecasts could be developed that combined Eroski's knowledge of the dynamics of individual retail outlets and the impact of promotion at these outlets, with Henkel's knowledge of the individual products and the impact of external factors on these product sales [68].

11.5 SUPPLY CHAIN MANAGEMENT SYSTEM COMPONENTS

In the previous section, we covered developments in information technology without focusing on supply chain management. The infrastructure issues, which ERP systems attempt to resolve, bring all business functions together and make an enterprise more efficient. They do not, however, help answer the fundamental questions of what should be made, where, when, and for whom. This is the role played by human planners with the aid of various analytical tools such as decision-support systems (DSSs), as discussed in Chapter 12.

As we saw in Section 11.2, where we analyzed the goals of IT, the first two goals, collecting and accessing data, require enterprise as well as interenterprise systems, which are not yet available in many industries. The third supply chain management goal, data analysis, may be the most achievable and the one with the highest and most immediate *return on investment (ROI)*. Such systems are much faster to implement and cause little disruption across the company since fewer people need to be trained to use a dedicated DSS.

The DSS that various companies and industries employ depends, among other things, on manufacturing characteristics, demand fluctuation, transportation costs, and inventory costs. For instance, if a company's predominant cost is transportation, the first DSS implementation would be a fleet routing system or a network design project. On the other hand, if there is a high variability in demand and complex manufacturing processes requiring setups when switching between products, demand planning and production scheduling systems may be the most urgent.

As we will discuss in more detail in Chapter 12, these systems typically support the strategic, tactical, and operational levels. Some of the supply chain components

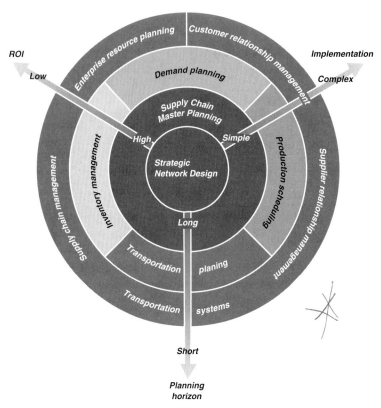

FIGURE 11-7 Capabilities required to acheive supply chain excellence.

predominantly support one level while others may support more than one, depending on how they are defined and utilized. The case study described at the beginning of Chapter 12 illustrates a typical application of supply chain optimization.

In this section, we describe the main IT capabilities required for supply chain excellence as well as the relationships between the different capabilities. These capabilities are described in Figure 11-7. As you can see, IT capabilities are partitioned into four layers:

- **Strategic network design** allows planners to pick the optimal number, location, and size of warehouses and/or plants; to determine optimal sourcing strategy, that is, which plant/vendor should produce which product; and to determine the best distribution channels, that is, which warehouses should service which customers. The objective is to minimize total costs, including sourcing, production, transportation, warehousing, and inventory, by identifying the optimal trade-offs between the number of facilities and service levels. The planning horizon for these systems is typically a few months to a few years using aggregated data and long-term forecasts. The method most often used is optimization.
- **Supply chain master planning** coordinates production, distribution strategies, and storage requirements by efficiently allocating supply chain resources to maximize profit or minimize systemwide cost. This allows companies to plan ahead for seasonality, promotions, and tight capacities. The planning horizon for these systems is typically weekly to monthly. See Chapter 5 for a detailed discussion.

- **Operational planning** systems enable efficiencies in production, distribution, inventory, and transportation for short-term planning. The planning horizon is typically daily to weekly and the focus is on one function; that is, each system focuses on only one function, for example, production. Therefore, these systems focus on generating feasible strategies, not optimized solutions, because of the lack of integration with other functions, the detailed level of the analysis, and the short horizon.

  Operational planning systems include four factors:

  —*Demand planning* generates demand forecasts based on various historical and other pertinent information. It also allows users to analyze the impact of promotions, new product introduction, and other business plans. The method used is mostly statistical analysis.

  —*Production scheduling* generates detailed production schedules based on the supply chain master plan or demand forecasts. The method used is constraint-based feasibility analysis that satisfies all production constraints.

  —*Inventory management* generates inventory plans for the various facilities in the supply chain based on average demand, demand variability, and source material lead times. The methods used are statistical and computational.

  —*Transportation planning* produces transportation routes and schedules based on availability of transportation on a lane, cost, and customer delivery schedules. There are a large variety of transportation planning options, so these systems can vary from fleet planning, transportation mode selection to routing and distribution planning. The methods used are mostly heuristic.

- **Operational execution** systems provide the data, transaction processing, user access, and infrastructure for running a company. These systems tend to be real-time in the sense that the data are current and are constantly being updated by users and events. These systems include five factors:

  —*Enterprise resource planning* traditionally spans manufacturing, human resources, and financials but is now the backbone of most companys' IT infrastructure. These systems are expanding to include new functionality covered by other components we discuss. They are also providing Web-based access and services and becoming more open to integration of other components.

  —*Customer relationship management* involves systems that update and track interaction with customers. These systems connect to order tracking and other back-end systems to provide better information for customers and the service representatives who are trying to assist them.

  —*Supplier relationship management* provides the interface to suppliers for transaction exchange as well as collaborative activities.

  —*Supply chain management* systems provide tracking of distribution activities in plants and warehouses as well as the event management that tracks exceptions based on performance measures. In addition, they provide lead time quotations based on current supply chain status—called available-to-promise (ATP) or capable-to-promise (CTP).

  —*Transportation systems* provide internal and external access and tracking of goods in transport. There may be some ability to route and plan at this level, but it would be on a smaller scale in terms of scope and horizon than the transportation planning systems.

  Figure 11-7 illustrates the difference between the various layers of capabilities:

- **Planning horizon** for strategic network design is much longer than for an operational system. Indeed, companies typically make long-term investments in facilities over a few years. On the other hand, supply chain master planning develops a strategy for a few months to a year. Finally, operational systems have a very short horizon of days to weeks.

- **Return on investment** for strategic systems can be very high since the decisions impact large capital investments and major distribution decisions. Typically, companies report 5 to 15 percent cost reduction due to strategic network design implementation. Consider now operational planning and execution, which can have a significant cost impact as well. Unfortunately, they require a much larger investment for much smaller gain.
- **Implementation complexity** of a strategic network design is not high since the tools that are used and the processes employed do need to integrate with other systems or processes. Similarly, strategic network design does not require real-time updates and few people in the company interact with it. Operational systems, on the other hand, are notoriously difficult to implement and integrate and require real-time data and extensive training.

11.6 INTEGRATING SUPPLY CHAIN INFORMATION TECHNOLOGY

How do all the elements of information technology (IT) come together? Supply chain management is extremely complex, so there is no simple or cheap solution to the issues we have raised. Many companies do not think it is cost-effective to introduce certain IT innovations because they are not sure there will be a significant return on investment. Trucking companies do not purchase sophisticated tracking systems because few clients would actually want to receive such detailed information. Warehouse managers do not invest in radio frequency (RF) technology because it is too expensive.

The key is to analyze what each component can contribute to the enterprise and then plan the investment according to the specific needs of the company and the demands of the industry. It should be noted, however, that the holistic solution is frequently greater than the arithmetic sum of the parts—that is, installation of a warehouse control system and a transportation management system can do wonders for customer service performance.

Companies need to decide whether to automate their internal processes or agree to some industry conventions—which usually happens when investing in an ERP system from one of the major vendors (e.g., SAP, PeopleSoft, Oracle, Baan). As more and more companies share information such as order entry, requisition, bills of material, and so forth and take part in joint planning, one can expect standard approaches to sharing this information will lower everyone's cost of doing business. In supply chain management, no single standard has yet emerged, as each ERP vendor continues to set its own de facto standards.

Due to the lack of standards, it is quite likely that in the near future middleware in the form of message brokers whose objective is to mediate between different systems and different standards will be developed. Eventually supply chain standards will become part of the basic systems that constitute the infrastructure.

In the following sections, we will review some important aspects of supply chain system integration. First, we review SAP's "Stages of Excellence" model, a model designed for evaluating a company's stage of development in IT and its impact on supply chain management. As a major vendor of supply chain systems, SAP helps clients pinpoint their current state of development as well as points them toward goals for the future based on their industry and unique needs. In the next section, we discuss implementation of ERP and DSS. What are the priorities in implementation? What should a company invest in first? Finally, we will review the "best-of-breed" compared with the single-vendor package dilemma and illustrate the dilemma with an example of two companies engaged in the same business that are taking divergent routes.

11.6.1 Stages of Development[3]

SAP, the leading ERP vendor, provides a Supply Chain Management Value Calculator that can tell by a company's industry, stage of development, revenue, and profit margin how much they can save from an investment in various SCM systems. The "Stages of Excellence," as the development stages are called, are divided into four levels (see www.sap.com/scm/). Note that, at any point in time, different parts of a company's business may be in different stages of development. The model defines the IT capabilities of an organization in each stage. Thus, the model is useful in evaluating current development and identifying where other companies are heading and where future competitive advantages lie.

Stage I: Disconnected systems.   Companies at this stage are characterized by the proliferation of many independent systems, manual and inefficient communications, and digitized internal data. Companies in Stage I typically focus on automating existing functions and tasks. Companies are organized functionally, with a low degree of integration and nonleveraged Web capabilities. Organizations at this stage of excellence must focus on internal process standardization and address Internet readiness.
   Characteristics of this stage include

- Functional (silo) strategies.
- Lack of clear, consistent supply chain management processes.
- Lack of qualified supply chain leadership.
- Disconnected systems.
- Measurements lacking or not aligned with company objectives.

Stage II: Internal and external interfaces.   In this stage, companies are organized functionally, with a high degree of integration and nonleveraged Web capabilities. These companies operate with functionally focused e-business solutions, disparate information systems, functional "flow through" of data, and decentralized external links. Trading partners can exchange information and interact via the Internet. Organizations at this stage are transaction-focused on both buy-side and sell-side activities.
   Characteristics of this stage include

- Integration of some functional information to decrease inventory and improve efficiency.
- Documented processes that are followed.
- Leaders who are supply chain professionals, and people providing data who are well-directed.
- Systems that are connected and generally provide accurate information about what is needed where.
- Key measurements that are used departmentally.

---

[3]SAP and mySAP.com are trademarks of SAPAktiengesellschaft, Systems, Applications and Products in Data Processing, Neurottstrasse 16, 69190 Walldorf, Germany. The authors gratefully acknowledges SAPs kind permission to use its trademark in this publication.

Stage III: Internal integration and limited external integration efficiency. In this stage, companies are cross-functionally organized. These companies operate with integrated systems within the enterprise, with limited external value chain integration. One-to-one trading partner interactions have been established. Organizations at this stage have linked suppliers to their back-end systems and integrated with buyer front-end systems.

Characteristics of this stage include

- Visionary organization that integrates information from whole supply chain to plan product movement from supplier to customer.
- Sophisticated processes that involve all affected organizations.
- Visionary, professional leadership.
- Highly capable systems that provide supply chain information to affected departments.
- Sophisticated systems that provide real-time guidance.

Stage IV: Multienterprise integration. Multienterprise systems/processes, common business objectives, seamless information sharing, knowledge organizations, and automated and interactive collaborations are included in this stage.

In this stage, companies are cross-functionally organized. These companies operate with integrated systems within the enterprise, with maximum external value chain integration. Total visibility into the value network is available as a result of end-to-end integration. Collaboration links trading partners and enables them to operate as one virtual corporation.

Characteristics of this stage include

- Collaboration across the supply chain.
- Internal collaborative supply chain management's focus on key service and financial goals.
- Executive leaders who foresee needs for functional and process skills that impact the supply chain and proactively drive skills development.
- Systems that integrate appropriate information across the whole company.
- Fully integrated performance management system that links supply chain results to company goals.

Table 11-3 presents examples of different capabilities of supply chain management IT and how they evolve through the different stages of IT development. Of course, a company can be in a mix of different stages, based on its investment strategy and importance of a certain aspect to the business.

As we have mentioned before, the ultimate goal is to standardize processes across an industry so companies can collaborate and cut costs. The ability to interact with as many business partners as possible in e-commerce projects makes this goal attractive. However, many companies report that the success of an application such as EDI requires that a large number of suppliers and customers utilize the system, a "critical mass"; otherwise the expected cost savings cannot be achieved and the system is not cost-effective.

11.6.2 Implementation of ERP and DSS

Implementation of a system that supports supply chain integration involves infrastructure and decision-support systems. The ERP systems that are typically part of the infrastructure are different in many ways from the supply chain DSS. Table 11-4

TABLE 11-3

SAP STAGES OF EXCELLENCE

Stage ⇒ Capability ⇓	I: Disconnected	II: Interfaces	III: Integrated internally	IV: Multienterprise integrated
Internet	Visibility	Catalogs	Exchanges	Unattended trading
Integration	None	Batch	Interenterprise	Supply chain networks
Supply chain planning	None	Informal demand planning	Formal global demand planning	Integrated global planning
Production scheduling	None	Basic MRP	Constraint-based	Advanced planning systems (APS)
Integration with suppliers	FAX/phone	EDI/FAX/phone	EDI with all large suppliers	VMI, on-line RFQ
Customer delivery	Research	Local inventory	Available to promise(ATP)	Capable to promise (CTP)

compares enterprise resource planning (ERP) and decision-support systems based on various implementation issues.

The question is what strategy should a company use in deciding what system to implement and when. IT goals (see Section 11.2) suggest that a company first must install an ERP system so that the data will be accessible and complete. Only then can it start analysis of its entire supply chain processes using various DSS tools. This may be the ideal, but in reality the data needed to achieve supply chain efficiencies already exist—maybe not in a single easy-to-access database, but it is worth the time it takes to assemble the database compared to the cost of waiting for installation of the ERP system.

These issues are illustrated in Table 11-4. An ERP implementation is typically much longer than a DSS implementation. The value of an ERP system to the enterprise involves the first two goals—visibility and single point of contact—and, while these can imply improved operations, DSSs impact the ability to perform strategic and tactical planning as well. This means that DSS projects have a much better ROI. Finally, DSS installations are typically cheaper and easier to implement and they affect a smaller number of highly trained users compared with those of an ERP system, which has a large number of users who require less extensive training.

Indeed, as we saw in the Starbucks case study at the beginning of this chapter, companies do not necessarily wait for an ERP implementation to proceed with DSS projects. Indeed, in many cases it makes sense to first implement DSS projects that

TABLE 11-4

ERP AND DSS FOR SUPPLY CHAIN MANAGEMENT

Implementation issue	ERP	DSS
Length	18–48 months	6–12 months
Value	Operational	Strategic, tactical, operational
ROI	2–5-year payback	1-year payback
Users	All end users	Small group
Training	Simple	Complex

TABLE 11-5

PRIORITIES WHEN IMPLEMENTING DSS

Industry	DSS
Soft drink distributor	Network and transportation
Computer manufacturer	Demand and manufacturing
Consumer products	Demand and distribution
Apparel	Demand, capacity, and distribution

provide a more immediate and observable return. Of course, companies examine their financial and human resources before they decide on the order and number of projects they will tackle at a time.

The type of DSS implemented depends on the industry and the potential impact on the business. Table 11-5 includes some examples from various industries. In the soft drink industry, where distribution is a major cost factor, priorities are different than those of a computer manufacturer, which has a complex manufacturing process with many different products and whose distribution cost is only a fraction of product cost. Thus, in the latter case, the manufacturer can utilize expensive shipping solutions.

11.6.3 "Best-of-Breed" versus Single-Vendor ERP Solutions

Supply chain IT solutions consist of many pieces that need to be assembled in order to achieve a competitive edge. They include infrastructure (ERP) and various systems to support decision making (DSS). Two extreme approaches can be taken: The first is to purchase the ERP and supply chain DSS as a total solution from one vendor; the second is to build a "best-of-breed" solution, which purchases the best-fit solution in each category from a different vendor, thus producing a system that better fits each function in the company. While the best-of-breed solution is more complex and takes longer to implement, it may be an investment that provides greater long-term flexibility and better solutions to the company's problems. Of course, the long period of implementation can also cause the solution to be less useful at the end and cause difficulty maintaining IT staff and enthusiasm for the project. Many companies choose an interim approach that includes a dominant ERP provider; the functionality that cannot be provided by the vendor, or does not suit the company, is provided through best-of-breed or in-house systems. Finally, there are companies (e.g., Wal-Mart) that still prefer in-house, proprietary software development [24]. This probably makes sense for extremely large companies with expert IT departments and systems that already serve the company well. Table 11-6 summarizes the pros and cons of these approaches.

TABLE 11-6

"BEST OF BREED" VERSUS SINGLE VENDOR AND PROPRIETARY

Implementation issue	Best of breed	Single vendor	Proprietary
Length	2–4 years	12–24 months	Not known
Cost	Higher	Lower	Depends on expertise
Flexibility	Higher	Lower	Highest
Complexity	Higher	Lower	Highest
Quality of solution	Higher	Lower	Not sure
Fit to enterprise	Higher	Lower	Highest
Staff training	Longer	Shorter	Shortest

In the introductory case study to this chapter, we introduced two coffee producers who chose completely different routes to implement their systems. Starbucks is implementing "best-of-breed" enterprise resource planning and decision-support systems while Green Mountain Coffee is implementing a one-vendor ERP solution. Note how the points mentioned in Table 11-6 come into play in the implementation experiences of the two companies.

SUMMARY

We have identified four major goals for IT:

1. Information availability on each product from production to delivery point.
2. Single point of contact.
3. Decision making based on total supply chain information.
4. Collaboration with supply chain partners.

How are the four major goals achieved? More importantly, what is the impact of achieving these goals on the logistics manager?

First, standardization of processes, communications, data, and interfaces bring about cheaper and easier methods to implement the basic infrastructure. IT infrastructure will become more accessible for companies of any size and in the future will work across companies in an almost seamless way. This will allow access to IT and integration of the systems at every level of the supply chain—therefore, there will be more information and tracking of products at each level. New technologies such as Auto-ID will allow products to be tagged and tracked through the supply chain and will be as easy to locate as a Federal Express package.

Second, data display and access in various forms are becoming more integrated in systems that do not require any specialized knowledge. This makes system interfaces more intuitive and relevant to the task at hand. The portal technology described in this chapter is one such example.

Third, various systems will interact in a way that will blur the current boundaries; Web service technologies, recently introduced by major vendors such as IBM, Microsoft, and Sun, are emerging technologies that allow different functions to integrate with no, or minimal, programming effort. As a result, systems purchased as "best of breed" by different people at various levels in the organization will become better integrated and use common interfaces. Similarly, there will be a proliferation of applications that can plug into a company's enterprise system to provide specialized functionality. The third goal will be achieved through development of decision-support systems and intelligent agents that are more sophisticated, rely on real-time data, and are interoperable.

Finally, electronic commerce is changing the way we work, interact, and do business. E-commerce provides an interface to businesses and government that allows meaningful data comparison, and transactions that follow through with error checking and correction capability. It enables access to data that exist in government, educational, and private databases and the ability to modify or correct these data. Private (and public) e-marketplaces now allow buyers to integrate their suppliers into their information systems. In the future, businesses will be able to expand their intercompany transactions into more sophisticated applications that can perform some basic processes and pass the information on to other applications. In a process as complicated as supply chain management, systems that not only perform their own function but also alert others in the system will be especially beneficial to fulfill the four goals we have outlined.

We end with a quote from Lou Gerstner, former IBM CEO (see [98]):

The payoff from information technology is going to be in making transactions and processes more effective and efficient, so it's not about creating a new economy, it's not about creating new models of behavior or new models of industry. It's about taking a tool, a powerful tool, and saying, "How can I make my supply chain more effective and efficient, how can I make my purchasing process more efficient, how can I make my internal employee communications more effective and efficient, how can I as a government deliver services to constituents more efficiently and more effectively?"

DISCUSSION QUESTIONS

1. Is the ERP industry fragmented? Explain why or why not?
2. What is the impact of Web service technology on supply chain management? Specifically, how can a third-party logistics provider use this technology to either improve services or provide new services?
3. In the last three years, a number of software vendors have offered their DSS in an ASP (application service provider) mode. In this case, the vendor hosts the client data and application and allows the client to access the website on an as-needed basis. What are the risks and benefits that the firm needs to consider when evaluating these services?
4. How can ERP vendors take advantage of Internet technology?
5. Compare the capabilities required to achieve supply chain excellence (see Figure 11-7) according to
   a. Decision focus.
   b. Data aggregation level.
   c. Time to implement.
   d. The number of users involved in the analysis.

CHAPTER 12

Decision-Support Systems for Supply Chain Management

CASE

Supply Chain Management Smooths Production Flow

As a manufacturer of wings and wing components for commercial and military aircraft, the Aerostructures Corp.'s build-to-order machine shops used to run into a lot of turbulence trying to move components through its fabrication processes.

Thanks to its recent use of Rhythm—a supply-chain management system from i2 Technologies, Inc., in Irving, Texas—Aerostructures has leveled out its work flow and has knocked $500,000 off its inventory costs.

In the past, when the Nashville-based company accepted a large order to build 50 "stringers," the stringers might get fitted for material one day and then sit idle for a few days before being heat-treated and contoured in a stringer oven. Stringers are pieces of contoured metal used to connect the top of a wing with a support structure and are up to 50 feet long.

The old setup wasted time. The stringer ovens and other manufacturing equipment often weren't being used efficiently because Aerostructures couldn't schedule any smaller jobs around lapses in production. The company's antiquated manufacturing resource planning (MRP) system wasn't designed to pinpoint work schedules for manufacturing equipment.

And because Aerostructures' custom-made products typically move through 220 operations before they are completed, the company couldn't afford to let its unfinished products sit around for too long.

"If an order was due tomorrow, the system could recognize that, but it couldn't tell you that you could run two smaller jobs in the same amount of time," said Julie Peeler, corporate vice president of manufacturing and information systems.

Aerostructures uses a 10-year-old MRP-II system from McCormack & Dodge called Production Inventory Optimization System (PIOS) running on an IBM S/390 MVS mainframe.

Aerostructures' legacy setup also threw its build-to-order inventory management out of whack because the MRP system was backing up the company's lead times on production runs. That made it difficult for Aerostructures to order aluminum, titanium, and other materials.

Rhythm, which has been up and running since the middle of last year, has helped Aerostructures schedule jobs more effectively. The PIOS system feeds

---

Source: Thomas Hoffman, *ComputerWorld*, December 10, 1997. Copied with permission.

planning information into the IBM RS/6000–based Rhythm system at night, using its Computer Associates International, Inc., CA-IDMS database as a gateway.

Rhythm then calculates how work orders should be prioritized and uploads that information back to the PIOS system before the next morning's MRP run, Peeler said.

Aerostructures has invested $650,000 in hardware, software, and support.

Aerostructures' use of Rhythm reflects just how hot these manufacturing optimization systems are right now, analysts said. "The win for a company like Aerostructures is being able to smooth out their interenterprise supply-chain operations," said Dennis Byron, an analyst at International Data Corp. in Framingham, Massachusetts.

Still, installing such a system is half the battle, said Barry Wilderman, an analyst at Meta Group, Inc., in Stamford, Connecticut. That's because systems such as Rhythm or manufacturing scheduling software from Rockville, Maryland–based Manugistics, Inc., are so complex.

Peeler agreed.

She said it took i2 most of the summer of 1996 to refine the system to meet Aerostructures' specs. "If optimization was easy, lots of people would do it," she said.

Aerostructures is midway through replacing its McCormack & Dodge MRP system with the Baan Co.'s enterprise resource planning (ERP) system.

Peeler said it isn't clear if Aerostructures will keep the i2 system, because Rhythm can be interfaced to, but not integrated with, the Baan ERP system.

By the end of this chapter, you should be able to answer the following questions:

- What are the goals of a software installation like the one described at Aerostructures?
- What type of decision support tools were selected for the system and why? What other types of tools might be appropriate?
- What is the relationship between Aerostructures' systems and its Rhythm supply chain optimization software?
- How will current trends in the information technology area affect Aerostructures' decision-support systems implementation? What about other kinds of companies?

12.1 INTRODUCTION

Many of the advances in the control and management of supply chains are driven by advancing computer technology. In Chapter 11, we considered this *information technology* and all of its many facets. In the current chapter, we focus on *decision-support systems (DSS)*.

Like many complex business systems, supply chain management problems are not so rigid and well defined that they can be delegated entirely to computers. Instead, in almost every case, the flexibility, intuition, and wisdom that are unique characteristics of humans are essential to manage the systems effectively. However, there are many aspects of these systems that can only be analyzed and understood effectively with the aid of a computer. It is exactly this type of assistance that decision-support systems are designed to provide. As the name implies, these systems do not make decisions. Instead, they assist and support the human decision maker in his or her decision-making process.

Decision-support systems range from spreadsheets, in which users perform their own analysis, to expert systems, which attempt to incorporate the knowledge of experts in various fields and suggest possible alternatives. The appropriate DSS for a particular situation depends on the nature of the problem, the planning horizon, and the type of decisions that need to be made. In addition, there is frequently a trade-off between generic tools that are not problem-specific and allow analysis of many different kinds of data, and often more expensive systems that are tailored to a specific application.

Within the various disciplines that make up supply chain management, DSSs are used to address various problems, from strategic problems such as logistics network design to tactical problems such as the assignment of products to warehouses and manufacturing facilities, all the way through to day-to-day operational problems such as production scheduling, delivery mode selection, and vehicle routing. The inherent size and complexity of many of these systems make DSSs essential for effective decision making.

Typically, decision-support systems use the quantifiable information available to illustrate various possible solutions and allow the decision maker to decide which one is most appropriate, based on other, possibly nonquantifiable, factors. Often, DSSs allow the decision maker to analyze the consequences of decisions, depending on different possible scenarios. This kind of what-if analysis can help decision makers to recognize potential problems before they occur.

Many decision-support systems use mathematical tools to assist in the decision-making process. These tools, often from the mathematical discipline of *operations research* (OR), were first developed to assist the armed forces with the enormous logistical challenges of World War II. Since then, improvements in these techniques, as well as ever-increasing computer power, have helped to improve these tools and make them more accessible to others. Other tools such as artificial intelligence (AI) are also employed in the design of decision-support systems but have not been as dominant as the OR methods.

As massive *data warehouses* that integrate the databases of entire firms become more popular, decision-support systems are performing analyses of these databases to assist with decision making. These DSSs employ sophisticated statistical tools to analyze data warehouse information. Recently, the tools of *data mining*, which comb through data in an attempt to find patterns and relationships in unexpected places, are proving increasingly valuable. These tools are currently used to find unexpected marketing relationships, but they could also be utilized to analyze supply chain relationships such as those existing between transportation and inventory (see Chapter 3).

In Chapter 11 we introduced a framework for supply chain management systems based on planning horizon; see Figure 11-7. It includes four layers, starting with the longest planning horizon, which includes **strategic network design**. The second layer is the tactical level of **supply chain master planning**. The third is the **operational planning** level that includes demand planning, inventory management, production scheduling, and transportation planning systems. The tactical and operational planning tools are sometimes called advanced planning and scheduling (APS) systems. Although there is no generally agreed-upon definition for this term, it is intended to describe systems that attempt to resolve the shortcomings of the ERP systems as a planning tool.

The last layer includes **operational execution** systems such as enterprise resource planning, customer relationship management, supplier relationship management, supply chain management, and transportation systems. This last layer is mostly transactional in nature and provides the infrastructure and databases to which decision-support systems in the other three layers are connected. This layer also includes event management, which provides alerts for decision makers when certain events occur—these do not typically involve a high level of sophistication because they rely on current data.

The scope of DSS is very wide. Thus, in this chapter we attempt to cover many of the models, concepts, and issues important when selecting and implementing DSS. First, we consider the challenge of modeling and using DSS, then we discuss the structure including the interfaces and solver technologies, and finally we go into more detailed descriptions and examples of the tactical and operational systems that form the heart of supply chain DSS.

12.2 THE CHALLENGES OF MODELING

The heart of any DSS is the model, or representation of reality within the system. Since any DSS involves some degree of human interaction, to effectively utilize a DSS, the user must possess both an understanding of modeling, as well as an understanding of the subject matter being modeled. The more strategic the DSS, the more critical it is for the user to think through various modeling options and scenarios. However, even in operational DSSs, in which this is less critical, it is still important to understand some aspects of the modeling process in order to qualify the system recommendations and know when to override them.

The following are the major questions that arise when modeling supply chains:

- *What part of reality should be modeled?* How do DSSs capture reality yet keep the models simple enough to be useful? This is the one of the main challenges of modeling. On the one hand there is a need for enough detail to allow the model to correctly represent reality, and on the other hand there is a need to keep the model simple enough to understand, manipulate, and solve. As Michael Pidd [120] suggests: "Model simple, think complicated." Indeed, it is the combination of the user and the model that comprises the decision-making process. The need for simplicity stems from the need for transparency, meaning anyone using the DSS should be able to understand it. Another important driver of simplicity is ease of manipulation—the ability to easily change data, run scenarios, and analyze the results. Finally, the mathematical models used in DSS may have limitations in the size of problems they can handle and there may be a need to reduce constraints in order to generate results in a reasonable amount of time. Of course, there is no way to know how complex a model needs to be, which is why it is important to be very clear about the purpose and objectives of the model.
- *What is the process of modeling?* The process of modeling is not a rational, linear one. Therefore, there is a need to employ an iterative process when developing models. Our experience with complex models is that it is best to make initial assumptions, develop a simple model, and then relax the assumptions later. Indeed, "Start with a simplified model and add complexity later" is an important rule of modeling. Using a prototyping approach enables decision makers to develop their understanding and intuition regarding the model. A simplified model should first be built and tested, and complexity should be slowly added as simpler models are analyzed. Similarly, a complex problem can be decomposed into simpler models. Of course, the way the model is broken up can be critical to the success of this process. If the modules do not take into account certain overall constraints, this approach may not produce the correct results.
- *What level of data and detail is required?* Modeling decisions should drive data collection, not the other way round. Although companies now have plenty of raw data, there is still a need for matching the correct data to the model and interpretation.

Strategic models require aggregated data, while operational models require more detailed data. In either case, decisions need to be made about what data to collect and use, and how to integrate and update the data and model various less quantitative issues. Typically, data need to be collected from many sources. In order to provide a comfort level with the data, a baseline model is created to compare the quantities and costs to ones that decision makers are familiar with. The baseline also provides a way to compare new scenarios to the current status.

We summarize the three most important rules of modeling:

1. Model simple, think complicated.
2. Start with a simplified model and add complexity later.
3. Modeling needs drive data collection, not the other way around.

For a more detailed discussion of the process behind modeling, see [120].

12.3 STRUCTURE OF DECISION-SUPPORT SYSTEMS

To effectively select and use decision-support systems, it helps to understand the essential pieces of a properly configured system. The three major components of a DSS are the input databases and parameters, the analytical tools, and the presentation mechanism.

- The *input database* contains the basic information needed for decision making. This can be a PC-based database extract designed for the specific problem, a data warehouse with an accumulation of a company's transactions, or distributed databases accessed through a network. This database can also include certain parameters and rules, such as the desired service level, hard-coded restrictions, and various other constraints.
- The data analysis usually involves embedded knowledge of the problem while also allowing the user to fine-tune certain parameters. The *analytical tools* employed are operations research and artificial intelligence–based algorithms, cost calculators, simulation, flow analysis, and other embedded logic procedures. This component is the most complex, because there are few off-the-shelf solvers that can deal with the huge variety of problems that companies face.
- Various database and spreadsheet *presentation tools* can be used to display the results of DSS analysis. Often, however, the output contains too much information, such as lists and tables, which may be difficult for the decision maker to absorb. Therefore, various *data visualization techniques* are employed to enable the user to comprehend the vast quantity of output data. For example, location, routing, and sales DSSs use geographic information systems (GISs) to display complex geographic data in problems such as site location, routing, and supply chain analysis. Similarly, scheduling systems use Gantt charts to display factory schedules, and simulations use animation to illustrate the relationships in the model.

All of these components are markedly affected by the planning horizon of the problem being considered. As we have seen, strategic decisions typically require long-term planning and may involve the aggregation of historical data and forecasting considerations, while their analysis and presentation do not need to be particularly rapid because immediate response is not an issue. In contrast, operational decisions typically involve short-term planning, require current data, and demand fast response from the DSS.

12.3.1 Input Data

As in all kinds of analyses, the data used as input to the DSS are critical to the quality of the analysis. Until fairly recently, acquiring the appropriate information was a complicated feat in itself. By and large, the information collection battle has now been won in corporate America. Extensive deployment of information technology such as ERP, bar coding, point-of-sale, and electronic commerce has provided companies with large business databases. These are now often collected into huge data warehouses or smaller data marts that, along with the appropriate tools, facilitate the analysis of the data. In addition, the proliferation of networks and network access tools means that accessing various geographically distributed databases is now feasible.

Depending on the type of analysis, a DSS may require collecting information from various parts of a company. For example, supply chain network design requires both static and dynamic information from different parts of a company. The static data include plant production rates, plant locations, warehouses, and customers as well as warehousing and transportation costs. The dynamic data involve forecasts, orders, and current deliveries. This type of information will not usually be found in a single database, or within one department or division of a company.

To evaluate the quality of the data and the quality of the models built into the system, it may be possible to load the current data and models into the system to see whether these correspond to reality. For example, consider a truck routing decision-support system. Ultimately, the goal of such a system is to provide routes that enable the trucks to make deliveries and pickups efficiently at the required times. However, the model can be tested by loading the current truck routes into the system, and observing if travel times, for example, are the same as the travel times actually experienced by the truck drivers. Similarly, projected costs from the model can be compared with actual financial and accounting records. This process, typically known as *model and data validation*, is essential to ensure that the model and data are *accurate enough*. Of course, the meaning of "accurate enough" depends on the decisions being made. For more information on this issue, see Chapter 2, Section 2.3.

In addition, the decision planning horizon affects the detail of the data required. For strategic planning, it often makes sense to aggregate yearly data while recent raw daily or weekly data may be best for short-term planning. The accuracy of the solution depends on the input data; therefore, the quality of the input data will determine to some extent the tools needed for the analysis.

EXAMPLE 12-1

A DSS is often used at the strategic level to help with logistics network design. The DSS assists in deciding on the number of warehouses required, their size, and the customer allocation to each warehouse. The DSS uses information about the distribution system to calculate the various costs related to site selection and customer allocation. The data required for this problem involve the manufacturers, warehouses, customers, and the transportation between them. Since this is a long-term planning tool, yearly demand data and costs are typically used, but sometimes the user may need to determine how to account for seasonality. In addition, for this kind of DSS to be utilized successfully, the user needs to break the products into product families and to specify inventory policies. This will allow calculations of the warehouse sizes and frequency of deliveries. Some of the required input data are summarized in Table 12-1.

This type of data may not be readily available in the company database. Even if the data are accessible, they may not be in the required format, particularly if the DSS involves geographic display and analysis. As one might expect, collecting, tabulating, and verifying the data can take considerable time.

Example 12-1 *Continued*

TABLE 12-1

INPUT DATA FOR LOGISTICS NETWORK DESIGN

Component	Data
Manufacturer	Location Production lines, capacities, and costs Transportation costs to warehouses
Warehouse	Location Fixed costs Variable costs (labor, utilities) Inventory turnover Transportation costs to retailers
Retailer	Location Annual demand by product
Product	Volume Weight Holding cost

EXAMPLE 12-2

Supply chain master plan is typically developed using tools that analyze the push portion, see Chapter 5, of the supply chain over multiple time periods. The objective is to minimize transportation, inventory, and production costs or maximize profit. The plan considers all capacities, lead times, bill-of-material structures, forecast demand, product shelf life, and the various cost parameters. Some of the required input data in this case are summarized in Table 12-2.

TABLE 12-2

INPUT DATA FOR SUPPLY CHAIN MASTER PLANNING

Component	Data
Manufacturer	Location Production lines, production rates, capacities, and costs by time period Production rules and constraints, including batching, setups, tooling Transportation costs to warehouses
Warehouse	Location Variable costs (inbound, outbound, storage) Days of coverage (for safety stock calculations) Transportation costs to retailers
Retailer	Location Demand by product by time period Revenue by product by time period
Product	Volume Weight Shelf life, including minimum and maximum values Holding cost
Time Periods	Weeks, months

12.3.2 Analytical Tools

To successfully use a DSS, appropriate performance measures need to be selected. For example, reducing total cost may be a goal, but in some cases improving customer service level may be more pertinent. DSS interfaces usually allow the user to select the relative importance of different objectives.

Once data have been collected, they must be analyzed and presented. Depending on the DSS and the particular decision being made, there are many different ways to analyze the data. It is important for the decision makers to *understand* how the DSS analyzes the data in order to assess the validity and accuracy of the decision-support system's recommendations. Of course, depending on the analysis, statistics can tell many different stories. (See [140] for an interesting discussion of these issues.) It is up to the decision maker to determine which analysis is most appropriate.

In Section 12.4, we discuss specific types of supply chain management DSSs. In this section, we consider common DSS analysis tools and techniques in general.

Queries.   Often vast quantities of data make manual analysis difficult. Decisions are often facilitated by simply allowing decision makers to ask specific questions about the data, such as "How many clients do we service in California?" and "How many clients purchased over $3,000 of a certain product by state?"

Statistical analysis.   Sometimes asking questions is not enough. In this case, statistical techniques can sometimes be used to determine trends and patterns in the data. For example, statistical data such as the average inventory in a warehouse, the average number of stops and length of a route, and the variability of customer demand can often be useful to decision makers.

Data mining.   Recently, as corporate databases have become larger and more all-encompassing, new tools have been developed to look for "hidden" patterns, trends, and relationships in the data. Data mining, for example, produced the marketing gem that men purchase beer and diapers on Friday afternoon, suggesting to retailers that these items should be displayed close to each other in the store.

On-line analytical processing (OLAP) tools.   On-line analytical processing tools provide an intuitive way to view corporate data, typically stored in data warehouses. OLAP tools aggregate data along common business dimensions and let users navigate through the hierarchies and dimensions by drilling down, up, or across levels. OLAP tools also provide sophisticated statistical tools to analyze these data and tools to present them. Mostly they are generic tools—more sophisticated than spreadsheets and easier to use than database tools—for the analysis of large amounts of data.

Calculators.   Simple decision-support tools can facilitate specialized calculations such as accounting costs. In many cases, more than simple calculations may not be warranted, especially if the changes are predictable and easy to evaluate. This may be the case for forecasting or inventory management, for some product types, while others may need more sophisticated tools.

Simulation.   All business processes have random components. Sales may take one value or another. A machine may or may not fail. Often these random, or stochastic, elements of a problem make analyzing it very difficult. In these cases, *simulation* is frequently an effective tool to help in decision making. In simulation, a model of the process is created on a computer. Each of the random elements of the model (e.g., sales, failures) is specified with a probability distribution. When the model is "run," the computer simulates carrying out the process. Each time a random event occurs, the computer uses the specified probability distribution to randomly "decide" what happens.

Consider, for example, a simulation model of a production line. As the computer runs the model, a series of decisions is made. How long does a job take on machine 1? On machine 2? Does machine 3 break while job 4 is being processed on it? As the model runs, statistical data (e.g., utilization rates, completion times) are collected and analyzed. Since this is a random model, each time the model is run, the results may be different. Statistical techniques are used to determine the model's average outcome and the variability of this outcome. Also, by varying input parameters, different models and decisions can be compared. For example, different distribution systems can be compared, utilizing the same simulated customer demand. Simulation is often a useful tool to understand very complex systems that are difficult to analyze analytically.

Artificial intelligence. As we discussed in Section 12.1, artificial intelligence tools may be employed in the analysis of DSS input data. For example, *intelligent agents* use AI to assist in decision making, especially in real-time decisions, such as determining how to supply a customer in the shortest possible time or to quote a delivery lead time as the customer waits on the phone. Following Fox, Chionglo, and Barbuceanu [57], we define an *agent* as a software process whose goal is to communicate and interact with other agents, so that decisions affecting the entire supply chain can be made on a global level. For example, the intelligent agent that assists the customer service representative in determining the appropriate lead time could interact with the intelligent agent that schedules production to help ensure that the lead time is met [159].

Expert systems also fall under the umbrella of artificial intelligence. These systems capture an expert's knowledge in a database and use it to solve problems. Expert systems rely on an extensive database of knowledge, usually expressed as a set of rules. Solving a problem involves applying the rules in the knowledge base and producing a conclusion that has the ability to explain how it was reached. Within the context of a decision-support system, this kind of expert system might suggest alternative solutions that the human decision maker has neither the time nor expertise to recognize. Although not extensively used in logistics practice, these systems have an important role because of their capability to capture and explain expert reasoning.

Indeed, a number of DSSs for supply chain management can be viewed as using intelligent agents to plan and execute different activities in the supply chain. These systems are characterized by the following interrelated issues [57]:

- The activities allocated to each intelligent agent (i.e., software processor).
- The level and nature of interactions between the different agents.
- The level of knowledge embedded within each agent.

For instance, a real-time supply chain planning tool involves the following components: intelligent agents that are located at each facility and collect information and enable planning and scheduling for the facility. In this case, facilities include manufacturing plants and distribution centers. Each agent interacts with other agents so that they can balance excess capacity at different plants, find missing parts, or coordinate production and distribution. A central planning agent communicates with agents that are located at each facility to collect status information and relate central planning decisions. The type and level of decisions made by the agents—as opposed to human operators—and the frequency and level of communications between agents depend on the specific implementation.

Mathematical models and algorithms.   As we discussed in Section 12.1, mathematical tools, often from the discipline of operations research, can be applied to the data to determine potential solutions to problems. For example, these tools may generate the best set of locations for new warehouses, an efficient route for a truck to take, or an effective inventory policy for a retail store. These algorithms fall into two categories:

- *Exact algorithms.* Given a particular problem, these algorithms will find a solution that is mathematically the "best possible solution." In general, these kinds of algorithms may take a long time to run, especially if a problem is complex. In many cases, it is impossible to find the optimal, or very best, solution. In other cases, it may be possible but not worth the effort. This happens because the input data to these algorithms are often approximated or aggregated, so *exact solutions to approximate problems may be worth no more than approximate solutions to approximate problems.*
- *Heuristics.* These are algorithms that provide good, but not necessarily optimal, solutions to problems. Heuristics typically run much faster than exact algorithms. Most DSSs that use mathematical algorithms employ heuristics. A good heuristic will rapidly give a solution that is very close to the optimal solution. Heuristic design often involves a trade-off between the quality of a solution and speed. It is often useful if in addition to the solution, the heuristic provides an estimate of *how far the heuristic solution is from the optimal solution.*

See Chapter 2 for additional discussion of exact and heuristic algorithms.

The analytical tools used in practice are typically a hybrid of many of the tools described above. Almost all decision-support systems employ a combination of tools, and many will allow further analysis using generic tools such as spreadsheets. In addition, some of the tools listed above may be embedded in generic tools (e.g., spreadsheets).

Most DSSs employ analytical tools that have some specific embedded knowledge of the problem being solved. Since these problems are usually complex, the DSS employs its problem knowledge to find efficient solutions. These are solutions that minimize cost and satisfy service-level requirements.

There are many factors that dictate the appropriate analytical tools to use for a particular decision-support system. These include

- The type of problem being considered.
- The required accuracy of the solution—there may be no need to find the optimal solution.
- Problem complexity—some tools may not be appropriate for very complex problems, while others may be an overkill for relatively simple problems.
- The number and type of quantifiable output measures.
- The required speed of the DSS—for operational systems such as lead-time quotation and vehicle routing, speed may be essential.
- The number of objectives or goals of the decision maker—for example, a DSS for truck routing may need to find a solution with the minimum number of vehicles and the least total distance traveled.

TABLE 12-3

APPLICATIONS AND ANALYTICAL TOOLS

Problem	Tools used
Marketing	Query, statistics, data mining
Routing	Heuristics, exact algorithms
Production scheduling	Simulation, heuristics, dispatch rules
Logistics network configuration	Simulation, heuristics, exact algorithms
Mode selection	Heuristics, exact algorithms

Table 12-3 shows a number of problems and the analytical tools that are appropriate for them.

EXAMPLE 12-3

Consider the logistics network design problem described in Example 12-1. For this problem, heuristic approaches and optimization-based techniques have been developed in the past few years. The choice between heuristics and optimization depends on the complexity of the specific problem and on the various modeling issues (e.g., service level) that the user wishes to consider. For instance, optimization-based techniques may be limited in the size of problem they can handle and in the number of parameters and special cases they can consider. Finally, some DSSs combine heuristic and optimization approaches.

12.3.3 Presentation Tools

These tools are used to display the data to the decision maker. There are a varied number of formats including

- Reports.
- Charts.
- Spreadsheet tables.
- Animation.
- Specialized graphic formats, such as a layout of a floor plan.
- Geographic information systems.

The reader is likely to be familiar with most of these items—reports, charts, and tables are very common. Animation is often used as a tool to present output of the simulation models described above; this helps the user verify the validity of the simulation model and understand the simulation results. Specialized graphic formats are extremely dependent on the nature of the problem being solved. For example, a facility layout DSS may present a suggested floor plan for a new facility.

In supply chain management, much of the output of a DSS is geographic in nature. For example, logistics network design software, sales territory analysis software, and truck routing software all include geography-related output. In the last few years, the *geographic information system* (GIS) has become more common as the presentation vehicle of choice for many supply chain management decision-support systems.

Geographic Information Systems   A geographic information system (GIS) is an integrated computer mapping and spatial database management system that provides a broad array of functions for the storage, retrieval, management, analysis, and display of geographically referenced data.

Some typical GIS capabilities are listed below:

- Mapping and thematic mapping.
- Database management.
- Interactive data query.
- Spatial data retrieval.
- Geographic data manipulation.
- Spatial data analysis.
- Geocoding.
- Geographic data import/export.
- Buffering/polygon overlay.

The advantage of a GIS platform is that it combines database, query, and reporting tools in addition to geographic display and analysis. In logistics modeling, GIS has the further advantage of allowing automated distance and travel time calculations. Some limited forms of GIS are now included in spreadsheets (Excel 7.0) but are not as extensive as the full-blown packages. These systems originally existed only on high-end UNIX workstations, but there are now many excellent, relatively inexpensive systems that run on PC platforms and networks. A major issue in deploying GIS is the availability and quality of the geographic data. Excellent data, with information about the geography, street networks, and demography, are available for the United States at a very low price. In other countries, however, the data may not exist or may be tightly held so that their use can be a major expense and deterrent to the effective use of GIS. Even in the United States, these data may not be perfect for every application, or they may be outdated and need to be constantly upgraded to be of any use.

Originally, GIS was extensively used in applications such as

- Market analysis.
- Census and demographic data analysis.
- Real estate.
- Geology.
- Forestry.

More recently, however, GIS has found application in areas of potentially more interest to the supply chain manager, such as

- Network analysis—transportation, telecommunications.
- Site selection.
- Routing.
- Supply chain management.

Figure 12-1 presents a typical GIS interface for supply chain management. The screen includes information about suppliers' warehouses, customers, and the flow of material throughout the logistics network.

Not surprisingly, there are special considerations in the use of GIS for logistics modeling. Often, time must be spent *geocoding* and *estimating travel time*. Geocoding is the translation of addresses into geographic coordinates. Geocoding requires databases that can assist in the translation. Although widely available in the United States, these data may be hard to come by in other countries. To prepare customer data for use by a DSS, this step is required and may be lengthy, depending on the quality of the address data.

In most logistics applications, it is necessary to use the distance between two locations in order to estimate travel time and transportation costs. This can be done in

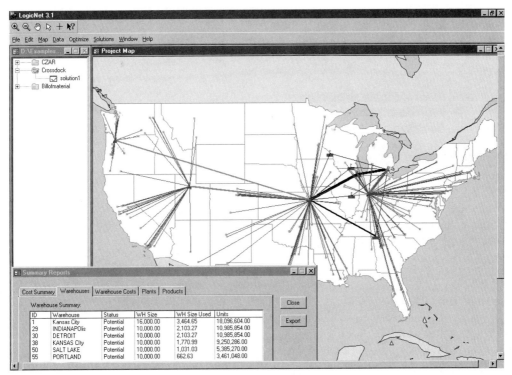

FIGURE 12-1 A typical GIS interface for supply chain management.

several ways. One is to calculate the straight-line distance between the two coordinates and multiply it by a factor that estimates the circuity of the roads between the two points. This, of course, is a very simplistic approach and does not require more information than the coordinates. In this case, the DSS typically applies different factors for different zones. Another way to calculate travel distance is to use the actual road network, identify the best route, and determine the distance. This requires extensive and accurate information about the road network, including one-way streets and similar details. It is also an extremely time-consuming process to calculate the network even for a moderate-sized problem. Table 12-4 compares the two alternatives. More on these two techniques can be found in Chapter 2.

In both types of calculations, assumptions need to be made about the speed of travel in order to estimate travel time. It is always possible to let the user enter the travel time between each pair of locations in the model, but this is usually impractical in large problems.

TABLE 12-4

ROAD AND ESTIMATED DISTANCE

Item	Estimated distance	Road distance
Data	Cheap	Expensive
Complexity	Low	High
Accuracy	Medium	High
Speed	High	Low

Although users of routing systems may demand a road network because it seems to provide a more accurate solution, experience has shown that this approach may not produce significantly better results than an approach that uses estimates of the distance. This is true even in short-haul distances and inner-city routing, such as school bus routing.

DSS may come with an embedded GIS or use a commercial GIS as a platform or server for presentation of geographic data. Geographic data available for the United States are mostly based on TIGER/Line files. The acronym TIGER stands for *Topologically Integrated Geographic Encoding and Referencing*, which is the name for the system and digital database developed at the U.S. Census Bureau to support its mapping needs for the decennial census and other bureau programs. The TIGER/Line files are extracts from the TIGER database and are available to the public. Most GIS vendors allow the user to load these files or distribute their own versions and formats based on these data. Otherwise there are no agreed-upon standards for geographic data representation apart from the leading vendors' formats, which can usually be converted from one system to another.

Integrating Algorithms and GIS   As mentioned earlier, GIS has found application in areas important to supply chain management. These include logistics network design, routing, mode selection, and so forth. The idea in all these applications is to integrate the GIS with mathematical models and algorithms. Figure 12-2 provides a schematic representation of such a system.

In this type of system, geographic data are provided by the GIS while attribute data, including demand information, costs, production, and storage capacities, are downloaded from standard databases. These data are sent to the GIS engine that is the heart of the system. The engine constructs a *symbolic network* that represents the various relationships between the components of the supply chain. The network is then used with either exact or heuristic algorithms to generate a number of solutions or strategies that achieve the objectives and satisfy the constraints in the system. These solutions can be viewed, modified, and analyzed by the user in order to implement the most appropriate one.

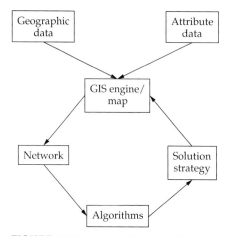

FIGURE 12-2 A general framework for integrating algorithms and GIS.

What are the advantages of integrating GIS and mathematical models and algorithms? This approach

1. Allows the user to visualize the data and the model to verify that they truly represent the supply chain environment.
2. Provides an accurate street-level database (if needed), including one-way streets and turn difficulties.
3. Allows the user to visualize the solution and strategies generated by the system.
4. Allows for sensitivity (i.e., what-if) analysis.

12.4 SUPPLY CHAIN DECISION-SUPPORT SYSTEMS

In Section 12.1 we discussed the different layers of supply chain management tools. In this section we will review some of these systems and how they relate to each other in more detail.

Logistics network design. We have already discussed logistics network design in previous examples. Network design involves the determination of warehouse and factory locations and the assignment of retailers or customers to warehouses. Typical input data include candidate locations, transportation costs, aggregate demand forecasts, and so on. Heuristic or exact algorithms are used to suggest network designs. Not all criteria can be quantified, so the decision maker must ultimately use his or her judgment.

EXAMPLE 12-4

The mid-Atlantic region of the American Red Cross [74] utilized a decision-support system based on optimization models to determine the effect of a proposed relocation on blood distribution and collection. Initially, the mid-Atlantic region had three sites for blood processing, two of which collected and distributed blood and one of which collected blood only. A new facility was being considered, and several scenarios, some of which involved closing an old facility and others of which involved reallocating resources, were considered. Mathematical models were used to support this decision by determining the effects of labor and transportation costs in each of the alternatives. In the end, the new facility was not built because, by more efficiently utilizing the currently existing facilities, the mid-Atlantic region was able to meet its goals without the capital expense of building a new facility.

Supply chain master planning. As observed in Chapter 5, supply chain master planning is applied to the push portion of the supply chain, with the objective of allocating production, transportation, and inventory resources effectively. Supply chain master planning can be defined as the process of

> coordinating production, distribution strategies, and storage requirements to efficiently allocate supply chain resources to maximize profit or minimize systemwide cost. Supply chain master planning allows companies to plan ahead for seasonality, promotions, and tight capacities.

The challenge of allocating production, transportation and inventory resources in order to satisfy demand can be daunting. This is especially true when the firm is faced with seasonal demand, limited capacities, competitive promotions, or high volatility in forecasting. Indeed, decisions such as when and how much to produce, where to store inventory, and whether to lease additional warehouse space may have enormous impact on supply chain performance.

It is therefore not surprising that supply chain master planning cannot be done effectively manually, or with a spreadsheet. To optimize these decisions, taking

FIGURE 12-3 A typical interface of a tactical planning tool that generates a supply chain master plan.

into account the interaction between the various levels of the supply chain, the firm needs to use an **optimization-based** decision-support system. These systems, which model the supply chain as large-scale **mixed-integer linear programs**, are the only analytical tools capable of considering the complexity and dynamic nature of the supply chain. For an example of an interface to this type of system, see Figure 12-3. Typically, the output from the tool is an effective supply chain strategy that coordinates production, warehousing, transportation, and inventory decisions. The resulting plan provides information on production quantities, shipment sizes, and storage requirements by product, location, and time period. This is typically referred to as the **supply chain master plan.**

In some applications, the supply chain master plan serves as an input for a detailed production scheduling system. In this case, the production scheduling system employs information about production quantities and due dates received from the supply chain master plan. This information is used to propose a detailed manufacturing sequence and schedule. This allows the planner to integrate the back end of the supply chain, that is, manufacturing and production, and the front end of the supply chain, that is, demand planning and order replenishment; see Figure 12-4. This figure illustrates an important issue: the focus of order replenishment systems, which are part of the pull portion of the supply chain, is on service level, while the focus of tactical planning, which is in the push portion of the supply chain, is on cost minimization or profit maximization. On top of this, the focus in the detailed manufacturing scheduling portion of the supply chain is on **feasibility**. That is, the focus is on generating a detailed production schedule that satisfies all production constraints and meets all the due date requirements generated by the supply chain master plan.

FIGURE 12-4 The extended supply chain: from manufacturing to order fulfillment.

Of course, the output from the tactical planning process should be shared with all of the supply chain participants to improve coordination and collaboration. For example, the distribution center managers can now better use this information to plan their labor and shipping needs. Distributors can share plans with their suppliers and customers in order to decrease costs for all partners in the supply chain and promote savings. Specifically, distributors can realign territories to better serve customers, store adequate amounts of inventory at the customer site, and coordinate overtime production with suppliers.

In addition, supply chain master planning tools can identify potential supply chain bottlenecks *early* in the planning process, allowing the planner to answer questions such as

- Will leased warehouse space alleviate capacity problems?
- When and where should the inventory for seasonal or promotional demand be built and stored?
- Can capacity problems be alleviated by rearranging warehouse territories?
- What impact do changes in the forecast have on the supply chain?
- What will be the impact of running overtime at the plants or out-sourcing production?
- What plant should replenish each warehouse?
- Should the firm ship by sea or by air. Shipping by sea implies long lead times and therefore requires high inventory levels. On the other hand, using air carriers reduces lead times and hence inventory levels but significantly increases transportation cost.
- Should inventory be rebalanced between warehouses, or replenished from plants, in order to meet unexpected regional changes in demand?

Another important capability that supply chain master planning tools have is the ability to analyze demand plans and resource utilization to maximize profit. This enables balancing the effect of promotions, new product introductions and other planned changes in demand patterns and supply chain costs. Planners now are able to analyze the impact of various pricing strategies as well as identify markets, stores, or customers that do not provide the desired profit margins.

A natural question is: when should one focus on cost minimization and when on profit maximization? While the answer to this question will vary from instance to instance, it is clear that cost minimization is important when the structure of the supply chain is fixed or at a time of recession and therefore oversupply. In this case the focus is on satisfying all demand at the lowest cost by allocating resources effectively. On the other hand, profit maximization is important at a time of growth, that is, at a time when demand exceeds supply. In this case, deciding who to serve and for how much is more critical than cost savings.

Finally, an effective supply chain master planning tool must be able to help planners improve the accuracy of the supply chain model. This is counter intuitive, since the accuracy of the tactical planning model depends on the accuracy of the demand forecast that is an input to the model. However, the accuracy of the demand forecast is typically time dependent. That is, the accuracy of forecast demand for the first few time periods, say the first 10 weeks, is much higher than the accuracy of demand forecast for later time periods. This suggests that the planner should model the early portion of the demand forecast at a great level of detail, that is, apply weekly demand information. On the other hand, demand forecasts for later time periods are not as accurate and hence the planner should model the later demand forecast month by month or by groups of two to three weeks each. This implies that later demand forecasts are aggregated into longer time buckets and, hence, due to the risk-pooling concept, the overall accuracy of forecasts improves. Thus, effective tools adapt to the specifics of the data.

EXAMPLE 12-5

This example illustrates how supply chain master planning can be used dynamically and consistently to help a large food manufacturer manage the supply chain. The food manufacturer makes production and distribution decisions at the division level. Even at the division level, the problems tend to be large-scale. Indeed, a typical division may include hundreds of products, multiple plants, many production lines within a plant, multiple warehouses (including overflow facilities), bill-of-material structures to account for different packaging options, and a 52-week demand forecast for each product for each region. The forecast accounts for seasonality and planned promotions. The annual forecast is important because a promotion late in the year may require production resources relatively early in the year. Production and warehousing capacities are tight and products have limited shelf life that need to be integrated into the analysis. Finally, the scope of the plan spans many functional areas, including purchasing, production, transportation, distribution, and inventory management.

Traditionally, the supply chain planning process was performed manually with a spreadsheet and was done by each function in the company. That is, the production plan would be done at the plant, independently from the inventory plan, and would typically require the two plans to be somehow coordinated at a later time. This implies that divisions typically end up "optimizing" just one parameter, usually production costs. The tactical planning DSS introduced in the company allows the planners to reduce systemwide cost and better utilize resources such as manufacturing and warehousing. Indeed, a detailed comparison of the plan generated by the tactical tool with the spreadsheet strategy suggests that the optimization-based tool is capable of reducing total costs across the entire supply chain. See Figure 12-5 for illustrative results.

FIGURE 12-5 Comparison of manual versus optimized scenarios.

Example 12-5 *Continued*

In practice, each week, the planners use an optimization-based tactical DSS to create a plan for the next 52 weeks; this is done on a rolling-horizon basis and thus allows the planner to take into account forecast updates or changes in supply. The new plan also accounts for starting inventory by SKU and by location, remaining shelf life, frozen production plan by SKU by week by line as well as all production constraints and supply chain costs. This allows the planner to determine how to best use the existing and future states of the supply chain to meet future requirements. The plan output includes new production plans and order quantities from suppliers, interfacility moves, and a new inventory strategy. Therefore, as the supply chain evolves and changes over time, the food manufacturer always has an up-to-date and complete supply chain plan.

Operational planning systems. This layer of systems includes different types of systems, ranging from demand planning tools to tools that assist with the details of production and sourcing strategies. Unlike strategic network design and supply chain master planning systems, these systems typically provide feasible solutions but not optimized ones. The reasons for this include the type of problem, its size, and in some cases the need for quick results. For instance, routing problems are typically solved with heuristics; finding optimal solutions would be too time-consuming.

Demand planning. Demand planning tools allow supply chain executives to apply two different processes:

- **Demand forecast:** A process in which historical demand data are used to develop long-term estimates of expected demand, that is, forecasts.
- **Demand shaping:** A process in which the firm determines the impact of various marketing plans such as promotion, pricing discounts, rebates, new product introduction, and product withdrawal on demand forecasts.

As we have seen, demand forecasts play an important role in many supply chain decisions. Typically, forecasts are made using various statistical techniques that take into account the history of the item, stability of demand, and other product-specific data. The impact of various marketing strategies is also analyzed using statistical techniques, as well as the behavior of similar products under the same marketing plan. See Chapter 3 for more details on forecasting.

The demand planning process is particularly difficult because so many of the departments involved in the supply chain play a role in determining forecasts, as well as in determining final sales. For instance, the sales group typically builds business plans to hit geographic quotas. Similarly, marketing works to meet specific market-share goals, and operations coordinates the production and distribution of products. Each of these areas utilizes different levels of detail and relies on unique pockets of information to make decisions.

These kinds of decisions all affect final sales, but they are often made independently of each other. Clearly, to develop effective demand plans, each area must have real-time visibility into both the information driving these decisions and the actual decisions made by the other groups. Indeed, to truly make decisions that benefit the entire supply chain, a collaborative process in which each group contributes information to the ultimate demand plan is needed. In this way, the separate business functions can agree on a demand plan that reflects all of the available information and meets all of their needs.

In addition, demand planning can go beyond a single enterprise to a collaborative effort among different companies. CPFR and other e-commerce initiatives for sharing information will be a major factor in how these systems are developed; see more on CPFR and e-commerce initiatives in Chapter 11.

EXAMPLE 12-6

In 1991, Unilever merged three business units. Each used software from Manugistics, but each implemented it differently. The current system, which also uses Manugistics software, blends historical shipment data with promotional data and allows information sharing and collaboration with key customers.

The company realized the statistical information was completely ineffective for the part of the forecast driven by events, promotions, rollouts, and special packages. The company has designed a process through which planners augment statistical forecasts with sales systems that plan promotions. For each promotion, the sales planning system predicts the "lift," or projected increase in sales, and routes it to the demand planning system, which applies it to appropriate stockkeeping units and distribution centers each week. Planners review those forecasts and make adjustments. Unilever also uses external market research in sales planning but not in the demand planning system. The company is experimenting with point-of-sale (POS) data as well. It compares POS data and forecasts that come directly from customers with its own forecasts. Those data help drive the final forecast but aren't incorporated into the model yet. Unilever collaborates with a few large customers on statistical and market promotion forecasts for key products, which are negotiated in weekly meetings and fed into the demand planning system. The benefits have been worthwhile, but the process was hard, expensive tools comprising only a small part of the total cost. The system has reduced inventory and improved customer service and the company hopes to see dramatic improvements through more customer collaboration and use of POS data [110].

Inventory management. When a facility holds many different items in inventory, managing that inventory can be extremely difficult. An inventory management DSS uses transportation and holding cost information, along with transportation lead times, facility processing time, committed respond time to the upstream facilities as well as service level by product by customer. The objective of these DSSs is to use transportation and inventory holding costs, demand forecasts and forecast error, and service levels to determine the levels of inventory, in particular, safety stock levels, to keep in each location in each period. In almost all cases, the DSS apply a heuristic algorithm to generate suggested policies.

EXAMPLE 12-7

Amoco Chemical Corporation [45] was confronted with a set of common inventory management challenges:

1. Identifying appropriate inventory levels at different echelons in the supply chain.
2. Dealing with capacity constraints of capital, equipment, and people.
3. Dealing with conflicting organizational objectives between sales, production, and inventory managers. These objectives include

- Relocate working capital to fund growth.
- Maintain or improve customer service levels.
- Improve operational efficiency.
- Push to be the best in industry.

Together with Mercer Management Consulting Inc., Amoco developed a custom DSS to address these issues. The system models Amoco's multiechelon logistics network, costs, and objectives. It uses both optimization and simulation techniques in the analysis. Optimization is used to determine inventory targets. Once inventory targets are determined, simulation is applied to test the stocking policy, associated cost, and customer service. According to Amoco, implementation of the system has provided the following benefits:

- Understanding of inventory costs, including shortage cost.
- The discovery of inefficient practices since they are no longer covered up with excess inventory.
- Better planning, coordination, and communication.

Transportation planning.   Transportation planning typically involves not only the dispatching of a company's own fleet but also decisions regarding selection of a commercial carrier on certain routes. Since rate structures can often be very complex, and speed and reliability may vary from carrier to carrier, transportation *mode selection* is frequently a difficult problem. In addition, input data such as rate structures need to be frequently updated.

An important component in transportation planning is fleet routing. Here we distinguish between two systems: static and dynamic. In static systems, daily routes are typically planned in the morning and weekly routes are drawn up at the beginning of the week. These routes are not changed during the day or the week. In dynamic systems, routes are updated during the planning horizon (i.e., day or week). For example, consider telephone repair crews. Calls may come in during the day, and work can be assigned as they come in. These systems are more complex than their static counterparts, since the DSS has to try to minimize operating costs on the fly.

EXAMPLE 12-8

Tanner Companies, Inc. [16], is a manufacturer of quality women's clothing. In the early 1990s, the company had problems with poor on-time delivery rates (around 74 percent) and high levels of work in process. To address these issues, the company turned to a scheduling decision-support system. The system takes input from a database that describes in detail the material and labor requirements for each of the many hundreds of items that Tanner manufactures. One of the most time-consuming parts of the implementation involved assembling this database, because the information was not readily available.

Based on the input data as well as incoming orders, the system generates manufacturing schedules. In particular, the system generates schedules that minimize shortages and finished goods inventory within the given production and demand constraints. Since these are conflicting objectives, there may be many schedules that reduce shortages, for example, but raise the level of finished goods inventory. Thus, the system generates a set of potential nondominated schedules, or schedules in which the performance based on one objective cannot be improved except by hurting the performance based on the others. Given this set of schedules, management must ultimately decide which schedule to use. Initially prototypes used mathematical programming techniques, but ultimately heuristics had to be used because of the magnitude of the problem.

The system utilized an intuitive menu-driven interface, so training time was minimal and user confidence was high from the beginning. By the end of the one-year period in which the system was developed, revised, and implemented, on-time deliveries increased to 90 percent and work-in-process inventory was reduced by more than $200,000. Also, the scheduler was freed from mundane and repetitive scheduling tasks, and was able to focus more on planning issues.

Production scheduling.   Given a series of products to make, information about their production processes, and due dates for the product, production scheduling DSSs propose manufacturing sequences and schedules. A production scheduling DSS can use artificial intelligence and mathematical and simulation techniques to develop schedules. Artificial intelligence–based production schedules typically involve rules that were previously used by the human schedulers who scheduled the particular processes in question. Optimization-based scheduling systems use algorithms to develop schedules that maximize or minimize some set of objectives. Finally, simulation-based scheduling systems typically allow the user to select a simple set of scheduling rules and "test" them in the simulation system. For example, the user might decide to test the impact of scheduling all jobs in the order of their due dates. The system would simulate the production process using this rule, and the decision maker could view the outcome. For example, the system can predict the

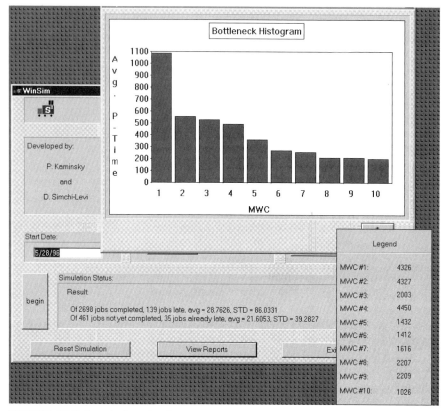

FIGURE 12-6 A typical production scheduling interface.

number of late jobs or the average time late jobs are delivered after their due date. Figure 12-6 illustrates a typical production scheduling interface.

A related planning system is the material requirements planning described below.

Material requirements planning (MRP). MRP systems use a product's bill of materials and component lead times to plan when manufacturing of a particular product should begin. Although these DSSs typically do not use sophisticated mathematical approaches, they are very popular in industry. These DSSs can serve as a good example of why the decision maker should only use the output of a DSS as a *possible* problem solution. Often MRP systems propose *impossible* schedules because they typically do not take production capacities into account. It is up to the decision maker to modify the plan in such a way that it becomes a feasible schedule without becoming too expensive.

EXAMPLE 12-9

Mobil Oil Corporation, see [12], uses a decision-support system to consolidate and dispatch shipments of lubricant products. Mobil has 10 plants and receives hundreds of orders every day. These orders are filled using either a vehicle from Mobil's dedicated fleet of trucks or a dedicated truck from one of Mobil's suppliers.

Mobil's dispatchers had to address many issues, including the selection and dispatching of private vehicles instead of contract carriers, the consolidation of orders, and when to ship orders early to take advantage of consolidated resources.

Example 12-9 *Continued*

To address these issues, Mobil collaborated with Insight, Inc., and developed the heavy-products computer-assisted dispatch (HPCAD) system. This system takes order, distance, and trucking rate information and prepares a set of feasible work schedules. The system calculates costs for each of these schedules. Then an optimization module uses this information to determine a detailed, cost-effective dispatch plan. The DSS is designed so that the dispatcher can interact with the system in developing the dispatch plan.

Mobil's internal audits have concluded that by utilizing delivery resources more effectively, the HPCAD system saves the company over $1 million annually. The company estimates that 77 percent of dispatches generated by means of HPCAD are different than the dispatches would have been employing a completely manual system.

Operational execution systems. These are real-time systems that allow executives to run their business efficiently. Of course, some of the decisions made in real time require those at the front end of the supply chain to have information and visibility to the back end of the supply chain. For instance, in many manufacturing operations, sales representatives commonly take orders over the phone and thus are able to immediately quote delivery lead times. In the past, sales representatives often quoted long lead times to ensure that these lead times could be met. Lead time quotation DSSs allow the quotation of shorter lead times by determining exactly how long a particular order will take to deliver. This is done by taking current production schedules, manufacturing times, and delivery times into account. Typically, the sales representative still needs to use his or her judgment about the importance of an order. If a customer is not regarded as significant as certain other customers, it might be worthwhile for the sales rep to quote a later due date than the DSS suggests. This allows leeway to quote shorter lead times for future orders.

The DSS that supports this process can provide three levels of sophistication

- Available to promise (ATP) involves time-phased functionality where a manufacturer is able to consider available finished goods inventory as well as work in process in determining ability to deliver products by a specific date.
- Capable to promise (CTP) involves time-phased functionality used by some manufacturing systems that will check component availability far down the supply chain as well as available materials to determine if delivery of a particular product can be made by a specific date.
- Profitable to promise (PTP) looks not only on the capability but also on the profitability of completing an order. This can include price determination. See Chapter 10 for a discussion on dynamic pricing.

12.5 SELECTING A SUPPLY CHAIN DSS

For each of the supply chain problems and issues listed above, decision-support systems are available in many configurations, platforms, and price ranges. DSS platforms have evolved in the last 15 years from relatively inflexible mainframe systems, to isolated PC tools, to client/server processes; lately, there is a new breed of high-performance and extensible enterprise decision-support applications. These systems come in a wide range of pricing from PC systems costing several thousand dollars to companywide installations costing a few million dollars [41].

When evaluating a particular DSS, the following issues should be considered:

- The scope of the problem addressed by the decision maker, including the planning horizon.
- The data required by the decision-support system.
- User interface capabilities.
- Analysis requirements, including accuracy of the model, ability to quantify performance measures, desired analytic tools—that is, optimization, heuristics, simulation, and computational speed needed.
- The system's ability to generate a variety of solutions so that the user can select the most appropriate one, typically based on issues that cannot be quantified.
- The presentation requirements, including issues such as user-friendliness, graphic interface, geographic abilities, tables, reports, and so on.
- Compatibility and integration with existing systems; this includes the ability of the database interface to accept and produce standard file formats.
- Hardware and software system requirements, including platform requirements, flexibility to changes, user interfaces, and technical support.
- The overall price, including the basic model, customization, and long-term upgrades; note that support and customization are often far more expensive than the initial investment.
- Complementary systems. Does the vendor have suites of products that make it easier to purchase from one source? For example, in some cases a routing DSS also includes load planning.

EXAMPLE 12-10

A small steel manufacturer in the Chicago area needs to review the location of its distribution centers (DCs). Some customers in the South are not receiving next-day service and there are extensive transportation costs. Management has asked the logistics team to come up with an analysis and plan of where to open new DCs and to close down some existing facilities.

This is a strategic issue that is required for long-term planning. The logistics team has decided to review the software packages on the market and purchase or lease the appropriate tool to assist in the analysis. One M.B.A. on the team tried to model the problem as a *linear-programming model*, but there were many factors that could not be taken into account.

The team quickly realized that annual data would be required in this analysis and, because the manufacturer has many clients, aggregating data is essential. They would prefer a stand-alone PC tool that could be operated from their desktops. They did not care about integration with other systems but wanted the database interface to accept standard PC file formats and to provide the resulting output in standard formats.

Using various logistics magazines and the Internet, the logistics team found five or six vendors who provide these types of systems. Unfortunately, no comparison was available for the different systems—at most some anecdotal evidence from customers was provided by each software vendor.

The team proceeded to collect literature and demos, and came up with the following list of requirements and issues to be discussed with each vendor:

- Database requirements.
- Geographic information system (GIS) capabilities.
- Transportation modeling requirements.
- Distribution center cost structures.
- Model assumptions and flexibility.
- Manufacturing cost structures.
- Optimization methods used.
- Reporting capabilities.
- Customization options.

Example 12-10 *Continued*

- Pricing, leasing, and purchasing costs.
- Support and training.
- Company experience and references.

Finally, they reviewed and rated the different systems and decided on the vendor that seemed to have the system most appropriate for their requirements. They decided to lease the product with an option to purchase.

There is a confusing array of supply chain DSSs or APSs, as they are sometimes called, on the market. The terminology can vary from one supplier to another, as can the scope, quality, and price of the solution offered. Of course, it is important for users to understand their requirements and the value of the systems to their organization. They should also have an understanding of their firm's internal capabilities, so that they can decide whether they want to take responsibility for integrating the DSS into their information systems or purchase supply chain capabilities that are modules of their ERP system.

SUMMARY

Decision-support systems for supply chain management are a fast-growing sector of the logistics software industry. DSSs will continue to evolve and to adopt standard features and interfaces in order to adapt to the competitive environment and provide the flexible solutions required in today's markets [41]. Since the basic data that are required to make decisions are being collected, there is a strong drive to utilize this information in sophisticated ways to gain competitive advantage by improving service and cutting supply chain costs. The major trends in DSS, and especially in supply chain DSSs and advanced planning systems, are

1. **Integration with and between ERP systems.** DSSs will be easier to integrate with ERP systems through standard interfaces, and in many cases there will be embedded DSS logic in ERP systems. Most ERP vendors already boast of having supply chain planning functionality. SAP offers its mySAP Supply Chain Management component, which was at first called Advanced Planner and Optimizer. Oracle and PeopleSoft also have added supply chain DSS functionality to their systems. ERP companies are also trying to create open interfaces that will allow linking of different ERPs for easier cross-company integration.
2. **Improved optimization.** Many DSSs lack a true optimization capability—either these systems use heuristics to generate feasible strategies, not necessarily the best one, or the systems are typically limited to optimizing fairly small problems. For instance, most existing supply chain master planning and MRP systems do not optimize at all and in many cases do not take capacities into account.
3. **Impact of standards.** As we noted in Chapter 11, development of standards is an important prerequisite to reducing the complexity and cost of systems. The current market includes many DSSs that are not compatible and difficult to integrate. In addition, strategic partnering forces the various partners to define standards so that they can efficiently integrate processes.
4. **Improved collaboration.** Using the CPFR process, companies are collaborating and jointly processing results received from demand planning systems. We have seen that collaboration can enhance production planning, inventory management, and other

supply chain processes. Systems that provide visibility, and enable collaboration, are now starting to appear on the market, often in the form of public and private exchanges. As companies begin to focus more on collaboration, these tools will become more and more valuable.

DISCUSSION QUESTIONS

1. What are the issues important in evaluating a DSS for supply chain master planning?
2. In the chapter we described a variety of DSSs for supply chain management. When is it important that a particular DSS will be based on Web technology?
3. How can DSS bridge the gap between supply chain planning and supply chain execution?
4. In the last few years many companies and software vendors have used benchmarking to prioritize technology investments. Discuss
   a. The value of benchmarking.
   b. The type of issues and questions that can be addressed with benchmarking.
   c. The supply chain areas in which you expect benchmarking to have a significant impact.

Computerized Beer Game

A.1 INTRODUCTION[1]

If you've taken an operations management course in the last 20 years, you are no doubt familiar with the Beer Game. This role-playing simulation of a simple production and distribution system has been used in countless undergraduate, graduate, and executive education courses since it was first developed at MIT in the 1960s.

The Computerized Beer Game, included with this text, is similar in many respects to the traditional Beer Game. As you will learn in the following pages, however, it has many options and features that enable you to explore a variety of simple and advanced supply chain management concepts that cannot be easily taught using the traditional game.

Windows 95 or later is required to operate the game. To install the software, place the included CD in your CD-ROM drive. If the installation program doesn't run automatically, open Windows Explorer, select the CD, and double click on the setup program.

A.2 THE TRADITIONAL BEER GAME

For comparative purposes, we will briefly review the traditional manual Beer Game, which is typically played on a large board. Locations on the board represent four components, or stages, of the beer supply chain: the factory, the distributor, the wholesaler, and the retailer. Orders placed by each of the component managers, as well as inventory in transit and at each of the locations, are represented by markers and pennies that are placed at the appropriate locations on the board. External demand is represented by a stack of cards.

One player manages each of the supply chain components. Each week, the retail manger observes external demand (by drawing the next "demand card"), fills as much of this demand as possible, records back orders to be filled, and places an order with the wholesaler. In turn, the manager of the wholesaler observes demand from the retailer, fills as much of this demand as possible, records back orders, and places an order with the distributor. The distributor manager repeats this process, ordering from the

---

[1] A Web-based version of the Beer Game can be found at the MIT Forum for Supply Chain Innovation, http://supplychain.mit.edu/innovation

factory. Finally, the factory manager, after observing and filling demand and back orders, begins production. Order processing and filling delays are incorporated into the game to represent order processing, transportation, and manufacturing lead times. The rules of the game require all back orders to be filled as soon as possible. At each stage of the supply chain, the manager at that stage has only local information; only the retail manager knows customer demand. The goal of the game is to minimize the total holding and back-order costs at the stage you are managing. Each week a cost of $0.50 for each unit in inventory and $1.00 for each unit of back order is accrued.

A typical game is played 25 to 50 "weeks." During the game, communication between players is limited. Inventory and back-order levels usually vary dramatically from week to week. At the end of the game, the players are asked to estimate customer demand. Except for the retail manager, who knows the demand, players often estimate wildly varying demand. After being informed that demand was constant at four units per week for the first four weeks, and then eight units per week for the remaining weeks, players are often surprised. Instinctively, they blame the other players for following inappropriate strategies.

A.2.1 The Difficulties with the Traditional Beer Game

When the Beer Game was first introduced in the 1960s, the concept of *integrated supply chain management*—as well as advanced information systems that support this concept—was not yet developed. In many cases, the supply chain was managed by different managers at each stage based on their individual intuition, experience, and objectives. Since then, however, both the theory and the practice of supply chain management have improved significantly. Unfortunately, as traditionally played, the Beer Game does not necessarily reflect current supply chain practices. Perhaps more importantly, the Beer Game does not necessarily provide students with insight on how to *better manage the supply chain*.

These weaknesses of the traditional Beer Game can be attributed to several of its characteristics. Our experience with the game suggests that the students typically are so occupied with the mechanics of the game, making sure that they correctly follow the rules of the game, that they have no time to develop an effective strategy. Even if a participant uses a sophisticated strategy, he or she may tend to attribute inventory and back-order problems, as well as higher-than-expected cost, to the other participants' strategies, rather than to search for potential flaws in his or her own strategic decisions.

In addition, the demand pattern exhibited in the Beer Game does not reflect a realistic supply chain scenario. In the traditional game, demand unexpectedly doubles in the fifth week of play and remains at that level until the end of the game. In real life, it is unrealistic to expect that managers of each of the supply chain facilities would not be informed of such a huge change in demand patterns.

Finally, the traditional Beer Game doesn't demonstrate several other important supply chain management issues. For example, in many real-world supply chains, several (or all) of the stages have a single owner. Thus, the real objective is to minimize the total system cost, not individual performance. Unfortunately, in the traditional Beer Game, there is no way to judge how much is lost by managing stages individually.

Many of the difficulties in managing the supply chain that are highlighted by the Beer Game can be addressed by shortening cycle times and centralizing information and decision making. Unfortunately, these approaches to solving many supply chain management problems cannot be demonstrated in the traditional Beer Game—students can learn about them only in the lecture following game play.

The Computerized Beer Game was developed precisely to address the difficulties inherent in the traditional Beer Game. In the following sections, we describe the scenario, the commands and options available, and, finally, several supply chain management concepts that we have taught successfully using the Computerized Beer Game.

A.3 THE SCENARIOS

The Beer Game (computerized and traditional) models the following scenarios. First, consider a simplified beer supply chain, consisting of a single retailer, a single wholesaler that supplies this retailer, a single distributor that supplies the wholesaler, and a single factory with unlimited raw materials that brews the beer and supplies the distributor. Each component in the supply chain has unlimited storage capacity, and there is a fixed supply lead time and order delay time between each component.

Every week, each component in the supply chain tries to meet the demand of the downstream component. Any orders that cannot be met are recorded as back orders and met as soon as possible. No orders will be ignored, and all orders must eventually be met. At each week, each component in the supply chain is charged a $1.00 shortage cost per back-ordered item. Also at each week, each component owns the inventory at that facility. In addition, the wholesaler owns inventory in transit to the retailer, the distributor owns inventory in transit to the wholesaler, and the factory owns both items being manufactured and items in transit to the distributor. Each location is charged a $0.50 inventory holding cost per inventory item that it owns. Also, each supply chain member orders some amount from its upstream supplier. An order placed at the end of one week arrives at the supplier at the start of the next week. Once the order arrives, the supplier attempts to fill it with available inventory. Thus, an order placed at the end of week w arrives at the supplier at the start of week $w + 1$. The material is shipped (if it is in stock) at the start of week $w + 1$ and arrives at the supply chain member who placed the order no earlier than the start of week $w + 3$. This implies that the actual order lead time is two weeks. Each supply chain member has no knowledge of the external demand (except, of course, the retailer) or the orders and inventory of the other members. The goal of the retailer, wholesaler, distributor, and factory is to minimize total cost, either individually or for the system.

The Computerized Beer Game has other options that model various situations. These differing options enable the instructor to illustrate and compare concepts such as lead-time reduction, global information sharing, and centralized management. For instance, consider a scenario exactly as described above, except that each supply chain member has full knowledge of the external demand, orders, and inventories of all other supply chain members. In another possible scenario, lead times are reduced from the two weeks described above to only one week.

Finally, in a centralized scenario, the game is changed as follows: The manager of the factory controls the entire supply chain and has information about all of the inventory levels throughout the supply chain, as well as the external demand. Because the system is centralized, stages other than the factory do not place orders; all inventory is moved through the system as quickly as possible. In addition, because there can be no back order at any stage except the first one, the retailer pays a $4.00 shortage cost for each back-ordered item. This enables a fair comparison between the decentralized scenario described above and the centralized scenario. Because three sets of orders are eliminated, the product moves through this supply chain three weeks faster than in the supply chain described above. These are the main scenarios modeled by the

Computerized Beer Game. In the following sections, we describe specifically how to use the software to model these situations.

A.4 PLAYING A ROUND

In this section, we describe how to play a round of the Computerized Beer Game, using the default settings, to model the first scenario described above. In the next section, we describe each of the menu commands in detail, so that a variety of scenarios also can be modeled.

A.4.1 Introducing the Game

When the Computerized Beer Game software is started, the following screen appears:

In this simulation, the player takes the role of manager of one of the components of the beer supply chain, either the retailer, the supplier, the distributor, or the factory. This will be called the *interactive* role. The computer takes the remaining roles. On the game display, the interactive role is displayed in color, and the remaining roles are displayed in gray. The information for the interactive roles is also displayed, but the information for other roles is hidden (with the exception of back orders at the supply chain member immediately upstream from the interactive supply chain member and the two outgoing trucks). In the example screen displayed above, the distributor is the interactive role. *Downstream* means the direction of the supply chain leading to the external demand while *upstream* means the direction of the factory. In addition, we refer to components of the supply chain as *facilities*.

Order of Events   The simulation is run as a series of weeks. Within each week, first the retailer, then the wholesaler, then the distributor, and finally the factory, executes the following series of events, as the simulation proceeds upstream. For each facility:

Step 1. The contents of *delay 2* are moved to *delay 1*, and the contents of *delay 1* are moved to inventory. *Delay 2* is 0 at this point.

Step 2. Orders from the immediate downstream facility (in the case of the retailer, external customers) are filled to the extent possible. Remember that an order consists of the current order and all accumulated back orders. Remaining orders (equal to current inventory minus the sum of the current orders and back orders) are backlogged, to be met as soon as possible. Except for retailers, which ship orders outside the system, the orders are filled to the *delay 2* location of the immediate downstream facility. This is the start of the two-week delay.

Step 3. Back-order and inventory costs are calculated and added to accumulated total costs from previous periods. This incremental cost is calculated as follows: The total inventory at the facility and in transit to the next downstream facility is multiplied by the holding cost, $0.50, while the total back order is multiplied by the shortage cost, $1.00.

Step 4. Orders are placed. If this is the interactive role, the user indicates the desired order amount. If this is one of the automatic roles, the computer places an order using one of several typical inventory control schemes. The schemes can be controlled by the instructor, as we will explain in the next section.

Delays and Order Filling   This sequence of events implies several things. First, once the downstream facility places an order at the end of a week, this order will be filled no earlier than the start of the week three weeks later (that is, if the order is placed at the end of week w, the material will be received no earlier than the start of period $w + 3$, a two-week lead time). *Also, once an order is placed at the end of a week, it is not received until the start of the next week. This means that if, for example, the retailer places an order for 5 units at the end of this period, the wholesaler does not even attempt to fill the order until the start of the next period. This period, the wholesaler attempts to fill the order from the previous period.*

Recall also that there is no guarantee that an order will be met, even with this lag. An upstream supplier can fill an order only if it has the necessary inventory. Otherwise it will backlog that order and attempt to fill it as soon as possible. *The exception to this is the factory. There is no limit to production capacity, so the factory's order will always be filled in its entirety after the appropriate delay.*

A.4.2 Understanding the Screen

Each facility in the supply chain is represented on the display. As an example, the *Distributor* is displayed below:

On the left of the screen, the number of items in inventory is displayed. The next two elements (from left to right) represent items in transit to inventory; that is, the numbers in the box labeled *delay 1* represent the number of items that will arrive in inventory in one week, and similarly for *delay 2*. The box on the right lists (1) the total inventory and shortage cost up to the current time; (2) the back order, that is, the demands that have been received at this facility but have not been filled yet due to lack of inventory; and (3) the most recent order placed by this facility, in this example, the *Distributor* to its upstream facility, the *Factory*. Note that in this case, back order refers to orders received by the *Distributor* but not yet met from inventory. To find out the orders placed by the *Distributor* that have been backlogged—that is, not yet met by the factory—check the back order at the *Factory*. Also, the recent order number displayed in the box represents the most recent order sent by the *Distributor* to the *Factory*. This order will arrive at the upstream supplier at the start of the next period.

A.4.3 Playing the Game

To start the game, select **Start** from the **Play** menu, or push the start button on the toolbar. The computer will automatically play the first round for the automatic facilities downstream from the interactive facility. For example, if the *Distributor* is the interactive facility, the computer will play for the *Retailer* and the *Wholesaler*, in that order.

Once this is completed, the first round for the interactive facility is played. Steps 1 and 2 (advance inventories and fill orders, described in the section labeled "Order of Events") are completed. At this point, inventory numbers are updated on the screen, and the Order Entry dialog box appears. The screen looks as follows:

Examine this screen in detail. Recall (you can see this from the previous screen shown on page 322) that the initial inventory was 4, and both *delay 1* and *delay 2* contained 4 units. This holds true for each of the supply chain facilities. Now, steps 1 and 2 have been completed. As you can see from the Order Entry dialog box, there is initially no back order and no order from the *Wholesaler*. Since the starting inventory was 8 (the initial 4 plus 4 from *delay 1*), 8 remain in inventory. *Delay 2* is now empty. In *delay 1* at the *Wholesaler*, there are 4 units, for which the *Distributor* will pay holding costs for this period. This is the first round, so there are no previous orders from the *Distributor* to the *Factory*. Thus, the *recent order* box reads 0. However, if this was a later round and an order was placed by the *Distributor* to the *Factory* during the previous round, it would appear in the *recent order* box.

The Order Entry dialog box indicates how much total back order and order was faced by the interactive player in this round (again, in our example, the *Distributor*), and how much of it was successfully filled. Note that the back-order box on the right side of the screen indicates the current level of back order, while the dialog box shows the level of back order at the beginning of this round, before the player (in this case, the *Distributor*) attempted to fill downstream orders (in this case, from the *Wholesaler*).

At this point, enter a demand amount. This can be zero or any other integer. Remember that you are trying to balance inventory holding costs and shortage costs. Also, by looking at the back-order box at your supplier (in this example, the *Factory*), you can see how much back order your upstream supplier already has to fill; that is, how many items you have ordered in prior rounds but have not yet received. Once an amount has been entered, the remaining upstream supply chain members play automatically, and the screen is updated. If you enter an order of 3 for the *Distributor*, the remainder of Week 1 play is carried out, and the *Distributor* portion of the screen looks like

The order of 3 is reflected in the recent order box, and the total cost box reflects holding cost charged due to the 8 units in inventory and the 4 units in *delay 1* at the *Wholesaler*.

To play the next round, select **Next round** from the **Play** menu, or push the *next round button* on the toolbar. The computer again automatically plays the next round for the automatic facility downstream from the interactive facility. Once again, the order entry dialog appears. At this point, both *delay 1* and *delay 2* show an inventory of 0, since the inventory was advanced and *delay 2* was initially 0. Recall that after you input an order, the upstream supplier (in this case the *Factory*) will try to meet last period's order of 3. If you order 6 this period and the remaining upstream supply chain members play automatically, the distributor portion of the screen at the end of Week 2 will look like

Continue play by selecting **Next round** from the **Play** menu, or pushing the *next round button* at the beginning of each round. At any time, you can view a graph of your performance to date by selecting **Player** from the **Graphs** menu, or pushing the *player graph button*. This graph will display orders, back order, inventory, and total cost over time. A sample graph follows:

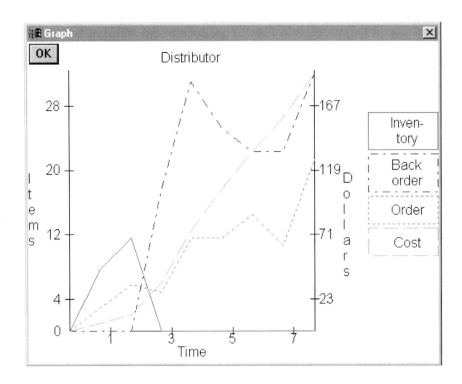

You can also view a list of your orders to date by selecting **Player** from the **Reports** menu.

A.4.4 Other Features

In addition to playing the Computerized Beer Game as we have just described it, it is possible to play the game in three other modes: the *Global Information Mode*, in which inventory levels and orders at all facilities and external demand are available to the interactive player; the *Short Lead Time Mode*, in which lead time through the system is reduced by eliminating *delay 2* at each of the facilities; and the *Centralized Mode*, in which all information is available to the interactive player and orders are placed at the *Factory* and sent through the system to the *Retailer* as soon as possible. These options will be described in the next section.

The software also has additional functions. Most of these selections are made from the **Options** menu and control game setup options. For example, they allow the selection of inventory policies used by the computer for the automatic players and selection of the interactive player. In addition, graphs and reports of the performance of each of the supply chain members and of the system as a whole can be viewed. These options will also described in more detail in the next section.

A.5 OPTIONS AND SETTINGS

This section follows the menu in the Computerized Beer Game, and describes the function of each of the parameters and options that the user can set. In the following subsections, the convention **menu—selection** item is used to describe menu selections.

A.5.1 File Commands

These commands are used to stop and reset play, and exit the system:

File—Reset. This command resets the game. All data from the previous game are lost.

File—Exit. This command exits the Computerized Beer Game and returns you to the Windows environment.

A.5.2 Options Commands

These commands allow the game options to be set, so that different scenarios can be modeled.

Options—Player. This command displays the following Player dialog in order to select the *interactive player*. This is the role that the player will take. The computer takes the other three roles.

Click on the player button or name to select a player, and then select OK. To cancel the command, select Cancel. Note that if None is selected, the computer will take all of the roles, so that the results can be observed.

Options—Policy. This command displays the following Policy dialog so that policies for each of the automatic players can be selected.

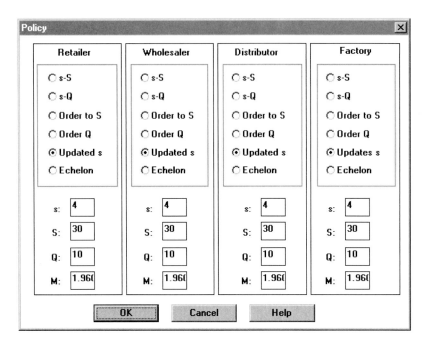

These policies and parameters apply only to computer-controlled players. Different policies can be selected for each of the automatic players. Six policies are available (note that by inventory position in the following, we mean the sum of inventory at a location, back order owed to that location, items being transported to that location, and back order owed by that location):

s-S. When inventory falls below s, the system places an order to bring inventory to S. In this example, s is set to 4, and S is set to 30.

s-Q. When inventory falls below s, the system places an order for Q.

Order to S. Each week, the system places an order to bring inventory to S.

Order Q. The system orders Q each week.

Updated s. The order-up-to level s is continuously updated to the following value: the moving average of demand received by that player over the past 10 weeks (or fewer if 10 periods have not yet been played) times the lead time for an order placed by that player, plus M times an estimate of the standard deviation during the lead time (based on the same 10-week period). When the inventory level falls below s, the system orders up to s. However, the maximum possible order size is S. Also, the ordering for the first four weeks is adjusted to account for start-up by not ordering (or including in the moving average) demand during the first week at the wholesaler, the first two weeks at the distributor, and the first three weeks at the factory.

Echelon. This is a modified version of the periodic review echelon inventory policy. The value of s for each of the players is determined as follows. Let $AVG(D)$ be the 10-week moving average of external customer demand, let $STD(D)$ be the standard deviation of that external demand, and let $L + r$ equal 3 in the regular game (where the lead time is 2 as previously discussed and the reorder interval is 1 week) and 2 in the short lead time game (described below). Then, at each period at each stage, s is determined as follows:

retailer: $\quad s = (L + r) * AVG(D) + M * STD(D) * (L + r)^{.5}$

wholesaler: $\quad s = (L + L + r) * AVG(D)$

$\quad\quad\quad\quad + M * STD(D) * (L + L + r)^{.5}$

distributor: $\quad s = (2 * L + L + r) * AVG(D)$

$\quad\quad\quad\quad + M * STD(D) * (2 * L + L + r)^{.5}$

factory: $\quad s = (3 * L + L + r) * AVG(D)$

$\quad\quad\quad\quad + M * STD(D) * (3 * L + L + r)^{.5}$

When the inventory position falls below s, the system orders up to s. However, the maximum possible order size is S.

Options—Short Lead Time. This command shortens system lead times by eliminating *delay 2* from the system. Each lead time is thus shortened by one week, and the system display is changed as follows:

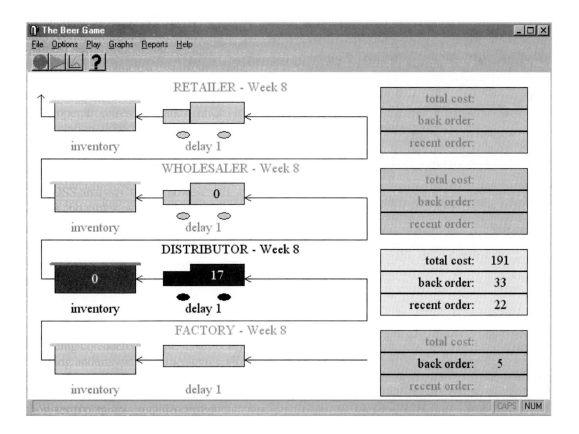

Options—Centralized.   This command toggles between standard play and centralized play. In centralized play, the interactive player manages the factory. External demand can be observed and the factory manager can react to it. In addition, when inventory reaches a stage, it is immediately sent forward to the next stage so that inventory is only held by the *Retailer*. This implies that more information is available to the player and that lead time is shortened, since there is no order delay at any stage except the *Factory*.

Options—Demand.   This command displays the demand dialog in order to set the external customer demand.

Using this dialog, play can be switched between random normal and deterministic demand. For the deterministic demand, a different constant demand can be selected for a number of initial weeks and the remainder of play. Similarly, for random normal demand, a different mean and standard deviation can be selected for the initial weeks and the remainder of play.

Options—Global Information.   This command displays inventory and cost information at all of the stages, not just the interactive stage. External demand is also displayed. This is the default setting for centralized play.

A.5.3 The Play Commands

These commands enable the start and continuation of play.

Play—Start.   This command starts play. It can also be called by using the *play toolbar button.*

Play—Next Round.   Once play has started, this command continues play. Each week, this command must be selected for play to continue. It also can be called using the *next round* toolbar button.

A.5.4 The Graphs Commands

These commands present status information graphically.

Graphs—Player. This command displays a graph of orders, back orders, inventory, and cost for the current interactive player. This command can also be called using the *graphs* toolbar button. An example follows:

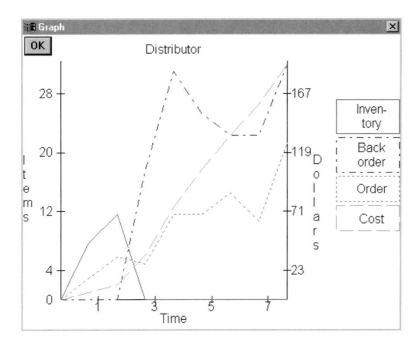

Graphs—Others. When this command is selected, you are first asked to select a player on the following dialog:

A graph of orders, back orders, inventory, and cost for the selected player is then displayed. This differs from the preceding Graphs—Player command, which displays a graph only for the current interactive player.

Graphs—System. This command displays a graph of orders for each stage.

A.5.5 The Reports Commands

These commands display a series of reports on the status of the system when the command is selected.

Reports—Player. This command displays the Status Report for the current interactive player. A sample report follows:

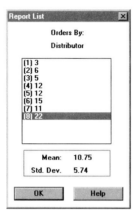

This report lists all orders placed by the player listed at the top of the dialog, as well as the mean and standard deviation of these orders.

Reports—Other. When this command is selected, you are first asked to select a player on the following dialog:

A status report for the selected player is then displayed. This differs from the preceding **Reports—Player** command, which displays a status report only for the current interactive player.

Reports—System. This command displays the System Summary Report:

This report summarizes the mean and standard deviation of orders placed by each player up to this point, the total cost experienced by each player, and the total system cost (at the bottom of the dialog).

The Risk Pool Game

B.1 INTRODUCTION

One of the most important concepts in supply chain management is "risk pooling." Recall that risk pooling involves the use of centralized inventory to take advantage of the fact that if demand is higher than average at some retailers, it is likely to be lower than average at others. Thus, if each retailer maintains separate inventory and safety stock, a higher level of inventory has to be maintained than if the inventory and safety stock are pooled. Therefore, the system with risk pooling has less overall inventory and is thus cheaper to operate with the same service level.

We developed the Risk Pool Game, included with this text, to illustrate risk pooling concepts. In the game, you simultaneously manage both a system with risk pooling (we also call this a centralized system) and a system without risk pooling (a decentralized system). The system records the profits of both systems, so you can compare performance.

Windows 95 or later is required to operate the game. To install the software, place the included CD in your CD-ROM drive. If the installation program doesn't run automatically, open Windows Explorer, select the CD, and double click on the setup program.

B.2 THE SCENARIOS

The Risk Pool Game models the following scenarios. The top half of the screen, the centralized game, consists of the following supply chain: A supplier serves a warehouse, which in turn serves three retailers. It takes two time periods for material to arrive from the supplier at the warehouse. This material can be shipped out during the same period or held in inventory. Once shipped, it takes an additional two periods for material to arrive at the retailers. The retailers then fill all the demand that they can. If demand cannot be met at the time it arrives, it is lost.

The bottom half of the screen represents the decentralized system. Three retailers order separately from the supplier, and the supplier ships material directly to each retailer. This takes four periods from the time the order is placed, the same length of time as the minimum total lead time in the centralized system. As in the centralized system, the retailers fill as much demand as possible—demand that if not met is lost. In each system, total holding cost, materials costs, and revenue are tracked. The goal in both systems is to maximize profit.

B.3 PLAYING SEVERAL ROUNDS

In this section, we describe how to play several rounds of the Risk Pool Game using the default settings. In the next section, we describe each of the menu settings and options so that you can customize the game play.

B.3.1 Introducing the Game

When the Risk Pool Game software is started, the following screen appears:

Order of Events   During each period or round of the game, several events occur.

Step 1. *To start this step, press the* **Start Round** *button.* The inventory is advanced. In the centralized game, this means that inventory four periods away moves to three periods away, inventory three periods away is added to the warehouse inventory, inventory two periods away is moved to one period away, and inventory one period away is added to retailer inventory. In the decentralized game, inventory four, three, and two periods away is moved, respectively, three, two, and one period away. Inventory one period away is added to retailer inventory.

Step 2. *This step starts automatically.* Demand is met. Each retailer experiences demand and fills as much as possible. Note that the top retailer in both the centralized and decentralized systems faces the same demand; the same is true for the middle and bottom retailers. Also, demand is not back ordered. Demand that cannot be met immediately is lost.

Step 3. *Place orders.* In the centralized system, enter an order for the supplier in the box closest to the supplier. Allocate the warehouse inventory to the three retailers in the three boxes closest to the retailers. Note that the allocation amount must be less than or equal to the total warehouse inventory. In the decentralized system, enter an order for each retailer. The system will present a default selection for each entry. You can keep the default or type in new values. As we describe in the next section, you have control over how the system selects default values. When entries are completed (or the decision has been made to keep the default values), *press the* **Place Orders** *button.*

Step 4. *This step starts automatically.* Orders are filled. The amount ordered is moved into the inventory slots four weeks away. In the centralized system, the amount allocated to each retailer is moved into the inventory slots two weeks away.

Step 5. *This step starts automatically.* Cost, revenue, and service level: A holding cost is charged for each unit in inventory, revenue is realized for each unit sold, and the cost of each item sold is subtracted from revenue. Service level is calculated as the fraction of demand met over total demand. For that reason, we refer to service level in the game as the *fill rate*.

Lead Times Note that in both systems, it takes a minimum of four periods for material that has been ordered to reach the retailer. In the centralized system, it can take longer if inventory is held in the warehouse.

B.3.2 Understanding the Screen

At the start of each round, the screen looks like this:

On the top half of the screen, the supplier is represented by the box at the left. The two vertical dotted lines labeled *4* and *3* have boxes on them representing inventory at least four or three periods away from the retailers, respectively. The large middle box represents the warehouse. The top line in the warehouse indicates the inventory contained there; the other boxes are used to enter an order from the supplier and allocation to the warehouse when appropriate. Note that the button in the lower right-hand corner of the screen initially says *Start Round*. This indicates that it is not the appropriate time to enter the orders and allocation. The two vertical dotted lines to the right of the warehouse are labeled *2* and *1*, indicating inventory two and one period from the retailers, respectively. Note that unlike the *3* and *4* lines to the left of the warehouse, lines *1* and *2* can have up to three inventory boxes, representing inventory going to each of the three retailers. To the right of these lines are the three boxes representing the retailers—the numbers in these boxes represent retailer inventory. The right-hand side of the screen contains cost and profit data. Holding costs and cost of goods sold (COGS) are subtracted from revenue to get profit. Service level and period number are also indicated.

The bottom half of the screen is similar to the top half, except that there is no warehouse. Also, when appropriate, orders are entered directly at the retailers.

The button in the lower right-hand corner initially reads *Start Round*. After the round has started, it looks like this:

Place Orders

B.3.3 Playing the Game

The game follows the order of events listed above. To start each round, press the *Start Round* button. Inventory is advanced, and then as much demand as possible is met. At this point, the button in the lower right-hand corner of the screen will change to read *Place Orders*. Do so either by accepting the default choices that are displayed or by typing in new ones. Recall that in the centralized game, you can allocate up to the total amount of inventory in the warehouse to the retailers. Once orders are placed, press the *Place Orders* button. Orders are filled, and cost, revenue, and service level are calculated. You can continue playing for any number of rounds.

B.3.4 Other Features

The game has several other features, which we discuss in detail in the next section. The **Play** menu has options that allow you to set various game parameters. The **Reports** menu allows you to display lists of demands and orders for all of the periods up to the current one.

B.4 OPTIONS AND SETTINGS

This section follows the menu in the Risk Pool Game and describes the function of each of the parameters and options that can be set by the user or instructor. In the following subsections, the convention **menu—selection** item is used to describe menu selections.

B.4.1 File Commands

These commands are used to stop and reset play and exit the system.

File—Reset.   This command resets the game. All data from the previous game are lost.

File—Exit.   This command exits the game.

B.4.2 Play Commands

These commands control game play and allow various parameters to be set.

Play—Start Round.   This command duplicates the *Start Round* button on the lower right-hand corner of the screen. Selecting it starts each round.

Play—Place Orders.   This command duplicates the **Place Orders** button on the lower right-hand corner of the screen. Select it after entering orders and allocations.

Play—Options.   This command displays a submenu with the following choices:

Initial Conditions.   This command displays the following dialog box:

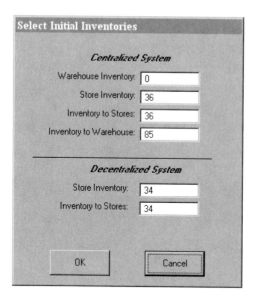

This enables you to select starting inventories throughout both systems. Note that in the centralized system, each retailer must have the same initial inventory level, and the inventory in transit from the warehouse to the retailer must be the same level for each of the retailers and for both periods. Similar restrictions exist for the decentralized system. After making changes, enter **OK** to accept the changes or **Cancel** to keep the current levels. Note that this option can only be used before the first round is played.

Demand. This command displays the following dialog box:

This enables you to control the demand faced by each of the retailers. The demand is normally distributed, with the mean and standard deviation that can be entered on the dialog box. The slider control at the top of the box enables you to control the correlation of the demand at the retailers. If the slider is in the center of its range, demand will be independent. At the right, demand is strongly positively correlated while at the left, demand is strongly negatively correlated. Intermediate positions allow correlation between these extremes.[1] After making changes, select **OK** to accept the changes or **Cancel** to keep the current levels. Note that this option can only be used before the first round is played.

Inventory Policy. This command displays the following dialog box:

---

[1] If demand is positively correlated, it is likely that if one retailer has high demand, all of them will; if one retailer has low demand, all of them will. If demand is negatively correlated, it is likely that if one retailer has high demand, at least one other will have low demand.

This enables you to control the inventory policy that displays the default order and allocation quantities. Note that you can always override the default suggestions when you are playing, but having good defaults speeds up game play. There are two types of default policies, the *Safety Stock* policy and the *Weeks of Inventory* policy. Select between them using the radio buttons at the top of the dialog box. The Safety Stock policy allows you to select order-up-to levels for the warehouse and retailers in the centralized system and the retailers in the decentralized system as a function of demand mean and standard deviation. There are three input boxes for each level: the first box is the mean multiplier, and the second and third are multiplied by the standard deviation. These quantities are then summed to get the final order-up-to level.

When the Weeks of Inventory policy is used, a single value multiplied by the mean demand is used to determine the order-up-to level.

To determine default orders, the system does the following: For the centralized system, warehouse echelon inventory (i.e., inventory in transit to the warehouse, inventory at the warehouse, inventory in transit to the retailers, and inventory at the retailers) is subtracted from the order-up-to levels to determine order quantity. Inventory at the retailers and in transit from the warehouse to the retailers is subtracted from the retailer order-up-to level to determine allocations. If insufficient inventory is available at the warehouse, the available inventory is allocated so that the same fraction of desired level is sent to each retailer. For the decentralized system, inventory at each retailer plus inventory in transit to the retailer is raised to the order-up-to level.

After making changes, select **OK** to accept the changes or **Cancel** to keep the current levels. Note that this option can be used at the start of any round.

Costs. This command displays the following dialog:

You can adjust costs using this dialog. Holding cost is per item per period; cost and revenue are per item. After making changes, select **OK** to accept the changes or **Cancel** to keep the current levels. Note that this option can only be used before the first round is played.

B.4.3 The Reports Commands

These commands display game-related information.

Reports—Orders. This command displays the following report, which lists orders placed by the warehouse in the centralized game and retailers in the decentralized game:

Week	Decentralized Retailer 1	Decentralized Retailer 2	Decentralized Retailer 3	Centralized Warehouse
1	0	0	0	0
2	11	10	9	28
3	23	29	2	54
4	6	25	43	74
5	37	25	36	88
6	27	8	15	50
7	26	24	23	73

Order Report — *Done*

Select **Done** to hide the report.

Reports—Demands. This command displays the following report, which lists demand faced by the retailers since the start of the game:

Demand History

Week	Retailer 1	Retailer 2	Retailer 3
1	31	30	29
2	28	28	28
3	23	29	2
4	6	25	43
5	37	25	36
6	27	8	15
7	26	24	23
8	24	27	17

Done

Select **Done** to hide the report.

The Inventory Spreadsheet

C.1 INTRODUCTION

We have created an Excel spreadsheet, inventory.xls, that implements many of the examples from Chapter 3. *Windows 98* or later and Microsoft Excel 2000 or later are required to use this spreadsheet. To install the software, place the included CD in your CD-ROM drive. If the installation program doesn't run automatically, open Windows Explorer, select the CD, and double click on the setup program.

C.2 THE SPREADSHEET

This spreadsheet is quite self-explanatory. It consists of five sheets, the contents of which are detailed below. We encourage you to experiment with different parameter values and see how these values affect the system.

The sheets are

- **Demand Scenarios.** This sheet contains the probabilistic demand forecast described in the swimsuit production case in Chapter 3.
- **Inventory Calculations.** This sheet contains the single-stage inventory calculations from the swimsuit production case.
- **Buy-Back Contract.** This is the two-stage buy-back contract example from Example 3-3 in Chapter 3.
- **Revenue-Sharing Contract.** This is the revenue-sharing contract example from Example 3-4 in Chapter 3.
- **Global Optimization.** This is an example of globally optimizing the two-stage swimsuit production system, as described in Example 3-5 in Chapter 3.

Bibliography

1. Agrawal, V., and A. Kambil. "Dynamic Pricing Strategies in Electronic Commerce." Working paper, Stern Business School, New York University, 2000.
2. Andel, T. "There's Power in Numbers." *Transportation & Distribution* 36 (1995), pp. 67–72.
3. Andel, T. "Manage Inventory, Own Information." *Transportation & Distribution* 37 (1996), p. 54.
4. Andreoli, T. "VMI Confab Examines Value-Added Services." *Discount Store News* 34 (1995), pp. 4–61.
5. Anonymous. "Divorce: Third-Party Style." *Distribution* 94 (1995), pp. 46–51.
6. Anonymous. "Choosing Service Providers." *Transportation & Distribution* 36 (1995), pp. 74–76.
7. Anonymous. "Supply Disruptions May Linger as Quake Aftershock." http://www.eetimes.com, September 22, 1999.
8. Anonymous. "Idapta: At the Core of E-Markets." *ASCET* 3 (2001), pp. 145–47.
9. Artman, L. B. "The Paradigm Shift from 'Push' to 'Pull' Logistics—What's the Impact on Manufacturing?" Northwestern University, Manufacturing Management Symposium, Evanston, IL, May 1995.
10. Baker, W.; M. Marn; and C. Zawada. "Price Smarter on the Net." *Harvard Business Review* 79, no. 2 (2001), pp. 122–27.
11. Ballou, R. H. *Business Logistics Management.* 3rd ed. Englewood Cliffs, NJ: Prentice Hall, 1992.
12. Bausch, D. O.; G. G. Brown; and D. Ronen. "Consolidating and Dispatching Truck Shipments of Mobil Heavy Petroleum Products." *Interfaces* 25 (1995), pp. 1–17.
13. Billington, C. "HP Cuts Risk with Portfolio Approach." *Purchasing Magazine Online,* February 21, 2002.
14. Blumenfeld, D. E.; L. D. Burns; C. F. Daganzo; M. C. Frick; and R. W. Hall. "Reducing Logistics Costs at General Motors." *Interfaces* 17 (1987), pp. 26–47.
15. Bovet, D., and Y. Sheffi. "The Brave New World of Supply Chain Management." *Supply Chain Management Review,* Spring 1998, pp. 14–22.
16. Bowers, M. R., and A. Agarwal. "Lower In-Process Inventories and Better On-Time Performance at Tanner Companies, Inc." *Interfaces* 25 (1995), pp. 30–43.
17. Bowman, R. "A High Wire Act." *Distribution* 94 (1995), pp. 36–39.
18. Bramel, J., and D. Simchi-Levi. *The Logic of Logistics: Theory, Algorithms and Applications for Logistics Management.* New York: Springer, 1997.
19. Brynjolfsson, E., and M. D. Smith. "Frictionless Commerce? A Comparison of Internet and Conventional Retailers." *Management Science* 46 (2000), pp. 563–85.
20. Buzzell, R. D., and G. Ortmeyer. "Channel Partnerships Streamline Distribution." *Sloan Management Review* 36 (1995), p. 85.
21. Byrne, P., and W. Markham. "Global Logistics: Only 10 Percent of Companies Satisfy Customers." *Transportation and Distribution* 34 (1993), pp. 41–45.
22. Cachon, G. P. "Supply Coordination with Contracts." To appear in *Handbooks in Operations Research and Management Science,* ed. Steve Graves and Ton de Kok. Amsterdam: North-Holland, 2002.
23. Cachon, G. P., and M. A. Lariviere. "Supply Chain Coordination with Revenue Sharing Contracts: Strengths and Limitations." Working paper, the Wharton School, University of Pennsylvania, 2000.
24. Caldwell B. "Wal-Mart Ups the Pace." http://www.informationweek.com, December 9, 1996.
25. Camm, J. D.; T. E. Chorman; F. A. Dill; J. R. Evans; D. J. Sweeney; and G. W. Wegryn. "Blending OR/MS, Judgement, and GIS: Restructuring P&G's Supply Chain." *Interfaces* 27 (1997), pp. 128–42.

26. Chambers, J. C.; S. K. Mullick; and D. D. Smith. "How to Choose the Right Forecasting Technique." *Harvard Business Review* 49, no. 4 (1971), pp. 45–69.

27. Chan, L. M. A.; D. Simchi-Levi; and J. Swann. "Effective Dynamic Pricing Strategies with Stochastic Demand." Working paper, Massachusetts Institute of Technology, 2001.

28. Chen, F. Y.; J. K. Ryan; and D. Simchi-Levi. "The Impact of Exponential Smoothing Forecasts on the Bullwhip Effect." *Naval Research Logistics* 47 (2000), pp. 269–86.

29. Chen, F. Y.; Z. Drezner; J. K. Ryan; and D. Simchi-Levi. "The Bullwhip Effect: Managerial Insights on the Impact of Forecasting and Information on Variability in the Supply Chain." In *Quantitative Models for Supply Chain Management*, ed. S. Tayur, R. Ganeshan, and M. Magazine. Norwell, MA: Kluwer Academic Publishing, 1998, chap. 14.

30. Chen, Y. F.; Z. Drezner; J. K. Ryan; and D. Simchi-Levi. "Quantifying the Bullwhip Effect: The Impact of Forecasting, Leadtime and Information." *Management Science* 46 (2000), pp. 436–43.

31. Chesbrough, H., and D. Teece. "When Is Virtual Virtuous: Organizing for Innovation." *Harvard Business Review* 74, no. 1 (1996), pp. 65–74.

32. Clark, T. "Campbell Soup Company: A Leader in Continuous Replenishment Innovations." Harvard Business School Case 9-195-124, 1994.

33. Clemmet, A. "Demanding Supply." *Work Study* 44 (1995), pp. 23–24.

34. Cook, T. "SABRE Soars." *ORMS Today*, June 1998, pp. 26–31.

35. Cook, T. "Creating Competitive Advantage in the Airline Industry." Seminar sponsored by the MIT Global Airline Industry Program and the MIT Operations Research Center, 2000.

36. Copacino, W. C., and R. W. Dik. "Why B2B e-Markets Are Here to Stay. Part I: Public Independent Trading Exchanges." http://TechnologyEvaluation.Com, March 18, 2002.

37. Crawford, F, and R. Mathews. *The Myth of Excellence.* New York: Crown Business, 2001.

38. Davis, D., and T. Foster. "Bulk Squeezes Shipping Costs." *Distribution Worldwide* 78, no. 8 (1979), pp. 25–30.

39. Davis, D. "State of a New Art." *Manufacturing Systems* 13 (1995), pp. 2–10.

40. ———. "Third Parties Deliver." *Manufacturing Systems* 13 (1995), pp. 66–68.

41. Deutsch, C. H. "New Software Manages Supply to Match Demand." *New York Times*, December 16, 1996.

42. Disabatino, J. "Priceline.com Reports $1.3 Million Q4 Loss." *Computerworld*, February 4, 2002.

43. Dornier, P.; R. Ernst; M. Fender; and P. Kouvelis. *Global Operations and Logistics: Text and Cases.* New York: John Wiley, 1998.

44. Duadel, S., and G. Vialle. *Yield Management: Applications to Transport and Other Service Industries.* Paris: ITA, 1994.

45. Eid, M. K.; D. J. Seith; and M. A. Tomazic. "Developing a Truly Effective Way to Manage Inventory." Council of Logistics Management Conference, October 5–8, 1997.

46. Federgruen, A., and A. Heching. "Combined Pricing and Inventory Control under Uncertainty." *Operations Research* 47 (1999), pp. 454–75.

47. Feitzinger, E., and H. Lee. "Mass Customization at Hewlett-Packard: The Power of Postponement." *Harvard Business Review* 75, no. 1 (1977), pp. 116–21.

48. Fernie, J. "International Comparisons of Supply Chain Management in Grocery Retailing." *Service Industries Journal* 15 (1995), pp. 134–47.

49. Figueroa, Claudia. "Local Reps See Temporary Delays after India Quake." http:// www.Apparelnews.net, March 9, 2001.

50. Fine, C. H. *Clock Speed: Winning Industry Control in the Age of Temporary Advantage.* Reading, MA: Pereus Books, 1998.

51. Fine, C. H., and D. E. Whitney. "Is the Make-Buy Decision Process a Core Competence?" Working paper, Massachusetts Institute of Technology, 1996.

52. Fisher, M. L. "National Bicycle Industrial Co.: A Case Study." The Wharton School, University of Pennsylvania, 1993.

53. Fisher, M. L.; J. Hammond; W. Obermeyer; and A. Raman. "Making Supply Meet Demand in an Uncertain World." *Harvard Business Review*, May–June 1994, pp. 83–93.

54. Fisher, M. L. "What Is the Right Supply Chain for Your Product?" *Harvard Business Review*, March–April 1997, pp. 105–17.

55. Fites, D. "Make Your Dealers Your Partners." *Harvard Business Review*, March–April 1996, pp. 84–95.

56. Flickinger, B. H., and T. E. Baker. "Supply Chain Management in the 1990's." http://www.chesapeake.com/supchain.html.

57. Fox, M. S.; J. F. Chionglo; and M. Barbuceanu. "The Integrated Supply Chain Management System." Working paper, University of Toronto, 1993.

58. Gamble, R. "Financially Efficient Partnerships." *Corporate Cashflow* 15 (1994), pp. 29–34.

59. Geary, S., and J. P. Zonnenberg. "What It Means to Be Best in Class." *Supply Chain Management Review*, July/August 2000, pp. 42–48.

60. Geoffrion, A., and T. J. Van Roy. "Caution: Common Sense Planning Methods Can Be Hazardous to Your Corporate Health." *Sloan Management Review* 20 (1979), pp. 30–42.

61. Georgoff, D. M., and R. G. Murdick. "Managers' Guide to Forecasting." *Harvard Business Review* 64, no. 1 (1986), pp. 1–9.

62. Guengerich, S., and V. G. Green. *Introduction to Client/Server Computing.* Deanborn, MI: SME Blue Book Series, 1996.

63. Hagel, J., III, and J. S. Brown. "Your Next IT Strategy." *Harvard Business Review* 79, no. 10 (2001).

64. Handfield, R., and B. Withers. "A Comparison of Logistics Management in Hungary, China, Korea, and Japan." *Journal of Business Logistics* 14 (1993), pp. 81–109.

65. Hannon, D. "Online Buy Gains Speed." *Purchasing Magazine Online*, February 7, 2002.

66. Harrington, L. "Logistics Assets: Should You Own or Manage?" *Transportation & Distribution* 37 (1996), pp. 51–54.

67. Hax, A. C., and D. Candea. *Production and Inventory Management.* Englewood Cliffs, NJ: Prentice Hall, 1984.

68. "Henkel-Eroski CPFR Pilot Case Study." Compiled by Thierry Jouenne, copyright 2000 by Jowen Editions, 2000, available at cpfr.org.

69. Henkoff, R. "Delivering the Goods." *Fortune*, November 28, 1994, pp. 64–78.

70. Hof, R. "How Amazon Cleared That Hurdle." *Business Week*, February 4, 2002, p. 60–61.

71. Hopp, W., and M. Spearman. *Factory Physics.* Burr Ridge, IL: Richard D. Irwin, 1996.

72. House, R. G., and K. D. Jamie. "Measuring the Impact of Alternative Market Classification Systems in Distribution Planning." *Journal of Business Logistics* 2 (1981), pp. 1–31.

73. Huang, Y.; A. Federgruen; O. Bakkalbasi; R. Desiraju; and R. Kranski. "Vendor-Managed-Replenishment in an Agile Manufacturing Environment." Working paper, Philips Research.

74. Jacobs, D. A.; M. N. Silan; and B. A. Clemson. "An Analysis of Alternative Locations and Service Areas of American Red Cross Blood Facilities." *Interfaces* 26 (1996), pp. 40–50.

75. Johnson, J. C., and D. F. Wood. *Contemporary Physical Distribution and Logistics.* 3rd ed. New York: Macmillan, 1986.

76. Johnson, E. M. "Money for Nothing." *CIO Magazine*, September 15, 2000.

77. Jones, H. "Ikea's Global Strategy Is a Winning Formula." *Marketing Week* 18, no. 50 (1996), p. 22.

78. Kaufman, L. "Wal-Mart's Huge Slice of American Pie." *New York Times*, February 16, 2000.

79. Kay, E. "Flexed Pricing." *Datamation* 44, no. 2 (1998), pp. 58–62.

80. Keenan, F. "One Smart Cookie." *Business Week E.Biz*, November 20, 2000.

81. Kerrigan, R.; E. V. Roegner; D. D. Swinford; and C. C. Zawada. "B2Basics." McKinsey and Company Report, 2001.

82. Kimes, S. E. "A Tool for Capacity-Constrained Service Firms." *Journal of Operations Management* 8 (1989), pp. 348–63.

83. King, J. "The Service Advantage." *Computerworld*, October 28, 1998.

84. Kogut, B. "Designing Global Strategies: Profiting from Operational Flexibility." *Sloan Management Review* 27 (1985), pp. 27–38.

85. Koloszyc, G. "Retailers, Suppliers Push Joint Sales Forecasting." *Stores*, June 1998.

86. Lakenan, B.; D. Boyd; and E. Frey. "Why Outsourcing and Its Perils?" *Strategy + Business*, no. 24 (2001).

87. Lawrence, J. A., and B. A. Pasternack. *Applied Management Science: A Computer Integrated Approach for Decision Making.* New York: John Wiley, 1998.

88. Leahy, S.; P. Murphy; and R. Poist. "Determinants of Successful Logistical Relationships: A Third Party Provider Perspective." *Transportation Journal* 35 (1995), pp. 5–13.

89. Lee, H. L., and C. Billington. "Managing Supply Chain Inventory: Pitfalls and Opportunities." *Sloan Management Review*, Spring 1992, pp. 65–73.

90. Lee, H.; P. Padmanabhan; and S. Whang. "The Paralyzing Curse of the Bullwhip Effect in a Supply Chain." *Sloan Management Review*, Spring 1997, pp. 93–102.

91. ———. "Information Distortion in a Supply Chain: The Bullwhip Effect." *Management Science* 43 (1996), pp. 546–58.

92. Lee, H. "Design for Supply Chain Management: Concepts and Examples." Working paper, Department of Industrial Engineering and Engineering Management, Stanford University, 1992.

93. Leibs, S. "Deskbound for Glory." *CFO Magazine*, March 14, 2002.

94. Lessard, D., and J. Lightstone. "Volatile Exchange Rates Put Operations at Risk." *Harvard Business Review* 64 (1986), pp. 107–14.

95. Levitt, T. "The Globalization of Markets." *Harvard Business Review* 61 (1983), pp. 92–102.

96. Lewis, J. *Partnerships for Profit.* New York: Free Press, 1990.

97. Lindsey. *A Communication to the AGIS-L List Server.*

98. Lohr, S. "He Loves to Win. At I.B.M., He Did," *New York Times* March 10, 2002.

99. Magretta, J. "The Power of Virtual Integration: An Interview with Dell Computer's Michael Dell." *Harvard Business Review*, March–April 1998, pp. 72–84.

100. Maltz, A. "Why You Outsource Dictates How." *Transportation & Distribution* 36 (1995), pp. 73–80.

101. "Management Brief: Furnishing the World." *The Economist*, November 19, 1994, pp. 79–80.

102. Manrodt, K. B.; M. C. Holcomb; and R. H. Thompson. "What's Missing in Supply Chain Management?" *Supply Chain Management Review*, Fall 1997, pp. 80–86.

103. Markides, C., and N. Berg. "Manufacturing Offshore Is Bad Business." *Harvard Business Review* 66 (1988), pp. 113–20.

104. Mathews, R. "Spartan Pulls the Plug on VMI." *Progressive Grocer* 74 (1995), pp. 64–65.

105. McGrath, M., and R. Hoole. "Manufacturing's New Economies of Scale." *Harvard Business Review* 70 (1992), pp. 94–102.

106. McKay, J. "The SCOR Model." Presented in *Designing and Managing the Supply Chain*, an Executive Program at Northwestern University, James L. Allen Center, 1998.

107. McWilliams, G. "Whirlwind on the Web." *Business Week*, April 7, 1997, pp. 132–36.

108. McWilliams, G. "Dell Fine-Tuned Its Pricing to Gain an Edge in Slow Market." *The Wall Street Journal*, June 8, 2001.

109. Mische, M. "EDI in the EC: Easier Said Than Done." *Journal of European Business* 4 (1992), pp. 19–22.

110. Mitchell, R. L. "Unilever Crosses the Data Streams." *Computerworld*, December 17, 2001.

111. Monczka, R.; G. Ragatz; R. Handfield; R. Trent; and D. Frayer. "Executive Summary: Supplier Integration into New Product Development: A Strategy for Competitive Advantage." *The Global Procurement and Supply Chain Benchmarking Initiative*, Michigan State University, The Eli Broad Graduate School of Management, 1997.

112. Mottley, R. "Dead in Nine Months." *American Shipper*, December 1998, pp. 30–33.

113. Nahmias, S. *Production and Operations Analysis*. 3rd ed. Burr Ridge, IL: Irwin/McGraw-Hill, 1997.

114. Narus, J., and J. Anderson. "Turn Your Industrial Distributors into Partners." *Harvard Business Review*, March–April 1986, pp. 66–71.

115. ——. "Rethinking Distribution: Adaptive Channels." *Harvard Business Review*, July–August 1986, pp. 112–20.

116. Nussbaum, B. "Designs for Living." *Business Week*, June 2, 1997, p. 99.

117. Ohmae, K. "Managing in a Borderless World." *Harvard Business Review* 67 (1989), pp. 152–61.

118. Patton, E. P. "Carrier Rates and Tariffs." In *The Distribution Management Handbook*, ed. J. A. Tompkins and D. Harmelink. New York: McGraw-Hill, 1994, chap. 12.

119. Peppers, D., and M. Rogers. *Enterprise One to One*. New York: Doubleday, 1997.

120. Pidd M. "Just Modeling Through: A Rough Guide to Modeling." *Interfaces* 29, no. 2 (March–April 1999), pp. 118–32.

121. Pike, H. "IKEA Still Committed to U.S., Despite Uncertain Economy." *Discount Store News* 33, no. 8 (1994), pp. 17–19.

122. Pine, J. B., II, and J. Gilmore. "Welcome to the Experience Economy." *Harvard Business Review*, July–August 1998, pp. 97–108.

123. Pine, J. B., II; D. Peppers; and M. Rogers. "Do You Want to Keep Your Customers Forever?" *Harvard Business Review*, March–April 1995, pp. 103–15.

124. Pine, J. B., II. *Mass Customization*. Boston: Harvard University Business School Press, 1993.

125. Pine, J. B., II, and A. Boynton. "Making Mass Customization Work." *Harvard Business Review* 71, no. 5 (1993), pp. 108–19.

126. Pollack, E. "Partnership: Buzzword or Best Practice?" *Chain Store Age Executive* 71 (1995), pp. 11A–12A.

127. Quinn, J. B., and F. Hilmer. "Strategic Outsourcing." *Sloan Management Review* 1994, pp. 9–21.

128. Rayport, J. F., and J. J. Sviokla. "Exploiting the Virtual Value Chain." *Harvard Business Review*, November–December 1995, pp. 75–85.

129. Reichheld, F. F. "Learning from Customer Defections." *Harvard Business Review*, March–April 1996, pp. 57–69.

130. Ries, A., and L. Ries. *The 22 Immutable Laws of Branding*. New York: HarperBusiness, 1998.

131. Rifkin, G. "Technology Brings the Music Giant a Whole New Spin." *Forbes ASAP*, February 27, 1995, p. 32.

132. Robeson, J. F., and W. C. Copacino, eds. *The Logistics Handbook*. New York: Free Press, 1994.

133. Robins, G. "Pushing the Limits of VMI." *Stores* 77 (1995), pp. 42–44.

134. Ross, D. F. *Competing through Supply Chain Management*. New York: Chapman & Hall, 1998.

135. SAP. "Stages of Excellence." www.sap.com/scm/.

136. Schoneberger, R. J. "Strategic Collaboration: Breaching the Castle Walls." *Business Horizons* 39 (1996), p. 20.

137. Schrader, C. "Speeding Build and Buy Processes across a Collaborative Manufacturing Network." *ASCET* 3 (2001), pp. 82–88.

138. Schwind, G. "A Systems Approach to Docks and Cross-Docking." *Material Handling Engineering* 51, no. 2 (1996), pp. 59–62.

139. Seybold, P. B. *The Customer Revolution*. New York: Crown Business, 2001.

140. Shenk, D. *Data Smog: Surviving the Information Glut*. New York: HarperCollins, 1997.

141. Singh, A. Private communication.

142. Signorelli, S., and J. Heskett. "Benetton (A)." Harvard University Business School Case (1984) Case No. 9-685-014.

143. Sliwa, C. "Beyond IT: Business Strategy Was a Problem, Too." *Computerworld*, January 25, 2002.

144. Songini, M. L. "Nike Says Profit Woes IT-Based." *Computerworld*, March 5, 2001.

145. Stalk, G.; P. Evans; and L. E. Shulman. "Competing on Capabilities: The New Rule of Corporate Strategy." *Harvard Business Review*, March–April 1992, pp. 57–69.

146. Supply Chain Council. "SCOR Introduction." Release 2.0, August 1, 1997.

147. Stein, T., and J. Sweat. "Killer Supply Chains." http://www.informationweek.com, November 9, 1988.

148. Streitfeld, D. "Amazon Pays a Price for Marketing Test." *Washington Post*, October 2000.

149. Swaminathan, J. M. "Enabling Customization Using Standardized Operations." *California Management Review* 43(3) (Spring 2001), pp. 125–35.

150. Temkin, B. "Preparing for the Coming Shake-Out in Online Markets." *ASCET* 3 (2001), pp. 102–7.

151. Troyer, T., and D. Denny. "Quick Response Evolution." *Discount Merchandiser* 32 (1992), pp. 104–7.

152. Troyer, C., and R. Cooper. "Smart Moves in Supply Chain Integration." *Transportation & Distribution* 36 (1995), pp. 55–62.

153. Trunnick, P.; H. Richardson; and L. Harrington. "CLM: Breakthroughs of Champions." *Transportation & Distribution* 35 (1994), pp. 41–50.

154. Ulrich, K. T. "The Role of Product Architecture in the Manufacturing Firm." *Research Policy* 24 (1995), pp. 419–40.

155. Varon, E. "What You Need to Know about Public and Private Exchanges." *CIO Magazine*, September 1, 2001.

156. Verity, J. "Clearing the Cobwebs from the Stockroom." *Business Week*, October 21, 1996.

157. Wood, D.; A. Barone; P. Murphy; and D. Wardlow. *International Logistics*. New York: Chapman & Hall, 1995.

158. Yannis, B. J. "The Emerging Role of Electronic Marketplaces on the Internet." *Comm. ACM* 41, no. 9 (1998), pp. 35–42.

159. Zweben, M. "Delivering on Every Promise." *APICS*, March 1996, p. 50.

160. *Journal of Business Strategy*, October–November 1997.

161. *The Wall Street Journal*, October 23, 1997.

162. *U.S. Surgical Quarterly Report*, July 15, 1993.

163. *The Wall Street Journal*, October 7, 1994.

164. *The Wall Street Journal*, August 1993.
    *(Dell Computer ref.)

165. *The Wall Street Journal*, July 15, 1993.
    *(Liz Claiborne ref.)

166. *The Wall Street Journal*, October 7, 1994.
    *(IBM ThinkPad ref.)

167. *The Wall Street Journal*, February 22, 2000.

Brief topical reference.

Index